Regulation, Deregulation, Reregulation

ADVANCES IN NEW INSTITUTIONAL ANALYSIS

Series Editor: Claude Ménard, *Professor of Economics, CES (Centre d'Economie de la Sorbonne), University of Paris Panthéon-Sorbonne, France*

Understanding the nature and role of institutions in the dynamics and failures of modern economies is an increasing concern among scholars and policy makers. Substantial progress has been made in economics as well as in other social sciences, particularly political science, history, sociology and the managerial sciences. New institutional scholars have been, and remain, at the forefront of this movement. Alternative views have also been proposed that deserve consideration. This series intends to promote the development and diffusion of these analyses with books from leading contributors as well as younger up-and-coming scholars.

The series will include topics such as:

- Institutions and growth
- Transaction cost economics
- The role of formal rules and legal institutions
- Regulation and deregulation
- Political institutions and the state
- Institutions and modes of governance
- Contracting issues
- Customs, beliefs and institutional changes.

The series will be essential reading for researchers in economics, the social and managerial sciences, as well as policymakers.

Titles in the series include:

Institutions and Development
Mary M. Shirley

Regulation, Deregulation, Reregulation
Institutional Perspectives
Edited by Claude Ménard and Michel Ghertman

Regulation, Deregulation, Reregulation

Institutional Perspectives

Edited by

Claude Ménard

Professor of Economics, University of Paris (Panthéon-Sorbonne), France

Michel Ghertman

University of Nice-Sophia Antipolis and GREDEG, France

ADVANCES IN NEW INSTITUTIONAL ANALYSIS

Edward Elgar

Cheltenham, UK • Northampton, MA, USA

Published by
Edward Elgar Publishing Limited
The Lypiatts
15 Lansdown Road
Cheltenham
Glos GL50 2JA
UK

Edward Elgar Publishing, Inc.
William Pratt House
9 Dewey Court
Northampton
Massachusetts 01060
USA

A catalogue record for this book
is available from the British Library

Library of Congress Control Number: 2009928601

PEFC
PEFC/16-33-111
CATG-PEFC-052
www.pefc.org

ISBN 978 1 84720 968 9 (cased)

Printed and bound by MPG Books Group, UK

Contents

Figures

Tables

Contributors

Luis Andres, Infrastructure Economist, Latin America and Caribbean Region, World Bank.

Magali Delmas, Associate Professor, UCLA Institute of the Environment, University of California, Los Angeles.

Adam Fremeth, University of Minnesota, Curtis Carlson School of Management.

R. Richard Geddes, Associate Professor, Department of Policy Analysis and Management Cornell University.

Michel Ghertman, Professor, HEC-Paris (1968–2003), University of Nice and Groupe de Recherche en Droit, Economie et Gestion (GREDEG, 2004–7), Distinguished Overseas Professor, Xi'an Jiaotong University (2004–7).

Jean-Michel Glachant, Director, Florence School of Regulation and Loyola de Palacio Programme, European University Institute.

José Luis Guasch, Senior Adviser on Regulation and Competitiveness, Latin America and Caribbean Region, World Bank and Professor of Economics, University of California, San Diego.

Guy L. F. Holburn, Associate Professor, University of Western Ontario, Richard Ivey School of Business.

Jackie Krafft, Groupe de Recherche en Droit, Economie et Gestion (GREDEG), University of Nice – Sophia Antipolis, CNRS.

Gary D. Libecap, Bren School of Environmental Science and Management and Economics Department, University of California, Santa Barbara; National Bureau of Economic Research; and Hoover Institution.

Sebastián Lopez Azumendi, consultant, Latin America and Caribbean Region, World Bank.

Claude Ménard, Full Professor of Economics, Université de Paris (Panthéon Sorbonne).

Maria J. Montes-Sancho, Professor, Department of Business Administration, University of Carlos III, Madrid.

Yannick Perez, Associate Professor, ADIS -Groupe Réseaux Jean-Monnet, Université de Paris Sud.

Roberta Romano, Oscar M. Ruebhausen Professor of Law, Yale Law School and Director, Yale Law School Center for the Study of Corporate Law, Research Associate, National Bureau of Economic Research, and Fellow, European Corporate Governance Institute.

Michael Russo, Professor, Lundquist College of Business, University of Oregon, Eugene, Oregon.

Evens Salies, Observatoire Français des Conjonctures Economiques (OFCE), Institut de Sciences Politiques.

Howard A. Shelanski, Professor of Law, University of California, Berkeley.

Pablo T. Spiller, Jeffrey A. Jacobs Distinguished Professor of Business and Technology, Haas School of Business, University of California, Berkeley, and Research Associate, NBER.

Steven Tadelis, Associate Professor, Haas School of Business, University of California, Berkeley.

Yesim Tokat, Vice President and Director, Research, Bernstein Global Wealth Management, USA.

Dean V. Williamson, Antitrust Division, United States Department of Justice, Economic Analysis Group.

Oliver E. Williamson, Professor of the Graduate School and Edgar F. Kaiser Professor Emeritus of Business, Economics, and Law, University of California, Berkeley.

Acknowledgements

This book originates from a workshop organized in Nice, in June 2007, in honour of Oliver E. Williamson. Participation to the workshop was restricted to the contributors, to favour intense discussions. All chapters were revised after the conference before going through a refereeing process, with at least two referees reporting on each chapter, and they were lastly all reviewed for final adjustments by Claude Ménard. We would like to express our gratitude to the referees, listed below, who did a wonderful job, several of them through one, two, even three rounds of revision.

We would also like to thank for their financial and logistic support the Groupe de Recherche en Droit, Economie et Gestion (GREDEG, Centre National de la Recherche Scientifique), and particularly Professors Jean-Luc Gaffard and Jacques-Laurent Ravix, respectively the former and current directors of GREDEG; the Region of Provence-Alpes-Cote d'Azur (PACA); the city of Nice; and the University of Nice. We also owe a special debt to Nadine Tournois, Professor at the Institut d'Administration des Entreprises (IAE) and vice-president of the University of Nice, and to Jacques Spendler, director of the IAE.

List of Referees (in Alphabetical Order)

Lee Alston (University of Colorado at Boulder)
Jean-Paul Bonardi (Université de Lausanne)
Eschien Chong (University of Paris Sud)
Aad Correlje (TU Delft)
Sandra Eckert (European University Institute, Firenze)
John de Figueiredo (University of California at Los Angeles)
Matthias Finger (Ecole Polytechnique Fédérale de Lausanne)
Christopher Garbacz (Consultant, Flora, Mississippi)
Michel Ghertman (Professor – retired, HEC-Paris; and University of Nice)
Richard Green (University of Birmingham)
John Groenewegen (TU Delft)
Deepak Hedge (University of California, Berkeley)
William H. Hogan (Harvard University)
Thomas Hubbard (Kellogg School of Management, Northwestern University)

Paul L. Joskow (Massachusetts Institute of Technology)
Rolf Kunneke (TU Delft)
Patricia Luis-Manso (Ecole Polytechnique Fédérale de Lausanne)
Chrysostomos Mantzavinos (Witten/Herdecke University)
Bernardo Mueller (Universidade de Brasilia)
Troy A. Parades (Washington University in St Louis)
Jean-François Sattin (Institut d'Administration des Entreprises, Valenciennes)
Robert C. Seamans, University of California, Berkeley
Mary Shirley (Ronald Coase Institute)
Tomas Sjostrom (Rutgers – State University of New Jersey)
Carine Staropoli (Université de Paris – Panthéon Sorbonne)
Stephane Straub (University of Edinburgh)
Joelle Toledano (Agence de Régulation des Communications Electroniques)
Bernhard Truffer (Swiss Federal Institute for Aquatic Science and Technology – EAWAG)
Scott Wallsten (Vice President for Research and Senior Fellow, Technology Policy Institute)
Michael Waterson (University of Warwick)
Hagen Worch (Swiss Federal Institute for Aquatic Science and Technology – EAWAG)

Introduction

Claude Ménard

On a sunny week of June 2007, a small group of economists locked themselves in a meeting room in Nice for a workshop intended to prepare a book on regulatory issues in order to express their deep admiration for Oliver E. Williamson, his work, and the stream of research he has inspired in that area. However, in preparing the meeting as well as this book, Michel Ghertman and I did not intend to deliver a traditional festschrift. We rather wanted the authors to explore some of the avenues opened by Professor Williamson, and to introduce new ideas and perspectives. In order to make this possible, we restricted the audience to the contributors, so as to facilitate extensive discussions and exchanges. After the conference, all chapters were rewritten, submitted to referees, and revised (several of them more than once).

The strong red thread interweaving the different contributions thus prepared comes from transaction costs economics and, more generally, from new institutional economics and the powerful tools it provides for analysing public policies. Regulatory issues offer a particularly favourable ground in that respect. The deregulation movement that developed since the early 1980s, the controversies it has raised and that it continues to face, and the obstacles encountered in the reforms of public utilities that it epitomizes, can gain enormously, on both theoretical and empirical sides, in using transaction cost lenses. At the same time, diverging experiences in different countries and different sectors have substantially enriched our experience and our databases, thus providing opportunities to proceed comparatively, which is a major lesson carried by Ronald Coase, Douglass North, Oliver Williamson and others. The chapters in this book are clearly impregnated by their view, but in an active and exploratory way.

The book is organized in three parts.

Part I ('Analytical framework') assembles chapters that push the conceptual framework, without losing sight of the contributions of the past or neglecting the 'real' world to which this framework applies. Honour where honour is due, the opening chapter is from Oliver Williamson. It reassesses the basic contribution of transaction cost economics in revisiting its precursors, thus putting the theory in perspective. However, this is not a purely historical piece. Professor Williamson emphasizes the need to take into account governance issues, with a more specific attention to the role of contracts, since this is where substantial transaction costs are embedded, determining what solutions are feasible. The 'benign neglect' in which too many reformers of public utilities have held these aspects might well explain why there are so many flaws and failures in deregulation experiences.

Chapter 2, by Gary Libecap, develops another key concept in new institutional economics, property rights, with a special attention to the difficulties involved in the allocation of these rights because of their distributional implications. The chapter analyses alternative allocation mechanisms (first-possession rules, uniform-allocation rules, auction rules), exhibiting their respective strength and weaknesses. The discussion is then extended to specific areas, namely: subsurface oil and gas reservoirs, air pollution emission permits and the allocation of ITQs in fisheries, all domains in which Professor Libecap expertise is widely acknowledged.

In Chapter 3, Pablo Spiller develops the contractual approach initiated by Williamson to exhibit the differences between private and public contracting. Going further than his previous analysis of uncertainties associated to government opportunism, which plagues so many reforms, he shows the complementary uncertainties resulting from third party opportunism, that is, the influence of interest groups. His analysis demonstrates the major impact they can have on the characteristics of contracts in reforming public utilities, particularly the rigidity it introduces, and how they may push towards the implementation of modes of organization with low incentives. Empirical evidence is briefly introduced that suggests the significance of these problems.

Chapter 4, by Steve Tadelis, fits nicely in that pattern since it focuses on incentive issues faced by public procurement. Contrasting competitive bidding in the private sector with that in the public sector, Tadelis shows that the possibility the private sector has to negotiate with selected supplier(s) before a contractual arrangement is agreed upon tends to be denied in the public sector, for reasons that Spiller's chapter helps understanding. One result is that public procurement operates within a more rigid framework, adding additional constraints for the parties, which translate into costs. Negotiated contracts may be less effective in selecting lowest costs bidders, but they might economize significantly on *ex post* transaction costs, thus being an important source of costs savings.

In Chapter 5, which concludes this section, Claude Ménard combines a control engineering perspective on public utilities with a transaction costs approach, exhibiting the difficulties in aligning modes of organization with technical functions in a way that maintain the integrity of the system, which also conditions its effectiveness. He argues that beyond the general rules of the game, 'micro-institutions' play a central role in guaranteeing that core transactions are monitored within a coherent framework. The status of some of these micro-institutions is then examined and discussed. The analysis is supported by casual evidence, mainly based on extensive case studies of the reform of urban water systems.

Part II ('Governance and performance') then turns to a close examination of governance, its difficult reform in what Ménard would call 'critical infrastructures', and its impact on performance of substantially distinct sectors. By governance, one can understand 'means by which to infuse order, thereby to mitigate conflict and realize mutual gain' (Williamson, this volume, p. 12). In Chapter 6, Luis Andres, José Luis Guasch and Sebastián Lopez Azumendi explore the impact of regulatory agencies on the performance of electricity distribution. Based on an index of regulatory governance that they tested on an extensive database from reforms in the electricity sector in Latin America, they show that the existence, experience, and governance of regulatory agencies make a very significant difference in how electricity systems perform. Their chapter is also full of methodological insights on how to measure this complex relationship between regulation and performance.

Chapter 7, by Howard Shelanski, examines the controversial issue of how relationships between network owners and application providers in broadband communications should be regulated, if they should be regulated at all. Indeed, because networks are characterized by market power, since there is most of the time no more than two or three competitors in the last-mile network market, the question arises about whether free and unmediated access for any provider is the optimal solution. Having confronted and discussed the arguments of defenders of the 'neutrality' in the rules of access to networks, and of proponents of discrimination rights that would allow networks to impose constraints on application providers, he concludes that long-term structural problems are at stake, and that our knowledge remains quite limited for dealing with these complex issues.

This is also one of the messages that readers can get from Chapter 8, by Magali Delmas, Michael Russo, Maria Montes-Sancho and Yesim Tokat. Comparing the performance of the deregulation of the US electric utility sector along two dimensions, productive efficiency and environmental results, they show that firms have reconfigured their assets and proceeded to significant organizational adjustments. Provisory results suggest that deregulation has been associated with a negative impact on efficiency and a positive impact on renewable energy. Thus, deregulation has complex, multidirectional effects. In order to better understand long-term consequences, different aspects of deregulation must be disentangled, and more data collected on specific effects.

Chapter 9, by Jean-Michel Glachant and Yannick Perez, endorse a different perspective in that they proceed comparatively. Starting from problems of modularity in the reform of the electricity sector, they confront two different modes of governance implemented in the transmission system: the 'Independent System Operator' model adopted in the US and the 'Transmission System Operator' model that prevails in Europe. The main lesson they draw from this comparison is that different institutional frameworks are compatible with the governance of complex systems like transmission, and that reforms must proceed sequentially when they concern a set of interdependent and nevertheless distinct blocks. As for the impact of alternative solutions on performance, their measure remains a task ahead of us.

The last chapter of this section (Chapter 10), by Richard Geddes, is a perfect illustration that poor performance does not necessarily generate institutional reform. The US postal service, in that respect typical of most postal services worldwide, has shown a remarkable resistance to change. Notwithstanding pressures to liberalize, only some segments have been opened to competition, making the USPS an 'organizational hybrid'. In that arrangement, worksharing rather than straightforward privatization has been the main solution adopted to introduce some competition in the system. The chapter discusses alternative explanations to this slow movement towards reform, with no simple one being fully convincing. However, in a pattern different from what Spiller explored in Chapter 3, a combination of governmental opportunism and interest group opportunism likely played a key role.

Part III ('Adaptation and changes') explores ambiguities of the deregulation movement and how, under some circumstances, it may even end up in reregulation. Chapter 11, by Roberta Romano, illustrates this through the saga of the Sarbanes–Oxley Act. Adopted in the context of the Enron scandal, with all the attention of the media it has crystallized, feeding political incentives to control, this law has progressively generated distortions in the running of financial markets and imposed costs hardly bearable on small firms. The question then becomes: how to go around a regulation that can hardly be changed at the legislative level because of its political dimension and the attention it could attract from the media? Romano shows the importance of the discretionary power of regulators, in this case the Securities and Exchange Commission (SEC), first in implementing, than in self-limiting the implementation of a regulation. She also illustrates, with the House bill prohibiting the SEC from expanding funds on the enforcement of section 404 against small firms, how political forces can reach an institutional agreement to circumscribe regulations that went out of control.

At a more micro level, Chapter 12 by Adam Fremeth and Guy Holburn provides another example of the complex adaptation of regulation to changing circumstances. Looking at rate reviews that concerned two important players in the electricity sector in the US, they explore the relationship between regulator's knowledge of regulated firms and the policy decisions they make. They exhibit the combination of mechanisms that allow regulators to reduce asymmetric information, namely: tacit knowledge based on the past experience of the regulator; codified knowledge made available through rules forcing firms to reveal information; and information provided by organized interest groups. This last point reveals the positive side of third-party opportunism. One nice thing with this chapter comes from the data that the authors were able to collect on aspects rarely measured, contrasting two stylized cases along the three mechanisms.

Chapter 13, by Dean Williamson, also looks at adaptation devices in the electricity sector, but in a different environment, that of contractual relationships between producers and marketers. Focusing on four instruments in the hands of contracting parties, duration, veto rights, risk sharing rules, and trade-off between debt and equity, he emphasizes the fact that duration, a favourite variable in many empirical studies, is only one of the four tools. Working out of a dataset of 101 marketing contracts, he exhibits the complementarity of these tools when important investments in generation capacities are at stake. Parties do combine these tools because they are aware of potential contractual hazards, due to risks of opportunism once important specific investments are made, which is very much in line with a fundamental lesson from transaction cost economics.

Jackie Krafft and Evens Saliens develop a very different perspective in Chapter 14. Focusing on retail broadband Internet markets, they argue that high switching costs for consumers may prevent competition to be effective. Their analysis is based on a discussion of the effects of the deregulation movement in the communication industries in France over the last decade. A key element of their discussion is based on the slow rate of penetration of cable connections, which they relate to switching costs. Challenging the idea that beneficial outcomes can be expected from self-regulation through competition in innovative industries, they wonder if a more active competition policy and some reregulation could be needed in order to break dominant positions that high switching costs contribute to maintain. This view might gain in being confronted to the positions expressed in Shelanski's chapter.

The last chapter of this section and of the book, by Michel Ghertman, intends to put discussions on regulation and deregulation in an historical perspective. Chapter 15 identifies three successive conceptualization of regulation (that we could call 'Pigovian', 'Stiglerian', and 'Williamsonian', respectively). Ghertman argues that the empirical content of these approaches is quite weak, with a possible exception for transaction cost economics, because economists have neglected the lessons accumulated in political science about the role of politicians, interest groups and, more generally social forces. His call is therefore for a multidisciplinary approach, which is exactly what Oliver Williamson concluded in his chapter.

To sum up, the contributions of this book largely complement each other, providing a stimulating view on progress accomplished from a transaction cost perspective in the analysis of regulation, the reform of public utilities, and the complex governance, of which contracting is an important component, of network industries. Because they are deeply rooted in sector analyses, the chapters also illustrate very well a central and deep message of leading new institutional economists, among which Oliver Williamson is a key figure, which is that theory should be continuously confronted to facts, and reformed or revolutionized accordingly.

PART I

Analytical framework

1. Transaction cost economics: the precursors

Oliver E. Williamson

INTRODUCTION

The first stage of the natural progression in the development of transaction cost economics is herein described. The period in question is 1920–70, especially the decade of the 1930s, during which period economists, organization theorists, and legal scholars were all taking exception with their respective orthodoxies.

As developed herein, dissents of all three kinds had a bearing on the overuse of the resource allocation paradigm, according to which firms were described not as hierarchies but as production functions whereby inputs were transformed into output according to the laws of technology. Markets, moreover, were mainly described as simple market exchange where 'faceless buyers and sellers . . . meet . . . for an instant to exchange standardized goods at equilibrium prices' (Ben-Porath, 1980: 4). There being neither a need nor a place for hierarchy, the study of organization was relegated to sociologists and organization theorists. Prices and output, supply and demand were made the focus of attention. Never the twain shall meet.[1]

Objections were raised, but cogent and cumulative criticism does not, without more, carry the day. Here as elsewhere, it takes a theory to beat a theory. It was not until the 1970s that new theories of firm and market organization began to take shape.[2] Transaction cost economics was one of these.

Contrary to the standard assumption in economic theory circa 1970 that transactions costs were zero, transaction cost economics makes express provision for positive transaction costs. Contrary also to the standard presumption in applied microeconomics circa 1970 that nonstandard and unfamiliar contractual practices and organizational structures have monopoly purpose and effect, provision is expressly made for efficiency purposes. Economizing on positive transaction costs becomes the basic engine of analysis. A huge number of economic phenomena are reinterpreted in the process.

That said, an implementation obstacle was encountered by the proliferation of transaction cost types. Once the black boxes of firm and market organization had been opened, positive transaction costs turned out to be 'everywhere'. Awaiting operationalization, any outcome whatsoever could be 'explained' by invoking some type of transaction cost to fit the need – as a result of which transaction cost reasoning earned a 'well-deserved bad name' (Fischer, 1977: 322). Dealing with this vast buzzing, blooming confusion of transaction costs in a disciplined way was the challenge.

My purpose here is to describe the three crucial conceptual moves that undergird the operationalization project: use of the lens of contract/governance; express provision for economizing on transaction costs as these relate to adaptation; and selective appeal to the contiguous social sciences. Each of these is described in sequence, followed by a summary. The implementation of a predictive theory of firm and market organization is the objective, although 'knowledge for its own sake' is the ultimate purpose (Georgescu-Roegen, 1971: 37).

THE LENS OF CONTRACT/GOVERNANCE

James Buchanan avers that 'mutuality of advantage from voluntary exchange is . . . the most fundamental of all understandings in economics' (2001, p. 29). He further contends that this fundamental understanding is better realized by examining economics through the underused lens of contract rather than the overused lens of choice (Buchanan, 1975) – where, by the latter, he means the neoclassical resource allocation paradigm. Indeed, Buchanan (1975: 225) holds that economics as a discipline went 'wrong' in its preoccupation with the science of choice and the optimization apparatus associated therewith. Wrong or not, the parallel development of a science of contract was slow to develop and is still a work in progress.

As perceived by Buchanan, the principal needs for a science of contract were in the field of public finance and took the form of public ordering: 'Politics is a structure of complex exchange among individuals, a structure within which persons seek to secure collectively their own privately defined objectives that cannot be efficiently secured through simple market exchanges' (1987: 296). Thinking contractually in the public ordering domain leads in to focus on the rules of the game. Constitutional economics issues are posed (Buchanan and Tullock, 1962; Brennan and Buchanan, 1983).

Whatever the rules of the game, the lens of contract is also usefully brought to bear on the play of the game. This latter is what I refer to as

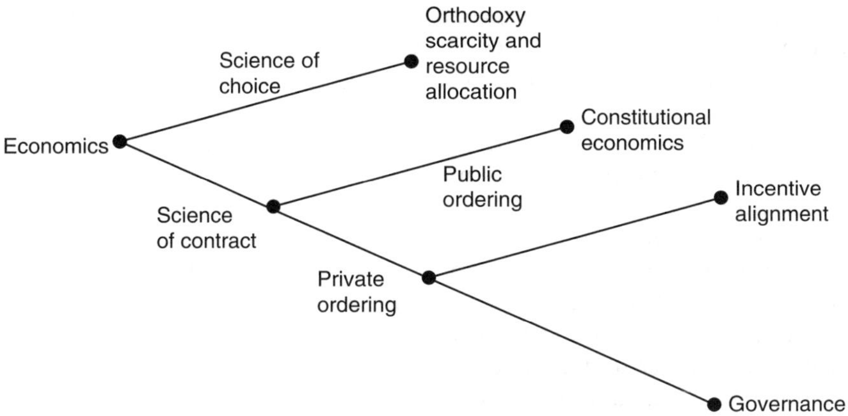

Figure 1.1 The sciences of choice and contract

private ordering, which entails efforts by the immediate parties to a transaction to align incentives and to craft governance structures that are better attuned to their exchange needs.

Figure 1.1 sets out the main distinctions (Williamson, 2002). The initial divide is between the science of choice (orthodoxy) and the science of contract. The latter divides into public ordering (constitutional economics) and private ordering parts, where the second is split into two related branches. One branch concentrates on the study of *ex ante* incentive alignment. The second branch deals with *ex post* governance, with emphasis on 'good order and workable arrangements' (Fuller, 1954: 477), to include both spontaneous order in the market and purposeful order, if and as needed, in both markets and hierarchies.

The study of governance as herein described was prefigured by John R. Commons, who was one of the leaders of older-style institutional economics in the United States. Of the many good ideas that originated with Commons, none was more important to the economics of governance than his abiding interest in 'going concerns'. As against the preoccupation of orthodoxy with simple market exchange, Commons observed that the continuity of an exchange relationship was often important, whereupon he reformulated the problem of economic organization as follows: 'the ultimate unit of activity . . . must contain in itself the three principles of conflict, mutuality, and order. This unit is a transaction' (Commons, 1932: 4). Commons thereafter recommended that 'theories of economics center on transactions and working rules, on problems of organization, and on the . . . [ways] the organization of activity is . . . stabilized' (1950: 21).

Operationalizing these prescient ideas nevertheless eluded Commons and his students and colleagues. How, if at all, can the Commons Triple of conflict, mutuality and order be implemented? I take the position that governance is the unifying concept, where governance is taken to be the means by which to infuse order, thereby to mitigate conflict and realize mutual gains. The transaction, moreover, is the unit of analysis out of which transaction costs economics works. In both respects, the study of economic organization is moved to a more microanalytic level of analysis than had been customary – broadly in the spirit of Herbert Simon's observation that 'In the physical sciences, when errors of measurement and other noise are found to be of the same order of magnitude as the phenomena under study, the response is not to try to squeeze more information out of the data by statistical means; it is instead to find techniques for observing the phenomena at a higher level of resolution. The corresponding strategy for economics is obvious: to secure new kinds of data at the micro level' (1984: 40).

If and as economics attempts to move beyond prices and output, supply and demand to deal with the modern corporation and to explain nonstandard and unfamiliar contractual practices, all-purpose reliance on the resource allocation paradigm is, to say the least, strained. As Harold Demsetz observed, it is a 'mistake to confuse the firm of [neoclassical] economic theory with its real world namesake. The chief mission of neoclassical economics is to understand how the price system coordinates the use of resources, *not the inner workings of real firms*' (1983: 377; emphasis added). Similar considerations apply to markets, where the mechanisms of simple market exchange and of complex market exchange differ consequentially in ways and for reasons that need to be uncovered and explicated.

David Kreps captures the spirit of what is different about the transaction cost economics enterprise by noting that the firm is akin to the agent (consumer) in textbook economics but is of the genus of the market in transaction cost economics. Thus (Kreps, 1990: 96):

> The [neoclassical] firm is like individual agents in textbook economics . . . Agents have utility functions, firms have a profit motive; agents have consumption sets, firms have production possibility sets. But in transaction-cost economics, firms are more like markets – both are arenas within which the individual can transact.

Plainly, the lens of contract/governance and the orthodox lens of choice work out of different conceptual setups, on which account it should come as no surprise that they employ different apparatus and, sometimes, interpret puzzling phenomena differently.

ECONOMIZING ON POSITIVE TRANSACTION COSTS

The assumption of standard economic theory that transaction costs were zero was a great analytical convenience and, for a long time, went unquestioned. Upon pushing the logic of zero transaction costs to completion, however, serious gaps, errors, and anomalies were exposed by Ronald Coase (1937, 1960, 1964, 1972), who was the first to perceive and demonstrate the conceptual problems that resided therein.

The basic insight that Coase employed in reformulating 'The nature of the firm' (1937) and 'The problem of social cost' (1960) and in his discussions of regulation (1964) and antitrust (1972) was that the assumption that transaction costs were zero was neither reasonable nor innocuous. If firm and market are properly viewed as 'alternative methods of coordinating production' (Coase, 1937: 388), then the decision to use one mode rather than the other should not be taken as given (as was the prevailing practice) but should be derived. Accordingly, Coase advised economists that they needed (1937: 389):

> to bridge what appears to be a gap in [standard] economic theory between the assumption (made for some purposes) that resources are allocated by means of the price mechanism and the assumption (made for other purposes) that this allocation is dependent on the entrepreneur-coordinator. We have to explain the basis on which, in practice, this choice between alternatives is effected.

Coase thereafter averred that 'the main reason why it is profitable to establish a firm would seem to be that there is a cost of using the price mechanism,' the most obvious of which is 'that of discovering what the relevant prices are' (1937: 390).[3,4] Coase also described the different mechanisms through which firm and market work: outsourcing is accomplished by an arm's length contract between buyer and supplier whereas an employment contract is used if a firm produces to its own needs. The latter entails creating an authority relation according to which the employee 'agrees to obey the directions of an entrepreneur *within certain limits*' (p. 391; emphasis in original). Vertical integration occurs when 'transactions [previously] organized by two or more entrepreneurs become organized as one' (pp. 397–8).

Although the 1937 article would be 'little used' over the next 35 years (Coase, 1972: 67), Coase's 1960 article on 'The problem of social cost' had an immediate and massive impact on law and economics literature. The latter uncovered an embarrassing lapse, in that Coase showed that 'Pigou's conclusion and that of most economists *using standard economic theory* . . . that some kind of government action (usually the imposition of taxes) was required to restrain those whose actions had harmful effects on others (often termed negative externalities)' was incorrect (Coase, 1992: 717, emphasis added). Upon reformulating the tort problem (more generally, the externality problem) in contractual terms, Coase demonstrated what is now, but was not then, obvious: parties to tort transactions will costlessly bargain to an efficient result if transaction costs are assumed to be zero. Proof, externalities and frictions of other kinds would vanish. That being preposterous, the real message was this: 'study the world of positive transaction costs' (Coase, 1992: 717).

Relatedly, Coase criticized the then-common practice among regulatory economists to contrast an actual condition with a hypothetical ideal. 'This has directed economists' attention away from the main question, which is how alternative [feasible] arrangements will actually work in practice . . . It is no accident that in the literature we find a category "market failure" but no category "government failure" . . . [We need to] realize that we are choosing between social arrangements which are all more or less failures' (1964: 195). The market failure literature in general and the regulatory literature in particular (as witness the chapters appearing in this volume) would eventually adopt this orientation.

Kenneth Arrow's contributions to the transaction cost economics project include both zero transaction cost analysis, as with the Arrow and Debreu (1954) model of general equilibrium,[5] and positive transaction cost constructions, as with his arguments that market failure: (a) is more general than externalities; (b) is an organizational rather than technological phenomenon; and (c) is subsumed by transaction costs, which (d) has ramifications for vertical integration (Arrow, 1969: 48):[6]

> market failure is not absolute; it is better to consider a broader category, that of transaction costs, which in general impede and in particular cases completely block the formation of markets. It is usually though not always emphasized that transaction costs are costs of running the economic system. An incentive for vertical integration is replacement of the costs of buying and selling on the market by the costs of intrafirm transfers; the existence of vertical integration may suggest that the costs of operating competitive markets are not zero, as is usually assumed in our theoretical analysis.

Implementing the Coase and Arrow message to study the world of positive transaction costs was accomplished in part by taking economizing on transaction costs to be the 'main case', broadly in the spirit of Frank Knight's views on efficiency (1941: 252; emphasis added):

> Men in general, and within limits, wish to behave economically, to make their activities *and their organization* 'efficient' rather than wasteful. This fact does deserve the utmost emphasis; and an adequate definition of the science of economics . . . might well make it explicit that the main relevance of the discussion is found in its relation to social policy, assumed to be directed toward the end indicated, or increasing economic efficiency, of reducing waste.

Transaction cost economizing is congruent with this prescription and provides analytical focus. But it also leaves considerable latitude. Which transaction costs are the more important? Interestingly, the economist Friederich Hayek (1945) and the organization theorist Chester Barnard (1938) were in agreement that adaptation was the central problem of economic organization, albeit with differences. Hayek focused on the adaptations of autonomous economic actors who adjusted spontaneously to changes in the market, mainly as signalled by changes in relative prices. The marvel of the market thus resides in 'how little the individual participants need to know to be able to take the right action' (1945: 526–7). By contrast, Barnard featured coordinated adaptation among economic actors working through administration. In his view, the marvel of hierarchy is that coordinated adaptation is accomplished not spontaneously but in a 'conscious, deliberate, purposeful' way (1938: 4). Transaction cost economics concurs with Hayek and Barnard that adaptation is the central problem of economic organization and makes provision for adaptations of both autonomous and coordinated kinds. To the widely celebrated 'marvel of the market' (Hayek) is now therefore joined the hitherto scorned 'marvel of hierarchy' (Barnard).

The upshot is that the problem of economic organization is properly posed not in terms of the old ideological divide of markets or hierarchies but rather as the combined use of markets and hierarchies. As developed herein, there is a place for each generic mode of organization and each should be kept in its place – depending on the attributes of the transactions.

INTERDISCIPLINARY

Although it is obvious from the foregoing that economics is the central discipline out of which the economics of governance works, organization theory and law also figure prominently. If the firm works out of different mechanisms than the market, as Barnard contends, then presumably organization theory is relevant. And if the lens of contract is to be adopted and if ownership matters, contract law and property law are pertinent.

Organization Theory

The faculty of the Graduate School of Industrial Organization at Carnegie Mellon University made path-breaking contributions to interdisciplinary research over the period 1950–1970 and since.[7] What I have elsewhere referred to as the 'Carnegie Triple' was this: be disciplined; be interdisciplinary; and have an active mind (Williamson, 1996: 151). The admonition to be disciplined means taking your project seriously and working up the logic in a modest, slow, molecular, definitive way. If and when problems spill over from the discipline where they originate, the interdisciplinary researcher will follow the problems into the contiguous social sciences (of which organization theory is one). Having an active mind entails being curious. As against working out of the imperative, 'This is the law here!', ask instead, 'What is going on here?' (D'Andrade, 1986). Carnegie urged the student of organization to be curious and to eschew fanciful constructions by addressing problems on their own terms.[8]

Organization theory is a huge subject and I will address only three aspects of it here: human actors, near-decomposability, and the pervasive importance of intertemporal transformations. Interestingly, the economist Frank Knight prefigured the first of these in 1921, when he advised economists to come to terms with 'human nature as we know it' (1965: 270), and distinguished 'five variable elements in individual attributes and capacities', the first three of which are (1965: 241–2):

> (1) Men *differ in their capacity* by perception and inference *to form correct judgments* as to the future course of events in the environment. This capacity, furthermore, is far from homogeneous, some persons excelling in foresight in one kind of problem situations, others in other kinds, in almost endless variety. Of especial importance is the variation in the power of *reading* human nature, of *forecasting* the conduct of other men, as contrasted with scientific judgment in regard to natural phenomena. (2) Another, though related, difference is found in men's capacities to *judge means* and discern and plan the steps and adjustments necessary to meet the anticipated future situation. (3) There is a similar variation in the power to *execute* the plans and adjustments believed to be requisite and desirable.

A fundamental but much neglected lesson, as I interpret these human attribute and capacity differences (in foresight; reading and forecasting human conduct; ascertaining the requisite means; planning, implementation, and adaptation), is that organization is an instrument by which to harness the specialization of labour in all of these respects. Rather, therefore, then assume, implicitly if not explicitly, that the cognitive, leadership, and conduct attributes of human actors are uniform throughout the population, variance in the capacity of human actors is where much of the interesting economizing action resides.

There is no more persistent critic of the overuse of hyperrationality reasoning in economics than Simon, whose general position on human actors is that 'Nothing is more fundamental in setting our research agenda and informing our research methods than our view of the nature of the human beings whose behavior we are studying' (1985: 303) – to include cognition and self-interestedness. In cognitive respects, Simon describes human actors as possessing 'bounded rationality', by which he means that they are 'intendedly rational, but only limitedly so' (1957: xxiv). Self-interest is described in relatively benign terms as 'frailty of motive' (1985: 303); and evolutionary fitness is ascribed to docility, which Simon describes as tractable, manageable, and teachable (1991: 35).

Bounded rationality directly challenges concepts of omniscience and optimality and reveals a need to examine the architecture of complexity. Simon's treatment of nearly decomposable systems is such an effort, where '(a) in a nearly decomposable system, the short-run behavior of each of the component subsystems is approximately independent of the other components; (b) in the long run, the behavior of any one of the components depends only in an aggregate way on the behavior of the other components' (Simon, 1962: 474). Modular designs have these properties. More generally Simon concludes that 'Hierarchy . . . is one of the central structural schemes that the architect of complexity uses' (1962: 468).

Transaction cost economics expressly appeals to bounded rationality in describing complex contracts as incomplete and views firms as an assemblage of nearly decomposable stages. I take exception, however, with the nonstrategic way in which Simon describes self-interest. Robert Michels' early and influential study of oligarchy is revealing in this respect.[9]

Michels' famous book on *Political Parties* (1962) is a sociological study of the oligarchical tendencies of modern democracy. Original democratic intentions notwithstanding, organization, like the law, has a life of its own – one manifestation of which is that the leadership uses the instruments of organization to gain and maintain control. 'Reduced to its most concise expression, the fundamental sociological law of political parties . . . [is this]: It is organization which gives birth to the dominion of the elected over the electors, of the mandatories over the mandators, of the delegates over the delegators. *Who says organization, says oligarchy*' (Michels, 1962: 365; emphasis added). Entrenchment efforts by the leadership is what explains the Iron Law of Oligarchy.

This grim assessment is not, however, the end of the story. Upon discovering a regularity, the lesson is not to accept the condition but rather to ascertain the mechanisms through which it works and take cost-effective countervailing measures: 'nothing but a serene and frank examination of the oligarchical dangers of democracy *will enable us to minimize these dangers*' (Michels, 1962: 370; emphasis added).[10] Michels the sociologist thus makes 'rational spirit' recommendations that were 50 years ahead of his time. Much of the mid-century strain between economics and sociology to which Paul Samuelson and James Duesenberry referred[11] would vanish if Michels' practice of uncovering organizational regularities and working out the ramifications by pushing the logic to completion had been widely adopted.

Barnard's contributions to the study of hierarchy went beyond the use of formal organization (to accomplish coordinated adaptations of a 'conscious, deliberate, purposeful' kind) to include informal organization, where the latter was largely of a spontaneous kind. Indeed, 'formal organizations are vitalized and conditioned by informal organization . . . [T]here cannot be one without the other' (Barnard, 1938: 120). Informal organization contributes to the viability of formal organization in three significant respects: 'One of the indispensable functions of informal organizations in formal organizations . . . [is] that of communication . . . Another function is that of maintaining the cohesiveness in formal organizations through regulating the willingness to serve and the stability of objective authority. A third function is the maintenance of the feeling of personal integrity, of self-respect, and independent choice' (Barnard: 122). Taken together, formal and informal organization provide internal organization with many of the attributes of 'private ordering' (on more of which later).

Alfred D. Chandler, Jr. was neither an economist nor an organization theorist but was a business historian. Author of a series of pathbreaking books in his field,[12] the one to which I would call particular attention is *Strategy and Structure* (1962). On my reading, Chandler's studies of nineteenth- and twentieth-century organizational innovations breathe contemporary significance into Arrow's contention that 'Truly among man's innovations, the use of organization to accomplish his ends is among both his greatest and earliest' (1971: 224).

Of special significance was Chandler's examination of managerial discretion in connection with the organizational innovation (by Pierre DuPont, Alfred P. Sloan, Jr., Donaldson Brown, and others) of the multidivisional form organization in the 1920s. As compared with the earlier unitary (U-form) form of organization, in which strategic and operating decisions were joined, the multidivisional (M-form) structure worked out of a logic of organization in which operating and strategic decisions were separated – broadly in the spirit of double-feedback (Ashby, 1960).[13]

Law

My treatment of the law focuses on contract law, although TCE also relates to antitrust, regulation, corporate governance, and other aspects of the law. Interestingly, John R. Commons appealed to W. N. Hohfeld's analysis, terminology, and classification of legal relations in his efforts to introduce operational content into institutional economics.[14] Alas, what Hohfeld provided was a vocabulary of 'jural opposites' and 'jural correlatives' that are classified as to rights, privilege, power, and immunity (Commons, 1924: 91–134). These concepts provided an elaborate taxonomy, but a theory replete with refutable implications never materialized. As with the legal realism movement in the United States (Schlegel, 1979, p. 459), so with older style institutional economics: for lack of operationalization, both movements ran themselves 'into the sand'.

This is not, however, to say that neither left a trace. As described above, Commons had deep insights into economic organization, and the same is true of the legal realists, of which Karl Llewellyn was one of the earliest and most important. Llewellyn's early critique of the 'legal rules' contracting tradition, according to which twentieth-century law students learned contract law in the nineteenth-century casebook manner (Feldman, 2004: 476–8), is that this made limited contact with contract in practice. More instructive for many purposes was the concept of 'contract as framework' (Llewellyn, 1931: 736–7):

> [T]he major importance of legal contract is to provide a framework for well-nigh every type of group organization and for well-nigh every type of passing or permanent relation between individuals and groups . . . a framework highly adjustable, a framework which almost never accurately indicates real working relations, but which affords a rough indication around which such relations vary, an occasional guide in cases of doubt, and a norm of ultimate appeal when the relations cease in fact to work.

The views of the 'industrial pluralists' in the field of labour law are broadly in this same spirit. Thus whereas some labour lawyers advise that the Wagner Act of 1935 should be interpreted in a legalistic way (Stone, 1981), Harry Shulman urged that the Act provided a 'bare legal framework' that permitted management and labour to devise workable mechanisms suited to their needs (1955: 1000).[15] Grievance and arbitration procedures were thus favoured over judicial disposition of disputes because of the corrosive effects on continuing relationships that adversarial proceedings encouraged (Shulman, 1955: p. 1024). Archibald Cox likewise held that the collective bargaining agreement should be understood as an instrument of governance, as well as an instrument of exchange: 'The collective agreement governs complex, many-sided relations between large numbers of people in a going concern for very substantial periods of time' (1958: 22). Provision for unforeseeable contingencies is made by writing the contract in general, flexible terms and supplying the parties with a special arbitration machinery. 'One simply cannot spell out every detail of life in an industrial establishment, or even of that portion which both management and labor agree is a matter of mutual concern' (Cox, 1958: 23).

The technical versus purposive distinction made by Llewellyn was elaborated by Clyde Summers, who distinguished between 'black letter law' on the one hand and a more circumstantial approach to law on the other. 'The epitome of abstraction is the *Restatement*, which illustrates its black letter rules by transactions suspended in midair, creating the illusion that contract rules can be stated without reference to surrounding circumstances and are therefore generally applicable to all contractual transactions' (Summers, 1969: 566). Such a conception does not and cannot provide a 'framework for integrating rules and principles applicable to all contractual transactions' (Summers, 1969: 566). A broader conception of contract, with emphasis on the affirmative purposes of the law and effective governance relations, is needed if that is to be realized. Summers conjectured in this connection that 'the principles common to the whole range of contractual transactions are relatively few and of such generality and competing character that they should not be stated as legal rules at all' (1969: 527).

Stewart Macaulay's empirical studies of commercial contract are corroborative. Macaulay reported that outsourcing is normally a much more informal and cooperative venture than legalistic approaches to contracting would suggest. He cited one businessman to the effect that 'you can settle any dispute if you keep the lawyers and accountants out of it. They just do not understand the give-and-take needed in business' (1963: 61). More generally, Macaulay's studies of contractual practices support the view that contractual disputes and ambiguities are more often settled by private ordering than by appeal to the courts.

Marc Galanter likewise took exception with 'legal centralism' and emphasized the importance of 'private ordering' (1981). Thus whereas the legal centralist approach to contract holds that disputes 'require "access" to a forum external to the original social setting of the dispute [whereby] remedies will be provided as prescribed in some body of authoritative learning and dispensed by experts who operate under the auspices of the state' (1981: 1), the facts disclose otherwise. Most disputes including many that under current rules could be brought to a court, are resolved by avoidance, self-help, and the like (p. 2). This is because in 'many instances the participants can devise more satisfactory solutions to their disputes than can professionals constrained to apply general rules on the basis of limited knowledge of the dispute' (p. 4).

Ian Macneil's examination of contract similarly describes the discrete transaction paradigm – 'sharp in by clear agreement, sharp out by clear performance' (1974: 738) – as an important but special case. Thus although reliance on legal rules, formal documents, and self-liquidating transactions describes the ideal transaction in both law and economics, deviations from this ideal are common among contracts in practice. 'Two common characteristics of long-term contracts are the existence of gaps in their planning and the presence of a range of processes and techniques used by contract planners to create flexibility in lieu of either leaving gaps or trying to plan rigidly' (Macneil, 1978: 865). Incomplete contracts supported by the mechanisms of governance are plainly contemplated. Black letter law has its place, but business lawyers, for many purposes, are better described as transaction cost engineers (Gilson, 1984: 255).

SUMMARIZING

The realization that the resource allocation paradigm was self-limiting and that the black boxes of firm and market organization needed to be opened up, thereby to examine the purposes served by the mechanisms inside, had begun to take hold by 1970. A variety of responses took shape, of which transaction cost economics is one – according to which markets and hierarchies are examined in a unified way through the lens of contract, with emphasis on the governance of contractual relations.

This move from choice to contract is accomplished by recognizing that more veridical descriptions of human actors in cognitive and self-interestedness respects have massive ramifications for our research methods and our research agenda. But there is more. The lens of contract/governance approach to economic organization focuses especially on ongoing contractual relations, with emphasis on adaptations of both autonomous and coordinated kinds – where markets enjoy the advantage in autonomous adaptation and hierarchy in coordinated adaptation. The upshot is that economic organization is examined at a more microanalytic level of detail, in both transactional and governance respects, than had been customary under the orthodox setup. Predictions and empirical testing ensued.

This interdisciplinary project moves beyond economics to draw selectively on organization theory and contract law. In addition to human actor considerations, organization theory also calls attention to consequential intertemporal regularities that attend economic organization.

Upon uncovering a potentially significant regularity, the object is to ascertain the mechanisms through which it operates and work out the organizational design ramifications – whereupon the hazards and benefits that attend 'organization' can be mitigated or enhanced, as the case may be.

As for contract law, the basic move here is to supplant the idea of a single, all-purpose form of contract law by recognizing that the operative law of contract varies among governance structures. Court ordering remains important, but private ordering is where much of the more interesting and relevant action resides. Recourse to principled courts for purposes of ultimate appeal nevertheless serves salutary purposes.

ACKNOWLEDGEMENTS

This chapter is a slightly revised version of a paper previously published by Blackwell Publishing Ltd as 'Transaction cost economics: the precursors' by Oliver E. Williamson in *Economic Affairs* **28**(3), 7–14. © Institute of Economic Affairs 2008. Reproduced with permission.

NOTES

1. Thus although Oskar Lange regarded bureaucratization rather than resource allocation to be the 'real danger of socialism', bureaucratization was thereafter ignored because 'this argument belongs to the field of sociology rather than economic theory and must therefore be dispensed with here' (1938: 109). Such a property rights view was also held by other leading economists. Paul Samuelson (1947), for example, distinguished between economics and sociology by ascribing rationality to the former and nonrationality to the latter; and James Duesenberry subsequently quipped (1960) that while economics was preoccupied with how individuals made choices, sociology maintained that individuals did not have any choices to make.
2. The new theories included mechanism design, agency theory, resource-based theory, property rights theory, evolutionary economics, and transaction cost economics. Earlier efforts in the 1960s include the behavioural theory of the firm (Cyert and March, 1963) and managerial discretion theories (Baumol, 1959; Marris, 1964; Williamson, 1964).
3. Although this oversimplifies, the basic analysis survives if choice of technology is made a decision variable (Riordan and Williamson, 1985).
4. The 'obvious' advantage of internal production over outsourcing in price discovery respects is that the firm avoids the need to consult the market about prices because it uses internal accounting prices of a formulaic kind (say, of a cost-plus kind) when transferring a good or service from one internal stage to another. If, however, that is the source of the advantage of internal organization over market procurement, the obvious lesson is to apply this same practice to outside procurement. The firm simply advises its purchasing office to turn a blind eye to the market by placing orders, period by period, with a qualified sole-source external supplier who agrees to sell on cost-plus terms. In that event, firm and market are put on a parity in price discovery respects – which is to say that the price discovery burden that Coase ascribes to the market does not survive comparative institutional scrutiny.

To be sure, one could object that cost-plus contracting differs within firms and between firms – which indeed is correct. But then the issue is what is responsible for these differences. As described elsewhere (Williamson, 1991), firm and market differ in discrete structural ways. Incentive differences, administrative command and control differences, and dispute settlement differences as between firm and market are where the crucial action resides.

5. Although the former may appear to be alien to the transaction cost economics project, in that it examines general equilibrium under the assumption that state contingent contracting can be costlessly implemented, Arrow–Debreu introduces a new framework for thinking about contracts that was hitherto missing. A different appreciation for where transaction costs arise and how this matters results.
6. Arrow's interim treatment of medical care is also noteworthy. His examination of medical care begins by insisting that price and output are not the only relevant data: 'the institutional organization and the observable mores of the medical profession are included among the data to be used in assessing the competitiveness of the medical care market. I shall also examine the presence or absence of the preconditions for the equivalence of competitive equilibrium and optimal states' (1971: 180–1). The non-marketability of certain identifiable, technologically feasible, welfare enhancing actions (Arrow, 1971: 182) is relevant to the latter, where non-marketability is explained by the attributes of human actors.
7. As Jacques Dreze recalls his visit to Carnegie in the late 1950s, 'Never since then have I experienced such intellectual excitement' (1995: 123). That was my experience as well.
8. I also associate this lesson with Kenneth Arrow (see pp. 13–15).
9. 'One of the earliest analyses, and in many ways still the best, of how some participants may seek to preserve an organization even at the sacrifice of the goals for which it was originally established is that provided by Robert Michels' (Scott, 1987: 53).
10. Michels can thus be interpreted as an early practitioner of 'feasible foresight' – which is a concept that many organization theorists regard with grave scepticism. Such scepticism can lead to a truncated treatment of complex economic organization. Note also that some unanticipated regularities can take the form of benefits. In that event, the challenge is to take ex ante actions to enhance (rather than mitigate) the beneficial effects.
11. See note 1, supra.
12. In addition to *Strategy and Structure* (1962), Chandler's books, *The Visible Hand* (1977) and *Scale and Scope* (1990) were also very influential.
13. Thus whereas disturbances in degree are dealt with in the primary feedback loop by the application of 'routines', disturbances in kind are dealt with in the secondary feedback loop and entail a more strategic view of the enterprise. The move from the centralized U-form structure to the decentralized M-form structure has ramifications for the separation of ownership from control to which Adolf Berle and Gardiner Means (1932) called attention. If managerial discretion in the large corporation is the problem to which Berle and Means had reference and if the 'central office' within the M-form structure is used to bring managerial discretion under control, then management is both the problem and (part of) the solution!
14. Both George Stigler (1983: 169–70) and Ronald Coase (1964: 230) take the earlier style institutional economics to task for its failure to develop a positive research agenda. I agree. But whereas Stigler and especially Coase treat older institutional economists as anti-theoretical and lacking in promising ideas, I contend that Commons had profoundly important insights that contained the seeds of a positive research agenda.
15. This and the next two paragraphs are from Williamson (1985: 16).

REFERENCES

Arrow, Kenneth J. (1969), 'The organization of economic activity: issues pertinent to the choice of market versus nonmarket allocation', in *The Analysis and Evaluation of Public Expenditure: The PPB System*, Vol. 1, US Joint Economic Committee, 91st Congress, 1st Session, Washington, DC: US Government Printing Office, pp. 59–73.

Arrow, Kenneth J. (1971), *Essays in the Theory of Risk-Bearing*, Chicago, IL: Markham.

Arrow, Kenneth J. and Gerard Debreu (1954), 'Existence of an Equilibrium for a Competitive Economy', *Econometrica*, **22**, 265–90.

Ashby, W. Ross (1960), *Design for a Brain*, New York: John Wiley & Sons.

Barnard, Chester (1938), *The Functions of the Executive*, Cambridge, MA: Harvard University Press (fifteenth printing, 1962).

Baumol, W. J. (1959), *Business Behavior, Value and Growth*, New York: Macmillan.

Ben-Porath, Yoram (1980), 'The F-connection: families, friends, and firms and the organization of exchange', *Population and Development Review*, **6** (March), 1–30.

Berle, Adolph A. and Gardner C. Means, Jr. (1932), *The Modern Corporation and Private Property*, New York: Macmillan.

Brennan, Geoffrey and James Buchanan (1983), 'Predictive power and choice among regimes', *Economic Journal*, **93** (March), 89–105.

Buchanan, James (1975), 'A contractarian paradigm for applying economic theory', in *Microeconomic Theory: Conflict and Contract: Papers and Proceedings*', *American Economic Review*, **65** (May), 225–30.

Buchanan, James (1987), 'The Constitution of Economic Policy', *American Economic Review*, **77** (June), 243–50.

Buchanan, James (2001), 'Game Theory, Mathematics, and Economics', *Journal of Economic Methodology*, **8** (March), 27–32.

Buchanan, James and Gordon Tullock (1962), *The Calculus of Consent*, Ann Arbor, MI: University of Michigan Press.

Chandler, Alfred D., Jr. (1962), *Strategy and Structure*, Cambridge, MA: MIT Press.

Chandler, Alfred D., Jr. (1977), *The Visible Hand: The Managerial Revolution in American Business*, Cambridge, MA: Harvard University Press.

Chandler, Alfred D., Jr. (1990), *Scale and Scope: the Dynamics of Industrial Capitalism*, Cambridge, MA: Harvard University Press.

Coase, Ronald H. (1937), 'The Nature of the Firm', *Economica N.S.*, *4*: 386–405, Reprinted in Oliver E. Williamson and Sidney Winter (eds), (1991), *The Nature of the Firm: Origins, Evolution, Development*, New York: Oxford University Press, pp. 18–33.

Coase, Ronald H. (1960), 'The Problem of Social Cost', *Journal of Law and Economics*, **3** (October), 1–44.

Coase, Ronald H. (1964), 'The regulated industries: discussion', *American Economic Review*, **54** (May), 194–7.

Coase, Ronald H. (1972), 'Industrial organization: a proposal for research', in V. R. Fuchs (ed.), *Policy Issues and Research Opportunities in Industrial Organization*, New York: National Bureau of Economic Research, pp. 59–73.

Coase, Ronald H. (1992), 'The institutional structure of production', *American Economic Review*, **82** (September), 713–19.
Commons, John R. (1924), *Legal Foundations of Capitalism*, New York: Macmillan.
Commons, John R. (1932), 'The problem of correlating law, economics, and ethics', *Wisconsin Law Review*, **8**, 3–26.
Commons, John R. (1950), *The Economics of Collective Action*, Madison, WI: University of Wisconsin Press.
Cox, A. (1958), 'The legal nature of collective bargaining agreements', *Michigan Law Review*, **57** (November), 1–36.
Cyert, Richard M. and James G. March (1963), *A Behavioral Theory of the Firm*, Englewood Cliffs, NJ: Prentice-Hall.
D'Andrade, Roy (1986), 'Three scientific world views and the covering law model', in Donald W. Fiske and Richard A. Schweder (eds), *Metatheory in Social Science: Pluralisms and Subjectivities*, Chicago, IL: University of Chicago Press.
Demsetz, Harold (1983), 'The structure of ownership and the theory of the firm', *Journal of Law & Economics*, **26** (June), 375–90.
Dreze, Jacques (1995), '40 years of public economics – a personal perspective', *Journal of Economic Perspectives*, **9** (2), 111–30.
Duesenberry, James (1960), 'An economic analysis of fertility: comment', in *Demographic Change and Economic Change in Developed Countries*, National Bureau of Economic Research. Princeton, NJ: Princeton University Press.
Feldman, Stephen M. (2004), 'The Transformation of an Academic Discipline', *Journal of Legal Education*, **54** (December), 471–98.
Fischer, Stanley (1977), 'Long-term contracting, sticky prices, and monetary policy: comment', *Journal of Monetary Economics*, **3**, 317–24.
Fuller, Lon L. (1954), 'American legal philosophy at mid-century', *Journal of Legal Education*, **6** (4), 457–85.
Galanter, Marc (1981), 'Justice in many rooms: courts, private ordering, and indigenous law', *Journal of Legal Pluralism*, **19**, 1–47.
Georgescu-Roegen, Nicholas (1971), *The Entropy Law and Economic Process*, Cambridge, MA: Harvard University Press.
Gilson, Ronald (1984), 'Value creation by business lawyers: legal skills and asset pricing', *Yale Law Journal*, **94** (December), 239–313.
Hayek, Friedrich (1945), 'The use of knowledge in society', *American Economic Review*, **35** (September), 519–30.
Knight, Frank H. (1941), 'Review of Melville J. Herskovits' "Economic Anthropology"', *Journal of Political Economy*, **49** (April), 247–58.
Knight, Frank H. (1965), *Risk, Uncertainty, and Profit*, New York: Harper & Row.
Kreps, David M. (1990), 'Corporate culture and economic theory', in James Alt and Kenneth Shepsle (eds), *Perspectives on Positive Political Economy*, New York: Cambridge University Press, pp. 90–143.
Lange, Oskar (1938), 'On the theory of economic socialism', in Benjamin Lippincott (ed.), *On the Economic Theory of Socialism*, Minneapolis, MN: University of Minnesota Press, pp. 55–143.
Llewellyn, Karl N. (1931), 'What price contract? An essay in perspective', *Yale Law Journal*, **40**, 704–51.
Macaulay, Stewart (1963), 'Non-contractual relations in business', *American Sociological Review*, **28**, 55–70.

Macneil, Ian R. (1974), 'The many futures of contracts', *Southern California Law Review*, **47** (May), 691–816.
Macneil, Ian R. (1978), 'Contracts: adjustments of long-term economic relations under classical, neoclassical and relational contracts', *Northwestern University Law Review*, **72**: 854–906.
Marris, Robin (1964), *The Economic Theory of Managerial Capitalism*, New York: Free Press.
Michels, Robert (1962), *Political Parties*, Glencoe, IL: Free Press.
Riordan, Michael and Oliver Williamson (1985), 'Asset specificity and economic organization', *International Journal of Industrial Organization*, **3**, 365–78.
Samuelson, Paul A. (1947), *Foundations of Economic Analysis*, Cambridge, MA: Harvard University Press.
Schlegel, John Henry (1979), 'American legal realism and empirical science: from the Yale experience', *Buffalo Law Review*, **28** (Summer), 459–586.
Scott, W. Richard (1987), *Organizations*, Englewood Cliffs, NJ: Prentice-Hall (2nd edn).
Shulman, Harry (1955), 'Reason, contract, and law in labor relations', *Harvard Law Review*, **68** (June), 999–1036.
Simon, Herbert (1957), *Administrative Behavior*, New York: Macmillan, 2nd edn.
Simon, Herbert (1962), 'The architecture of complexity', *Proceedings of the American Philosophical Society*, **106** (December), 467–82.
Simon, Herbert (1984), 'On the behavioral and rational foundations of economic dynamics', *Journal of Economic Behavior and Organization*, **5** (March), 35–56.
Simon, Herbert (1985), 'Human nature in politics: the dialogue of psychology with political science', *American Political Science Review*, **79**, 293–304.
Simon, Herbert (1991), 'Organizations and markets', *Journal of Economic Perspectives*, **5** (Spring), 25–44.
Stigler, George J. (1983), 'Remarks appearing in "The Fire of Truth", Edmund Kitch (ed.)', *Journal of Law and Economics*, **26**, 163–233.
Stone, K. (1981), 'The postwar paradigm in American labor law', *Yale Law Journal*, **90** (June), 1509–80.
Summers, Clyde (1969), 'Collective agreements and the law of contracts', *Yale Law Journal*, **78** (March), 537–75.
Williamson, Oliver E. (1964), *The Economics of Discretionary Behavior: Managerial Objectives in a Theory of the Firm*, Englewood Cliffs, NJ: Prentice-Hall.
Williamson, Oliver E. (1985), *The Economic Institutions of Capitalism*, New York: Free Press.
Williamson, Oliver E. (1991), 'Comparative economic organization: the analysis of discrete structural alternatives', *Administrative Science Quarterly*, **36** (June), 269–96.
Williamson, Oliver E. (1996), *The Mechanisms of Governance*, New York: Oxford University Press.
Williamson, Oliver E. (2002), 'The theory of the firm as governance structure: from choice to contract', *Journal of Economic Perspective*, **16** (Summer), 171–95.

2. Property rights allocation of common pool resources

Gary D. Libecap

INTRODUCTION

Command and control regulation typically has been the first formal government response to mitigate the losses of the common pool.[1] Dissatisfaction with the subsequent performance of regulation, however, has resulted in a search for alternative institutional responses, including deregulation and the corresponding assignment of property rights of some type as part of market-based reforms.[2] For instance, Tietenberg (2007: 69) reported that tradable use permits were now used in nine applications in air pollution control, seventy-five in fisheries, three in water and five in land use control that previously had been regulated. Property rights approaches offer more flexibility, cost savings, information generation, migration to high-valued uses, and better alignment of incentives for conservation or investment in the resource. The more complete are property rights, the more the private and social net benefits of resource use are meshed, eliminating externalities and the losses of the common pool.[3] By contrast, centralized regulation relies more upon uniform standards, arbitrary controls on access, constraints on timing of use, and/or limits on technology or production capital, and hence, suffers from high cost, inflexibility, ineffectiveness and industry capture. Further, regulatory decisions take place in the absence of information about alternative uses that market trades generate. Finally, centralized state regulatory rules may or may not align with the incentives of actual users of the resource. Generally, no party involved – actual users, regulators, politicians – is a residual claimant to the social gains from investment or trade.[4]

Deregulation through the use of property rights, however, requires adoption of an allocation mechanism. Because of distributional implications, allocation can be very controversial and conflict over distribution limits the adoption of property rights and their effectiveness in mitigating the losses of the common pool. At least some constituencies, including regulators, who benefited from the previous regulatory arrangement, will be disadvantaged under a new rights system and have incentive to resist the new arrangement. Other parties that previously used the resource will be denied access. Production under a property rights regime has a different composition of inputs and timing than what occurs under open-access or regulation, with negative impacts on certain groups of labor, input sellers, service organizations and processors. These production changes are inherent in the efficiency gains of privatization. Further, as the resource rebounds and becomes more valuable, new owners have wealth, status and political influence not available to those without access privileges. These distributional factors, along with the costs of bounding, measurement, and enforcement constrain the extent and timing of the assignment of property rights to address the potential losses of the common pool as part of a process of deregulation.

OPEN-ACCESS, REGULATION, AND THE ALLOCATION OF PROPERTY RIGHTS

The Losses of the Commons

The losses of the commons are well known. Garrett Hardin's (1968), 'The Tragedy of the Commons' made clear in the popular scientific press what resource users had always understood, that open-access can result in important economic and social costs.[5] Hardin was not the first to call attention to the tragedy of the commons, however. More than a decade before his article, H. Scott Gordon (1954) clearly outlined similar logic in another classic: 'The Economic Theory of a Common-Property Resource: The Fishery'. Gordon's analysis was extended by Scott (1955), Cheung (1970), among others.

Central State (Command and Control) Regulation

The first formal response to the commons generally has been central, command and control regulation of entry and production to include: (a) restrictions on access or time of use, such as limits placed on non-citizens or non-residents in fisheries; (b) equipment controls, such as on vessel size or technology used in fisheries and uniform requirements for scrubbers on power plants; and (c) extraction regulations, such as prorationing in oil production and air pollution emission controls. The aim of these regulations is to constrain output to more optimal levels and thereby avoid some rent dissipation.

State regulation is the initial resort for a number of reasons. One is that it avoids the complex, costly and controversial allocation of more definite property rights, which could directly address the problem of externalities. Second, state regulation may involve lower costs of measurement, bounding, and enforcement, and if the resource is of relatively low value, more definite property rights may be too costly to be an option.[6] For example, in the western United States when water was plentiful relative to demand, there was little effort to precisely define property rights to water and water allocation and management largely was regulated by the state. As water values have risen, rights have been made more precise and water markets have emerged as an alternative to state regulation of distribution.[7] Another reason is that state regulation is consistent with the notion that many natural resources are rightly 'public' with ownership reserved in the state rather than in private parties. This notion is part of arguments made for wildlife and freshwater sports fisheries.[8] Similarly, if there are important public goods associated with the resource, then state ownership and regulation of access may be optimal. This is a rationale for the establishment of national parks and wilderness areas. Finally, state regulation can advantage certain influential political constituencies who mold regulatory policy in their behalf. While market processes are relatively transparent, political and bureaucratic processes are less so, facilitating preferential treatment to certain parties.[9]

Allocation of Property Rights

Often, state regulation involves high cost and inflexibility and is ineffective in stemming open-access losses. If the resource is of high enough value to warrant adoption of more definite property rights and resort to more flexible market processes, then deregulation can occur. But property rights arrangements are costly and how they are implemented affects their timing and efficacy in addressing the losses of the commons. There are several allocation mechanisms.

First-possession rules

As we will see, first-possession is the dominant method of establishing property rights.[10] It assigns ownership on a first-come, first-served basis or first-in-time, first-in-right. First-possession rules are attractive because they recognize incumbent parties, who have experience in exploiting the resource and hence, may be the low-cost, high-valued users. Incumbents also have a direct stake in access to the resource and will be important constituents in any property rights distribution. They are concerned about past investment in specific assets, which otherwise would not be deployable to other uses. Since first-possession rules recognize these investments, this security should encourage future outlays. Allocations that do not consider the position of incumbents likely will face opposition, raising the costs of rights assignment and enforcement.

First-possession rules also recognize valuable risk taking by innovators and entrepreneurs, who first experiment with and use a resource. Further, under first-possession the market determines optimal claim size, whereas under other allocation arrangements bureaucratic or political objectives define the assignments. If these are not consistent with optimal production size then further trade is required. Hence, first-possession can economize on transaction costs.[11] Examples of first-possession rules include allocating property rights based on historical catch in fisheries, on past fuel use in emission permits, prior appropriation in water rights, and on novelty in patent and copyright assignment.

A criticism of first-possession is that it can encourage competing parties to race for ownership and to dissipate rents. If the parties are homogeneous in the costs of claiming the resource, then full dissipation is possible as competitive conflicts continue until all rents are exhausted. If, on the other hand, the parties are heterogeneous and the property rights are long-term and secure, then allocation losses will be more limited.[12] Those who can claim the asset at lower cost will do so and limit access by higher-cost claimants so that some rents, at least, are protected. There are costs with any rights allocation rule, and the 'winners' of such a race for control may also be the most efficient producers or subsequently trade their claims to such producers. Accordingly, first-possession may not be more costly than other assignments. Generally, if the transaction costs of exchange are high, then it makes sense to assign rights to low-cost users with histories of past involvement in the resource. If incumbents are not the low-cost or most efficient users and first-possession allocation is used, then it is important to lower transaction costs in order to facilitate subsequent exchange.

Despite their ubiquity, first-possession rules can conflict with fairness considerations, and this situation raises political opposition to them in the assignment of property rights. First-possession discriminates against new entrants who do not have a history of past use. Accordingly, incumbents earn windfall gains as new entrants purchase rights to the asset. If first-possession ownership is viewed as rewarding those who by luck and connections initially were allocated the right, then they may be opposed or their returns taxed.[13]

Uniform allocation rules

Equal sharing rules avoid the distributional concerns associated with first-possession and better reflect egalitarian goals. If there are no restrictions on subsequent exchange of property rights and transaction costs are low, there are few efficiency implications. The resource still migrates to high-valued users. Uniform allocations also avoid the measurement costs of verifying claims of past production or use or of documenting precedence claims that are part of first-possession assignments. They can also avoid the costly pursuit of property rights when first-possession is known to be the allocation rule. Lotteries are examples of uniform allocations because each claimant is given an equal, random draw in the assignment of rights to the resource. Uniform allocations are most effective when applied to new resources where there are no incumbent claims and all parties are relatively homogeneous.

Auction allocation

A third allocation mechanism is auction. It can directly place asset into the hands of those who have the highest value for the asset. It thereby avoids the transaction costs of re-allocation. Auctions also generate resources for the state and avoid the windfalls that might be considered unearned and divisive. Auction returns can be used to cover the costs of defining and enforcing property rights and other costs of resource management. As with lotteries, auctions work best for new, unallocated resources where there are no incumbent claimants and where resource values are very high. By granting more of the rents to the state, auctions reduce the distributional implications of first-possession or uniform-allocation. As with other allocation arrangements, there are costs to auctions. The state must be able to measure and enforce resource boundaries and individual allocations secured by auction. The terms of the auction may also be influenced by competing claimants who lobby for rules that provide them with specific advantages. Because of their design costs and opposition by incumbent users, auctions are not used as often as economists have predicted.[14] With these concepts in mind, we now turn to environmental and natural resources where rights institutions have been adopted to augment or replace central regulation: oil and natural gas, air pollution emission permits, and fisheries.

ALLOCATION OF RIGHTS TO SUBSURFACE OIL AND GAS RESERVOIRS IN NORTH AMERICA

In the United States and Canada rights to access oil, natural gas and other minerals generally are assigned to surface land owners based on first-possession. Actual ownership of the flow of oil and natural gas comes through the common law rule of capture, which creates conditions for competitive open-access extraction if there are multiple surface owners above the deposit. In this sense, first-possession allocation of rights to the flow was costly. Had rights to the stock also been assigned based on first-possession claims, as was done with hard-rock minerals, then more rent dissipation could have been avoided and claims could have been exchanged to achieve optimal production size as technological conditions changed.[15] Oil and natural gas stocks, however, are migratory and subject to competitive extraction.

One alternative arrangement to reduce dissipation was withholding mineral rights by the state, but this was not consistent with US land policy that emphasized private ownership of natural resources. Another was mandatory unitization for coordinated extraction. This option is discussed below. Where there were incumbent resource claimants, *ex post* auctions to reallocate or more formally allocate the asset generally were not feasible due to opposition from existing claimants due to the distributional implications of such actions.

The first response to open-access was state regulation of production, with most regulations adopted in the US between the late 1920s and 1960. Libecap and Smith (2002) describe the pattern of state regulation of oil and gas production. Overall production 'allowables' were determined each year in each state based on geologic conditions and more importantly, on estimated oil demand and supply. These allowables were then prorated among the regulated firms as annual production quotas. Quotas were based on past production and investment, such as the number and depth of existing wells on a lease. The latter variables encouraged denser drilling of deep, costly wells in order to increase quota size, and thereby shifted regulated production from low to high-cost producers. Further to gain their political support for regulation, the owners of numerous small, high-cost firms in Texas were able to obtain exemption from prorationing rules for their so-called 'stripper' wells (very high-cost, low-production wells). These and other preferences to high-cost small firms reduced the overall benefits of regulation by over $2 billion annually by the early 1960s. As a result, state regulation (prorationing) was criticized as being very costly.[16] There were calls for less reliance upon regulation and more on private production controls through unitization through deregulation.

Under unitization, production is delegated through negotiation to a single firm, the unit operator, with net revenues apportioned among all parties on the field (including those that would otherwise be producing). As the only producer on the field and a residual profit claimant, the unit operator has incentive to maximize field rents. Accordingly, unitization results in important economic gains: a time stream of output that more closely approximates the rent-maximizing pattern, increased oil recovery, and reduced wells and other capital costs.

Despite these attractions and advantages over central state regulation, conflicts over the allocation of unit shares or property rights have slowed unitization.[17] Wiggins and Libecap (1985) examine the bargaining problem underlying unit formation and Libecap and Smith (1999) describe the nature of a complete unit contract. As a result of conflicts over allocation, unit agreements can take a very long time to negotiate or breakdown and result in incomplete units that cover only part of a field. In their detailed analysis of seven units in Texas and New Mexico, Wiggins and Libecap found that they required from four to nine years from the time negotiations began until agreements could be reached. Moreover, in five of the seven cases the acreage in the final unit was less than that involved in the early negotiations. With incomplete units, part of the reservoir remains open-access or is organized into competitive subunits with significant losses. In the case of Prudhoe Bay, North America's largest producing field, Libecap and Smith describe a lengthy and contentious bargaining process. The field was discovered in 1968 and unit negotiations began in 1969. The first unit agreement was not reached until 1977 and was revised at least seven times due to disputes among the key producers over natural gas and oil valuation, investment, and production. In 1999 British Petroleum, one of the largest producers on the field, purchased ARCO, the other major operator, to effectively complete unitization of the field.

To speed the process of unitization and deregulation, states have intervened with so-called compulsory or forced unitization statutes as the costs of reliance solely on prorationing became apparent. These statutes relaxed unanimity voting requirements for share allocations. Between the late 1940s and the 1960s, all oil-producing states, except Texas adopted some form of forced unitization law to facilitate unit formation. Only in Texas was the power of small firms sufficiently great to block the legislation. Not surprisingly, Texas has a lower share of production from fully-unitized fields than does other states. It also has had more high-cost producers than other states.

ALLOCATION OF AIR POLLUTION EMISSION PERMITS

Early regulatory efforts to reduce air pollution in the US generally were costly and not effective. They relied on relatively inflexible, uniform air quality standards and required that polluting firms meet them. Regulation included rules on emissions, equipment to be used, such as types of scrubbers and performance standards. The uniform rules did not recognize that the costs of controlling emissions varied across and within firms.

Traditional regulation gave advantages to old plants and technology. There were few incentives to develop new technologies, and central regulation was often used politically to disadvantage certain firms and regions at the behest of entrenched interests with little environmental benefit.[18] Beginning in the mid-1970s dissatisfaction with the costs and performance of centralized air pollution regulation led to deregulation and adoption of emission trading programs, despite some resistance from regulatory agencies.[19]

Under deregulation, an annual targeted level of emissions is set and then prorated across permit holders, who are allowed to discharge a specified amount of pollution. The permits have been allocated through first-possession, based on past electricity production, heat generation, fuel use or emissions, free of charge. In some cases, a small portion, about 2 percent, have been auctioned to provide flexibility and to allow new entry by firms that did not have production histories. These emission permits are a right to use the air to discharge waste products in production. They can be traded and an active market has developed in most emission systems where tradable permits have been used successfully.[20] Rather than equating pollution levels across firms, these instruments equalize incremental abatement costs. Those firms with pollution below their allowable allotments can sell the residual emission rights, apply them to offset excess emissions in other parts of their operations, or bank them. As an example, consider SO_2 deregulation and trading under the 1990 Clean Air Act Amendments. There are various estimates of the cost savings of the program, but they range from \$5 to \$12 billion over the command and control regulation alternative.

The objective was to reduce SO_2 and NO_x emissions by 10 million and 2 million tons respectively from their 1980 levels. These are the principle gases associated with acid rain and they largely were emitted by electrical utilities. Two phases were used. Phase I, which ran through 1995, assigned emission permits to over 400 electrical generating plants and Phase II, which extended regulation to almost all generating units.[21] Total emissions were gradually reduced each year to achieve the targeted level.

Emission permits were granted on first-possession so that existing polluters were grandfathered and newer units were disadvantaged. There is no available information on how negotiations over pollution rights may have slowed the process of deregulation. Nevertheless, politics clearly played a role. Utilities that began operating in 1996 and thereafter had to purchase their allowances on the open market. Phase I allowances were allocated free of charge based on past power generation as indicated by heat input. The allocation formula granted emission rates of 2.5 lb of SO_2/mmBtu (million British thermal units) of heat input, multiplied by the unit's baseline, mm Btu (the average fossil fuel consumed from 1985 through 1987). Utilities in key states such as Illinois, Indiana, and Ohio were allocated an additional 200 000 allowances annually during Phase I. In these states there were important coal interests and all had ranking members or chairs of key Congressional subcommittees.[22] Additional allowances were granted to plants where scrubbers had been installed that reduced SO_2 emissions by 90 percent and to plants where emissions were reduced through use of renewable energy. A small portion of the allowances, 2.8 percent of the total allowances for a year, were auctioned by the EPA.[23]

Phase II allowances are part of a tighter overall annual emissions cap. The formula used in determining the initial allocation took an emission rate of 1.2 lb of SO_2/mmBtu of heat input, times the unit's baseline. As with phase I, exceptions and additional allowances were made for political and technical reasons. Additional allowances were allocated to units that did not perform at their capacity during the base year due to equipment malfunctions. Greater allowance allocations were granted to smaller units.[24] An opt-in program also was used to encourage very low-polluting utilities to enter by granting them allowances which could be traded to others.

ALLOCATION OF ITQS IN FISHERIES

Wild ocean fisheries are classic open-access resources. Over entry, over fishing, over capitalization, falling catch per unit of effort, and depleted stocks follow from the fugitive nature of most species, distances involved, overlapping political jurisdictions and large numbers of heterogeneous, competing fishers.[25] The implications of open access have been understood for a very long time (Gordon, 1954), yet Grafton *et al.* (2000) described the dramatic wastes of over fishing and regulation in the Pacific Northwest halibut fishery, and a 2003 *Nature* article by Myers and Worm (2003) reported that the world's major predatory fish populations were in a state of serious depletion.[26]

Historically, the initial response has been command and control regulation with denial of access to certain groups – non-citizens with expansion of the Exclusive Economic Zones (EEZs), sports versus commercial fishers, inshore versus offshore fishers, large-vessel versus small-vessel fishers, or vice-versa, and so on. This action temporarily reduced fishing pressure, but it did not solve the fundamental problem which is that rents exist for those who can find ways around the regulations.

As these failed, new command and control regulations such as fixed seasons, area closures and gear restrictions were put into place. These arrangements are politically attractive to regulators because they do not upset status quo rankings, minimize existing transaction costs, and call for major regulatory mandates, which are attractive to regulators and politicians. But they have not been successful. They do not align the incentives of fishers with protection of the stock. Further, given heterogeneous fishers and limited and asymmetric information about the stock and the contribution of fishing relative to natural factors, there are disputes about the design and efficacy of these regulations. Finally, there is no basis for fishers to contract among themselves to reduce fishing pressure and thereby to capture the returns from an improved stock. There are no property rights to exchange.

With deregulation, there has been a turn to individual transferable quotas (ITQs) in some fisheries, after continued declines in the stock under centralized regulation. ITQs require restrictions on entry, the setting of an annual total allowable catch, TAC, the allocation of rights or quotas to a share of the TAC, and enforcement.

The more secure, definite, durable, divisible, and permanent the ITQ, the stronger is the property right. And stronger property rights better link the incentives of fishers with the goal of maximizing the economic value of the fishery. The value of each quota as a share of the TAC depends on the state of fish stocks and the sustainability of the fishery.[27] Enforcement costs may decline relative to those under other forms of regulation because fishers have a stake in the preservation of the stock as shareholders in the right to fish and self-monitor.

There are efficiency advantages to first possession. Assigning quotas to those with knowledge and past experience in the fishery is consistent with granting rights to the low-cost users. This practice reduces the need for subsequent reallocation and therefore, economizes on transaction costs. Reserving the fishery rents to fishers, rather than granting them to the state via auctions, also, enhances long-term incentives of fishers for protection of the stock and provides incentives for investment. Collaboration between fishers and regulators in setting the TAC not only reduces resistance to the catch limit, but incorporates stock and habitat information collected by the industry.[28]

Other parties, such as processors and other input suppliers (crews, dock owners, boat and equipment sellers and support providers) and their communities, however, may be adversely affected by changes in harvest patterns made possible by ITQ regimes. There are additional concerns that transferability of quotas and associated consolidation of the industry, which also bring efficiency gains, will gradually squeeze out small vessel owners. Regulators also may resist ITQs because of a potentially reduced regulatory mandate or diminished ties to specific constituents that become less active in the fishery under the ITQ. The following summarizes selected

ITQ allocation issues in fisheries in five countries, Australia, Canada, Chile, Iceland, New Zealand, and the United States.

Australia

There are at least 20 ITQ-managed fisheries in Australia, covering about 34 percent of the volume and 22 percent of the value of the country's fisheries.[29] The dominant allocation method is first-possession based on historical catch. Prior investment plays a smaller role. There are equity considerations in certain fisheries leading to equal or uniform quota distributions and/or restrictions on the maximum and minimum amounts of quotas that can be held as well as requirements that quotas be exchanged only among license holders. ITQs in Australia are comparatively strong property rights, being permanent, divisible, and transferable, and apparently can serve as collateral for long-term loans.

Canada

There are ITQs in about 40 fisheries in Canada, accounting for over 50 percent of the value and volume of landings.[30] In established fisheries, allocations are based on historical catch, modified by vessel size, capacity and recent investment. The quotas are granted without charge. Most quotas, such as those for Pacific halibut (1991) and sablefish (1990), were adopted between 1982 and 1998. In one newer fishery, the North Atlantic shrimp fishery, a uniform quota allocation of the TAC was used. In that fishery there were only a small number of licenses and limited historical catch records. In Canada, ITQs as property are weaker than in Australia. They do not have the legal status of property, but rather held as a use privilege, subject to renewal and regulation. In most fisheries there are no limits on number of quotas that can be held, but there are no guarantees of permanence. Their term is the same as the fishing license, which generally is more or less automatically renewed.

Chile

In 2002, there were four ITQ fisheries in Chile, the squat lobster, yellow prawn, black hack and orange roughy.[31] Unlike the Australian and Canadian systems, initial allocation was by auction, followed by annual auctions of 10 percent of the outstanding quota shares. There are few participants (less than 10) in each of these fisheries so that allocation issues may have been less contentious. The ITQs are transferable, divisible, and are not linked to a vessel. There are no maximum limits on the number of quotas that can be held by a firm, but during the annual auctions no firm can bid for more than 50 percent of the TAC. Based on the success of these ITQs, they are being extended to other established fisheries, and are to be allocated through first-possession, based roughly on 50 percent weight on historical catch for the past four years for purse seiners and past two years for trawlers, and 50 percent vessel hold capacity. There are restrictions on transferability to existing fishers.

Iceland

Iceland is one of the first countries to adopt ITQs.[32] Herring quotas were implemented in 1975 and 1979; quotas in the capelin fishery in 1980 and 1986; quotas in the demersal fisheries in 1984; and ITQs to all fisheries in 1991. Sixteen species are covered for 95 percent of the volume of the total catch. The quotas were granted without charge and include a right to catch a given proportion of the TAC every year. TAC shares are divisible and transferable. In the demersal, lobster, scallop and deep-sea shrimp fisheries, ITQs were allocated on the basis of vessel historical catch, three years prior to quota system adoption. In the herring and inshore shrimp fisheries, where smaller vessels may have predominated, there were initially equal shares for eligible vessels. There have been some restrictions on the transfer of annual quotas between geographical regions to protect local employment, and recent requirements that vessels holding quotas must be involved in harvest.

New Zealand

New Zealand is also one of the first countries to adopt ITQ systems.[33] After declines in deep water stocks within the 200-mile EEZ, New Zealand adopted ITQs in 1983 based on 1982 catch volume and vessel capacity. In 1986 an inshore ITQ system was adopted for vessels active in 1985 based on 1982–84 catch histories. In both the offshore and inshore fisheries ITQs initially were fixed quantities, but these were changed to shares in 1990. Equity concerns led to assignment of 40 percent of the quota to the Maori. The ITQs are permanent, divisible and transferable, with no restrictions on trade among participants. The rights apparently are as secure as those that exist for land. The rights security is similar to that found in Australia.

United States

ITQs are more limited and are a weaker property right in the US than in many other major fishing countries.[34] Only four US marine fisheries operate under such regimes: the Mid-Atlantic surf clam and ocean quahog fishery, the Alaskan halibut and sablefish fishery, and the South Atlantic wreckfish fishery, all adopted in the early 1900s. Two extensions were under consideration in 1995 for the Gulf of Mexico red snapper and Pacific sablefish fisheries, but tabled with the 1996 Congressional four-year moratorium on further ITQs.[35] The ITQs are a permanent share of the TAC, divisible and tradable. They are allocated on the basis of historical catch at no charge.

In the Alaska halibut and sable fish fisheries, allocations went only to vessel owners who had landings during 1988–90 (historical catch) and were based on the best five of seven harvest years between 1984 and 1990 for halibut and best five of six harvest years between 1985 and 1990 for sable fish. Quotas go the vessels and owners must be on the vessels (a type of beneficial use requirement). Part of the halibut TAC is reserved for community development quotas. ITQs in these two fisheries are weaker than in the others. There are restrictions of transferability to those in same management area and vessel class involving fishers with 150 days commercial fishing and there are minimum and maximum quota limits. Moreover, only transfers from larger to smaller vessel classes are permitted, and no individual is allowed to own more than 0.5 percent of the total quota. There are other controls on share consolidation to limit holdings and to maintain a targeted number of vessels in the halibut fleet.[36]

CONCLUDING REMARKS

Deregulation of many common pool resources has taken place through the adoption of property rights arrangements of some type. This institutional change has occurred as central regulation has failed to stem the losses of open access. Allocation of property rights, however, has been a major issue in determining the timing and extent of deregulation. Table 2.1 summarizes the distribution of property rights for oil and gas unit shares, air pollution emission permits, and individual transferable fishing quotas in six countries. As shown, first-possession allocation rules dominate where incumbent users existed at the time of establishing the rights regime under deregulation. Auctions are adopted very infrequently. Although first-possession is criticized by many economists as being inefficient, its empirical regularity suggests that there are efficiency advantages beyond political expediency. Equity issues, however, often have constrained the type of property right assigned. The more limited the property right, the less effective it will be in addressing the losses of the commons.

Table 2.1 Summary of allocation mechanisms in deregulation of natural resources

Resource	Nature of the property right	Allocation	Allocation constraints
Oil and gas unit shares	Full, legal property right	First Possession (Rule of Capture)	No restrictions on trade Small producers granted preferences in regulation and restrictions on mandatory unitization laws in Texas
Air emission permits	Use rights Explicitly, not a property right	First Possession Limited (2.8%) Auction in Phase I	Some preferences to coal using states in SO_2 permits. More restrictions on banking in RECLAIM
Certain fishery ITQs			
Australia	Use rights Legal property right	First Possession (historical catch, some past investment)	Some quota trade restrictions
Canada	Use rights Not property	First Possession (historical catch and past investment and vessel size) Uniform allocation	Some quota trade restrictions
Chile	Use rights	Auction First Possession (historical catch and vessel size)	Some quota trade restrictions
Iceland	Use rights Fairly strong property right	First possession (historical catch, vessel size)	Some quota trade restrictions
New Zealand	Use rights Legal property right	First Possession (historical catch and past investment)	Some quota trade restrictions Reservation of quota share for Maori
US	Use rights Uncertain	First Possession (historical catch)	Some quota trade restrictions Community quota reservations Actual fishers

There is the potential for waste due to a race to establish credentials for the subsequent assignment of use rights if first-possession is known to be the allocation rule and the parties are homogeneous in the costs of claiming. Just how important this problem is depends on the empirical case at hand. In general, for most of the resources examined here, there was a long history of prior use before the introduction of rights-based institutions and the claimants were heterogeneous. In the absence of binding controls on entry, at least in oil and gas and fisheries, low-cost claimants would have likely out-competed their higher-cost rivals and saved resource rents. Hence, the real costs of the race to establish property rights may have been considerably lower than would have been the case had the parties been more similar.

In every case except for oil and gas unit shares, the rights granted are use rights only. They are not a right to the resource itself. In general, ownership of the stock is much more difficult to define and enforce than to the flow of use. Political factors also have influenced the nature of the rights system. In oil and gas, regulatory advantages were granted to small, high-cost producers that appear to have limited subsequent adoption of unitization in Texas, and in fisheries preferential assignments to certain groups of fishers (small, community) and accompanying restrictions on exchange would lower the value of the rights and the value of the fishery.

NOTES

1. This chapter draws directly from discussion in Libecap (2007, 2008). I thank two referees and the participants at the conference on 'Deregulation or Re-regulation: Institutional and Other Approaches' Nice, France 18–19 June, 2007 for their helpful comments. Support provided by the International Center for Economic Research (ICER), Turin, Italy.
2. See Hannesson (2004) for example for discussion of the process of regulation and subsequent shift to privatization in some previously open access fisheries. Stavins (1998b, 2007) provides discussion of the movement toward market-based instruments.
3. Libecap (1989), Dahlman (1972).
4. Johnson and Libecap (1994: 156–71)
5. Discussion drawn from Libecap (1998).
6. See Alston *et al.* (1996) for discussion of the emergence of property rights as resource values change.
7. For discussion of western water markets, see Brewer *et al.* (2008).
8. See Lueck (1989) for wildlife law.
9. For discussion of the problem of oversight when information is limited, see Johnson and Libecap (2001).
10. See discussion of first possession in Epstein (1979), Rose (1985), and especially, Lueck (1995, 1998).
11. See Epstein (1979).

12. Johnson and Libecap (1982) show that heterogeneity among fishers limits rent dissipation even under open-access and the rule of capture.
13. Alesina and Angeletos (2005: 960–80).
14. Lueck (1998: 136), McMillan (1994) point to the costs of auctions.
15. Transaction costs of subsequent exchange likely were low due to the close proximity of parties as well as the existence of stock exchanges in San Francisco, Denver and other urban areas near mining regions. See Libecap (2007a) for discussion of hard rock mineral rights and first-possession claims.
16. Libecap and Smith (2002: S595).
17. Libecap (1989: 93–114).
18. Pashigian (1985).
19. Dewees (1998).
20. Tietenberg (2007: 71), Stavins (2007: 23).
21. Stavins (1998b: 6–13).
22. Ellerman (2000: 40–3).
23. Ellerman (2000: 8–9)
24. Ellerman (2000: 43–8).
25. Libecap and Johnson (1982), Leal (2005) and Hannesson (2004) for discussion of the emergence of various regulatory/property regimes.
26. A similar conclusion for deep-sea fisheries was reported by Devine *et al.* (2006), also in *Nature.*
27. Arnason (2002: 1).
28. See criticism of grandfathering in Fullerton and Metcalf (2001). Their major concern is that valuable assets are allocated without charge to incumbents and that the rents should go to the state.
29. Arnason (2002: 3–11).
30. Arnason (2002: 12–17).
31. Arnason (2002: 18–23).
32. Arnason (2002: 24–33).
33. Arnason (2002: 45–51).
34. Arnason (2002: 52–7).
35. The Sustainable Fisheries Act (PL 104–297).
36. Doyle *et al.* (2005).

REFERENCES

Alberto Alesina and George-Marios Angeletos (2005), 'Fairness and redistribution', *American Economic Review*, **95**(4), 960–80.

Alston, Libecap and Schneider (1996), 'The determinants and impact of property rights on the frontier: land titles on the Brazilian frontier', *Journal of Law, Economics and Organization*, **12**(1), 25–61.

Arnason, Ragnar (2002), 'A review of international experiences with ITQ', Annex to *Future Options for UK Fishing Management*, Report to the Department for the Environment, Food and Rural Affairs, CEMARE, University of Portsmouth, UK.

Brewer, Jedidiah, Robert Glennon, Alan Ker and Gary Libecap (2008), 'Water markets in the west: prices, trading, and contractual forms', *Economic Inquiry*, **46**(2): 91–112.

Cheung, Stephen (1970), 'The structure of a contract and the theory of a non-exclusive resource', *Journal of Law and Economics* **13**(1), 49–70.

Dahlman, Carl (1979), 'The problem of externality', *Journal of Law and Economics* **22**, 141–62.

Devine, Jennifer A., Krista D. Baker and Richard L. Haedrich (2006), 'Fisheries: deep-sea fishes qualify as endangered', *Nature*, **29**, 5 January, 439.
Dewees, Donald N. (1998), 'Tradable pollution permits', in Peter Newman (Ed.), *The New Palgrave Dictionary of Economics and the Law*, Vol. 3, London: Macmillan pp. 596–601.
Doyle, Matthew, Rajesh Singh and Quinn Weninger (2005), 'Fisheries management with stock growth uncertainty and costly capital adjustment: extended appendix', Department of Economics Working Paper, Iowa State University.
Ellerman, Denny A. (2000), *Markets for Clean Air*, New York: Cambridge University Press.
Epstein, Richard (1979), 'Possession as the root of title,' *Georgia Law Review* **13** 1221.
Fullerton, Don and Gilbert E. Metcalf (2001), 'Environmental controls, scarcity rents, and pre-existing distortions', *Journal of Public Economics* **80**, 249–67.
Grafton, R. Quentin, Dale Squires and Kevin J. Fox (2000), 'Private property and economic efficiency: a study of a common-pool resource', *Journal of Law and Economics*, **43**, 679–713.
Gordon, H. Scott (1954), 'The economic theory of a common-property resource: the fishery', *Journal of Political Economy*, **62**(2), 124–42.
Hannesson, Rögnvaldur (2004), *The Privatization of the Oceans*, Cambridge, MA: MIT Press.
Hardin, Garrett (1968), 'The tragedy of the commons', *Science* **162**, 1243–8.
Johnson, Ronald N. and Gary D. Libecap (1982), 'Contracting problems and regulation: the case of the fishery', *American Economic Review* **72**, 1005–22.
Johnson, Ronald N. and Gary D. Libecap (1994), *The Federal Civil Service and the Problem of Bureaucracy: The Economics and Politics of Institutional Change*, Chicago, IL: University of Chicago Press.
Johnson, Ronald N. and Gary D. Libecap (2001), 'Information distortion and competitive remedies in government transfer programs: the case of ethanol', *Economics of Governance* **2**(2), 1001–34.
Leal, Donald R. (Ed.), (2005), *Evolving Property Rights in Marine Fisheries*, Lanham, MD: Rowman and Littlefield.
Libecap, Gary D. (1989), *Contracting for Property Rights*, New York: Cambridge University Press.
Libecap, Gary D. (2007a), 'The assignment of property rights on the Western Frontier: lessons for contemporary environmental and resource policy', *Journal of Economic History* **67**(2), 257–91.
Libecap, Gary D. (2007b), 'Assigning property rights in the common pool. Implications of the prevalence of first-possession rules for ITQs in fisheries', *Marine Resource Economics*, **22**: 407–23.
Libecap, Gary D. and James L. Smith (1999), 'The self-enforcing provisions of oil and gas unit operating agreements: theory and evidence', *Journal of Law, Economics, and Organization* **15**(2), 526–48.
Libecap, Gary D. and James L. Smith (2002), 'The economic evolution of petroleum property rights in the United States', *Journal of Legal Studies*, **31** (June), S589–608.
Lueck, Dean (1995), 'The rule of first possession and the design of the law', *Journal of Law and Economics* **38**(2) (October), 393–436.
Lueck, Dean (1998), 'The economic nature of wildlife law', *Journal of Legal Studies*, **18**: 291–324.

Lueck, Dean (1998), 'First possession', in Peter Newman (ed.) *The New Palgrave Dictionary of Economics and the Law* Vol. 2, London: Macmillan Press, pp. 132–44.

McMillan, John (1994), 'Selling spectrum rights', *Journal of Economic Perspectives*, **8**(3) April, 145–62.

Myers, Ransom A. and Boris Worm (2003), 'Rapid worldwide depletion of predatory fish communities', *Nature* **423**, 280–3.

Pashigian, B. Peter (1985), 'Environmental regulation: whose self-interests are being protected?' *Economic Inquiry*, **23** (4), 551–84.

Rose, Carol M. (1985), 'Possession as the origin of property', *University of Chicago Law Review* **52**, 73–87.

Stavins, Robert N. (1998a), 'What can we learn from the grand policy experiment? Lessons from SO_2 allowance trading', *Journal of Economic Perspectives*, **12**(3), 69–88.

Stavins, Robert N. (1998b) 'Economic incentives for environmental regulation', in Peter Newman (ed.) *The New Palgrave Dictionary of Economics and the Law* Vol. 2, London: Macmillan, pp. 6–13.

Stavins, Robert N. (2007), 'Market-based environmental policies: what can we learn from US experience (and related research)?' in Jody Freeman and Charles D. Kolstad (eds), *Moving to Markets in Environmental Regulation*, New York: Oxford University Press, 19–47.

Scott, Anthony (1955), 'The fishery: the objectives of sole ownership', *Journal of Political Economy* **63**, 116–24.

Tietenberg, Tom (2007), 'Tradable permits in principle and practice', in Jody Freeman and Charles D. Kolstad (eds), *Moving to Markets in Environmental Regulation*, New York: Oxford University Press, pp. 63–94.

Wiggins, Seven N. and Libecap, Gary D. (1985), 'Oil field unitization: contractual failure in the presence of imperfect information', *American Economic Review* **75**, 368–85.

3. An institutional theory of public contracts: regulatory implications

Pablo T. Spiller

INTRODUCTION

The fundamental feature of private contracting is its relational nature.[1] When faced with unforeseen or unexpected circumstances, private parties, as long as the relation remains worthwhile, adjust their required performance without the need for costly renegotiation or formal recontracting (Baker *et al.*, 2001).[2] Public contracting,[3] on the other hand, seems to be characterized by formalized, standardized, bureaucratic, rigid procedures (Greenstein, 1993).[4] Faced with unexpected circumstances, parties in a public contract may face, even when the relation remains worthwhile, the stark choice of litigation or performance. In fact, common wisdom sees public contracts as generally more inflexible, requiring more frequent formal renegotiation, having a higher tendency to litigate, and providing weaker incentives. In sum, public contracts are perceived to be less 'efficient'.

The main thrust of this chapter is twofold: first, just as in private contracting, the nature of contracting hazards is what determines the fundamental features of public contracting (Williamson, 1979). A fundamental difference between private and public contracts is that public contracts are in the public sphere, and thus, although politics is normally not necessary to understand private contracting,[5] it becomes fundamental to understanding public contracting. Second, the analysis of public contracting must be done within the proper institutional comparison (Coase, 1964) and with a heavy micro-analytic dose (Williamson, 1979). In fact, the supposed inefficiency of public contracting must be assessed in reference to all relevant alternatives (Williamson, 1996).

In this chapter I develop a theory of public contracting that accommodates these stark differences between private and public contracting. The thrust of the chapter is that these differences arise directly because of the different hazards present in public and purely private contracts, which directly impact the nature of the resulting contractual forms. A fundamental corollary of this result is that the perceived inefficiency of public or governmental contracting is simply the result of contractual adaptation to different inherent hazards, and as such is not directly remediable (Williamson, 1999). Finally, I apply the main insights from the general framework developed here to understand the characteristics of concession contracts.

THE FUNDAMENTAL BENCHMARK: PRIVATE CONTRACTING

I start from the fundamental point that contracts are always incomplete, and that, to a large extent, the degree of incompleteness is chosen by the parties. In the extreme, and in the absence of a third party enforcer, contracts, whether explicit or implicit, may be sustained exclusively via implicit or explicit threats of actions, such as discontinuation of a relationship,[6] executing implicit or explicit guarantees (Williamson, 1983), decentralized enforcement by market participants (Milgrom *et al.*, 1990), or expelling the breaching party from membership in a clan, sect or family.[7] In fact, even in the face of third party enforcement, companies normally rely on inter-firm relationships to support contracting (Macaulay, 1963), and in particular, on private ordering in a discriminating way (Williamson, 2002). Inter-firm relationships help manage conflicts that would otherwise be resolved via formal mechanisms (courts), with the corresponding uncertainties, delay and costs (Williamson, 1975). Macneil's (1978) three-way categorization of contracts into classical, neoclassical and relational properly highlights that as relations become long term and complex, the reference point for adaptations becomes less the original contract as specified, and more the entire relation as it developed, the 'relational web' as Macneil (1974: 595) puts it. In fact, 'adaptation is now taken to be the chief mission of economic organization', with cooperative adaptation being achieved via 'complex contractual modes' (Williamson, 2002).

Although informal and continuous adaptations may be enough to sustain a private contract over time, thereby reducing haggling and negotiating costs, they require the discriminating selection of governance structures, with 'more complex modes of governance [being] reserved for more hazardous transactions' (Williamson, 2002). Relational contracting, then, appears in highly complex transactions, transactions where parties have sunk highly specific investments (Williamson, 1985), and where parties have highly particular, detailed and tacit knowledge of their specific situations, which they can use to 'adapt to new information as it becomes available' (Baker *et al.*, 2002).

This, however, does not mean that formal adaptations and adjustments are not needed. In fact, large unexpected events may require wholesale

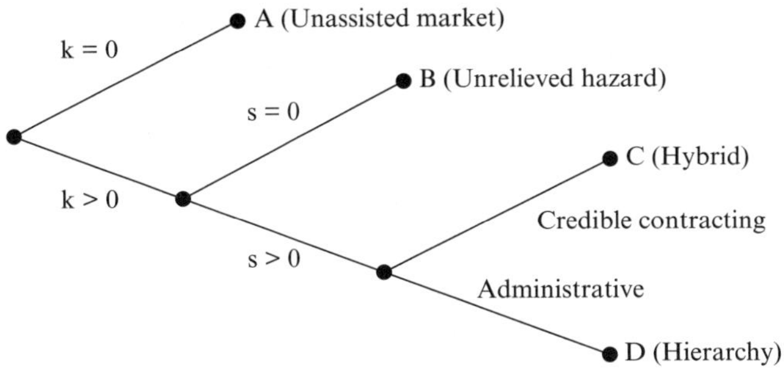

Source: Williamson (2005).

Figure 3.1 Williamson's simple contractual schema

re-contracting to provide further clarifications on how future adaptations will take place, or even termination of the relation.[8]

In sum, discriminating alignment is the foundation of private contract adaptability. The main risk facing the parties in complex transactions is opportunistic behavior by the trading party. Contractual governance is precisely designed to limit such behavior so as to successfully implement the transaction, or as Williamson (2002: 439) puts it, to 'infuse *order,* thereby to relieve *conflict*, and realize *mutual gain*'.

Figure 3.1 reproduces Williamson's famous 'simple contractual schema', whereby simple transactions ($k = 0$) get implemented via simple contractual methods such as unassisted market transactions, while complex transactions ($k > 0$) exposing the parties to transaction hazards require the design of complex governance structures. Figure 3.1 shows the existence of multiple governance structures – credible contracting at node (C) and hierarchy at node (D) – which counter entering into the transaction with unrelieved hazards (node B).

PUBLIC CONTRACTING

Public contracting is exposed to a larger set of hazards than purely private contracting, arising from three fundamental types of opportunistic behavior. As in private contracting, parties with idiosyncratic investments face the risk of opportunistic behavior by its partner, whether public or private, and will thus attempt to design the transaction's governance so as to limit the risk of opportunistic behavior by its trading partner. I will call this, the risks associated to standard opportunistic behavior.

Public contracting, on the other hand, generates peculiar types of hazards associated with the fact that one of the parties to the contract is the state, or a state institution. Here I will focus on two hazards: governmental opportunism and third-party opportunism. In previous writings, I emphasized governmental opportunism as the fundamental risk of investors in public utilities,[9] and how regulation by contract may limit such risk. Regulation by contract requires, however, a judiciary that not only will see such a contract as property and thus that cannot unilaterally be modified by the government, but also that will have the ability to enforce it. Facing these risks, then, private utilities may require that such regulatory contracts be highly specific, so as to limit opportunistic interpretations of contracts. In this section I will briefly deal with governmental opportunism,[10] and focus instead on what I believe is the fundamental risk faced by all public contracts – third party opportunism.

Public Contracting and Governmental Opportunism

The risk of governmental opportunism arises because, differing from private actors, governments can opportunistically change the rules of the game via the standard use of governmental powers to extract the quasi-rents of its contract partner.[11] Changes in the rules of the game can be done in multiple, subtle and not so subtle ways. Governments may issue legislation making illegal a particular type of contract, even a contract it may have originally designed. Such use of governmental powers may seem extreme, but is not unusual. Consider, for example, Venezuela's Decree No. 5.200/2007,[12] requiring that PDVSA, the Venezuelan public oil company, take operational control over oil projects in Venezuela, cancel all exploration, commercialization and production rights of the private/public association agreements originally set up between PDVSA and private oil companies (where private investors were the majority shareholders) to explore and develop those oil fields, and transfer those rights to mixed companies controlled by PDVSA. This Decree, known as the Nationalization Decree, came after private oil companies invested, by all accounts, billions of US dollars in developing these fields.[13] One may imagine multiple reasons for Venezuela's government issuing the Nationalization Decree, but it may not be wild speculation that the Decree would not have been issued if crude oil prices would have stayed in the low 10s or 20s, rather than increased as they did in 2002.[14]

Governmental opportunism, however, does not have to be so drastic as a law or Executive Decree cancelling or changing the nature of contracts, but can be achieved via the subtle works of administrative process. Consider, for example, the imposition of fines on a public utility for alleged quality deficiencies, or a regulatory decision denying a tariff increase. What may seem as innocuous acts of regulatory supervision, may actually be nothing else but governmental opportunism, attempting to extract part of the utility's quasi-rents. Consider, for example, the case of Compañía de Aguas del Aconquija, a water and sewage services concession granted by the Province of Tucumán, Argentina, in 1995 and terminated by the Province just two years later. The process that led to the contract termination, and described in unusual detail by the Arbitration Panel in its Award,[15] is a textbook, and probably an extreme, example of what I call governmental opportunism, whereby a government uses its regulatory and executive powers to achieve a tariff reduction not allowed by the regulatory framework. In fact, the *Aguas del Aconquija* Award shows the multiplicity of instruments governments have at their disposal to attempt to extract a utility's quasi-rents. In this case, the Provincial Government seems to have used all its formal powers – regulatory decisions, legislative acts, executive decrees, attorney general recommendations, even judicial decisions – and informal powers – press releases, Ombudsman's letters, public announcements, and the like – to force the company's hand.[16]

Investors facing the risk of governmental opportunism will either not invest, or demand up-front compensation for that risk. Either strategy, however, as the case of *Aguas del Aconquija* shows, may not alleviate the risk, but rather may exacerbate it.

Government opportunism affects not only private investors but public operators as well. Since the government has direct control over publicly owned companies, Savedoff and Spiller (1999) explain how the threat of governmental opportunism against publicly owned companies may lead those companies to protect their cash flows against such hazards by undertaking actions, such as hiring too many permanent or transitory employees, granting excessive benefits, and the like, which translate into low efficiency and quality levels.

The limits to governmental opportunism are, however, institutional (Spiller, 1996a, b). The potential for the opportunistic use of legislative powers depends, to a large extent, on the control the executive may exercise over the legislature. Thus, a fragmented polity may provide more assurances to investors than a highly centralized government. Similarly, a judiciary with a tradition of independence may put some limits on opportunistic governmental behavior. Concession contracts, as long as they are upheld by the local courts, may also provide a level of commitment against opportunistic behavior. It is, thus, not surprising that the UK, a country characterized by a centralized government but with a long tradition of judicial independence, would have adopted a regulatory system based on concession contracts, while the regulatory structure in the US, a country characterized by fragmented government, is based on judicial review of administrative procedures (Spiller 1996a).

Implications of Governmental Opportunism

Facing the threat of governmental opportunism, private agents would require stronger safeguards to undertake contracts with the state than they would in contracts with other private agents. These safeguards may involve making the contract even more complete and more specific so as to avoid opportunistic interpretations or the transfer of some of the specific investments to the state.

In the absence of strong judicial independence, and of procedural safeguards, the threat of governmental opportunism may simply imply the payment of substantial upfront rents, or that the private sector may not contract with the state. Thus, in the absence of safeguards against governmental opportunism, public integration (whereby the government provides the service directly) and public ownership become equilibrium outcomes (Spiller and Levy, 1994; Savedoff and Spiller, 1999).

Third Party Opportunism

The essence of public contracting is its publicity. Public contracting involves, directly or indirectly, the use of public monies, and thus it affects, although indirectly, the lives of all citizens. Reasonably working societies, then, will naturally develop ways for public contracts to be subject to public scrutiny so as to avoid corruption and graft.[17] Public contract scrutiny is normally undertaken by designated agencies in charge of contract supervision. In the United States, while individual departments have agencies in charge of auditing their procurement, the Office of Management and Budget, the Government Accountability Office, and the Congressional Budget Office routinely examine the procurement performance of government agencies and of the auditing agencies themselves.[18]

Apart from official agencies, a substantial amount of supervision and control is done by interested third parties (McCubbins and Schwartz, 1984; McCubbins *et al.*, 1987, 1989).[19] In fact, McCubbins and Schwartz (1984) in their seminal article argue that politicians can manage the bureaucracy via 'fire alarms', whereby interest groups (interested third parties) will 'pull the alarm' when agencies stray from the politician's preferred policy path. They further make the point that 'a predominantly fire-alarm oversight policy is likely to be more effective . . . than a predominantly police-patrol policy'.[20] Thus, third party supervision is fundamental in a democratic society.

A fundamental feature of interest groups as monitors, though, is that they are interested. In other words, they are biased. They provide information only when it is to their advantage. That is, the third party (or parties) may behave opportunistically. As it relates to public contracts, interested third parties may have incentives to challenge the 'probity' of a particular public agent when by such action they may benefit. Such incentives may exist when third parties compete with the public agent in another (political) market. Benefits may arise in the political and the economic sphere. In both it may involve the displacement of the incumbent (and competing) public agent. In the political sphere, the challenge may be deemed successful if because of the challenge the public agent is, eventually, replaced by an agent related or more to the liking of the interested third party. As it relates to the economic sphere, the challenge may be deemed successful if the private party is replaced or the terms of the contract are changed in ways that benefit the third party. But it is precisely because of competition in the political market that such challenges are particularly dangerous to the public agent.[21]

In a competitive political market environment third party opportunism, depending on the challenge's credibility, may entail significant costs to the public agent. The public agent may have to incur significant time and expense to defend its actions,[22] may have to leave its public position, or in the extreme, if the challenge is fully successful, may be prosecuted.[23]

Given the inherent informational asymmetries between the interested third party, the courts, and the public in general, the challenge may be exercised even if the action is ethical and/or legal. In fact, the more complex the public/private transaction, the higher the inherent informational asymmetries, and thus, the higher the probability of third-party opportunism.

The potential for successful challenges has different types of implications. Dal Bó and Di Tella (2006) show, for example, that the potential for threats of the type discussed here – that is, actions by third parties that may imply costs to public agents – impacts the selection of public agents. While the potential for positive transfers (that is, bribes) increases the competition to become a public agent, the potential for costly and credible threats reduces it, thus reducing the quality of public agents. I will not explore this issue further here.

Here I will explore the impact that potential challenges of this sort have on the nature of public contracting in general. The exposure to third-party opportunism increases the risk to both the public agent and the private party contracting with the state. In response, both will have incentives to increase the specificity of these contracts as compared to equivalent contracts among private parties. Moreover, to mitigate the risk of third-party opportunism, these contracts are likely to demand more rigid procedural processes, including formal procedures for renegotiation. Nevertheless, these adjustments are unlikely to mitigate third-party opportunism altogether, and the implementation of public contracts is more likely to experience a higher degree of conflict than contracts among private parties. In other words, the risk of third-party opportunism means that 'relational' contracting is less likely to evolve in the public sphere.

RELATED LITERATURE

Marshall *et al.* (1991, 1994), for example, show that allowing excluded bidders to challenge the outcome of a procurement process inefficiently reduces sole-sourcing. Kelman (1990) reports that following the enactment in 1984 of the Competition in Contracting Act (CICA), one-third of all major information technology federal procurements were protested including nearly all of the biggest procurements, leading to its reversal in 1995. Kelman (1990: 155) further suggests that, in response, contract agents 'think only about what's legally defensible. They bend over backwards to avoid appeals'. Greenstein (1993) emphasizes the costs associated with procedural rules designed to increase transparency. For example, procurement rules that restrict agencies to evaluating vendors only on the listed factors when they cannot write a complete specification list implies that vendors 'have incentives to shirk in the provision of those dimensions that are undervalued or are not explicitly requested in the RFP' (Greenstein, 1993: 167), thus lowering the quality of the delivered good.

Williamson (1999) raises the hazard of probity as the fundamental hazard distinguishing some public transactions, such as foreign affairs. Williamson (1999: 324) defines 'probity transactions' as those having a strong need for loyalty (to the leadership and to the mission) and process integrity, while having low potential for operational cost hazards. In this chapter I try to show that probity, and the suspicion of lack of probity, is what drives much of the features of public contracting.

BASIC FRAMEWORK OF THIRD-PARTY OPPORTUNISM

The following provides a basic framework to understand the workings of third-party opportunism and its impact on public contracting. Consider a political environment with four players:

(a) Incumbent public agent – who is of uncertain quality (her predisposition to corruption being a good example), is responsible to choose the nature of the contract with the private party (which for simplicity can be considered as high power or low power), and which may or not involve a payment to her.[24]
(b) Contractor – who could be a supplier or employee. The contractor's job is to accept or reject the contract offered by the incumbent public agent, and who will then share or not share the proceeds with the incumbent.
(c) Political competitor – the potential third party opportunist. This competitor's decision is whether to challenge the contract implementation. Challenges are, however, costly, so not all contract types will be challenged. The political competitor also is able to observe some signals concerning the realization of the contract which are not verifiable.
(d) The Public (which could be considered also as the court), who will, based on the actual realization of the contract and the challenge of the political competitor decide to retain or to replace the incumbent by the political competitor (if the challenge took place).[25]

In this environment it is straightforward to show that low power incentives will be preferred by public incumbents. By relating payments to verifiable incurred costs, low power contracts limit the potential for successful political challenges. Contracts with low power incentives, however, may generate fewer social benefits, or be more costly to the public, but avoid the potentially negative political consequences of high power incentive contracts. Similarly, high power incentives do not provide the same benefits they could provide in private transactions. Challenges have also risks to the private party. In fact, challenges may impede, *ex post*, the payment of high power compensation when it is due. Thus, third party opportunism also increases the risk to the private agent of transacting with the state.

The response to third-party opportunism for both the incumbent public agent and the private transacting party is to provide low power contracts, to increase the degree of contract specificity, to limit the potential discretion granted to the public agent, and to increase procedural rigidity. Since the potential for third-party opportunism increases with complexity, complex public contracting projects would then have more contractual rigidities than simpler public contracts.[26] Rigidity, however, when combined with complexity, will increase conflict. The potential for conflict, together with the potential for third party opportunism, then, favors low power incentives. High power incentives simply may not be implementable given the potential for third-party opportunism and the expected level of contractual conflict.

Thus, third party opportunism limits the potential for 'relational public contracting'. Public agencies will have difficulty entering into a close relation with a supplier, in which contract adaptation takes place without formal renegotiations, and/or litigation. Furthermore, public contracting will not only be more complex, involving multiple rules and procedures, but will also be more subject to litigation. The added complexity required to limit the potential for third-party opportunism will make public contracting look 'inefficient'. This inefficiency, however, does not pass Williamson's (1999) remediableness test. In other words, the perceived inefficiency of public contracting is an equilibrium response to its hazards, and in particular, to the hazard of third party opportunism, a defining feature of public contracting. In fact, to eliminate the alleged inefficiency, one could consider two options: one, to move the transaction within the public sphere completely, that is, to vertically integrate; second, to drive it off the public and into the private sector. Consider, first, moving the transaction within the public sphere completely. Public vertical integration does not solve the 'within the bureaucracy' contracting problems. In fact, similar types of concerns arise with the implementation of high power incentives within the bureaucracy itself. For the same reason that high power incentives are not appropriate for public contracting, high power incentives are not often appropriate for within the bureaucracy relations as high transfers to public employees will naturally raise probity questions, and will thus increase the risk of third party opportunism.[27]

Complete privatization of the government activity may not be feasible either. There is a public 'sphere of action' in which the government is the party best suited to engage in the transaction (Williamson, 1999). Privatizing key policy making aspects of a nation, for example, may expose the nation to serious probity hazards. Thus, the undertaking of basic public policies will have to be undertaken by Government, and that would naturally require an interface with the private sector – that is, public contracting.

Furthermore, most public contracts would be even less efficient if brought completely within the public sphere. That the state is more 'inefficient' in computer procurement than the private sector and has complex and rigid procurement procedures (Greenstein 1993) does not mean that the government should be in the business of making computers.

Thus, whether public contracting is, or not, inefficient cannot be inferred from the observation that it does not replicate private contracting. A proper comparison must be institutionally consistent and pass the Williamson's remediableness test. That can only be assessed on a case by case basis.

The potential for third-party opportunism, furthermore, may be exacerbated by the nature of the institutional environment in which the public contract takes place. To thrive, third party opportunism requires some political contestability and fragmentation. Although internal party politics could provide the environment for fragmentation, and for the type of political displacement required for third-party opportunists to prosper, centralized party power limits the upward mobility of political mavericks, and thus the potential for internal third party opportunists.[28] On the other hand, political instability, the caldron where governmental opportunism thrives, is also conducive for third-party opportunism as the cost of removing incumbent politicians falls. In the middle, between stable centralized party control and rampant political instability, is where most of the world democracies fall. 'Open access' states, following the nomenclature introduced by North *et al.* (2006), naturally facilitate the development and organization of third party interest groups. In these societies, public policies become depersonalized, and governments are constrained in their ability to limit – whether by withdrawing funding, political harassment or direct violence – the development and organization of such groups. It is in these societies where the threat of third-party opportunism becomes more credible, as such challenges may not be easily covered up by side payments or the direct threat of the recourse to violence. In 'natural' states, following again North *et al.* (2006) nomenclature, the public agent may have more instruments at her disposal to quash such challenges, and thus, it could be argued that her ability to overcome a third party challenge is increased.

This discussion, then, suggests that third-party opportunism and governmental opportunism may not appear in similar circumstances. While governmental opportunism requires the existence of important sunk investments, such is not the case for third-party opportunism. Third party opportunism may appear even when the contractor may move its assets costlessly elsewhere.[29] Furthermore, while the potential for governmental opportunism requires an institutional environment with few institutional limitations to governmental discretion, the essence of 'natural' states, the potential for third-party opportunism is limited in such environments by the same discretionary ability of governments. Third-party opportunism, then, would be more effective in open access states, thus suggesting that public agents would adapt public contracting further away from relational contracting in 'open access' than in 'natural' states.[30]

In sum, public contracting is plagued by third party and governmental opportunism. While the institutional environment most propitious for the development of both types of opportunism differ and so differ the nature of transactions which may generate each, the framework provided here suggests that both types of hazards interact in increasing the specificity and rigidity of public contracts causing difficulties in adapting to shocks and leading to low-powered incentives. Similarly, both types of hazards, and their combination, lead to more 'inefficient' termination of public than private contracts. These 'inefficiencies' persist in equilibrium, and thus public contracting cannot be simply compared to private contracting, nor can the standard measure of performance from private contracting be applied to public contracts. With this in mind, I proceed to analyze the implications of the framework to the use of concession contracts as regulatory instruments.

AN APPLICATION TO CONCESSION CONTRACTS

Concession contracts are part of the general set of licenses and permits through which states grant the right to a private organization to undertake a particular public-service activity. Concession contracts differ from other types of legal instruments in that while taking the form of operating licenses, they tend to embed the basic regulatory framework that will guide their evolution as it relates to basic features such as prices, quality, penalties, termination and the like. In that sense, the state that selects to grant a concession contract in essence is embedding the regulatory framework within a formal contract.

Concession contracts, then, differ from simple operating licenses, such as those common in the United States, as the latter are silent about the regulatory framework, leaving the management of the terms of operation of the licensee to other instruments, such as administrative procedures or specific legislation.[31] Since including the regulatory framework within the license makes it more rigid, as significant changes in the regulatory framework requires either the consent of the concessionaire or a judicial decision, the natural question to ask is why a state chooses such a restrictive legal instrument.

In Spiller (1996a) I provide a theory of regulatory instrument choice based on the need for regulatory credibility given the nature of the institutional environment in which the investment is undertaken. Concession contracts, then, arise as a mode for organizing provision of public services precisely because regulation by contracts sets limits to unilateral regulatory changes, and by doing that, it mitigates the potential for governmental opportunism (Levy and Spiller, 1994). In particular, regulation by contract is preferred in sectors with a high level of sunk assets (for example water, transport, natural gas, and electricity distribution), in politically unstable environments, and when regulation by law does not provide enough credibility to protect the investments of the service providers. In these cases the providers are vulnerable to governmental opportunism, and so private service providers will not enter the market or demand too high a premium on services under direct regulation. Concession contracts, by creating an individualized regulatory framework for the investments at hand, limit such opportunism.

The choice of regulatory contracts shows the inexorable trade-off between commitment and flexibility (Spiller, 1996a). To be credible, a regulatory contract must be specific – that is it must lay out in detail how the parties will deal with each eventuality. However, adjustments in the relationship require flexibility in the contract, which in turn requires that the contract be complex. Complexity is limited by administrative capability and negotiation costs (which depends on differences among potential investors and political incentives).

Concession contracts are rigid by 'origin'. A flexible concession contract that grants substantial discretion to the state would fail to provide the required commitment, and thus would not be seen by the investor as mitigating the risk of governmental opportunism. Thus, concession contracts are born with less flexibility than normal private contracts.

They are also not 'relational contracts'. In fact, adaptations to shocks seldom involve serious contractual deviations without triggering formal contractual adaptations.[32] In fact, Guasch (2004) finds that from a total of 942 concessions granted in Latin American countries from the mid-1980s, by year 2000 a full 42 percent of them were renegotiated. Figure 3.2 shows the distribution across sectors, showing that most transport and water concession contracts were renegotiated.

The large percentage of formally renegotiated contracts is only surprising if we look at it from the perspective of 'relational contracts'. But regulatory adaptations should not be surprising. Most concession contracts should be adapted over time, as by nature, these contracts are long term and incomplete. As a consequence, it is unreasonable to expect that through the long life of these concessions, there will be no economic (for example, an unexpected increase in external or internal costs) or political shocks (for example new political needs) that would call for a change in the agreed terms of the contract. An unadjusted contract may lead to unproductive actions or even default, generating unnecessary social losses.

In fact, while adaptation to new realities is necessary, informal adaptation, whereby the parties agree to deviate from the terms of the concession contract without formal renegotiation raises the risk of third party opportunism. As a consequence, adaptation, if needed, would mostly be done by formal renegotiation.

Here is, though, where governmental and third-party opportunism interact. Formal renegotiation raises the risk of third party opportunism, as the whiff of corruption can immediately be sensed. Thus, to generate a

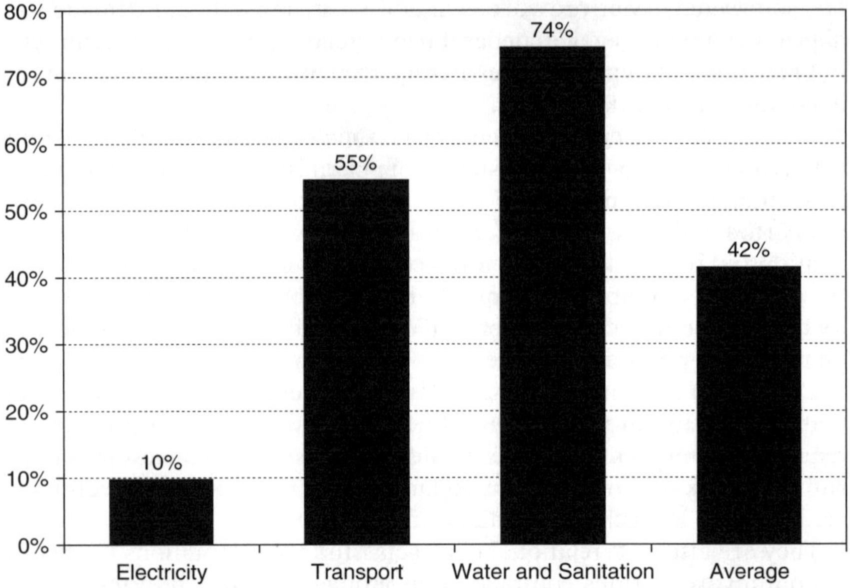

Source: Guasch (2004).

Figure 3.2 Latin America concession contracts renegotiated 1985–2000

formal renegotiation, the shock has to be large enough that the need for adaptation becomes clear to lay observers.

Long term concessions are exposed to different types of economic shocks. Internal shocks arise early in the life of the concession when concessionaires are granted the use of existing assets whose working conditions are difficult to ascertain. This is mostly the case in waterworks concessions, where operators are granted the use of a waterworks often without updated maps detailing routes, inventory of type of equipment, clients and so on. In fact, most water concessions get renegotiated in the initial two years.

External shocks are simply the normal types of demand and cost changes (devaluations, drastic increase in input costs not covered in the contract and so on) that may drastically impact the viability of the concession. This could be the case if the contract introduces high power incentives features, such as annual payments to the government for the right to operate the concession, minimum investment levels, or fixed prices over long periods of time.[33, 34] These conditions may become very onerous to implement if an economic shock lowers revenue expectations after the contract has been signed. By contrast, a regulatory mechanism characterized by lower-powered incentives, such as rate-of-return regulation, is less likely to trigger the need to renegotiate, as it generates adaptation more naturally.

Lack of adaptation following a shock that threatens the viability of the concession may in fact trigger contract termination. While termination may be 'socially inefficient',[35] it may be politically preferable for the public agent than bearing the third-party opportunism risks associated with renegotiating the contract.[36]

All other things being equal, it is reasonable to expect that the larger the investments undertaken in relation to future network expansion needs, the higher the government's incentive to terminate the concession (Troesken, 1997), both because of governmental opportunism and because of the difficulties of renegotiating given third-party opportunism hazards. Given the risk of early termination, concession contracts normally provide for very specific and explicit compensation at termination, whether early or normal. The degree of specificity of these clauses is obvious: the greater the ability of the state to manipulate the compensation, the higher the government's incentive to terminate.[37]

Although there are inherent[38] and institutional limits to governmental opportunism, third party opportunism may not be subject to these limitations. Even in contractual circumstances where the potential for governmental opportunism has been limited by expectations of future investments or institutional limitations, third party opportunism may still trigger 'inefficient' contract termination.

Consider, for example, waterworks in the US. A large number of municipalities across the United States use concession contracts to operate and manage their water works.[39] Not all contracts, though, are for city-wide service, with most covering only partial operations, such as operation of a particular pumping or treatment plant, or the provision of billing services (Water Science and Technology Board, 2002). These contracts are long term, often dealing with highly complex physical environments.[40] These contracts assign risks to the contractor and the city in highly complex and sophisticated fashions, providing for cost escalation clauses, and for renegotiation facing a large scale shock such a natural disaster.[41] The transfer of existing operations to a private contractor is, though, as complex in the United States as elsewhere.[42] Consider, for example, the breakdown of the Atlanta waterworks contract. In January 2003, the City of Atlanta terminated what was then a 22 year management and operation contract of the whole waterworks system of Atlanta, only four years after its transfer. Right after the transfer the parties entered into conflicts on the costs required to meet the standards agreed upon in the contract. United Water, the operator, claimed that much of the baseline data was inaccurate and thus, the targets and annual fees agreed upon were unrealistic, forcing it to lose $10 million a year out of a $20.8 million/year contract.[43] Renegotiation, then, would have to involve a substantially higher per year fee, as well as a modification of the service targets. The City, however, preferred to take back the contract at a cost of $40 million/year – against the $22 million/year of the contract, rather than having to handle the public criticism of its management of the contract. Following the reasoning in this chapter, renegotiation would have been 'in neither party's interest'.[44] It would not have been in the City's interest as it would be extremely difficult to explain that a contract drafted and crafted by the City just a few years ago was in such seeming disarray that it requires a substantial fee increase. For the City it would be much easier to blame all problems on the operator's bad performance. Similarly, it would not have been in the operator's interest, as, given the public perception of wrongful operator performance, it would be difficult to expect that the renegotiated contract would fully compensate it. At the end, the parties ended the contract 'amicably'.[45] The contract termination, however, was preceded by a series of corruption allegations involving an agreement to grant a $4 million/year for 17 years' payment increase following the operator's request for $80 million compensation for work not included in the contract,[46] and allegations that the Mayor had business relations with a competing water operator.[47]

The Atlanta case is an example of a contract falling apart not because of governmental opportunism – as seems to have been the case in Aguas del Aconquija, but rather by the inability of the parties to draft and implement contracts with sufficiently flexibility that can adapt to uncertain operating circumstances. Instead, the parties entered into a highly inflexible contract, forcing them to renegotiate or terminate. The City, however, was unwilling to pay the political price of renegotiation. The main thrust of this chapter is that contract inflexibility is inherent to public contracts, and that, facing the potential for third party opportunism, large shocks may trigger termination and/or litigation rather than renegotiation.

REGULATORY IMPLICATIONS

This analysis has some implications for regulation by contract. Regulation that requires high cash-flow fluctuations, such as price cap regulation or involving minimum investment requirements (rather than service targets), increases the potential of third-party opportunistic behavior. On the other hand, regulatory systems, such as rate-of-return regulation, which generate steadier cash flows, tend to limit third-party opportunism, and thus, reduce the overall cost of the service.[48]

FINAL COMMENTS

This chapter argues that public contracting is plagued by third party and governmental opportunism. Providing for both types of hazards results in highly specific and rigid contracts causing difficulties in adapting to shocks and leading to low-powered incentives. Nevertheless, there is likely to be more 'inefficient' termination of public than private contracts. High contract specificity, termination penalties and jurisdictional arrangements arise as safeguards. These 'inefficiencies' persist in equilibrium, and thus public contracting cannot be simply compared to private contracting, nor can the standard measure of performance from private contracting be applied to public contracts.

This framework has direct implications for the study of regulation. In particular, this framework suggests the need to reconsider the use of high-powered incentives in concession contracts and rethink the beauty of simple, less theoretically 'efficient' contracts that are likely to be more conducive to long term sustainability (Levy and Spiller, 1994). This framework also has direct implications for other types of public contracting, such as the organization of the bureaucracy, a subject left for another paper.

ACKNOWLEDGMENTS

This chapter benefited from comments received at various workshops and seminars, including the World Bank, the Nice Conference on Regulation and Deregulation, University of California, Irvine, and ISNIE, as well as from an anonymous referee and from conversations with Benito Arruñada, Bryan Hong, Claude Menard, Robert Seamans, Steve Tadelis, Richard Wang and Oliver Williamson. Bryan Hong, Richard Wang and Robert Seamans provided useful research assistance. This research benefited from funding from the Jeffrey A. Jacobs Distinguished Professorship Chair in Business and Technology at the Haas School of Business of the University of California, Berkeley.

NOTES

1. See, e.g., Mcaulay (1963), Macneil (1974), Williamson (2002).
2. Corporations, however, often move away from relational contracting endorsing highly formalized contracting procedures, only to reverse course. A case in point is GM's recent endorsement, jointly with the US Department of Defense, of highly bureaucratized IT procurement practices, the Capability Maturity Model Integration. See

Bernard *et al.* (2004). See also CIO.com report at http://www.cio.com/article/156400/New_Guidelines_for_IT_Procurement_May_Prove_Intimidating.

3. Hereafter, I refer to public contracting to the case when one of the parties to a transaction is a public entity, such as a governmental agency or company.
4. Although there is a large literature dealing indirectly with what I call public contracting (such as the literature on privatization of municipal services or bureaucracy), there is in fact no systematic study I know of comparing public versus private contracts on the dimensions mentioned here.
5. There is a large literature on influence in organizations, which started with the work of Milgrom and Roberts (1988). See, generally, Laffont and Tirole (1993).
6. A costly action if assets are not easily redeployed to alternative uses. See Telser (1981).
7. See, for example, Greif (1993), Landa (1981) and Richman (2006).
8. As Macaulay (1963: 65) represents, the use of courts is often relegated for the purpose of settling contract termination disputes, rather than contract adaptation.
9. By governmental opportunism I refer to the ability of governments to opportunistically change the rules of the game once the utility sunk its investments. See, Spiller (1996a, 1996b), and Levy and Spiller (1994).
10. For a more detailed treatment of governmental opportunism, see Spiller (1996a, b).
11. Spiller (1996a), Levy and Spiller (1994). This does not imply that the private contractor may not opportunistically withhold information, but such opportunism is of the 'standard' nature, discussed at length by the literature.
12. Published on 26 February 2007, as *Decreto Con Rango, Valor y Fuerza de Ley de Migración a Empresas Mixtas de los Convenios de Asociación de la Faja Petrolífera del Orinoco, así como de los Convenios de Exploración a Riesgo y Ganancias Compartidas.*
13. See, for example, *New York Times* '2 Oil Firms Are Defiant in Venezuela', 27 June 2007.
14. The fact that other governments (such as Argentina, Bolivia and Ecuador) took similar or related actions following the rapid raise in the price of crude oil may indicate that Venezuela's Nationalization Decree may be better characterized as opportunistic rather than ideological.
15. See, Award – 'In the arbitration between Compañia de Aguas del Aconquija S.A. and Vivendi Universal S.A. Claimants v. Argentine Republic, Respondent, Case No. ARB/97/3' issued on 20 August 2007.
16. At the end, the company attempted to rescind the contract due to governmental breach, at which point the Province terminated the concession. The service remained in the company's hand for another year, at which point it was taken over by ENHOSA, a federal water service entity. See, Award, at page 112 (Note 15).
17. Private contracts, on the other hand, are normally protected against public scrutiny, often requiring a judicial act to make a private contract subject to public scrutiny. Some private contracts, however, are public for obvious reasons. The registration of land ownership requires the registration of real estate transactions, making some aspects of real estate transactions then potentially open to public scrutiny.
18. For example, the Defense Contract Audit Agency, formed in 1965, is in charge of performing audits to all the US Defense Department contracts. The performance of the DCAA, in turn, is supervised by the OMB, while the GOA and the CBO routinely review specific programs of the Department of Defense. See, for example, CBO, 'Replacing and repairing equipment used in Iraq and Afghanistan: the Army's Reset Program,' Pub. No. 2809, September 2007; see also, GAO, *Defense Acquisitions: Department of Defense Actions on Program Manager Empowerment and Accountability,* 9 November 2007.
19. de Figueiredo *et al.* (1999) also show that politicians prefer not only a proliferation of interested interest groups monitoring agencies, but also prefer them to come from divergent perspectives.
20. McCubbins and Schwartz (1984: 171).

21. For example, the replacement of the private party may damage the political credibility of the incumbent public agent, weakening its position *vis-à-vis* a third party interested in its replacement.
22. Public agents would not be expected to leave their positions without a (political) fight. Multiple interest groups may be expected to contribute to the public discussion following a challenge. Some groups, aligned with the beneficiaries of the particular contract or policy, may come to the public agent defense, and help to limit the effectiveness, or credibility, of the challenge (de Figueiredo *et al.* 1999).
23. This effect works also in non-democratic environments, as long as there is competition for political power.
24. It is easier to consider the public incumbent as a politician, that is, someone whose appointment to the position depends on the result of an election. The public incumbent, however, can also be a political appointee or a high level bureaucrat. All that is necessary is for the incumbent to want to remain in position; where the support of higher level public agents and/or the public at large will be needed.
25. The decision of the 'public' will also depend on the performance of pro-incumbent interest groups.
26. This result is consistent with Bajari and Tadelis (2001).
27. There are many instances, though, of the introduction of some type of high power incentives in bureaucracies. For example, Mexico's higher bureaucratic echelon under the PRI has traditionally been composed of a high paid technocracy, linked by a network of personal and political relations to the members of cabinet. As a consequence, career advancement has been based on informal norms of reciprocity and loyalty, where bad performance implies disloyal behavior, leading to discontinuation either right away or when the bureau chief moves to another position. See, Grindle (1977).
28. Two interesting parallel examples are the demise of the PRI and the LDP in Mexico and Japan respectively. Both parties controlled their respective polities for more than half a century, providing internal party mechanisms for resolution of public conflicts, as well as for the rotation, displacement and succession of public agents. The framework provided in this section predicts that public contracting in Mexico and Japan became much more cumbersome and rigid since then. This is a topic for future research.
29. In this case, the contractor has less to fear from the consequences of third party opportunism, but that is not the case for the public agent.
30. This, however, does not mean that in 'natural states' public contracting will be relational. In such states, public contracting is subject to governmental opportunism requiring its types of own adaptations.
31. See, Spiller (1996a) for a discussion of this issue.
32. In a sense, it is possible to say that the frequency of contract renegotiation may provide concessions a 'relational' quality.
33. There are various types of price cap regulatory schemes. The UK style involves tariff reviews every five years. Others may set prices without a fixed term for review, relying instead on the initiation of extraordinary tariff reviews.
34. In fact, Guasch *et al.* (2003) show that the probability of renegotiation in Latin America increases with the presence of price caps, financial commitments and large scale investment requirements.
35. The concession would need to be taken over by the government, and then transferred again to a private operator, who, this time will not accept without further guarantees of proper governmental behavior.
36. Termination may also be the result of governmental opportunism. An economic shock may enable the government to expropriate the quasi-rents physically (via termination) that could not be obtained financially (by renegotiating on more favorable terms).
37. Governments may still attempt to manipulate compensation via the introduction of 'counter-claims' although that would naturally lead to litigation.
38. The government may benefit from a reputation for being a good contracting partner, especially if it takes the long-term view. There may also be a financial cost of

termination, including contractual termination clauses, the rules of contract law generally, or even international law.
39. Some commentators put the number of water systems operated by private operators in the United States above 1100 (see, for example, Arrandale, Tom, 2003. "Foreign Faucet," *Governing*. Available at <http://www.governing.com/archive/2003/jun/water.txt>).
40. This observation is based on a set of contracts obtained via directly contacting the municipalities and asking for copies of all such contracts they may have.
41. The 1997 Seattle Public Utilities Treatment Plant Contract, is such an example. See Appendix C to Water Science and Technology Board (2002).
42. See discussion of the Aguas del Aconquija contract termination above.
43. See, 'Water privatization becomes a signature issue in Atlanta,' The Center for Public Integrity. Available at < http://www.icij.org/Content.aspx?src=search&context=article&id=55 >. See, also, 'As cities move to privatize water, Atlanta steps back,' Great Lakes Article, by Douglas Jehl, 18 February 2003. Available at < http://www.greatlakesdirectory.org/zarticles/021803_great_lakes.htm>.
44. See 'As cities move to privatize water. . .'
45. The termination involved a net payment of $5 million from United Water to the City. See, 'Joint news release: City of Atlanta and United Water announce amicable dissolution of twenty-year water contract, 23 January 2003, available at < http://www.unitedwater.com/pr012403.htm>.
46. The agreement seems to have been signed by the then Mayor Bill Campbell in a series of letters, who later on the City attorneys claimed were invalid, and which Mr Campbell claimed did not sign. See, 'Water privatization becomes . . .'
47. *Ibid.*
48. Gilbert and Riordan (1995) emphasize, furthermore, that in environments with low technological change, high-powered-incentive regulation is not that necessary.

REFERENCES

Arrandale, Tom (2003), 'Foreign faucet', *Governing*, http://www.governing.com/archive/2003/jun/water.txt

Bajari, Patrick and Steve Tadelis (2001), 'Incentives versus transaction costs: a theory of procurement contracts', *Rand Journal of Economics*, **32**, 387–407.

Baker, George, Robert Gibbons and Kevin J. Murphy (2001), 'Bringing the market inside the firm?' *American Economic Review* **91**, 212–18.

Baker, George, Robert Gibbons and Kevin J. Murphy (2002), 'Relational contracts and the theory of the firm', *Quarterly Journal of Economics* **117**(1), 39.

Bernard, T., B. Gallagher, R. Bate and H. Wilson (2004), 'CMMI acquisition module (CMMI-AM) Version 1.0', Technical Report CMU/SEI-2004-TR-001, February.

Center for Public Integrity (2003), 'Water privatization becomes a signature issue in Atlanta', http://www.icij.org/Content.aspx?src=search&contect=article&id=55

Coase, Ronald (1964), 'The regulated industries: discussion', *American Economic Review*, **54**, 194–7.

Dal Bó, Ernesto and Rafael Di Tella (2006), 'Plata o Plomo? Bribe and punishment in a theory of political influence', *American Political Science Review* **100**, 41–53.

deFigueiredo Rui, Pablo T. Spiller and Santiago Urbiztondo (1999), 'An informational perspective on administrative procedures', *Journal of Law, Economics & Organization* **15**, 283–305.
Gilbert, Richard J. and Michael H. Riordan (1995), 'Regulating complementary products: a comparative institutional analysis', *RAND Journal of Economics* **26**, 243–56.
Greenstein, Shane (1993), 'Procedural rules and procurement regulations: complexity creates trade-offs', *Journal of Law, Economics and Organization* **9**, 159–79.
Greif, Avner (1993), 'Contract enforceability and economic institutions in early trade: the Maghribi Traders' Coalition', *American Economic Review* **83**, 525–48.
Grindle, Merilee S. (1977), 'Patrons and clients in the bureaucracy: career networks in Mexico', *Latin American Research Review* **12**(1), 37–66.
Guasch, J. Luis (2004), *Granting and Renegotiating Infrastructure Contracts: Doing It Right*, Washington, DC: World Bank Institute.
Guasch, J. Luis, Jean-Jacques Laffont, and Stéphane Straub (2003), 'Renegotiation of concession contracts in Latin America', *World Bank Policy Research Working Paper* 3011.
Jehl, Douglas (2003), 'As cities move to privatize water, Atlanta steps back', http://www.greatlakesdirectory.org/zarticles/021803_great_lakes.htm
Kelman, Steven (1990), *Procurement and Public Management: The Fear of Discretion and the Quality of Government Performance*, Washington, DC: American Enterprise Institute Press.
Laffont, Jean-Jacques and Tirole, Jean (1993), *A Theory of Incentives in Procurement and Regulation*, Cambridge, MA: MIT Press.
Landa, Janet T. (1981), 'A theory of the ethnically homogeneous middleman group: an institutional alternative to contract law', *Journal of Legal Studies* **10**, 349 62.
Levy, Brian and Pablo T. Spiller (1994), 'The institutional foundations of regulatory commitment: a comparative analysis of telecommunications regulation', *Journal of Law, Economics and Organization* **10**(2), 201–46.
Macaulay, Stewart (1963), 'Non-contractual relations in business: a preliminary study', *American Sociological Review*, **28**, 55–67.
Macneil, Ian R. (1974), 'Restatement (second) of contracts and presentation', *Virginia Law Review* **60**, 589–610.
Macneil, Ian R. (1978), 'Contracts: adjustment of long term economic relations under classical, neoclassical and relational contract law', *Northwestern University Law Review*, **72**, 854–905.
Marshall, Robert C., Michael J. Meurer and Jean-François Richard (1991), 'The private Attorney General meets public contract law: procurement oversight by protest', *Hofstra Law Review* **20**, 1–71.
Marshall, Robert C., Michael J. Meurer and Jean-François Richard (1994), 'Curbing agency problems in the procurement process by protest oversight', *Rand Journal of Economics* **25**, 297–318.
McCubbins, Matthew and Thomas Schwartz (1984), 'Congressional oversight overlooked: police patrols versus fire alarms', *American Journal of Political Science* **28**,165–79.
McCubbins, Matthew, Roger Noll and Barry Weingast (1987), 'Administrative procedures as instruments of political control', *Journal of Law, Economics and Organization*, **3**, 243–77.

McCubbins, Matthew, Roger Noll and Barry Weingast (1989), 'Structure and process, politics and policy: administrative arrangements and the political control of agencies', *Virginia Law Review* **75**, 431–82.
Milgrom, Paul and Roberts, John (1988), 'An economic approach to influence activities in organizations', *American Journal of Sociology* **94**, S154–S179.
Milgrom, P., D. North, and B. Weingast (1990), 'The role of instittutions in the revival of trade: the law merchant, private judges and the champagne fairs', *Economics and Politics* **2**, 1–23.
North, D., J. J. Wallis and B. R. Weingast (2006), 'A conceptual framework for understanding recorded human history', NBER Working Paper 12795.
Richman, Barak (2006), 'How community institutions create economic advantage: Jewish diamond merchants in New York', *Law and Social Inquiry* **31**, 383–420.
Savedoff, William, and Pablo Spiller (1999), *Spilled Water: Institutional Commitment in the Provision of Water Services in Latin America*, Washington, DC: Interamerican Development Bank.
Spiller, Pablo T. (1996a), 'A positive political theory of regulatory instruments: contracts, administrative law or regulatory specificity?' *Southern California Law Review* **69**, 477–515.
Spiller, Pablo T. (1996b), 'Institutions and commitment', *Industrial and Corporate Change* **5**, 421–52.
Telser, Lester (1981), 'A theory of self enforcing agreements', *Journal of Business* **53**, 27–44.
Troesken, Werner (1997), *Why Regulate Utilities? The New Institutional Economics and the Chicago Gas Industry, 1849–1924*, Ann Arbor, MI: University of Michigan Press.
United Water (2003), 'Joint news release: City of Atlanta and United Water announce amicable dissolution of twenty-year water contract', http://www.unitedwater.com/pr012403.htm.
Water Science and Technology Board (2002), *Privatization of Water Services in the United States: An Assessment of Issues and Experience*, Washington, DC: National Academy Press.
Williamson, O. E. (1975), *Markets and Hierarchies: Analysis and Antitrust Implications*, New York: Free Press.
Williamson, O. E. (1979), 'Transaction-cost economics: the governance of contractual relations', *Journal of Law and Economics* **22**, 233–61.
Williamson, O. E. (1983), 'Credible commitments: using hostages to support exchange', *American Economic Review* **73**, 519–40.
Williamson, O. E. (1985), *The Economic Institutions of Capitalism*, New York: Free Press.
Williamson, O. E. (1996), *The Mechanisms of Governance*, New York, Oxford University Press.
Williamson, O. E. (1999), 'Public and private bureaucracies: a transaction cost economics perspectives', *Journal of Law Economics and Organization* **15**, 306–42.
Williamson, O. E. (2002), 'The lens of contract: private ordering', *American Economic Review*, **92**, 438–43.
Williamson, O. E. (2005), 'The economics of governance', *American Economic Review* **95**, 1–18.

4. Incentives and transaction costs in public procurement

Steven Tadelis

INTRODUCTION

Standardized goods, such as computers, office supplies and automobiles are mass produced, have standard characteristics and are typically purchased at list price from a menu of prespecified characteristics. Custom made goods, such as new buildings, custom-software or legal services are tailored to fit a buyer's specific and often unique needs. To procure these customized goods, the buyer usually hires a contractor who supplies the good or service according to a set of desired specifications, referred to as the procurement problem.

The procurement problem has attracted much attention both in policy and in academic circles. The main focus of academic economists has been on procurement by the public sector, in part because of its sheer importance to the economy. For example, procurement by federal, state and local government accounts for more than 10 percent of gross domestic product in the United States.

When considering the procurement of goods and services, the buyer is faced with many challenges. First, she has to choose what exactly should be procured, and how to transmit her needs to the potential suppliers. Second, a contract must be laid out that includes contractual obligations and methods of compensation. Third, the buyer needs to decide how to award the procurement contract between the potential suppliers. Finally, the award mechanism should result in the selection of a qualified and desirable supplier and in the implementation of a cost-effective final product.

Procurement is often achieved with the buyer seeking, through competitive bidding, a low price to purchase the desired good or service. To achieve this low price, competitive bidding is widely recognized as an attractive award mechanism and is commonly advocated for several reasons. Most notably it is viewed as a procedure that stimulates and promotes competition. By their nature, open competitive bidding procedures invite potential suppliers from many venues, and fair market price discovery is often touted as a beneficial result of such bidding. Such award mechanisms are also known for their transparency, making it easier to prevent corruption in the public sector where procurement agents may have incentives to rig the system in return for bribes and other benefits. These characteristics, as well as arguments for equal opportunity, provide a justification for statutes such as the Federal Acquisition Regulations (FARs) that strongly favor the use of auctions in the US public sector.

Interestingly, in the private sector there is widespread use of *both* competitive bidding for fixed-price (or unit-priced) contracts, and of negotiations. Many negotiated contracts are cost-plus contracts that are negotiated with one potential supplier who is selected before the final contractual arrangements are in place. For example, Bajari *et al.* (2007) show that from 1995 to 2000, 44 percent of private sector non-residential building construction projects in Northern California were procured using negotiations, while only 18 percent were procured using open competitive bidding. The use of negotiations with single source suppliers is also common in high-tech and software, and used for defence procurement as well. This chapter offers a framework to compare competitive bidding for fixed-price contracts with negotiations over cost-plus contracts.

Most of the existing formal economic analysis describes the procurement problem as follows. The supplier has information about production costs that the buyer does not have. The buyer then has to consider clever ways to infer the supplier's costs, such as offering the supplier several potential projects to choose from, each with an associated price, and having the supplier select the one that will be produced. For an excellent summary of this literature see Laffont and Tirole (1993).

In contrast, the approach taken here is more in line with that of Transaction Cost Economics as advocated by Williamson (1975, 1985), and focuses on adaptation costs when contractual specifications are incomplete. This is in line with the concerns of scholars and practitioners of engineering and construction management. They argue that the central problem in procurement is not that suppliers know so much more than buyers at the onset of the project, but that instead, both buyers and suppliers share uncertainty about many important design changes that occur after the contract is signed and production begins. These changes are usually a consequence of design failures, unanticipated conditions, and changes in regulatory requirements.[1]

The framework described builds heavily on Bajari and Tadelis (2001) (henceforth, BT) who formalize the procurement problem as one of smoothing out or circumventing adaptations after the project begins rather than information revelation by the supplier before the project is selected. This chapter argues that the form of contracts and award mechanisms can be tailored in a way to help mitigate this procurement problem. In particular, a trade-off between incentives to reduce cost and incentives to facilitate changes and share information will be the key force in the arguments for contractual choice.

In particular, simple projects, which are defined as easy to design with little uncertainty about what needs to be produced, ought to be procured using fixed-price contracts, should be accompanied by high levels of design completeness (to prevent the need for adaptations), and are best awarded through competitive bidding. In contrast, complex projects, which are defined as hard to design with large scope for surprises in the final configuration, ought to be procured using cost-plus contracts, should be accompanied by low levels of design completeness (implying a high chance that adaptations to the contract will be needed), and should be awarded through a negotiation with a reputable and qualified supplier.

The intuition for these prescriptions stems from a tension between providing incentives to lower costs and avoiding costly and wasteful renegotiation that follows requests for changes. The strong incentives to reduce costs that are offered by fixed-price tendered contracts will lead the parties to dissipate valuable surplus when changes need to be renegotiated. This efficiency loss will often be due to haggling over prices when there is true lock-in of the current supplier who wishes to use the need for adaptation to his advantage. Cost-plus contracts, in contrast, discourage cost-saving efforts but ease the process of renegotiating changes and adaptation to the contract's original requirements.[2]

The choice of payment procedures, such as fixed-price and cost-plus contracts, is tied in with the follow-up decision that a buyer faces: whether to award a procurement contract by competitive bidding or by negotiating with a potential supplier. In the US the public sector statutes that govern procurement, typically based on FARs, strongly favor the use of competitive bidding. For example, Bajari *et al.* (2007) show that from 1995 to 2000, 97 percent of public sector building construction projects in Northern California were procured using competitive bidding. While competitive bidding does have the advantage of unbiased awarding of projects, it fails to respond optimally to ex post adaptation. This suggests that public procurement of complex projects are suffering from efficiency losses.

The analysis in the next section begins with a simple framework to describe the buyer's choice of devising a contract that will govern the procurement relationship with a selected supplier. The analysis then continues to describe how the contracts chosen will dictate the use of award mechanisms. A discussion of implications for public procurement is then offered.

THE CONTRACTING FRAMEWORK

Contractual Components: Design and Incentives

The precursor to awarding a contract is devising one, so consider a buyer who wishes to procure a project (good or service) from a supplier. To get what he desires the buyer must provide the supplier with plans and specifications that describe the project. If the project is built according to the buyer's needs, he will obtain a value of $\overline{v}$. Thus, the buyer's first dimension of contractual choice is how much design costs to invest at the onset, where more investment (and hence costs) in design creates a more detailed set of plans and specifications. Clearly, a more detailed and accurate design of a project reduces the need to renegotiate changes after the project starts taking shape.

It is often prohibitively expensive to draft a complete design that fully describe the project exactly as the buyer's needs dictate, and how production should take place as certain contingencies arise. There is always a chance that a contingency will arise for which their are no instructions, or for which the blueprints are insufficient. This implies that the specified design may not result in the successful completion of the project. This problem is referred to as contractual incompleteness because it is generally associated with the design and specifications not being a complete description of what needs to be done in the face of all future contingencies.

The contractual incompleteness of the project will also depend on how prone the type of project is to unforeseen changes. Such unforeseen changes can arise from technological or regulatory contingencies that are hard to predict or plan for, or alternatively too expensive to try and draft onto the design. To capture this idea, define the complexity of the project as how expensive it is to provide a rather complete set of plans and contingencies. The more complex a project is, the more expensive it will be to try and prevent contractual incompleteness.

Formally, it is instructive to consider a complete design as a list of instructions that fully describe the project. Let $\tau \in [0, 1]$ represent the fraction of instructions that are actually written down by the buyer, and interpret τ as the probability that ex post adaptations are not needed, or as the design completeness of the project's design. With probability $1 - \tau$, however, a contingency will arise for which their are no instructions, implying that following the prespecified plan will not result in the successful value v. In this case the buyer will only get a value of $\underline{v} < \overline{v}$, which will later depend on the type of payment-incentive scheme.

To model project complexity, I suppress the state space model of BT and focus on its reduced form. In particular, let $T \geq 0$ be a scalar that represents the complexity of the project, where higher values of T imply a more complex project. (A natural interpretation of T is the number of instructions required to completely specify the project.) Providing a design completeness $\tau \in [0, 1]$ for a project of complexity T costs the buyer $d(\tau, T)$. This can be thought of as the engineering and drafting costs that go into producing the set of design blueprints for the project. Assume that $d(\tau, T)$ satisfies three properties (that are rather intuitive, and are endogenously derived in BT). First, for a given level of complexity T, the costs of design are increasing in design completeness τ. Second, the cost of a fixed level of design completeness τ is increasing in complexity T. Finally, the more complex a project, the higher is the marginal cost of increasing the probability of specification, so that $\partial^2 d(\tau, T)/\partial\tau\partial T > 0$.

The buyer's second dimension of contractual choice is the payment and incentive scheme in the contract. Most procurement contracts are variants of simple fixed-price or cost-plus contracts. In fixed price contracts, the buyer offers the supplier a pre-specified price for completing the project as specified, and any changes are negotiated separately at the stage in which they arise. A cost plus contract does not specify a price, but rather reimburses the contractor for costs (time and material) with an additional stipulated fee (the 'plus'). Hence, in cost-plus contracts the costs of changes are automatically built into the original contract.[3]

Formally, Let $y \in \{0, 1\}$ represent the payment choice variable, where $y = 0$ is a cost plus incentive scheme, and $y = 1$ is a fixed price incentive scheme. It is customary to refer to fixed price contracts as having high powered incentives to reduce costs since he contractor is the residual claimant to every dollar saved on production costs (similarly, cost-plus contracts offer low-powered incentives). As Williamson (1985) suggested, the ease in which work adaptations are executed will depend on the contract employed. In particular, a cost-plus contract easily adapts to cover additional changes, while renegotiating a fixed-price contract generally involves more haggling and friction. I therefore assume that the value of the project when adaptation is needed, $\underline{\upsilon}(y)$, will depend on the incentive scheme so that $\underline{\upsilon}(0) > \underline{\upsilon}(1)$. This means that if changes are needed then the buyer's ex post surplus is lower with a fixed price contract than it is with a cost plus contract. (This inequality is derived more thoroughly in BT.)

The Costs and Benefits of Incentive Schemes

To compare the advantages of each incentive scheme, first start by ignoring any changes to the original design, and assume that the project will be executed exactly as the design specifies. If a fixed-price contract is in place then the supplier bears all of the costs of providing the project. This, of course, implies that the supplier has strong incentives to lower the cost of production, and some of these would pass on to the buyer through competitive pressures (that are discussed further in the next section).

In contrast, if a cost-plus contract is in place then the supplier knows that any extra costs he incurs will be fully compensated for, and may even generate a small profit if the fee is based on a percentage of the costs. Thus, the supplier will have no incentives to reduce the costs of production, and no such costs savings can therefore be transferred to the buyer.

Formally, the above argument suggests that one can describe the buyer's cost of a project, $c(y)$, as depending on the incentive contract that is used. Stronger (fixed-price) incentives imply a lower direct cost of production because contractors are the residual claimants of costs and they will make choices to reduce the costs of production, so that $c(0) > c(1)$.[4]

That said, cost-plus contracts have an appealing feature that has been recognized by scholars and practitioners in the area of construction management, in that they facilitate changes and modifications to the original specifications. Indeed, the most common sources of changes in building construction are defective plans and specifications, changes in project scope and differing conditions than expected at the site of construction. Conventional wisdom in the industry is that cost plus contracts are better suited to facilitate such change.

To see why, imagine a situation where at some advanced stage of the project's development it turned out that the plans and specifications are defective, or lacking some directive for an unforeseen issue that arises. In such an event the buyer will ask the contractor to adopt some changes to the original plan. First consider the effects of having a fixed price contract in place. The fixed price compensation binds the supplier to the original plans and does not oblige him to agree to the changes proposed by the buyer. Thus, the buyer will have to negotiate any changes with the supplier. The buyer's objective is to get the changes done in the most cost effective way according to his needs while the supplier wishes to make as high a profit as he can from the potential windfall. The supplier can then hold up the buyer as a consequence of being in the midst of the project, and he has no competitive pressure to discipline his behavior. Knowing this, the buyer may expect to be overcharged and the two parties are likely to engage in contentious adversarial negotiations.

Alternatively, consider the effects of having a cost-plus contract in place. Unlike the specific-performance nature of a fixed price contract, a cost-plus contract effectively has a built-in mechanism to compensate the supplier for any changes that are required. Namely, any additional costs that the supplier incurs are compensated for through the cost-plus structure.[5] In other words, the lack of cost-reducing incentives serves as a lubricant for smooth and cooperative implementation of changes when contractual incompleteness gives rise to the need for changes. This simple intuition is formally derived from the model above as follows:

Proposition 1: More complex projects will result in less design, are more likely to be renegotiated and are better procured with cost-plus incentives. Simpler projects are more likely to have more complete specifications and are better procured using fixed-price contracts.

It is worth explaining the reason for favoring savings on design for complex projects. At first it may seem that complex projects would require an extra effort in trying to provide more details into the design. However, the complexity of such projects implies that many changes are expected even if design efforts are high. Thus, if a cost-plus contract is in place to deal with such changes, the added benefits of extra design efforts are small. This follows because it will not be too costly to implement changes in the aftermath of unforeseen issues, which makes the benefits of a more complete design less pronounced. A caveat is that one would wish to avoid changes that will completely disrupt the project's production plan and cause expensive changes to the infrastructure as it develops. Thus, some initial investment in planning will be necessary to predict how complete the design ought to be to at least set the stage for proceeding with the project.

COMPETITIVE BIDDING VERSUS NEGOTIATIONS

The analysis above describes the relative benefits of cost plus versus fixed price contracts in the face of varying project complexity. Once a contract is specified, the next step is to award it to a qualified contractor. It turns out, as argued below, that the choice of a contract's payment structure should be tied to the choice of award mechanism, namely, the choice between a process of competitive bidding and a negotiation with a selected supplier. To set the stage, recall the many known benefits of competitive bidding. First, it promotes competition among potential suppliers. Second, it offers transparency that helps mitigate corruption. The question is then, what is the object over which bids are solicited and what form should these bids take?

Consider the contractual framework above and imagine that a simple project is at stake where our buyer produces a rather complete design that is accompanied by a fixed-price contract. In his case the buyer is fairly confident that changes to his design will not be needed, and would like to secure the design at the lowest possible price. A competitive bidding mechanism will offer the buyer all its benefits. Suppliers will compete their surplus away, and the buyer is getting exactly what he wants: a well defined project at the lowest possible price.

Now turn to the other case of a complex project with an incomplete design and which the buyer plans to award using a cost-plus contract. As most practitioners would readily agree, '[a] cost-plus contract does not lend itself well to competitive bidding' (Hinze, 1993: 144) and in the area of construction management, '[m]ost negotiated contracts are of the cost-plus-fee type' (Clough and Sears, 1994: 10).

To try and implement a competitive bidding process for a cost-plus contract one might suggest that bidders can bid over the 'plus' portion of the compensation. In this way the buyer can choose the supplier who requests the lowest compensation for his management, and the production costs of labor and material will be automatically paid for through the cost-plus structure. However, as the 'plus' is often only a small fraction of the costs, this can be quite a disastrous way to select a contractor for what is in essence a challenging and complex project. Clearly, a supplier will not wish to settle for less than he could obtain in some alternative job. If, as one would imagine, more cost efficient suppliers have better alternative opportunities, then their bid for a fee in a cost-plus contract will be higher than that of less cost efficient suppliers.[6] This argument implies that the highest cost and least able supplier will win such a competitive tender for a cost-plus fee. Furthermore, if complex projects that are tied to cost plus contracts require suppliers that have more expertise, then hiring the least able supplier can be devastating.

Another merit of negotiating a contract with one reputable seller is that buyers and contractors spend more time discussing the project and ironing out possible pitfalls before work begins. It is widely believed, however, that when competitive bidding is used to award a fixed-price contract, the contractors strategically read the plans and specifications to determine where they will fail. A contractor who sees a flaw in the plans can use this information to submit a low bid, and recover significant profits when necessary changes are implemented. Thus, competitive bidding may lead to adverse selection, which is more problematic when projects are complex. This disadvantage of auctions has been recognized in a seminal article by Goldberg (1977) who writes that 'in competitive bidding for complex contracts, conveyance of information at the pre-contract stage is likely to be a substantial problem' (p. 254). Therefore:

Corollary 1: For complex and incompletely specified projects favor a cost-plus contract to be awarded using a negotiation with a reputable supplier, while simple and mostly specified projects should be procured with fixed-price contracts and awarded sing competitive bidding.

Note that the analysis above does not consider projects that are not clearly categorized as simple or complex, and for which the choice of contract structure and award procedure is not obvious. For these, market conditions will play a role in favoring one or the other. It is well known that the benefits from a competitive bidding mechanism will generally depend on the number of qualified bidders who will participate. The more potential suppliers are available for bidding, the higher the benefits from promoting competition. As such,

Corollary 2: For moderately complex projects more potential competition will favor a more complete design and a fixed-price contract to be awarded using a competitive bidding. If potential suppliers are scarce then less design will be favored with a cost-plus contract that is negotiated with a qualified supplier.

Finally, consider the difference between an open competitive bidding mechanism in which any supplier can submit a bid to the procedure of 'invited bidders' in which only a handful of suppliers are invited to participate in the competitive bidding process. To analyze potential differences between these procedures consider the response of suppliers to a request for bids for a rather complex, but somewhat well specified project. Preparing thc bid will be more challenging and costly the more complex and large the project. If qualified suppliers expect that less qualified suppliers may try to compete and offer low bids, then this may deter the qualified suppliers from exerting the time and costs of preparing the bids. As a result, a buyer may not be able to attract qualified suppliers if price competition is expected to be fierce. Hence, it may be beneficial to prevent less qualified suppliers from bidding and in this way restrict competition to guarantee a reasonable rate of return then the qualified suppliers will have incentives to invest in preparing these bids and compete.[7]

THE COSTS OF ADAPTATION

The arguments above are based on the premise that the use of rigid fixed-price compensation schemes comes at the cost of inefficient adaptation, a process which would be smoother under more flexible compensation rules such as cost-plus contracts. An important next step would be to try and measure the inefficiency of rigid rules for the use of fixed price contracts. This is challenging because one would need to compare similar projects that are procured with different incentives and award mechanisms, and measure the total costs of completion, as well as the resulting quality. Some progress in this direction is found in a recent paper by Bajari *et al.* (2007) (henceforth, BHT).

In their paper, 414 public highway construction contracts from Northern California are analyzed. These are 'unit price' contracts, where government employed civil engineers that represent the California Department of Transportation (Caltrans) first prepare a list of items that describe the tasks and materials required for the job. For example, in the contracts studied by BHT, items include laying asphalt, installing new sidewalks and striping the highway. For each work item, the engineers provide an estimate of the quantity that they anticipate contractors will need in order to complete the job. For example, they might estimate 25 000 tons of asphalt, 10 000 square yards of sidewalk and 50 rumble strips. The itemized list is publicly advertised along with a detailed set of plans and specifications that describe how the project is to be completed.

A contractor that wishes to bid on the project will propose per unit prices for each of the work items on the engineer's list, so his bid is a vector of unit prices that specifies his price for each contract item. Table 1 shows the basic structure of a completed bid, which must be sealed and submitted prior to a set bid date. When the bids are opened, the contract is awarded to the contractor with the lowest estimated total bid, defined as the sum of the estimated individual line item bids (calculated by multiplying the estimated quantities of each item by the unit prices in the bid).

As a rule of thumb, final quantities are never equal to the estimated quantities. For example, the engineers might estimate that it will take 25 000 tons of asphalt to resurface the stretch of highway listed in the plans but 26 752 tons are actually used. As a result, final payments made to the contractor are almost never equal to the original bid. The determination of the final payment can be rather complicated because in many cases it is not the simple sum of actual item costs given the unit prices in the bid. Caltrans' *Standard Specifications* and its *Construction Manual* discuss the

Table 4.1 Unit price contract – an example

Item	Description	Estimated quantity	Per unit bid	Estimated item bid
1.	Asphalt (tons)	25000	\$25.00	\$625000.00
2.	Sidewalk (square yds)	10000	\$9.00	\$90000.00
3.	Rumble strips	50	\$5.00	\$250.00
			Final Bid:	\$715250.00

determination of the final payment at length. To a first approximation, there are three primary reasons that account for large enough adaptations that merit modifying the payments away from the simple vector product of unit prices and actual quantities.

First, if the difference between the estimated and actual quantities is small, then the contractor will indeed be paid the unit price times the actual quantity used. If the deviation is larger, however, or if it is thought to be due to negligence by one party, both sides will renegotiate an adjustment of compensation.

Second, in addition to changes in the estimated quantities, there may be a change in scope of the project. A change in scope is a change in the overall description and design of the project that needs to be completed. In most cases, the contractor and Caltrans will negotiate a change order that amends the scope of the contract as well as the final payment. If negotiations break down, this may lead to arbitration or a lawsuit. Payments from changes will appear in two ways. First, to the extent that the change in scope affects pre-specified contract items, changes in the actual ex post quantities of those items will compensate the contractor for the direct production costs. Second, extra payments may reflect the use of unanticipated materials or other adjustment costs, and they are recorded as extra work.

Finally, the payment may be altered because of deductions. If work is not completed on time or if it fails to meet specifications, Caltrans may deduct liquidated damages. Such deductions are often a source of disputes between Caltrans and the contractor. The contractor may argue that the source of the delay is poor planning or inadequate specifications provided by Caltrans, while Caltrans might argue that the contractor's negligence is the source of the problem. The final deductions imposed may be the outcome of heated negotiations or even lawsuits and arbitrations between contractors and Caltrans.

BMT use the data of these completed contracts to estimate the adaptation costs and conclude that they are substantial. The implied adaptation costs on the different changes to final payment range from $2 to over $10 for every dollar in change. When considering the amount of money awarded and deducted after the initial contract is signed, these costs are significant by any standard. These numbers might be surprising in the context of the existing economics literature which has emphasized private information and moral hazard as the main sources of departures from efficiency in procurement. However, this result is consistent with current thinking in Construction and Engineering Project Management (see Bartholomew, 1998; Clough and Sears, 1994; Hinze, 1993; Sweet, 1994. Also see Bajari and Tadelis (2001) for a more complete set of references and discussion of the literature). One of the central concerns emphasized in this literature are methods for minimizing the costs of disputes between contractors and buyers. The topic of controlling contractor margins by comparison receives relatively little emphasis in this literature.

Summing over all 414 projects, BMT calculate that the average ratio of the adaptation costs to the winning bid is just over 10 percent. Even half of this number would be substantial. Since contractors factor these costs into their bids, the procuring government, and hence the taxpayer, is ultimately responsible for expected adaptation costs on the project as they are directly passed on from the bidders.

LESSONS FOR REGULATION

In the public sector, statutes such as the US FARs (and the many statutes that are modeled after the FARs) strongly favor the use of competitive bidding, and particularly open competitive bidding when feasible. For instance, in a study of the building construction industry in Northern California (Bajari *et al.* 2007), 97 percent of the projects awarded in the public sector were awarded using open competitive bidding as compared to only 18 percent in the private sector. Since private sector firms are more sensitive to cost minimization and are not constrained by fixed rules, it is reasonable to conclude that the behavior of private sector firms is more responsive to optimal choices.

As mentioned above, competitive bidding is perceived to select the lowest cost bidder, prevent corruption and favoritism that are opposed to efficiency, and it offers a clear yardstick with which to compare offers. According to an Ohio Court, competitive bidding 'gives everyone an equal chance to bid, eliminates collusion, and saves taxpayers' money . . . It fosters honest competition in order to obtain the best work and supplies at the lowest possible price because taxpayers' money is being used. It is also necessary to guard against favoritism, impudence, extravagance, fraud and corruption' (Sweet, 1994: 379). This is the main rational for requiring competitive bidding in the public sector.

The analysis above suggests that for complex projects that have incomplete designs and specifications there is a downside to the use of fixed-price contracts awarded through competitive bidding. Instead, selecting and negotiating with a contractor may be the favorable course of action. This deficiency of open competitive bidding can arise from the expectations that *ex post* haggling and frictions might occur when changes are needed, from a lack of input by qualified and knowledgeable contractors at the design stage, or from the need to proceed quickly without the ability to complete detailed plans and specifications.

Bajari *et al.* (2007) studied how private sector, non-residential building construction contracts were awarded in Northern California between 1995 and 2000. In the private sector, unlike the public sector, buyers can more easily use mechanisms other than competitive bidding to select a contractor. As mentioned above, open competitive bidding is only used in 18 percent of the contracts while 44 percent of the contracts are negotiated. Also, Negotiated contracts are more commonly used for projects that ex ante appear to be the most complex and likely to change plans and specifications *ex post*.

A perceived advantage of negotiated contracts is that they allow the architect, buyer and contractor to discuss the project plans before construction begins, allowing information flows that would otherwise not be in the interest of the contractor, as Goldberg (1977) points out. Thus, the contractor can point out pitfalls and suggest modifications to the project design before work begins. In negotiated contracts, some form of cost plus contracting is often used. As discussed in Bajari and Tadelis (2001) and as illustrated in the framework on pp. 70–3, cost plus contracts have poor incentives for contractors to control overall project costs. However, they are simpler to renegotiate since when changes occur, the contractor presents his receipts for the additional expenses and is reimbursed this amount. Thus, the often acrimonious process of haggling over change orders to the contract is avoided. Negotiated contracts may be less effective in selecting the lowest cost bidder compared to open competitive bidding. However, the problems discussed in this chapter suggest that economizing on *ex post* transaction costs is an important potential source of cost savings and this may outweigh the benefits of competitive bidding in selecting the lowest cost contractor.

Since the source of these costs is the incompleteness of project design and specifications, one policy implication is to consider increasing the costs and efforts put in to estimating and specifying projects before they are let out for bidding. Since the magnitude of adaptation costs estimated in Bajari *et al.* (2007) is sizeable, there may be room to consider some experimentation with more careful and costly design efforts, and to carefully examine the results of any such added effort in ex ante engineering.

In the public sector, the use of negotiated contracts is problematic.[8] Allowing for greater discretion in contractor selection increases the possibility for favoritism, kick backs and political corruption. The competitive bidding system is less prone to corruption since it allows for free entry by qualified bidders and there is an objective criteria for selecting the winning bidder. An important policy issue is whether it is possible to construct a mechanism that minimizes the *ex post* cost of making changes and the potential for corruption. To date, this question has not been explored in the existing theoretical literature. The research described above suggests that developing such a mechanism could improve efficiency in public sector procurement.

NOTES

1. See Bartholomew (1998), Clough and Sears (1994), Hinze (1993) and Sweet (1994).
2. In fact, Williamson expresses the idea that 'low powered' incentives are good to accommodate adaptations and writes that 'low powered incentives have well known adaptability advantages. That, after all, is what commends cost plus contracting. But, such advantages are not had without cost which explains why cost plus contracting is embraced reluctantly' (1985: 140). It turns out that in many cases cost plus contracting is indeed embraced.
3. Intermediate types of contracts that are not often used can lie between fixed-price and cost-plus contracts (see, for example, the discussion in section 2 of Bajari and Tadelis, 2001). These reimburse only a fraction of the total cost to the supplier and can sometimes include quality performance incentives.
4. In BT this is endogenously generated by a standard moral hazard component (hidden cost-savings effort).
5. Furthermore, if the fee is a percentage fee then implementing costly changes includes a small increase to compensate the contractor for any opportunity costs of extra time and potential overhead. This, of course, adds the risk that the contractor has incentives to increase costs and get a higher fee, which favors fixed-fees. With fixed fees the procurer and contractor may need to bargain over a fair fee for the opportunity costs of time, but this is typically a fraction of the labor and material costs of change over which no bargaining is needed with a cost-plus contract.
6. Note that this adverse selection problem is not akin to that in Laffont and Tirole (1993). Unlike their setting, it is not assumed that the seller knows more about the cost of the particular project, but just that more able sellers have higher outside options, regardless of the projects actual costs.
7. Ye (2007) investigates the problem of costly bidding, and how restricting the number of bidders may help the procurer.
8. Of course, if the procured service is one that lasts over time, one way to control adaptation with cost-plus incentives is by procuring the service in government internally with its own employees. See Levin and Tadelis (2007) for a transaction-cost incentive approach to this problem of privatization versus government provision of services.

REFERENCES

Bajari, Patrick and Steven Tadelis (2001), 'Incentives versus transaction costs: a theory of procurement contracts', *RAND Journal of Economics*, **32**(3), 387–407.

Bajari, Patrick, Stephanie Houghton and Steven Tadelis (2008), 'Bidding for incomplete contracts', NBER Working Paper No. W12051.

Bajari, Patrick, Robert McMillan and Steven Tadelis (2007), 'Auctions versus negotiations in procurement: an empirical analysis', *Journal of Law, Economics and Organization* (forthcoming).

Bartholomew, Stuart H. (1998), *Construction Contracting: Business and Legal Principles*, Englewood Cliffs, NJ: Prentice-Hall, Inc.
Caltrans' *Construction Manual*, available at, http://www.dot.ca.gov/ohq/construc/manual2001/cmaug2005.pdf
Caltrans' *Standard Specifications*, available at, http://www.dot.ca.gov/ohq/esc/oe/specifications/std-specs/2002-Stdspecs/2002StdSpecs.pdf
Clough, R. and G. Sears (1994), *Construction Contracting*, New York: Wiley.
Goldberg, Victor P. (1977), 'Competitive bidding and the production of pre-contract information', *The RAND Journal of Economics*, **8** (1), 250–61.
Hinze, Jim (1993), *Construction Contracts*, McGraw-Hill Series in Construction Engineering and Project Management, Columbus, OH: Irwin/McGraw-Hill.
Laffont, Jean-Jacques and Jean Tirole (1993), *A Theory of Incentives in Procurement and Regulation*, Cambridge, MA: MIT Press.
Levin, Jonathan and Steven Tadelis (2007), 'Contracting for government services: theory and evidence from US cities', NBER Working Paper No. W13350.
Sweet, J. (1994), *Legal Aspects of Architecture, Engineering and the Construction Process*, Eagan, MN: West Publishing Company.
Williamson, Oliver E. (1975), *Markets and Hierarchies*, New York: Free Press.
Williamson, Oliver E. (1985), *The Economic Institutions of Capitalism*, New York: Free Press.
Ye, Lixin. (2007) 'Indicative bidding and a theory of two-stage auctions', *Games and Economic Behavior*, **58**, 181–207.

APPENDIX

Proof of Proposion 1

The buyer's objective function is given as,

$$\max_{\substack{y \in \{0,1\} \\ \tau \in \{0,1\}}} u_B(y, \tau; T) = r\overline{\upsilon} + (1 - \tau)\overline{\upsilon}(y) - c(y) - d(\tau, T) \qquad (4.1)$$

and monotone comparative statics imply the following. It is easy to see that $u_B(y,\tau; T)$ exhibits increasing differences in $(y, T),(-\tau, T)$ and $(-\tau, y)$ since

$$\frac{\partial u_B(1, \tau; T)}{\partial T} - \frac{\partial u_B(0, \tau; T)}{\partial \tau} = \underline{\upsilon}(1) - \upsilon(0) > 0$$

$\partial u_B(y,\tau;T)/\partial T$ is constant in y, and

$$\frac{\partial^2 u_B(y, \tau; T)}{\partial T \partial \tau} = \frac{\partial^2 d(\tau, T)}{\partial T \partial \tau} < 0$$

Hence, as T increases, the buyer is better off having (weakly) less design (lower τ) and and more likely to benefit from a cost plus contract. *Q.E.D.*

5. From technical integrity to institutional coherence: regulatory challenges in the water sector

Claude Ménard

INTRODUCTION

If we look at the deregulation movement of the last 25 years or so, the pace of reform in the water sector has been remarkably slow, and changes likely the less radical among public utilities. Water was never deregulated. Even in the most spectacular reforms, like that implemented in the UK at the end of the 1980s, the sector remained heavily regulated. Moreover, there was never a significant move towards privatization. At most there has been private participation, supervised by a very visible public hand. A recent survey of 973 major urban water and sanitation systems in developing countries showed only 136 of them involving private sector participation, with divestitures constituting 10 per cent of this subset, while 66 per cent were concessions, 19 per cent management contracts, and the remaining 5 per cent leases or 'affermages' (Gassner *et al.*, 2007: 16).[1]

This reference to the limited role of privatization or private participation does not intend to suggest that privatization would be *the* solution to water problems. It rather points out that resistance to changes in the regulation and mode of organization of the sector, beside other changes that may be needed as well, is particularly striking if we take into account the essential character of water provision for human beings and the huge needs in that respect. According to the UN Millenium project (2005), confirmed by several reports from the World Bank and other institutions, over one billion human beings do not have access to safe drinkable water (and even less have access to safe sanitation), with poor people and particularly children the first victims of this situation, paying a heavy toll in terms of death and illness. This situation has not significantly improved, notwithstanding heavy investments from international donors and NGOs. The World Bank alone invested more than $2 billion on average per year in the first half of the 1990s (World Bank, 2006), and it is estimated that over $100 billion will be needed in the coming ten years to guarantee safe access to water and sanitation.[2]

The magnitude of the problem, and of the investments required, does not tell the entire story. For those familiar with water systems and the difficulties of their reform, particularly in developing countries, explaining this situation requires understanding why inappropriate modes of organization embedded in inadequate institutions persist. This chapter aims at contributing to the explanation of this resistance to reforms universally perceived as urgently needed. The conventional economic approach assumes it is mostly due to political backwardness and, to a lesser degree, to poorly defined property rights and/or badly designed contracts. Although I do not deny the role of these factors, I emphasize more 'neutral' conditions, related to the difficulties in maintaining technical integrity of the water system and in finding organizational arrangements embedded in appropriate institutions, difficulties that lead to high risk-averse strategies against fundamental reforms. At the theoretical level, I capture these dimensions with the concept of 'critical infrastructures', which has to do with the technical integrity of the system, and the concept of 'core transactions', which concerns the alignment (or misalignment) of organizational arrangements with the transactions at stake. The fitness of the institutions framing interactions between these two dimensions and guaranteeing their coherence then becomes a central issue. At the empirical level, I argue that the high complexity, due to local diversity of conditions for keeping technical integrity under control, and the uncertainty plaguing core transactions, due to competition for alternative usage of a good that has no substitutes and to political interference, determine the key role of micro-institutions in getting feasible configurations. By micro-institutions, I understand specific institutions that operate at the local and/or sector level under the umbrella of the general rules of the game established by legal and political institutions and that transform these general rules into operational ones.

More specifically, the underlying argument of the chapter is twofold. Because of the technical as well as the organizational requirements for water systems to meet demand, regulation is almost unavoidable. Because of the characteristics of the water sector, particularly its geographical specificity, local and/or regional institutions play a key role in shaping regulatory conditions for the provision of water services, which is also an element that can generate risk aversion to reform. Naïve attempts at 'deregulating' without taking into account these micro-institutions will likely get stuck in the very first steps.

These arguments are developed as follows. The second section develops the concept of critical infrastructure in order to catch the technical and economic requirements for guaranteeing the coherence of water systems. The third section points at the core transactions, as distinct from peripheral ones, that are central in meeting these requirements. The fourth section discusses the complex set of interactions involved and introduces the key role of micro-institutions in providing adequate guarantees. The fifth section analyses more specifically regulatory arrangements in that perspective. The sixth section turns the attention towards other micro-institutions that are much neglected, although playing an important role. The final section concludes with an emphasis on the need to also consider the sequential dimension in the implementation and operation of these micro-institutions. My analysis focuses on the provision of drinkable water in urban environments, leaving aside issues related to alternative uses of water, to drinkable water in rural communities, and to sewerage systems.[3]

A CRITICAL INFRASTRUCTURE[4]

There is no reregulation problem in the urban water sector because there was never deregulation to begin with! Water systems have always been and remain either heavily regulated or directly in the hands of public authorities. It is so due to technical properties that combines with specific economic characteristics, a combination that makes water systems falling unambiguously in the category of critical infrastructure.

There is an ongoing debate about what 'critical' infrastructures are and whether there is such a thing. A first approach emphasizes the supply side, that is, the need to secure those infrastructures that provide goods or services potentially subject to major disruptions (Moteff *et al.*, 2003). A second approach focuses on the demand side, that is, the need to guarantee consumers access to infrastructures that provide what are considered 'essential services'[5] or 'services of general interest' (European Union, 2004).[6] Both intend to identify assets and services viewed as crucial to economic development (for example, an adequate road system), to the protection of socio-economic cohesion (for example, infrastructures exposed to a terrorist attack), or to meeting social goals considered consubstantial to a developed society (for example, providing access to basic telephone services). However, the concept remains relatively ambiguous, and subject to many different interpretations.[7]

In what follows I adopt a restrictive approach to 'critical infrastructures' which I limit to sets of interdependent physical assets defining technical systems that impose requirements conditioning the provision of goods or services essential for guaranteeing the continuity of vital economic (and social) functions. The technical combination of assets needed from an organization to collect and deliver drinkable water to all citizens, or to secure dykes to prevent flood, provides unambiguous examples.

Technical Integrity and its Requirements

In that respect, the provision and coordination of assets or services required for the running of critical infrastructures are key issues. From a control engineering perspective, four criteria must be satisfied by any technical system for guaranteeing its integrity, that is: its capacity as a whole to durably deliver the adequate outcome (Nightingale *et al.*, 2003; Kunneke *et al.*, 2008). First, there must be coordinating devices that have the adequate scope of control, encompassing a complex set of relevant parameters (technological, transactional, safety). Second, accurate control mechanisms must be implemented that provide appropriate coordination. Third, the system must be reliable: essential functions in the system must be satisfied when needed, with timing a key factor. Fourth, the system must be viable: in the long run, it must be cost efficient so as to remain sustainable.

The water sector unambiguously falls in the range of critical infrastructures, directly since water is essential to human survival, and indirectly since it commands agriculture and therefore the provision of food.[8] As such, water systems must meet the criteria identified above. Their examination shows that there is always an economic dimension involved.

On the demand side, reliability is crucial. Drinkable water is essential per se to human beings, since there is absolutely no substitute, and the continuity of its provision is also indispensable. Leakages due to bad maintenance or illegal connections, major disruptions due to underinvestment, may threaten the health and even the survival of large segments of the population. Because there is no substitute, accessibility is also central, notwithstanding the fact that a significant amount of water delivered through urban systems does not go to essential needs (for example, showering). Although unbundling may be possible for some activities (for example, agricultural or industrial usages), it is often impossible (for example, unbundling different domestic uses), so that essential needs can hardly be dissociated from less critical ones.[9] The need to access water may also explain why it is so heavily loaded with social values. These values include quality requirements; environmental issues, so that alternative uses such as irrigation are not threatening durable reliability; and even beliefs, with water often viewed as a gift from Mother Nature . . . or God. This already helps understanding resistances to reforms, particularly when they are challenging or perceived as challenging accessibility, as it is the case with full privatization.

On the supply side, specific characteristics of water systems also impose technical requirements on its infrastructures, with economic consequences. The origin of water available (for example, whether it is underground or surface) requires techniques that carry their own constraints, as when water comes from distinct sources requiring differentiated treatment, but may also represent an opportunity, as when it is provided from a clean and easily accessible underground source, notwithstanding the risk of depleting a valuable resources. In terms familiar to transaction cost economists, physical as well as site specificity largely determine the scope of control and accuracy of coordination mechanisms required.

However, economists too often neglect the physical specificity of water systems. Laws of turbulence impose tight coordination in the network and its subsystems, between production and distribution on the one hand, and between primary and secondary networks on the other hand. It also requires coordination with maintenance services in order to control systemic effects of leaks. Site specificity may well add to these constraints, or relax them! Having access to a river that flows through the city, to an underground water table, or to an artificial reservoir that requires building a dam determines the scope of control and frames the set of alternative modes of organization. A reservoir imposes a centralized treatment and distribution system that a water table may allow to avoid. Other geographical factors also matter. Having to pump water from sources located hundreds of kilometres away and thousands of metres below the Federal District of Mexico in order to reduce the depletion of the underground lake on which the city is built obviously imposes technical constraints and coordination devices that differ from those in Santiago-de-Chile which benefits from a major river flowing through the city. And there is little hope to circumvent these constraints through technological innovation: technologies for providing potable water remain so far remarkably stable, beside marginal progress in metering (reading meters at distance) and development of less costly techniques of desalinization that also faces constraints (and could hardly solve the problem of Mexico City).

Economic Consequences

Obviously, these technological components have an impact on costs. The viability of urban water systems depends on these technical constraints and their economic consequences, which deeply embed them in their political environment (Savedoff and Spiller, 1999: chapter 1). Water systems are networks, with characteristics as close as possible to pure natural monopolies.

1. They benefit from large economies of scale, particularly with respect to transportation and distribution,[10] which combine with economies of density: the larger the number of customers connected in the neighbourhood of a production system, the lower the costs.
2. Technological developments in other network industries may reinforce the advantages of integrated water systems by allowing economies of scope, for example installing insulated cables carrying information through the water network.
3. Such possibilities can help lowering costs, a particularly important issue since sunk costs in water systems are so high: they are usually estimated to represent as much as 80 per cent of total costs, far above other network industries. This situation has major consequences on the organization of the system, the role of regulation, and . . . the risk of political opportunism (Savedoff and Spiller, 1999; Menard and Shirley, 2002).
4. One last dimension that contributes to economic specificities of water systems has to do with their important *externalities* (Crocker and Masten, 2002). Rapid demographic changes may render a system obsolete, because population growth or population movements across urban areas make the system inadequately dimensioned. In that respect, urban planning and the capacity of the political power to implement an orderly development play an important role, as well illustrated by the example of Singapore. Another important externality relates to the extension and maintenance of the system, with its impact on other underground networks, on the road system, and on related economic activities. Last, but not least, a major externality has to do with the impact of water quality on health, which depends on the capacity to monitor the system, to fix leaks rapidly (bad maintenance can translate into quick diffusion of underground pollution), and so on.

These factors cumulate in determining the criticality of water infrastructures because of the absolute need for water: there is not one single individual who can survive without drinking regularly an adequate amount of water. These features of water systems explain the importance of their reliability and condition their economic viability. They also explain why politicians are so sensitive to its pricing, so that both politicians and investors want regulatory rules strict enough to make sure there are no surprises, such as sudden increases in prices (on the politician side) or price reductions (the investor problem).

CORE TRANSACTIONS

These characteristics of urban water systems define and delineate the attributes of key transactions involved in organizing the production, transportation and distribution of water. I call these transactions '*core transactions*', as opposed to peripheral transactions, for example those relating to connection, metering, billing, or collecting bills. Keeping the governance of core transactions in line with the requirements of critical infrastructure is a key issue. These transactions play a critical role: they are essential to maintain the integrity of technical functions while keeping the system economically viable. Keeping their governance in line with their attributes is therefore a key issue. Inappropriate modes of organizations for these transactions are disruptive for the entire system.[11]

Core transactions can adequately be examined through the lenses of transaction cost economics, which helps understanding why organizations in the sector are predominantly integrated and submitted to tight regulation. First, core transactions relate to highly specific investments, that is: investments required to support the technical integrity of the system. In urban water systems, physical assets and related human capabilities must guarantee that production meets the needs of the population, that an adequate primary distribution network is implemented and that there is appropriate interconnection with the secondary network, in due respect to the laws of turbulence and the geographic specificity of water available.[12] The criticality of these infrastructures then largely depends on the adequacy of the system to the density of the population and its spatial distribution, and on the existence and implementation of urban planning. The denser the population is, the more significant and specific are investments required in water infrastructure; the better the urban planning is, the less costly the coordination of these investments is.

Second, core transactions are particularly exposed to uncertainties, which reinforce the need for coordination. Factors of uncertainty are of variable magnitude and may come out of four sources:

1. The physical environment may generate uncertainties (for example, variations in quantity or quality because of geology or hydrology: in years of drought, the depletion of a reservoir makes critical the capacity to anticipate and to coordinate alternative resources).
2. Human activities may also generate uncertainties that require reactivity and coordination (for example, pollution due to industrial or agricultural activities).
3. In organizing transactions that link parts of water systems, uncertainties may be generated by asymmetric information among parties

regarding their status and role (for example, between public authorities and a private operator; or between an operator in charge of the primary network and the one responsible for the secondary network whatever the status of ownership is).

4. Last, the high level of sunk costs and the long-term nature of investments in water infrastructures can also generate uncertainty, particularly when the institutional environment allows public authorities to exert a lot of discretionary power (risks of opportunistic usage of regulation, possibility to capture rents or even take over assets without compensation).

The higher are uncertainties surrounding the core transactions, the lower is the level of specific investments. As a corollary, this will deeply affect the possibility of private participation and the form of contracts (for example, lease versus concession) as well as their duration, if there are contracts at all.

Third, the frequency of core transactions poses puzzling problems in the urban water sector. On the one hand, features that make water systems so close to a natural monopoly mean that most of these transactions tend to be internalized. Moreover, the importance of sunk costs and the very low rate of technical changes in the sector involve long term commitment. As a consequence, organizational solutions (including contracts with private operators) tend to be long term, with low frequency of turnover. At the same time, site specificity that plays such an important role in the sector induces a significant variety in arrangements adopted. This property explains the local or regional nature of most water systems, but also provides opportunities for some benchmarking.[13] Moreover, recent researches (Guasch, 2004: chapter 6) show the exceptionally high rate of renegotiations in the water sector when private operators are involved, which suggest that transactions need adaptation and/or impose periodic transformation. A result of these diverging trends is that when private operators are involved, the frequency of contracting is low, while the frequency of renegotiations within existing contracts is high.

These complex attributes of core transactions in the urban water sector cumulate in the difficulties in finding appropriate risk sharing rules, particularly when private operators are involved. On the one hand, incentive theory suggest that risky decisions should be systematically transferred to the party supporting risks: the better the alignment between decision rights and property rights in core transactions, the better the performance of the system should be. On the other hand, the radical absence of substitute on the demand side[14] combined with heavy sunk investments and the features of natural monopoly on the supply side make the allocation of rights particularly sensitive to political interference and renegotiations. As a consequence, coherence between organizational solutions for monitoring core transactions and the need to guarantee technical integrity of the system is a critical issue.

GUARANTEEING COHERENCE BETWEEN CORE TRANSACTIONS AND TECHNICAL FUNCTIONS: ALIGNMENT ISSUES

Indeed, a main hypothesis of this chapter is that the explanation to the existence of the heavy regulation observed in the water sector lies largely in the difficulties in implementing and monitoring an organizational solution that satisfies constraints associated to core transactions and maintains the technical integrity of the system. A corollary is that the institutions supporting the interactions between these dimensions are a key for understanding how urban water systems work and their performance. Figure 5.1 summarizes the set of interactions involved.

A Complex Set of Interactions

Notwithstanding their specific characteristics, urban water systems share with other critical infrastructures some key interactions that determine their capacity to meet their goals, and their performance in doing so. This chapter leaves aside the performance issue,[15] and I have already explored the role of technical requirements as well as the core transactions that must be organized in order to provide adequate infrastructures and to deliver proper services (for example, clean drinkable water on a continuous basis). Figure 5.1 also introduces more explicitly the political dimension. Indeed, the choice of a mode of organization and the institutional framework in which it is embedded is also tributary of social forces: the political economy of water systems matters greatly. These forces particularly show up at times of reforms, pushing towards changes or resisting them. Successes or failures in aligning the organization of core transactions with technical requirements also depend on the equilibrium between winners and losers and among users, for example farmers versus urbanites. Although I do not analyse political forces here, they clearly interact with the two other dimensions identified on the first level of the figure.

My main concern in what follows is the impact these three dimensions have on the alignment (or misalignment) between modes of organization and their institutional framework, that the shaded area capture. More precisely, from now on I focus on the missing link between modes of

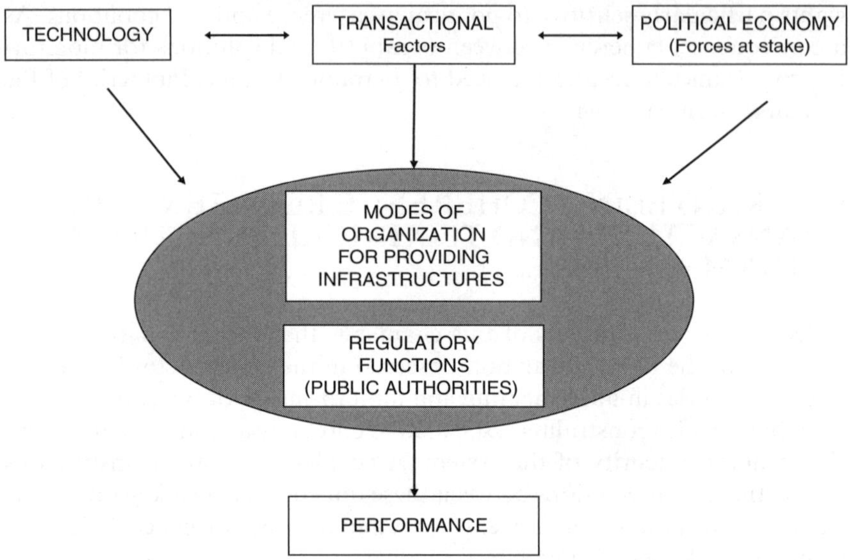

Figure 5.1 Interactions involved in critical infrastructures

organization and how regulatory functions operate, namely: the role of microinstitutions. The main point I want to make is that these micro-institutions, which tend to be ignored in the literature on critical infrastructures and their reform, are a major determinant in the capacity of urban water systems to meet their goals, and to do that efficiently.

Micro-institutions as Key to Coherence

Indeed the coherence of urban water systems (and of other critical infrastructures in that respect), their capacity to align their organization to the technical requirements as well as to the core transactions that support their functions, depends on intermediary devices that articulate the rules defined at the broad institutional level with the specific modes of organization adopted. I call 'micro-institutions' these intermediary devices determining the sustainability of water systems. These micro-institutions maintain a coherent system if they provide both formal and informal dispute resolution devices and coordination mechanisms between organizations involved while keeping transaction costs at a sustainable level.[16]

In order to capture the complex interactions between micro-institutions and the mode of organization chosen, it is helpful to distinguish horizontal and vertical interactions of micro-institutions. Indeed, a key problem in guaranteeing the coherence and adequate performance of water systems is the simultaneous presence of multiple principals and of multiple layers of regulation.

Horizontal challenges to coherence

The existence of multiple principals monitoring simultaneously the same public utilities tends to be a general phenomenon (Estache and Martimort, 2001). In the case of Manila, I have identified 32 bureaux and agencies involved in the regulation of water (World Bank, 2005; Xun Wu *et al.*, 2006). The phenomenon is particularly significant in the water sector because of the geographical decentralization of the system and the heterogeneity of users involved. A major trade-off is between domestic users, since water is essential to all human beings, and agriculture, which might arguably also be considered essential since water conditions the production of food. As a result there is tension everywhere between authorities in charge of delivering water to households and authorities in charge of agriculture. Moreover, increasing environmental concerns have led to new constraints most of the time implemented and monitored by either a specific ministry or an autonomous agency. Other administrative entities also interfere. Since quality standards matter so much for public health, relevant authorities are usually in charge of their control. Numerous industrial and commercial users are big consumers lobbying related ministries or bureaux. These entities, and possibly others, for example Ministries of Defence or authorities in charge of urban planning, hold some jurisdiction over water systems, and remain subject to pressures from groups of interest and political players.

An important consequence concerns the allocation of regulatory rights and how it could guarantee the coherence of the system. There is no simple solution to this problem. In many cases, particularly when it comes to major cities, conflicts among jurisdictions and bureaus tend to be solved at the highest level of government. In my sample,[17] most cases illustrate the activity of this very visible political hand, for example Abidjan, Buenos Aires, Manila, Vanuatu, and so on. Santiago-de-Chile is the exception in that respect, with relatively little political game among different authorities involved in the regulation of the sector. These interferences and overlapping generate high political transaction costs (Savedoff and Spiller, 1999: chapter 1).

Vertical challenges to coherence

Beside the distribution of responsibilities among different ministries or bureaux that may challenge the coherence of water systems, whether they are operated by a public entity or a private operator, there is also the problem of the multiple layers of institutions and decision-makers involved. Water provision presents physical and technical characteristics that impose some decentralization. The resulting trade-off between centralization and decentralization raises the issue of the optimal degree of decentralization and of the adequate micro-institutions. At an abstract level, this issue present similarities with the problems raised by fiscal federalism or, from a very different perspective, with the problem of delegation in organization theory.

Three aspects are particularly significant in that respect. First, regulatory responsibilities must be allocated among different levels of government. Centralized regulation and/or administrative supervision, as in unified political systems, present the advantage of lower transaction costs since agreements do not have to be negotiated and implemented among a large number of parties. However, it confronts the risks associated to 'one-size-fits-all': the temptation is pervasive for central authorities to impose a unique contractual model that does not fit local circumstances, thus giving way to cheating.[18] The other polar case, full decentralization, has the advantage of opening the door to diverse solutions, facilitating comparison and, ideally, benchmarking, which means regulatory mechanisms potentially more market-oriented. However, it also involves higher transaction costs (operators have to tailor different contracts for different municipalities, and local authorities must consider non-standard contracts as well), higher risks of conflict among the different layers of public decision-makers, and the multiplication of sources of political interferences. The Buenos Aires saga, which ended up with the operator breaching the contract, illustrates this all too well (Alcazar *et al.*, 2002).

Second, the very nature of the organizational arrangement, for example the characteristics of a contract, may challenge the vertical coherence of the system.[19] There is a trade-off between agreements that tightly constrain parties, for example detailed contracts that restrict arbitrary decisions in dispute resolution but also involve costly design and potentially harmful rigidities; and flexible arrangements that lower initial transaction costs but create room for discretionary power in the hands of regulator(s) and political decision-makers, making dispute resolution quite opaque. Contracts need to be adapted because circumstances are changing in the long run and because there is a continuing learning process that can favour better design but also feed lobbying by groups of interest, thus challenging the coherence of the arrangement. The case of the Manila concession, when operators were suddenly confronted by the Asian financial crisis, illustrates these tensions quite well (World Bank, 2005; Xun Wu *et al.*, 2006). A related issue is about whether local governance is more at risk of inconsistency in decision making, with political changes going in different directions at different levels of decision. In Buenos Aires, the presence of representatives of different levels of government with different political orientations on the regulatory board was a major source of conflicts, leaving the operator disoriented about what was expected, thus challenging the coherence of the system (Alcazar *et al.*, 2002).

Third, the administrative burden for local authorities of designing and monitoring reforms at the local level, particularly when resorting to contracts, amplifies the role of conflict resolution devices. New institutional economists have established a reputation in emphasizing the importance of ex post conditions in contractual arrangements, because of the risks of hold-up by opportunistic parties (Williamson, 1985: chapter 13). Building adequate micro-institutions to monitor complex arrangements is not a one-shot game. It has an inherently evolutionary character: effects are observed and discovered, they are articulated by interest groups, they are evaluated and brought in the regulatory and governance arena, opening doors to negotiation, arbitration, and so on. With respect to water systems a major aspect of these complex interactions concerns the level at which conflicts should be monitored: local, regional or central levels of government. Indeed, these levels tend to overlap, generating gaps, delays, and uncertainties in the interaction between regulation and organizational arrangements. An unambiguous indicator of these difficulties is the exceptionally high rate and frequency of renegotiations of contracts in the sector (Guasch, 2004: chapter 6). The multiplicity of layers involved also raises the underexplored question of whether a decentralized system is more prone to corruption or the reverse.[20]

REGULATORY DEVICES AS CENTRAL MICRO-INSTITUTIONS

My main argument so far has been that the technical functions making water infrastructures critical also determine the existence of core transactions, and that the institutions framing their interactions are crucial in guaranteeing, or failing to guarantee, the coherence and performance of water systems. These characteristics and their economic consequences also lighten the key role of the heavy visible hand regulating the sector. I now turn to the central micro-institutions that are regulatory devices.

Two polar forms of regulation border the field within which water systems operate: 'command-and-control'; and an independent regulator monitoring private entities. Most arrangements are actually in-between, defining 'hybrids' in which regulation leans towards integration, monitoring water systems through administrative rules; or towards market arrangements, providing critical infrastructures through contracts with variable delegation of rights to private participants. Urban water systems remain dominated by these hybrid institutional arrangements. Pure market forms (full privatization) remain the exception. According to the extensive sample from Gassner *et al.* (2007), pure divestiture in the water sector represents only 10 per cent of the 136 cases with private participation, which is itself a relatively minor case in the 973 entities of their study, against 43 per cent of the cases (and up to 89 per cent if we include all cases of Public-Private Participation) in the electricity sector. The Private Participation in Infrastructure Database confirms: of the 522 projects listed from 1991 to 2006, only 23 were divestiture. Similarly, Guasch (2004: 25) found that 89 per cent of infrastructure projects involving private participation in the water sector in Latin America for the period 1990–2000 were concessions. Moreover, private participation in water projects seems to have reached a peak in the second half of the 1990s (in 1997 according to the data collected by Guasch 2004: 151), with an observable decline more recently, a notable exception being the East Asia and Pacific region according to the PPI database.[21]

Command-and-Control

The 'command-and-control' mode of regulation[22] is mainly characterized by the direct monitoring of core transactions by public authorities that remain in charge of the coherence of the system. It takes the form of the provision of general laws, framing the organization and the running of the system, and of administrative rules shaping its operation.

These laws and rules do not have to be specific to the water system: they may determine the rules of the game for different public utilities simultaneously. When it comes to making them operational for a specific sector, they can be embedded in different arrangements, from direct implementation of these rules through a public bureau to decentralized organizations as when decision rights are delegated to public corporations. In this context, links between general rules and specific arrangements in charge of developing and maintaining adequate infrastructures raises typical agency problems: the coherence and reliability of the water system depends on the capacity of the principal – the public authorities – to supervise and control its agents, and to implement adequate incentives while keeping control over strategic decisions. Note that this does not tell us who the public authorities are, and therefore what are the actual institutions implementing the rules of the game. Note also that in these arrangements, regulators (if they exist) are almost always a branch of the principal (the public authorities), with very limited autonomy.

Regulation Through Contracts

Notwithstanding the fact that urban water systems remain largely State Owned Enterprises, the trend in the last two decades has been a shift towards a contractual approach (Guasch, 2004; Chapter 6 this volume). The story in this case differs from command-and-control. Most of the time, water systems are then submitted to laws not specific to the sector, for example laws framing the provision of 'essential services' through contracts and/or laws regulating competition. Specific rules complement the general framework by defining particular targets (such as rate of connections) or modalities adapted to the characteristics of the sector (for example price formulae intending to guarantee the provision of water to all segments of the population). The degree of overlapping of these laws and rules with the autonomy of the operator depends very much on the type of 'franchise' implemented.

The examination of the different modes of organization that can be endorsed under regulation through contracts largely exceeds the scope of this chapter. Figure 5.2 summarizes the main arrangements and how they relate, *grosso modo*, with regulatory devices.

The horizontal axis shows the allocation of property rights and of related decision rights, from public ownership to full divestiture. The vertical axis summarizes the autonomy of decision, with respect to policy makers, and the intensity of incentives associated with that autonomy. Predominant forms of regulation are associated with these different arrangements, from the pure form of command-and-control over a public bureau (typically waterworks department) to arrangements regulated by contracts, as with lease contracts, to full divestiture in which private operators are regulated by general laws (particularly competition policies). Frontiers, indicated

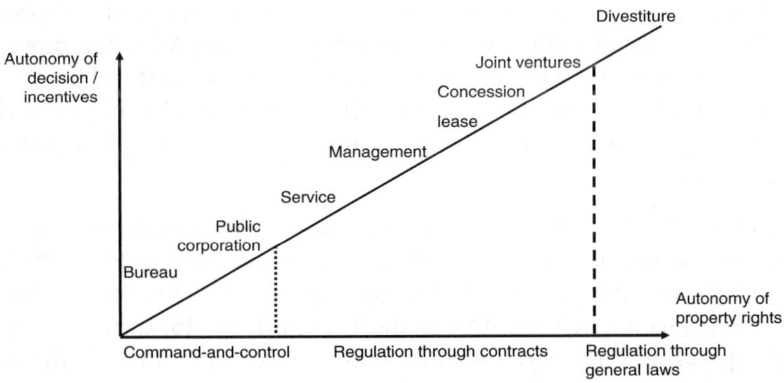

Figure 5.2 Regulation and modes of organization

with doted lines, can be blurred as with the provision of some services in the water system through outsourcing (for example, maintenance, or billing and recovering) while core transactions remain under the control of public authorities, or through concessions that bring the arrangement closer to integration by a private operator.

With the exception of full privatization, which remains an exception in the urban water sector, contractual arrangements ranking from services to joint ventures can be understood as forms of 'franchising': public authorities transfer some property rights and some decision rights to one or several private operators, while keeping rights over some core transactions. In my sample and for the period under review, most solutions implemented maintained public entities (Bogotá, Johannesburg, Lima, Mexico, Montana, Santiago – later privatized – and Tegucigalpa),[23] while contractual arrangements were predominantly concessions (Buenos Aires, Cancun, Manila, Vanuatu) or a mix of lease and concession (Abidjan, Cartagena, Conakry, Dakar).

The point I want to emphasize is the very specific role of regulatory entities as central micro-institutions in the context of contractual arrangements (the intermediary zone in Figure 5.2). Indeed, defining rights, enforcing and controlling implementation of agreements, which requires specific capabilities, become major tasks for these entities, particularly with respect to core transactions. These tasks increase in importance and complexity the closer we get to full privatization. Five characteristics of regulatory entities deserve particular attention in that respect:

1. How is their domain of action delineated?
2. What are the dominant traits of their internal governance (for example, how are regulators selected and appointed)?
3. What rules guide their action (public audit before making a decision, accountability after the decision is made)?
4. What is the scope of their discretionary power with respect to the contractual arrangement chosen (for example, what power of investigation and what capacities of enforcement do they have)?
5. How much do institutional and political factors influence their decisions (capacity of courts to intervene, capacity of political power to interfere)?

In discussing these issues, most economists have focused on the quest for optimal solutions. However, because of the multiple criteria involved, several equilibria are sustainable. Selecting one solution becomes an institutional/political choice. This choice is itself submitted to lobbying from interest groups as well as conditioned by market structures. Indeed, the water sector tends to be very polarized, with operators that are either relatively small autonomous entities operating at the local or regional level so that regulation needs adjusting to important local variations, or a small number of highly concentrated international operators competing for contracts and often combining in consortia, which reduces even more the number of competitors. In my sample, in the seven cases in which bidders competed, only two bidders remained until the last round (Buenos Aires being the exception, with three competitors). This is confirmed by other studies.[24]

Establishing adequate regulatory institutions to properly monitor these contractual arrangements and secure core transactions in order to guarantee the coherence of the system then becomes a key issue. An unambiguous indicator of the difficulties involved is the significance of renegotiations. According to Guasch (2004: 13), almost 75 per cent of the contracts in the water sector in Latin America are renegotiated, by far the highest rate among utilities operating under contracts. Moreover, on average renegotiations intervened only 1.6 year after signature, much earlier than what contractual clauses anticipated. The conventional view turns spontaneously to political interference, although data show that a significant per centage of renegotiations are initiated by private operators. Notwithstanding continuous efforts by highly qualified economists and lawyers to define optimal contracts, this situation clearly indicates how difficult the regulation by contracts is.

To sum up, the political sensibility of water issues combines with the relative decentralization of the provision of water to make the task of regulatory entities particularly complex. Monitoring core transactions involves several institutional levels and even several layers within the same regulatory entity. In Buenos Aires, the Board monitoring the concession was highly politicized, with representatives from the three levels of government, local, provincial, and federal (Alcazar *et al.*, 2002, chapter 3). In Manila, the bureau supervising the contract and operating as a regulator had different departments with personnel appointed by different ministries and also under political influence (World Bank, 2005; Xun Wu and Malaluan, 2006). The resulting risks may explain an apparent trend towards shorter duration of contracts, with reduced commitment from private operators or even switches back to the direct provision of water by public authorities.[25]

SOME OTHER KEY MICRO-INSTITUTIONS

Beside regulatory devices, several other institutions are involved in monitoring urban water systems. It is so for all public utilities, although it might be particularly significant in the water sector because of the three determinants encapsulated in Figure 5.1. Technology makes the provision of water essentially local or regional: it is technically complex to carry water on long distance and it requires costly infrastructures. Hence local and/ or regional authorities have more weight than in the provision of other critical infrastructures such as electricity or telecommunications. From a transactional point of view, the very high level of specific investments required and the uncertainty that would result from a lack of coherence in the system mean that tight coordination of the core transactions is needed. Last, the political economy of water, mainly characterized by the total overlapping between users and citizens and the multiplicity of usages, makes multi-levelled political interferences and conflicts of interest almost inevitable. As a result, dispute resolution devices play a particularly important role in maintaining conflicting interests under control while guaranteeing some continuity in the running of water systems. In what follows, I emphasize the role of three such devices.

Judicial Review

With the introduction of private operators and the development of contractual regulation, an increasing emphasis has been put on the key role of an independent judiciary that can review agreements and arbitrate conflicts among parties as well as audit consumers' complaints (for example, Savedoff and Spiller, 1999: chapter 1). The existence of efficient and competent courts is now ritually mentioned, although rarely analysed,[26] as a central piece of a successful reform of public utilities, especially water systems.

I do not intend to deny the importance and significance of an adequate legal system (see Hadfield, 2005). However, the literature may overstate the role of the judiciary. In my sample, for the period covered by the case studies, very few conflicts between public authorities (or regulators) and operators ended in courts. Contracts referred to courts as the key dispute-resolution device in seven cases, but actual conflicts were almost all solved through negotiations with superior levels of public authorities, or through international intermediation,[27] Santiago being an exception, with courts playing an active role. This mitigated role of the judiciary has at least four reasons:

1. Going to courts signals that parties have been unable to solve conflicts, which challenges the continuity of the relationship, a crucial ingredient when investments as highly specific as in urban water systems are needed.
2. Relying on the judiciary involves high transaction costs. There is no such a thing as a free lawyer! Judicial procedures are particularly costly for local authorities dealing with big operators who have the capacity to spread their legal fees over several contracts with different authorities.

3. The judiciary introduces an extra player in the game that interferes with regulation, which might increase uncertainty for all parties, particularly when respective jurisdictions are not well specified.
4. Last, one cannot ignore that most countries have poor legal competences.

Judges and lawyers apt to deal with commercial affairs are a very scarce resource, costly to develop (Hadfield, 2005). Incompetent, corrupt, or politically appointed judges represent a major source of uncertainty for private operators who often prefer to deal directly with the political power. Circumventing these difficulties by going to international courts makes uncertainty and costs even more significant.

It does not mean that the judiciary is unimportant. However, its role is mostly one of dissuasion in last resort against the risk of opportunistic behaviour, either from public authorities or from private operators.

Arbitration

Therefore, it is no surprise if in the context of contractual arrangements parties look for substitutes to the judiciary. A key micro-institution in that respect is arbitration. In my sample and for the period under review, going to court was indeed the exception while arbitration played a significant role in most cases. Ten contracts were challenged not long after they were signed, and all conflicts were referred to arbitrators, although satisfying solutions were not always found, as illustrated by the case of Buenos-Aires in which Suez ended up breaching the contract.

These cases refer only to formal arbitration. Rubin (2005), among others, suggests a sharp distinction between mediation and arbitration. The former refers to the role of private agents, either insiders or outsiders, who are jointly asked by the parties to help solve their conflicts. Most of the time conflicts solved in this way are not made public and are not registered, making very difficult to get data confirming the role of mediation. However, discussions and interviews with private operators as well as with public authorities substantiate their significance, which confirms Rubin's intuition about the significant role of this relatively informal institution in dispute resolution.

The alternative to mediation when it fails or when parties are too distrustful but do not want to go to courts is the more formal device embedded in many contracts, arbitration. This solution is also costly, particularly when it involves international experts. Its advantages over the judiciary are threefold: (a) it usually mobilizes experts in the field; (b) it is less disruptive for the contractual relationship since it signals that parties value its continuation; and (c) it can help circumventing situations in which there is no competent judicial system or the judiciary is either corrupt or too dependent on the political power. Unfortunately, I am not aware of empirical studies clarifying the role, functioning, and costs of arbitration as a dispute resolution device in contracts between public authorities and private operators.[28] Moreover, there is to my knowledge no empirical study on how conflicts are solved when public operators are endowed with large autonomy, as is the case with 'corporatization'.

Also, there is likely a size effect. Indeed, we can presume that contracts between large cities dealing with big private operators end up much more frequently in arbitration. This can be accentuated by flaws in contracts and in their implementation, due to the limited human capabilities available at the local level. As a result, the ex ante design and allocation of contracts through complex procedures and the *ex post* collection and processing of data to properly monitor operators by far exceeds local competences, so that disputes emerge that require resolution by third parties. Courts being expensive and procedures lengthy, arbitration offers a solution in case of failure of mediation, likely preferred by local authorities of limited size and/or operators that are not among the big ones. Here again we need more data about the respective role of these alternative devices.

Last, 'benchmarking' could facilitate dispute resolution and, more specifically, arbitration. In theory, water systems should benefit from an important advantage to do so, thanks to decentralization and the multiple cases it provides, notwithstanding adjustments required by variations in the physical environment, the density and/or distribution of population, the reliability of the existing system at time t_0, and so on. However, only one case in my sample, Santiago-de-Chile, has implemented benchmarking. The explanation might depend on several factors, among which an important one could be the scarcity of adequate human assets. There is some naivety among reformers, particularly international organizations, in their 'benign neglect' of the limited human competences required for monitoring complex contracts in developing countries, as well as in most medium and small cities of developed countries. Arbitrators and consultants offer a partial alternative, since they use and develop more or less general indicators, criteria, approaches, protocols or checklists. In that respect, arbitration also operates as a micro-institution.

Regional Institutions as Solutions?

Another possibility developed to circumvent scarcity of qualified human assets and reduce renegotiations and recourse to arbitration or courts is the building of micro-institutions at the regional level, regions being either infra-national, as with basin agencies, or supra-national, for example to allocate water from a source flowing across different countries. Regional institutions intend to maintain coherence in water systems while keeping transaction costs at reasonable levels.

At the infra-national level, there is a propensity to improve coherence in the allocation and provision of water to competing users by developing more concentrated micro-institutions, as can be observed in many countries, developed (Pezon, 2008) as well as developing ones (Perard, 2007). The French Basin Agencies provide an example. They are micro-institutions mixing regulatory functions with coordination among users of water resources. They are structured along the main river basins (with the exception of Corsica and overseas departments) in order to pool human resources for coordinating municipalities, providing support in the negotiation of contracts, implementing new environmental rules, and facilitating a more rational allocation of water among users. However these arrangements face the difficulties of coordinating different political institutions.

The same of course applies and is even amplified when it comes to building institutions for regulating water systems, and possibly contractual arrangements, at the supra-national level. Although it is becoming a major concern, and a strategic issue, for countries depending on a common resource, there are still few experiences of regional institutions operating across borders in the water sector.[29] Considering the high rate and frequency of renegotiations in the sector, regional institutions could also facilitate the implementation of adequate arbitration procedures, with arbitrators possibly covering different public utilities and/or several regions, thus relaxing constraints on local authorities. They could reduce arbitration costs; restrict the role of the judiciary while increasing its credibility; and limit risks of capture.[30]

CONCLUSION

In this chapter, I argued that water has been and remains a highly regulated sector because it is a 'critical infrastructure' that requires tight coordination of its core transactions in order to maintain technical integrity as well as economic coherence in the system. If one looks at the history of developed countries, they all have had at some point their water and sewerage systems developed either by public bureaux under political control or by private operators tightly supervised by public authorities. It is also noticeable that Public-Private Participation has become fashionable less because of failures in the running of water and sewerage systems in developed countries than because of constraints in public finances, particularly in developing countries. This is not to deny flaws and failures in many SOEs, but to temper their significance.

Once the necessity of regulating the provision of urban water is acknowledged, the problem becomes that of designing adequate institutions to regulate properly the system. I have argued that there are specific aspects of water infrastructures that impose making room for micro-institutions in order to align properly the modes of organization to the core transactions at stake. Two issues are of particular importance in that respect:

1. There are no substitutes for satisfying the need for safe drinkable water and for agricultural purposes. As a result, social goals (accessibility, sustainability) are inextricably interwoven with technological constraints and allocative efficiency, making political interference almost inevitable.
2. Because of the nature of water resources and the distribution of needs, decentralization tends to prevail, with water systems mostly managed at a local or regional level, which amplifies the role of micro-institutions.

In that respect, it might be necessary to get rid of the ideological aspect of the discussion on property rights. Incentives are of course an issue in the provision of water, but it cannot solve per se the required coherence for an infrastructure so critical to human beings. Contracts cannot do it all. Repeated adjustments of 'optimal contracts' inspired and monitored by very competent economists have not delivered fully convincing results. Adequate institutions need being designed. Those economists who have looked at this issue so far have almost exclusively focused on the global institutional environment: legal systems, political regimes, checks and balances, and so on. In this chapter I have argued that there may be serious gains in looking at intermediate institutions, or 'micro-institutions' as I called them, linking institutional environments to organizational arrangements. My attention has mainly concentrated the attention on conditions imposed by the characteristics of the system in a static perspective. Another important issue, which I have not taken into consideration, has to do with the sequential dimension in the implementation and operation of these micro-institutions. Of course, these problems by far exceed the urban water sector.

ACKNOWLEDGEMENTS

This is an exploratory essay, linked to an ongoing research on the role of micro-institutions in reforms of water systems in 15 major urban areas in 12 different developing countries. With a few exception, I have been involved in these case studies directly (field research) or indirectly (scientific adviser). I am deeply indebted to Aad Correlje, Michel Ghertman, Patricia Manso, Chris Shugart, Pablo Spiller, Bernhardt Truffer, Oliver Williamson and Hagen Worch, for their extremely helpful comments and suggestions: several ideas were borne out of our discussions and exchanges. However, the usual disclaimer fully applies.

NOTES

1. State Owned Enterprises (SOE) represented 837 out of the 973 entities in the sample. By comparison, in the same study there were 161 PSP and only 91 SOE in the electricity sector, which is another indicator of the weak involvement of private operators in the water sector.
2. For a very critical review of this situation, see Shirley (2008: Chapter 5).
3. These are not minor restrictions. Most water is for alternative uses (particularly the agri-food sector) and in many developing countries the provision of drinkable water is a particularly acute problem in rural areas. As for sewerage, epidemiologists have shown that without an adequate system, the provision of safe drinkable water does not prevent the development of significant epidemics and illnesses (Esrey, 1996).
4. This section and the next one draw from an ongoing project with John Groenewegen and Rolf Kunneke, from Delft University of Technology (TU Delft). I am grateful to this institution for its financial support.
5. See *Essential Services Commission Act*, Australia, 2001 (No. 62 of 2001). The Act explicitly lists such services.
6. This concept is an extension of the notion of 'services of general economic interest' used in Articles 18 and 86 (2) of the Treaty founding the European Union.
7. In that respect the report on critical infrastructures to the US Senate (Moteff *et al.*, 2003) is impressive by the extension of what is considered critical, from agriculture to chemical and nuclear power plants.
8. Hence the difficult and often conflicting trade-off between urban water systems and irrigation.
9. A related issue is that there is a wide variation in the appreciation and valuation of water by different types of users at different times, so that infrastructures must be designed in a way that allows dealing with some instability on the demand side (conflicting usages at a time of very hot weather) as well as on the supply side (possibility of shortage). It also means adequate modes of organization as well as appropriate institutions are required to translate this variability into investments.
10. Under some circumstances, for example an abundant underground water table, production might partially make exception, allowing diverse suppliers to operate, as when there are concessions to just manage a pump or a fountain.
11. Related to the distinction between the technical dimension and their economic consequences, it is possible to make a distinction between two types of effects associated to core transactions: (a) systemic effects, related to their capacity to secure the technical functions of the system (for example, guaranteeing adequate interconnections); (b) transaction-specific effects, related to their capacity to meet the goals they are assigned (for example, providing adequate incentives for highly specific investments). See Kunneke *et al.*, 2008.
12. Political and social factors might also contribute in making investments specific, for example military or geo-strategic issues (as with the Jordan Valley), religion, or other values imposing constraints and rules on usage of water.

13. It also favours learning, thus contributing to improve the capabilities of public authorities as well as private operators, particularly when it comes to negotiating and monitoring contracts.
14. The absence of substitute may also explain the importance of social values attached to water issues, the conflicts it might generate among users (for example, households and farmers), and the impact it may have in favouring political interference and creating unstable conditions in the system.
15. For a detailed examination of the relationship between institutions and performance, see Saleh and Dinar (2004), particularly Chapter 8.
16. Disputes can be associated to customers' complaints, political unrest, courts cases, etc.
17. See Note 4.
18. For example, before 1994 a unified law structured all contractual relationships in the French water sector, so that adjustments and adaptation proliferated in annexes and so forth, leaving room to political manipulation . . . and corruption.
19. A useful indicator for capturing problems of coherence in a system is the level of Unaccounted For Water (UFW), that is: the water that is pumped into the system but never reaches users. In my sample it runs from a high close to 66 per cent in Conakry to a low 13 per cent in Abidjan at the time reforms were implemented. On average in my sample UFW represents almost 33 per cent of the water produced.
20. In a study on corruption in the water sector in Germany and France, Domanski (2006) suggests that decentralized systems tend to have fewer and smaller cases of corruption than more centralized ones.
21. The decline is even more noticeable if one looks not only at the number of projects but also at total investment. See Private Participation in Infrastructure Database, http://ppi.worldbank.org (last consulted: 28 August 2007).
22. Also referred as 'institutional regulation'. 'Administrative regulation', as opposed to 'contractual regulation', could be more appropriate since institutional factors and modes of control are everywhere involved. The dominance of hybrid arrangements might explain why no polar characterization is fully satisfying. For example, regulators under contractual forms of regulation might well turn towards 'administrative' style of regulation!
23. For the purpose of this chapter I do not consider contracts by which a public corporation outsource some services as falling under the contractual mode of regulation.
24. In the extensive dataset for Latin America in Guasch (2004: 153), 93 projects in the water sector had three bidders at most (ten had only one, 54 only two), while only eight projects had more than three bidders (six had four, two had six).
25. A proxy to changes in duration could be switches from concession to lease and management contracts. We miss time series in that respect. Based on the PPI database, the trend is not obvious, particularly because of the development of concessions in the East Asia and Pacific region. A similar difficulty applies to measuring switches back to public entities.
26. But see Ménard and Shirley (eds), 2005, section III for several detailed contributions.
27. In the same vein, and significantly, there is almost no reference to any active role of the judiciary in the extensive study of conflicts and renegotiations in Guasch (2004).
28. Significantly, Guasch (2004) devotes only one explicit paragraph (p. 135) to this issue, recommending that arbitration clauses be extended to most contracts.
29. Administrative agreements among countries for monitoring shared water resources have existed for a long time (recent examples are provided in Perard, 2007). Here I am pointing at the newness of micro-institutions developed for monitoring relationships in the context of contractual regulations with private operators involved.
30. Formal regional regulators have been implemented in the telecoms to monitor operators in Southern Africa and in the Caribbean, the motivation largely stemming from the need to overcome scarcity of human resources at the national level as well as to deal with technologies that exceed national borders (Barendse, 2006). See also Baudrier (2007) for Europe.

REFERENCES

Alcazar, Lorena, Manuel A. Abdala and Mary M. Shirley (2002), 'The Buenos Aires Water Concession', in M. Shirley (ed.), *Thirsting for Efficiency: The Economics and Politics of Urban Water System Reform*, Oxford: Elsevier chapter 3; 65–102.

Arrandale, Tom (2003), 'Foreign faucet', available at, http://www.governing.com/archive/2003/jun/water.txt

Barendse, Andrew (2006), 'Regional regulation as a new form of telecom sector governance'; PhD: Delft University of Technology.

Baudrier, Audrey (2007), 'Coûts de coordination, structure de gouvernance réglementaire et environnement institutionnel: une analyse économique néo-institutionnelle de la mise en œuvre du cadre réglementaire européen des communications électroniques', PhD Université de Paris 1 (Panthéon-Sorbonne).

Center for Public Integrity (2003), 'Water privatization becomes a signature issue in Atlanta', available at, http://www.icij.org/Content.aspx?src=searchcontent=article&id=55

Crocker, Keith J. and Scott E. Masten (2002), 'Prospects for private water provision in developing countries: lessons from 19th-century America', in M. Shirley (ed.), *Thirsting for Efficiency: The Economics and Politics of Urban Water System Reform*, Oxford Elsevier Chapter 9, 317–48.

Domanski, Aleksandra (2006), 'Corruption and public utilities: the case of the water sector', Master Thesis, Université de Paris (Panthéon-Sorbonne).

Esrey, Steven A. (1996), 'Water, waste, and well-being: a multicountry study', *American Journal of Epidemiology*, 143(6), 608–23.

Estache, Antoine and David Martimort (2001) 'Transaction costs, politics, regulatory institutions and regulatory outcomes', in L. Manzetti (ed.), *Regulatory Policy in Latin America: Post-Privatization Realities*, Miami: North-South Press Center of the University of Miami, 49–82.

European Union (2004), *White Paper on Services of General Interest,* Commission of the European Communities, Com (2004) 374 Final.

Gassner, Katarina, Alexander Popov and Nataliya Pushak (2007), *An Empirical Assessment of Private Sector Participation in Electricity and Water Distribution in Developing Countries*, Washington, DC: Finance, Economics and Urban Department, World Bank. Version consulted: March 2007.

Guasch, Juan Luis (2004), *Granting and Renegotiating Infrastructure Concessions. Doing it Right*, Washington, DC: World Bank.

Hadfield, Gillian K. (2005), 'The many legal institutions that support contractual commitments', in Claude Ménard and Mary Shirley, *Handbook of New Institutional Economics*, Dordrecht-Berlin-New York: Springer, chapter 8, 175–204.

Jehl, Douglas (2003), 'As cities move to privatize water, Atlanta steps back', available at, http://www.greatlakesdirectory.org/zarticles/021803_great_lakes.htm

Kunneke, Rolf, John Groenewegen and Claude Ménard (2008), 'Aligning institutions with technology: Critical transactions in the reform of infrastructures', Working paper, TU Delft.

Ménard, Claude and Mary Shirley (2002), 'Cities awash: a synthesis of the country cases', in M. Shirley (ed.), *Thirsting for Efficiency*: *The Economics and Politics of Urban Water System Reform*, Oxford: Elsevier, Chapter 1: 1–42.

Ménard, Claude and Mary M. Shirley (2005), *Handbook of New Institutional Economics*, Dordrecht, Berlin, New York: Springer.
Moteff, John, Claudia Copeland and John Fischer (2003), *Critical Infrastructures: What Makes an Infrastructure Critical?* Report to the US Senate, (version of 29 January).
Nightingale, P., T. Brady, A. Davis, and J. Hall (2003), 'Capacity utilization revisited: software, control, and the growth of large technical systems', *Industrial and Corporate Change* **12**, 477–517.
Pérard, Edouard (2007) 'Private sector participation and regulatory reform in water supply: the southern mediterranean experience', OECD: Development Center Working Papers. September.
Pezon, Christelle (2008), 'Decentralization and delegation of water and sanitation services in France', Working paper, ENGREF-Montpellier.
Rubin, Paul H. (2005), 'Legal systems as frameworks for market exchanges', in Claude Ménard and Mary M. Shirley (eds), *Handbook of New Institutional Economics*, Dordrecht, Berlin, New York: Springer, Chapter 9, 205–28.
Saleh, R. Maria and Ariel Dinar (2004) *The Institutional Economics of Water. A Cross-country Analysis of Institutions and Performance*, Cheltenham: The World Bank & Edward Elgar.
Savedoff, William and Pablo Spiller (1999), 'Government opportunism and the provision of water', in William Savedoff and Pablo Spiller (eds), *Spilled Water: Institutional Commitment in the Provision of Water Services*, Washington, DC: InterAmerican Development Bank, Chapter 1, 1–34.
Shirley, Mary M. (2002), *Thirsting for Efficiency: The Economics and Politics of Urban Water System Reform*, Amsterdam, London, New York, Oxford, Paris, Shannon, Tokyo: Pergamon-Elsevier.
Shirley, Mary M. (2008), *Institutions and Development*, Cheltenham, UK and Northampton, MA, USA: Edward Elgar.
United Nations Millennium Project (2005), *Health, Dignity, and Development: What Will It Take?* New York: United Nations Millennium Project.
United Water (2003), 'Joint news release: City of Atlanta and United Water announce amicable dissolution of twenty-year water contract', available at, http://www.unitedwater.com/pr012403.htm
Williamson Oliver (1985), *The Economic Institutions of Capitalism,* New York, London: Macmillan Free Press.
World Bank (2005), *Case Study on the Metropolitan Waterworks and Sewerage System Regulatory System*, Washington, DC: World Bank.
World Bank (2006) 'World Bank: water supply and sanitation: project lending', http://www.worldbank.org/html/fpd/water/projectlending.html. Accessed 5 January 2007.
World Bank (n.d.) *Private Participation in Infrastructures* (http://ppi.worldbank.org).
Wu, Xun and Napomuceno A. Malaluan (2006), 'A tale of two concessionaires: a natural experiment of water privatization in Metro Manila', Working Paper, Lee Kuan Yew School of Public Policies, National University of Singapore.

PART II

Governance and performance

6. Regulatory governance and sector performance: methodology and evaluation for electricity distribution in Latin America

Luis Andres, José Luis Guasch and Sebastián Lopez Azumendi

INTRODUCTION

According to an increasing body of empirical evidence, institutions matter for growth and development (Aron, 2000; Rodrik, 2004). The infrastructure sector generally, and the electricity sector in particular, are not an exception to this finding. Research on the subject has associated better sector performance, represented by higher levels of electricity generation per capita, to the governance of institutions responsible for the conduct of regulatory decisions (Cubbin and Stern, 2006).

Despite the different approaches in the design of regulatory institutions, a separate agency from the government with reasonable levels of autonomy and technical expertise has emerged as the model and paradigm of a regulatory institution. The Latin America and the Caribbean (LAC) region has adopted that regulatory model. Beginning with Chile's National Energy Commission in 1978 and ending in 2001 with Barbados' Fair Trading Commission, the region presents a diverse spectrum of regulatory authorities and practices, today 70 percent of countries in the region have a separate entity – with varying degrees of independence – to regulate electricity markets (LAC Electricity Regulatory Governance Database, The World Bank, 2007).

Even though more than ten years have passed since the majority of LAC countries established independent agencies, the study of their governance and of its impact on sector performance has been limited and poorly focused. With some exceptions (Correa *et al.*, 2006; Brown *et al.*, 2006; Guasch and Spiller, 1999), the research on the subject has limited the assessment of regulatory agencies to a few governance indicators, specifically focusing on their independence from political authorities, and many of them have been case studies. This is particularly the case of the electricity sector of the LAC region where, beyond specific agency-based case studies, regional analyses that assess institutional design and governance behavior do not exist.

In a previous paper (Andres *et al.* 2007), we attempted to fill that gap. Based on selected literature on the subject, we defined and assessed electricity's agencies governance through four main characteristics of their governance design: (a) autonomy from political authorities and of their management and regulatory competencies; (b) transparency before institutional and non-institutional stakeholders; (c) accountability to the three branches of government (Executive, Legislative, and Judiciary); and (d) tools and capacities for the conduct of the regulatory policy and the improvement of its institutional development. We defined regulatory governance as the agency's institutional design and structure that allows it to carry its functions as an independent regulator.

Although we tried to capture as many governance variables as possible, some caveats need to be taken into account. Our assessment of the governance of regulatory agencies was based on the regulatory and institutional inputs that agencies need to implement their procedures and tools, but does not consider the outputs or outcomes of agencies' regulation.[1] In other words, the measurement of agencies' governance is not an indicator of the effectiveness of the use of their regulatory instruments (such as the methodology to calculate tariff readjustment) or the quality of stakeholders' involvement in public consultations. Rather it is aimed at capturing the institutional conditions necessary to achieve good regulation regardless of their scope and impact on the sector's performance (Correa *et al.*, 2006). While we considered some practices (informal regulation) of agencies' governance, the indicators used are referred to the operationalization of particular aspects of agencies' governance but did not measure their full effectiveness.

In this chapter we combine our data on electricity agencies' governance with data collected at the company level and assess the impact of regulatory agencies on utility performance in the electricity sector of the LAC region. This research fills a gap in the literature on the subject as previous attempts to interrelate the notions of governance of agencies and performance of the electricity sector have focused on very limited factors, affecting the scope and explanatory power of the research. On the governance side, previous research has only focused on the existence of an agency, a legal framework, or particular aspects of its governance, mainly its autonomy, emphasizing formal attributes. On the performance side, only electricity generation per capita was used as an indicator related to governance (Stern and Cubbin, 2005). Estache and Rossi have recently written a paper exploring the relationship between the establishment of an agency and the efficiency of the utilities as well as the welfare of the consumers (Estache and Rossi, 2007).

In this chapter, we go further as we create an aggregate index with different critical aspects of the governance of regulatory agencies and we relate it to several factors that represent the performance of utilities and assess its impact on sector performance. Based on the hypothesis that agencies (and their governance) have a positive impact on performance, we develop a methodology where we ran different models in order to explain the contributions of change in ownership and different characteristics of the regulatory agency and of its governance on the performance of the utilities. The results suggest that the mere existence of a regulatory agency, independent of the utilities' ownership has a significant impact on performance. Furthermore, after controlling for the existence of a regulatory agency, the ownership dummies are still significant and display the expected signs. We also proposed an experience measure in order to identify the gradual impact of the agency on performance. Our results confirm this hypothesis.

In measuring governance, we explore two different approaches: (a) we use an aggregated measure of regulatory governance (Electricity Regulatory Governance Index, ERGI); and (b) we decompose several dimensions of agencies governance into three main principal components related to both informal and formal aspects of autonomy, transparency and accountability; we also include agencies' attributes in setting tariff structure and levels as an independent variable together with the formal and informal dimensions of autonomy, transparency, accountability and tools. The results suggest that governance matters and that it has significant impacts on performance when we simulated a standard deviation in each of these indexes.

The chapter is organized as follows: the next section is a review of the literature on institutional design of independent agencies as well as on the impact of private sector participation on sector performance. The third section proposes an analytical framework for regulatory governance. The fourth section presents the empirical approach for measuring the impacts on performance and the fifth section describes the data. The sixth section provides a detailed description of the results. The final section of the chapter presents the conclusions and the final remarks.

LITERATURE REVIEW

This work will explore the relationship between two different literatures. The first is related to the impact of private sector participation on sector performance. The second is the literature related to the measurement of the governance of regulatory agencies. There is little knowledge on the relationship between these two. Some exceptions include a recent paper done by Sirtaine *et al.* (2004) and Estache and Rossi (2007).

The literature on change in ownership, most of it related to ownership change, has focused on other sectors than electricity, such as in transportation (for example, Ramamurti, 1996; Laurin and Bozec, 2000), telecommunications (for example, Ros, 1999; and Ramamurti, 1996) and manufacturing (for example, Frydman *et al.*, 1999; Boardman and Vining, 1989). In the case of privatization of the distribution of electricity, in particular for Latin American Countries, there is no comprehensive reference. Most of the articles that analyze this issue respond to case-studies or a country analysis (for example, see Galal *et al.*, 1994; La Porta and Lopez-de-Silanes, 1999), and only the telecommunications sector has been more deeply analyzed in the region (see for example Ros and Banerjee, 2000). Some exceptions in these sectors are Estache and Rossi (2004) for the case of Electricity Distribution.

For the case of the electrical sector in Latin America, there are broad descriptions of the reforms in the sector but no empirical analysis (see for example, Millan *et al.*, 2001; Dussan, 1996; Estache and Rodriguez-Pardina, 1998). Information on Latin America can also be found in studies on developing countries (see for example Bacon and Besant-Jones, 2001). The recent review of Joskow (2003) summarizes the lessons learned across countries in the electricity market.

The lack of available systematic data has prevented the development of empirical analysis in the subject. Nevertheless, some country analyses have been conducted. For example, Chisari *et al.* (1997) built a general equilibrium model in order to analyze the impact of privatizations in Argentina between 1993 and 1995. Among regional empirical research, Estache and Rossi (2004) analyze the impact of change in ownership on labor productivity and prices. They also evaluated how the different regulatory environments affected these outcomes in the region. They found that private firms use significantly less labor to produce a given bundle of output than public firms. Using similar data, Rossi (2004) also analyzed the firms' operating and maintenance expenses. He found that these costs did not change significantly after the reform, and argued that outsourcing, in part, may bias the results for the decrease in labor usage and labor productivity.

The literature on the governance of agencies in infrastructure has centered on the independent regulator model, which is reflected in the United States (US) independent commissions. An institutional design model that emphasizes agencies that make decisions independently from the Executive branch, are subject to the accountability of the Parliament, and budgeting autonomy has emerged as the paradigm of an infrastructure regulator. The first attempts to evaluate infrastructure regulatory agencies made use of frameworks to assess the independence of Central Banks (Stern and Cubbin, 2005; Oliveira *et al.*, 2005). This fact explains the original emphasis on agencies' independence and the reduced significance given to other aspects of their functioning such as accountability and transparency. The evolution of the subject and the initial stages of agencies functioning changed the original approach and introduced more comprehensive approaches to assessment.

The literature has focused on three main aspects of their design: (a) their independence from political authorities and the autonomy of their management; (b) mechanisms to make them accountable (both to other branches of government and to the public); and (c) the transparency of both their rule- and decision-making procedures. Within these categories, indicators range from simple measures to determine, for instance, independence (such as the legal instruments that created the agency) to more sophisticated mechanisms aimed, for example, at improving the quality of regulation (such as Regulatory Impact Analysis).

Research on the regulatory governance of independent agencies has evolved and changed. Despite the original focus on independence, a growing body of literature has been using more comprehensive approaches to address their institutional design. Good examples of this trend are the works of Correa *et al.* (2006), Brown *et al.* (2006) and Andres *et al.* (2007), which approach the assessment of independent regulatory agencies through the classic lens of autonomy, transparency and accountability, but include a wide array of indicators within these variables as well as innovative tools to understand and assess their functioning. Furthermore, this literature focuses not only on the formal aspects of regulation (provisions existing in agencies' statutes and laws) but also on informal regulation (aspects related to the implementation of the provisions' components). This approach is useful as it recognizes the broad nature of the role of regulatory agencies: they are not only institutions responsible for driving investment in infrastructure but also are decentralized administrative bodies in charge, such as delivering public service to citizens.

The following paragraphs review some of the literature on the subject. Stern and Holder (1999) develop a framework to assess the governance of economic regulators in several sectors (electricity, natural gas, telecom, transport and water) in six developing Asian economies. Their appraisal scheme is composed of two variables related to the formal (institutional design) and informal (regulatory processes and practices) aspects of regulation. Results indicate middle-low levels of regulatory governance for all the sectors and countries included in the research. Moreover, results are relatively uniform by country across the industries, with the exception of India. Gilardi (2002) develops an independence index, covering regulators from five sectors in seven European countries. The author attempts to prove that governments delegate their regulatory powers and competences to independent regulatory agencies to enhance the credibility of their policies. Johannsen (2003) measures the formal independence of energy regulators in eight European countries. Using information collected through surveys, she assesses the independence of energy regulatory agencies through four main variables: (a) independence from government; (b) independence from stakeholders; (c) independence in the decision-making process; and (d) organizational autonomy. The survey's questions reflect formal regulation with no consideration for the practices of regulatory agencies.

Gutierrez (2003) develops a Regulatory Framework Index (RFI) to assess the evolution of regulatory governance in the telecommunications sector during the period 1980–2001 in 25 LAC countries. According to Gutierrez, the RFI shows that most countries embraced strong regulatory reforms along the lines recommended by experts and practitioners. In another article, Gilardi (2005) proposes three ways of evaluating independent regulators: the impact of an agency's independence on regulatory quality, an agency's respect for accountability standards, and the impact of agency's independence on the performance of the market it regulates.

Few have been the efforts to measure the practices of agencies' governance, in addition to their formal design. In addition to Stern and Holder's attempt to measure informal regulation, Magetti (2005) develops a framework to assess the real independence of regulatory agencies. His framework is composed of two main features: (a) the degree of self-determination of agencies' preferences; and (b) the degree to which those preferences are translated into regulatory acts. He applies his approach to the Swiss Federal Banking Commission (SFBC), finding that the SFBC has higher levels of informal independence from political authorities than from the regulatees. With regards to the degree of influence of relevant actors on the legislative process, Magetti finds the informal independence of the SFBC to be quite low, particularly *vis-à-vis* political decision makers.

Three comprehensive approaches to assessing the governance of regulatory agencies have been those developed by Correa *et al.* (2006), Brown *et al.* (2006) and Andres *et al.* (2007). Correa *et al.* provide a detailed analysis of Brazilian regulatory agencies. The authors select four aspects of agencies' governance and, based on information collected through surveys, construct three indexes. The first index, the Regulatory Governance Index, is the base-line indicator and represents the most comprehensive dataset of all the indexes. The second index, the Parsimonious Index, captures those variables of the survey that are less subjective. The third index, the De Facto Index, is related to actual practices of regulatory agencies. The report finds that independence and accountability are more developed than regulatory means and instruments (particularly qualified personnel and regulatory tools) and decision-making procedures (particularly with respect to those mechanisms that can guarantee consistency of decisions and reduce arbitrariness). It also finds that there is a clear difference between federal and state regulatory agencies, with the former achieving higher results in the autonomy, decision-making, and decision tools components of the Regulatory Governance Index.

Brown *et al.* (2006) develop a framework to assess the effectiveness of a regulatory system. They aim to provide the policy-maker with different types of evaluations (quick, mid-level, and in-depth) to carry out these assessments. The authors include aspects related not only to the governance of the regulatory system (independence, transparency, and accountability of the regulator) but also to the substance or content of the regulation (decisions about tariff levels and structures, network access conditions for new and existing customers). Using the independent regulator model as the benchmark of analysis, they select ten principles that should be followed in order to create an independent regulatory agency. The principles are accompanied by standards that establish the details for their implementation.

In Andres *et al.* (2007) we evaluate and benchmark electricity agencies of the region based on four main attributes of their governance: autonomy, transparency, accountability, and tools/capacities. Using a unique database, we develop an index of regulatory governance and rank all the agencies in the LAC countries. The index is an aggregate number of the evaluation of four key governance characteristics: autonomy, transparency, accountability and regulatory tools, including not only formal aspects of regulation but also indicators related to actual implementation. Based on 18 different indexes, we analyze the positions of agencies with regard to different aspects of their regulatory governance, considering not only performance in each variable but also scores in the different components of each category. This evaluation allows for the identification of particular country shortcomings regarding governance, and indicates needed improvements.

A few papers have focused on the relationship between regulatory characteristics and performance. Sirtaine *et al.* (2004) define a Regulatory Quality Index, considering three key aspects of regulatory quality: legal solidity, financial strength and decision-making autonomy. Despite their small sample sizes, three out of the four models show that the regulatory quality variables are significant in overall terms, and that are on their own capable of explaining 20–25 percent of the internal rate of return of private investment in infrastructure projects in LAC. More recently, Estache and Rossi (2007) explored the causal relation between the establishment of a regulatory agency and the performance of the electricity sector. They exploit a unique dataset comprising firm-level information on a representative sample of 220 electric utilities from 51 developing and transition countries for the years 1985 to 2005. Their results indicate that regulatory agencies are associated with more efficient firms and with higher consumer welfare.

REGULATORY GOVERNANCE FRAMEWORK

We base on our work on the governance of electricity agencies. We selected a theoretical framework of analysis and designed a survey that was completed by 19 countries of the region. The evaluation of agencies' governance was done through several indexes that reflect different dimensions of agencies' organization and functioning.

Building upon Correa *et al.* (2006) and the majority of the research on the subject, we evaluate the electricity agencies' governance structure. We develop two related indexes of regulatory governance – an aggregated measure (Electricity Regulatory Governance Index, ERGI) and a principal components based governance index that includes autonomy, transparency and accountability – and evaluate the impact of agencies' governance on the performance of the sector. Exploring this dimension is the objective of this section.

Our conceptual framework or benchmark model of analysis is the independent regulator model. This decision was based on two main factors. The first factor is related to the use of independent regulatory agencies as the model for electricity regulation in the majority of the region. According to their database,[2] almost 70 percent of the countries in the region have adopted a separate regulator from the line ministry as the preferred institutional arrangement for electricity regulation. The second factor is related to empirical evidence that considers the independent regulator model as the most effective approach in the regulation of privatized infrastructure industries (Brown *et al.*, 2006).

Following our work on the subject, we conceive regulatory agencies as both public bodies that are part of the public administration – and as such in charge of the delivery of public services – and as instruments to implement regulatory policies. This approach to assessing electricity agencies' governance led us to consider not only existing research on infrastructure agencies' designs (documented in the literature review), but also notions and tools of public sector governance applied to decentralized structures of government.

The regulatory governance of independent agencies is defined and assessed according to four variables of their design and functioning: autonomy, transparency, accountability, and tools. Each of the variables, with the exception of accountability, is composed of several elements, reflecting different aspects of autonomy, transparency and tools. Variables for agencies' governance reflect not only formal aspects (procedures and tools established in the agency's statute or laws) but also the practices that derive from their implementation (informal regulation). Indicators for the informal elements of autonomy, accountability, and transparency represent the operationalization of some aspects of these variables. The variable 'tools' is excluded from this analysis as the mere existence of these instruments implies their actual implementation.

The first variable of agencies' regulatory governance is autonomy. We define autonomy as the procedures, mechanisms, and instruments aimed at guaranteeing the independence of the agency from political authorities (political autonomy), the autonomous management of its resources (managerial autonomy) and the regulation of the sector (regulatory autonomy). Political autonomy represents the level of independence of the agency from government authorities and is measured by indicators that reflect the autonomy of the agency's decision-making. Managerial autonomy involves the freedom of the agency to determine the administration of its resources and is measured by indicators that reflect the powers of the agency to determine its organizational structure and the use of its budget. Regulatory autonomy is defined by the extension of the agency's regulatory powers in the electricity sector and is represented by indicators that capture agencies' responsibilities in electricity regulation.

The second aspect of agency's governance is accountability, which we define as the procedures, mechanisms, and instruments aimed at guaranteeing an adequate level of control of the agency's budget and performance by political authorities, namely the Parliament. Despite the successful use of mechanisms to assess the performance of agencies by governments, we prioritize the accountability of the agency before the Parliament. We based this decision on two main reasons: first, the fact that the institutional design model we follow is that of a US independent commission, where agencies are subject to parliamentary oversight; second, the history of political interference of LAC line ministries in utilities underscores the importance of including other political stakeholders, such as the Parliament, in the regulatory process. We consider an institutional perspective of accountability only as defined by the relationships of the agency with the three branches of government (Executive, Legislative and the Judiciary) and do not further dissect the variable.

The third variable is transparency. We define transparency as the procedures, mechanisms, and instruments aimed at guaranteeing the disclosure and publication of relevant regulatory and institutional information, the participation of stakeholders in the agency's regulatory decisions and decision-making, and the application of rules aimed at governing the integrity and behavior of agency officials. We cover two dimensions of transparency: social transparency and institutional transparency. Social transparency is composed of indicators related to the involvement of non-institutional actors in the agency's policy-making, including their access to the agency's information. Institutional transparency is composed of indicators related to the transparent management of the agency that are not directly linked to stakeholder involvement, and includes issues such as the publication of the agency's annual report, the use of norms of ethics, and the existence of public exams for hiring employees.

The fourth variable is tools, which we define as the instruments and mechanisms that contribute to the strengthening of different aspects of an agency's functioning and the quality of its regulations. We include not only regulatory tools (for example mechanisms for tariff revision, regulatory accountability, instruments for monitoring technical standards), but also those instruments aimed at improving the institutional quality of the agency, or institutional tools (for example audits of agencies' accounts, electronic files for consumer complaints, performance-based payments for employees, regulatory quality standards). This is the only variable whose analysis does not consider its formal and informal aspects; the sole existence of agencies' tools implies their actual implementation.

The pooling together of these indicators defines the Electricity Regulatory Governance Index (ERGI). This index was the main indicator in Andres *et al.* (2007) and it is composed of 74 questions. The index is a single average of their seven main indexes: (a) formal autonomy; (b) informal autonomy; (c) formal transparency; (d) informal transparency; (e) formal accountability; (f) informal accountability; and (g) tools. The rankings across the regulatory agencies were tested with other weights across the indexes;[3] however, the rankings were similar to the one chosen in the paper as a simple average of the indexes.

According to our results, the region shows a reasonable governance design of their regulatory agencies. Nevertheless, the implementation of the independent regulator model still faces several challenges. This is particularly evident in political autonomy and in the informal aspects of governance, where the region shows the largest number of countries with the lowest scores. In our main index, ERGI, Trinidad and Tobago, Brazil, Bolivia and Peru show the best results and Ecuador, Honduras, and Chile the worst performances. The rest of the countries vary according to the different indexes. Table 6.1 presents their main results and rankings.

EMPIRICAL APPROACH

Ideally, to evaluate the impact of private sector participation and the characteristics of the regulation on the performance of a utility, privatized utilities should be compared to the performance of its 'counterfactual', a comparable firm in a similar environment that is still operated by the government and is not regulated. In most cases, it is hard to identify a comparable firm; hence, most of the literature compares the evolution of selected indicators before and after the change in ownership and regulation.

The majority of the literature focuses mainly on the impact of change in ownership. For these evaluations, two methodologies have been identified. The first methodology began with Megginson *et al.* (1994); and several subsequent studies have used the same approach to measure means and medians of the periods before and after change and to test the significance of the change between the periods. This methodology has also been applied in studies that considered different samples of state owned enterprises (SOEs) among countries and compared their performance to privatized firms. The second methodology is found in another branch of literature that assumes privatization policies to be an intervention. Following the literature of program evaluation (see Heckman *et al.*, 1985), this approach proposes a dummy for those periods where the SOE was privately owned, and checks the significance of this dummy, as well as the significance of various interactions specific to each paper (for example, Boardman and Vining, 1989; Ros, 1999).

This chapter follows the second methodology. We start with a simple version of the model, as specified in Equation 6.1:

$$\ln(y_{ijt}) = \beta^{*}PRIV_{ijt} + \delta^{*}X_{ijt} + \gamma^{*}(PRIV_{ijt}{}^{*}X_{ijt}) + \sum_{ij}\phi_{ij}D_{ij} + \upsilon_{ijt} \tag{6.1}$$

where y_{ijt} are the variables of interest (outputs, number of employees, labor productivity, efficiency, quality, coverage and prices). The main variables in this model are the dummy $PRIV_{ijt}$, that is equal to one if the utility i of country j has private ownership at time t and X_{ijt}, that is a vector of characteristics such as existence of regulatory agency, the agency's experience, and its regulatory governance that regulates the utility i of country j at time t. Hence, β will capture the effect of the private sector participation on the outcome of interest and δ will capture the effect of regulation on

Table 6.1 National regulatory agencies in the ERGI and the four main indexes

	ERGI		Autonomy		Transparency		Accountability		Tools	
	Position	Score	Position	Score	Position	Score	Position	Score	Position	Score
Argentina	7	0.80	6	0.85	8	0.71	10	0.71	8	0.83
Barbados	8	0.76	10	0.82	8	0.71	4	0.83	10	0.59
Bolivia	3	0.84	**1**	**0.912**	5	0.80	3	0.84	4	0.78
Brazil	2	0.85	5	0.87	6	0.79	2	0.87	2	0.90
Chile	18	**0.56**	**19**	**0.57**	12	0.63	**16**	**0.50**	12	0.52
Colombia	9	0.75	18	0.67	5	0.8	6	0.79	7	0.71
Costa Rica	12	0.74	8	0.84	7	0.74	10	0.71	10	0.59
Dominican Republic	10	0.75	3	0.90	8	0.71	8	0.74	12	0.51
Ecuador	17	0.60	17	0.70	15	0.57	12	0.65	13	0.40
El Salvador	5	0.82	7	0.84	2	0.86	5	0.81	7	0.71
Guatemala	6	0.79	12	0.80	13	0.62	2	0.87	**1**	**0.93**
Honduras	**19**	**0.56**	16	0.70	**16**	**0.53**	14	0.54	**14**	**0.37**
Jamaica	15	0.72	14	0.78	10	0.68	13	0.62	3	0.86
Mexico	14	0.72	15	0.75	4	0.83	7	0.75	**14**	**0.37**
Nicaragua	11	0.74	2	0.91	11	0.66	9	0.72	9	0.63
Panama	16	0.63	11	0.81	14	0.59	15	0.52	11	0.54
Peru	4	0.83	4	0.90	3	0.85	7	0.75	3	0.86
Trinidad and Tobago	**1**	**0.88**	9	0.82	**1**	**0.92**	**1**	**0.97**	5	0.76
Uruguay	13	0.72	13	0.80	9	0.69	11	0.67	6	0.72

Source: LAC Electricity Regulatory Governance Database, The World Bank (2007). Extracted from Andres *et al.* (2007b).

the outcomes. Then, γ will capture the interaction between private sector participation and the regulation. Several factors may affect this, such as initial conditions and geography. Hence, it is important to control for the firm's specific fixed effects to capture the characteristics of the firm not observed by the econometrician. Therefore ϕ_{ij} captures fixed effects defined by D_{ij}.

A second version of Equation (6.1) may also be estimated, introducing a firm-specific time trend:

$$\ln(y_{ijt}) = \beta_0 PRIV_{ijt} + \delta^* X_{ijt} + \gamma^*(PRIV_{ijt}{}^* X_{ijt}) + \sum_{ij} \phi_{ij} D_{ij} + \sum_{ij} \theta_{ij} t_{ij} + \upsilon_{ijt} \quad (6.2)$$

Equation 6.2 contains the same dependent variables, dummies and control variables used in the static model, but will include a coefficient that will capture the time trends specific for each utility of the variable of interest. As was described by Andres *et al.* (2008), it is important to account for these effects since the omission of these factors may cause erroneous results. For instance, coverage in LAC presents, in general, a natural trend. Ideally speaking, in order to identify an effect in the variable, we would like to get a significant break in this trend. If there is no such break and Equation 6.1 is applied, under the presence of a positive trend, it is likely that the dummies will result with significant and positive coefficients. When Equation 6.2 is estimated, these trends are corrected and the dummies should be read as an average break in the trend. These effects will be captured by θ_{ij}.

Most of the literature reviewed uses a basic approach similar to that in Equation 6.1, and in some cases accounts for specifications like those included in Equation 6.2. In other words, the utility is evaluated immediately before and after the change in ownership. This approach does not account for changes that may occur in preparation for the change in ownership or in response to it, perhaps through one-time decisions (for example a reduction in personnel). In this chapter, in order to isolate and identify the outcomes during the period around the change in ownership, specific dummies are defined for these transitional years. For these, the analysis will split the data into three main periods: first, the 'pure public' period, covering the years before transition; second, the 'transition' period, starting when the reform was announced and ending one year after the concession or privatization was awarded; and third, the years after the transition, or the "pure private" period. As will be described later, the transition period has some important effects on firms. Since it is not clear for all the cases when the process to change ownership was announced, we will assume that it started two years prior to the date of the award.[4] Therefore, we can define a dummy for the transition and a dummy for the post-transition period, so that Equations 6.1 and 6.2 become:

$$\ln(y_{ijt}) = \beta^{T}DUMMY\_TRAN_{ijt} + \beta^{P}DUMMY\_POST_{ijt} + \delta^{*}X_{ijt} + \gamma^{T} {}^{*}DUMMY\_TRAN_{ijt}{}^{*}X_{ijt} + \gamma^{P*}DUMMY\_POST_{ijt}{}^{*}X_{ijt} + \sum_{ij}\phi_{ij}D_{ij} + \upsilon_{ijt} \quad (6.3)$$

$$\ln(y_{ijt}) = \beta^{T}DUMMY\_TRAN_{ijt} + \beta^{P}DUMMY\_POST_{ijt} + \delta^{*}X_{ijt} + \gamma^{T} {}^{*}DUMMY\_TRAN_{ijt}{}^{*}X_{ijt} + \gamma^{P*}DUMMY\_POST_{ijt}{}^{*}X_{ijt} + \sum_{ij}\phi_{ij}D_{ij} + \sum_{ij}\theta_{ij}t_{ij} + \upsilon_{ijt} \quad (6.4)$$

where

$$DUM\_TRAN_{ijt}\begin{cases}1 & \text{if } s_{ijt} \geq -1\\ 0 & \text{otherwise}\end{cases}$$

and

$$DUM\_POST_{ijt}\begin{cases}1 & \text{if } s_{ijt} \geq 2\\ 0 & \text{otherwise}\end{cases}$$

where s_{ijt} is a time trend that has a value equal to zero for the year when the privatization or concession was awarded. In this sense, the first dummy will identify the average change in the dependent variable during the transition with respect to the average level prior to the transition years, during the pure public period. The second dummy will identify the average change of the dependent variable after the transition with respect to the transition period.

The first basic specification will be Equation 6.3 using the log level of the indicators. In particular, this will help to identify most of the conclusions. For those variables that present trends (for instance, number of connections), Equation 6.4 will be more enlightening. However, it relies on the assumption that trends among the three periods of analysis are the same.

Given the fact that we are using a semi-logarithmic functional form of these models for each of the indicators, it should be remembered that the percentage impact in each indicator is given by $e^{\delta} - 1$ (Halvorsen and Palmquist, 1980) when interpreting the coefficient estimates of the dummy.

In order to correct for potential non-spherical errors, a generalized least square (GLS) approach would be appropriate. However, the GLS estimation requires knowledge of the unconditional variance matrix of υ_{ijt}, Ω, up to scale. Hence, we must be able to write, $\Omega = \sigma^2 C$ where C is a known $G \times G$ positive definite matrix. But, in this case, as this matrix is not known, we will follow a Feasible GLS (FGLS) approach that replaces the unknown matrix Ω with a consistent estimator.

DATA

We work with two unique databases. In terms of performance, we use the Electricity Benchmarking data (World Bank, 2007). This benchmarking initiative contributes primarily with the collection and analysis of detailed data for 26 countries and 250 utilities that represent 88 percent of the electricity connections in the Latin American and Caribbean region. Through in-house and field data collection, this work compiled data on the electricity distribution sector based on accomplishments in output, coverage, labor productivity, input, operating performance, service quality and tariffs. Based on the results of these performance indicators, the World Bank (2007) benchmarks the performance of electricity distribution at the regional, country and utility level. Among the utilities in this database we selected those utilities that had a change in ownership and/or present a regulatory agency. Out of the 250 utilities 216 were retained. The definitions of the variables selected for this report can be found in Appendix 6.1.

For the data on regulatory governance we used the one collected in our previous work Andres *et al.* (2007). As previously stated, we designed a survey that was distributed to all electricity regulatory agencies in the region, including not only national but also provincial or state regulators (particularly in the cases of Argentina and Brazil). The questionnaire was composed of 97 questions (for the full version of the survey, see Appendix 1 in Andres *et al.*, 2007) reflecting the four variables of agencies' governance and both formal and informal aspects of their functioning. We also included a general section aimed at capturing characteristics of electricity markets such as the methodology for tariff calculation, the degree of market liberalization, and social tariffs. We received responses from 43 electricity regulatory agencies, whose coverage in terms of electricity consumers exceeds 90 percent of the region. Appendix 6.2 presents the list of the national regulatory agencies with some selected characteristics.

Each country or state was represented by its own regulatory agency, with the exception of Colombia and Chile, for which we assigned unique values since they each have two different agencies with regulatory functions. In both Colombia and Chile, regulatory responsibilities are shared between a National Energy Commission in charge of the main regulatory aspects

Table 6.2 Summary statistics of the regulatory governance database

Variable	Obs	Mean	Std. Dev.	Min	Max
Formal autonomy	40	0.780	0.120	0.386	0.939
Informal autonomy	40	0.800	0.115	0.400	0.950
Formal transparency	40	0.755	0.142	0.500	1.000
Informal transparency	40	0.652	0.158	0.200	0.909
Informal accountability	40	0.817	0.153	0.500	1.000
Formal accountability	40	0.522	0.197	0.100	0.950
Tools/capacities	40	0.623	0.171	0.315	0.936
ERGI	40	0.707	0.105	0.474	0.889

Source: Authors' calculations.

(tariffs, approval of contracts) and an Oversight Electricity Agency (in the case of Chile, the *Superintendencia de Electricidad y Combustibles* and in the case of Colombia, the *Superintendencia de Servicios Públicos*) in charge of the sector's oversight (service quality, sanctions' enforcing, consumer complaints). Considering that both agencies perform different tasks that in other countries are undertaken by only one regulator, we 'merged' both administrative bodies and assigned a unique value for the country. For those institutional aspects that should be reflected in both agencies, such as the independence of their decision-making (for example the appointment of directors) or the transparency of their management (for example account audits), we assigned the country an average score calculated from both agencies' scores on the same question. For instance, if the *Comisión Nacional de Energía* of Chile was assigned 0 for not auditing its accounts and the *Superintendencia de Electricidad y Combustibles* was assigned 1 for auditing its accounts, then Chile would obtain 0.5 in that question. In those aspects where the agencies had separate responsibilities (for example the regulation of tariffs by the *Comisión Reguladora de la Energía* of Colombia and the reception of consumers' claims by the *Superintendencia de Servicios Públicos*), we assigned the country the score achieved by the agency with responsibility in that issue, regardless of the score obtained by the other agency for the same issue. Table 6.2 presents the summary statistics.

RESULTS

This section describes the results with different specifications. As stated above, all the specifications were run using a semi-logarithmic functional form of these models for each of the indicators. It should be remembered that the percentage impact in each indicator is given by $e^{\delta} - 1$ when interpreting the coefficient estimates of the dummy.

First, we describe the results when only the change-in-ownership variables are included. Then we included a dummy for the existence of a regulatory agency as well as its interactions with the ownership dummies. After this, we included a quadratic form of experience of the regulatory agency. Following this, we introduced the ERGI in the specifications as well as its interactions with the ownership. Finally, we decomposed the regulatory index through a Principal Component approach and obtained three principal components that are introduced in the models.

Change in Ownership

We first explored the impact on performance of private sector participation. We do this because, together with the introduction of regulatory agencies, private participation was the main change in the sector. As described in Andres *et al.* (2008) and World Bank (2007), by 1993 only 3 percent of the total connections were in private hands. In contrast, by 2005, 61 percent of them were under private management.

Table 6.3 presents the results. Consistently with Andres *et al.* (2006), private sector participation exhibits significant effects in labor productivity, reduction of distributional losses, improvement in the quality of the service, reduction of the operational expenditures, increment in tariffs, and improvement in thc cost recovery ratio. However, most of these changes occurred during the transition period. Despite this, some additional improvements happened after this period. Not surprisingly, coverage of the service, when the estimation accounts for utility specific time trends, presents no significant change.

More specifically, labor productivity rose between 19.8 and 26.0 percent during the transition. After this period, an additional increase was observed between 2.4 and 6.9 percent with respect to the transition levels. This is a consequence of a significant reduction in the labor force as well as the natural positive trends that were observed in terms of the number of connections as well as their total consumption. Consistent with previous analyses, distributional losses have decreased significantly after the transition, resulting in a 13.2 percent reduction. As it is well understood in the sector, most of the improvements in this area have responded to investments in the network in order to reduce the technical losses as well as improvements in the cadastres and monitoring in order to limit the commercial losses. In general, these improvements are observed at least one year after the change; hence, it is expected to find no significant impact during the transition and a significant one afterwards. Quality of the

Table 6.3 Impact of change in ownership on performance of utilities

	Residen tial conn. per employee (1)	Energy sold per employee (2)	Distribut. losses (3)	Coverage (4)	Energy sold per conn. (5)	Duration of interrupt's (6)	Frequency of interrupt's (7)	OPEX per connection (in dollars) (8)	OPEX per MWH sold (in dollars) (9)	Avg resid. tariff (in dollars) (10)	Avg indust. tariff (in dollars) (11)	Cost recovery ratio (12)
Dummy transition of PSP	0.181*** (0.013)	0.231*** (0.015)	0.014 (0.012)	−0.008*** (0.002)	0.047*** (0.004)	−0.124*** (0.027)	−0.063* (0.033)	−0.484** (0.224)	−0.458** (0.230)	0.113*** (0.015)	0.037** (0.019)	0.024 (0.059)
Dummy post-transition of PSP	0.067*** (0.009)	0.024** (0.012)	−0.141*** (0.012)	0.004*** (0.001)	−0.002 (0.005)	−0.356*** (0.022)	−0.396*** (0.021)	−0.216*** (0.038)	−0.175*** (0.046)	0.013 (0.010)	−0.044** (0.020)	0.194*** (0.050)
Utility FE	Yes	Yes	Yes	Yes	Yes	Yes	Yes	Yes	Yes	Yes	Yes	Yes
Utility specific time trend	Yes	Yes	No	Yes	No	No	No	No	No	No	No	No
Observations	2000	1931	2073	1323	2515	1056	947	864	873	1728	840	669
number of utilities	199	198	190	144	213	144	132	131	131	175	90	103

Notes:
Standard errors in parentheses
* significant at 10%; ** significant at 5%; *** significant at 1%

service, measured as duration and frequency of the interruptions presents significant reductions in both indicators during the transition. During the former, a 11.7 and 6.1 percent reduction was observed for duration and frequency. After the transition, an improvement of 30.0 and 32.7 percent was observed, respectively. Similar to the case of distributional losses, the quality of service measured as the duration of interruptions may be improved with better management, whereas significant improvements in the frequency of interruptions require investments in the network.

With regards to operational expenditure per MWH sold, the amount was halved; possibly achieved with the reduction of the number of employees and its total labor costs, the reduction of the cost of the energy bought given the improvements in the generation segment, and finally because of some managerial improvements with the introduction of the private sector in the utility. Tariffs also presented some increase. While average residential tariffs increased by 12.0 percent and industrial ones by 3.8 percent, after the transition only industrial tariffs presented a significant change reducing them by 4.3 percent with respect to the transition. Finally, the cost recovery ratio resulted with a 21.4 percent improved after the transition indicating more alignment between the cost structure and the revenues, given by the average tariffs.

Existence of a Regulatory Agency

We defined a dummy with a value equal to one starting in the year when the regulatory agency was established.[5] We ran two different specifications. First, we ran the ownership dummies and the one for the existence of a regulatory agency (see Table 6.4). These specifications allowed for the identification of the impact of ownership when they were controlled by the existence of a regulatory agency and the effect of the existence of regulation when they were controlled by ownership. In a second set of specifications that was run, we interacted the ownership dummies with the one for existence. This allowed us to identify some complementarities between both phenomena (see Table 6.5).

Most of the results regarding the change in ownership from the previous description hold when they are controlled by the existence of a regulatory agency; however, their magnitude is slightly reduced. For instance, the effect on labor productivity is reduced by one fourth. Similar to the quality of the service, the result during the transition becomes non-significant. On the contrary, the results for the post-transition remain significant with a 10 and 17 percent reduction of the impact of the change in ownership, with respect to the results previously described when we did not account for the existence of an agency.

Table 6.4 Impact of the existence of regulatory agency on performance of utilities

	Residential conn. per employee (1)	Energy sold per employee (2)	Distribut. losses (3)	Coverage (4)	Energy sold per conn. (5)	Duration of interrupt's (6)	Frequency of interrupt's (7)	OPEX per connection (in dollars) (8)	OPEX per MWH sold (in dollars) (9)	Avg resid. tariff (in dollars) (10)	Avg indust. tariff (in dollars) (11)	Cost recovery ratio (12)
Dummy transition of PSP	0.131***	0.169***	0.043***	−0.011***	0.065***	−0.014	0.032	−0.314	−0.352	0.042**	0.064***	−0.005
	(0.012)	(0.014)	(0.013)	(0.002)	(0.003)	(0.032)	(0.037)	(0.223)	(0.224)	(0.019)	(0.023)	(0.059)
Dummy post-transition of PSP	0.045**	0.015	−0.131***	0.003*	0.003	−0.295***	−0.348***	−0.142***	−0.089**	−0.019**	−0.031	0.192***
	(0.008)	(0.010)	(0.012)	(0.002)	(0.005)	(0.024)	(0.023)	(0.034)	(0.036)	(0.009)	(0.021)	(0.050)
Existence of regulatory agency	0.177***	0.167***	−0.045***	0.004*	−0.031***	−0.210***	−0.190***	−0.387***	−0.320***	0.145***	−0.047**	0.125***
	(0.010)	(0.012)	(0.009)	(0.002)	(0.005)	(0.028)	(0.029)	(0.051)	(0.056)	(0.016)	(0.021)	(0.032)
Utility FE	Yes	Yes	Yes	Yes	Yes	Yes	Yes	Yes	Yes	Yes	Yes	Yes
Utility Specific Time trend	Yes	Yes	No	Yes	No	No	No	No	No	No	No	No
Observations	2000	1981	2073	1323	2515	1056	947	864	873	1728	840	669
Number of utilities	199	198	190	144	213	144	132	131	131	175	90	103

Notes:
Standard errors in parentheses
* significant at 10%; ** significant at 5%; *** significant at 1%

Table 6.5 Impact of the existence of regulatory agency on performance of utilities (with interactions)

	Residential conn.per employee	Energy sold per employee	Distribut. losses	Coverage	Energy sold per conn.	Duration of interrupt's	Frequency of interrupt's	OPEX per connection (in dollars)	OPEX per MWH sold (in dollars)	Avg Resid. tariff in dollars)	Avg indust. tariff (in dollars)	Cost recovery ratio
	(1)	(2)	(3)	(4)	(5)	(6)	(7)	(8)	(9)	(10)	(11)	(12)
Dummy transition of PSP	0.121*** (0.014)	0.170*** (0.016)	0.125*** (0.018)	−0.012*** (0.003)	−0.057*** (0.008)	−0.018 (0.040)	0.059 (0.046)	−0.278 (0.228)	−0.230 (0.229)	0.164*** (0.024)	0.055 (0.039)	−0.053 (0.107)
Dummy post-transition of PSP	0.018 (0.015)	−0.020 (0.025)	−0.123*** (0.035)	0.006 (0.004)	0.095*** (0.015)	−0.561*** (0.074)	−0.429 (0.064)	−0.110 (0.102)	−0.116 (0.099)	−0.087*** (0.018)	0.123 (0.100)	0.308*** (0.116)
Existence of regulatory agency	0.162*** (0.014)	0.175*** (0.017)	−0.008 (0.010)	0.002** (0.002)	−023*** (0.006)	−0.239*** (0.038)	−0.176*** (0.044)	−0.351*** (0.069)	−0.233*** (0.078)	0.286*** (0.024)	−0.039 (0.026)	0.146*** (0.042)
Transition * existence	0.026 (0.018)	−0.012 (0.022)	−0.144*** (0.022)	0.004 (0.004)	0.005 (0.011)	0.019 (0.054)	−0.016 (0.059)	−0.150 (0.121)	−0.315*** (0.129)	0.000 (0.033)	0.045 (0.045)	(0.144)
Post trans. * existence	0.032* (0.017)	0.041 (0.026)	0.020 (0.037)	−0.005 (0.005)	−0.102*** (0.016)	0.284*** (0.078)	0.107 (0.069)	−0.071 (0.109)	0.006 (0.108)	0.138*** (0.021)	−0.158 (0.102)	−0.123 (0.121)
Utility FE	Yes	Yes	Yes	Yes	Yes	Yes	Yes	Yes	Yes	Yes	Yes	Yes

Table 6.5 (continued)

	Residential conn.per employee	Energy sold per employee	Distribut. losses	Coverage	Energy sold per conn.	Duration of interrupt's	Frequency of interrupt's	OPEX per connection (in dollars)	OPEX per MWH sold (in dollars)	Avg Resid. tariff in dollars)	Avg indust. tariff (in dollars)	Cost recovery ratio
	(1)	(2)	(3)	(4)	(5)	(6)	(7)	(8)	(9)	(10)	(11)	(12)
Utility Specific Time trend	Yes	Yes	No	Yes	No	No	No	No	No	No	No	No
Observa tions	2000	1981	2073	1323	2515	1056	947	864	873	1728	840	669
Number of utilities	199	198	190	144	213	144	132	131	131	175	90	103

Notes:
Standard errors in parentheses
* significant at 10%; ** significant at 5%; ** significant at 1%

With respect to the existence of a regulatory agency when it was controlled by change in ownership we found a significant and desirable impact in most of the indicators. For instance, under the presence of a regulatory agency, utilities resulted with 19.4 and 18.2 percent higher labor productivity. Similarly, utilities reported 18.9 percent less average duration and 17.3 percent less frequency of interruptions. With respect to operational expenditures, utilities regulated by an agency resulted between 27.4 and 32.1 percent fewer expenditures. Residential tariffs reported a 13.5 percent increase under the presence of a regulatory agency while industrial ones presented a 4.6 percent reduction. Consistent with the previous results, the cost recovery ratio resulted significantly higher with 13.3 percent.

Experience of the Regulatory Agency

We defined an experience variable as the years since the establishment of the regulatory agency. We argue that agencies can learn 'by doing' in order to obtain the desired outcomes. We assumed a quadratic form for this experience acquisition. As expected, these results are correlated with those with the existence of a regulatory agency. However, these estimations support the hypothesis of gradual improvements of utilities' performance under the presence of regulatory agencies.

As before, most of the results on the change in ownership from the previous description hold when they are controlled by the experience of a regulatory agency; however, we also observed reductions in the magnitude of their effect when we introduced experience variables in the model. The linear coefficient of experience variables resulted significantly and with the expected signs in all the models. For instance, after controlling for the change in ownership, utilities resulted with 1.4 additional increments per year in labor productivity. Similarly, distributional losses and average consumption per connection reported a 1.8 percent reduction per year. Both quality indicators resulted with an annual improvement of 9.0 percent. Operational expenditures presented between 1.6 and 5.5 percent per year. Consistent with the previous results, residential tariffs reported an increase of 2.6 percent per year while industrial ones reported a 1.3 percent annual reduction. Consequently, the cost recovery ratio resulted with significant annual improvements (see Table 6.6).

Electricity Regulatory Governance Index

We included in the models the index developed in our previous work. The ERGI was defined as an index between zero and one. The average of this index was 0.483 with a standard deviation of 0.343. The purpose of these

Table 6.6 Impact of the experience of the regulatory agency on performance of utilities

	Residential conn.per employee	Distribut. losses	Coverage	Energy sold per conn.	Duration of interrupt's	Frequency of interrupt's	OPEX per connection (in dollars)	OPEX per MWH sold (in dollars)	Avg resid. tariff (in dollars)	Avg indust. tariff (in dollars)	Cost recovery ratio
	(1)	(2)	(3)	(4)	(5)	(6)	(7)	(8)	(9)	(10)	(11)
Dummy transition of PSP	0.175***	0.030***	−0.013***	0.062***	−0.022	0.044	−0.463**	−0.451**	0.053***	0.027	0.043
	(0.014)	(0.011)	(0.002)	(0.005)	(0.027)	(0.033)	(0.220)	(0.228)	(0.016)	(0.019)	(0.059)
Dummy post-transition of PSP	0.101***	−0.091***	0.006***	0.024***	−0.112***	−0.167***	−0.152***	−0.158***	−0.089***	−0.058***	0.157***
	(0.008)	(0.012)	(0.002)	(0.006)	(0.025)	(0.024)	(0.036)	(0.046)	(0.011)	(0.021)	(0.049)
Duration of the regulat. agency	−0.014***	−0.018***	0.004***	−0.018***	−0.094***	−0.094***	−0.057***	−0.016***	0.026***	−0.013***	0.040***
	(0.003)	(0.002)	(0.001)	(0.001)	(0.008)	(0.007)	(0.005)	(0.004)	(0.004)	(0.003)	(0.005)
Duration of the regulat. agency (Sq.)	−0.000	0.001***	−0.001***	0.001***	0.004***	0.004***	0.003***	0.001***	0.001***	0.002***	−0.001***
	(0.000)	(0.000)	(0.000)	(0.000)	(0.001)	(0.001)	(0.000)	(0.000)	(0.000)	(0.000)	(0.000)
Utility FE	Yes	Yes	Yes	Yes	Yes	Yes	Yes	Yes	Yes	Yes	Yes
Utility Specific Time trend	Yes	No	Yes	No	No	No	No	No	No	No	No
Observations	2000	2073	1323	2515	1056	947	864	873	1728	840	669
Number of utilities	199	190	144	213	144	132	131	131	175	90	103

Notes:
Standard errors in parentheses
* significant at 10%; ** significant at 5%; *** significant at 1%

models is to test not just the existence of a regulatory agency but also the governance of these agencies. As seen in the previous sections, the sole existence of a regulatory agency has a significant impact on performance. However, we would like to test if there are additional effects that protrude under the presence of an agency with good regulatory governance. For this end, this section reports the results with an increase of one standard deviation in governance. Our data is cross-section; hence, the underlying assumption is that once the agency was created it resulted with a similar institutional design and, therefore, its governance is assumed constant.

As in the previous sections, most of the results on change in ownership from the previous description hold when we control by the regulatory governance of a regulatory agency; however, we also observed some reduction in the magnitude of their effect when we introduce the ERGI in the model. A standard deviation in the ERGI is associated with a 8.7 and 9.1 percent additional increase in labor productivity, between a 7.5 and 8.2 percent reduction in duration and frequency of interruptions. Furthermore, operational expenditures resulted in more than a 10 percent reduction while a 5.7 percent increase was observed in residential tariffs. Consequently there was also an improvement in the cost recovery ratio (see Table 6.7).

Governance Principal Components of the Regulatory Agencies

Although the previous section illustrates the impacts of 'total' governance on performance, it is interesting to disentangle the different aspects of governance. As described before, the ERGI was defined as a combination of seven different indicators (see pp. 118–21). Although each of them had a particular scope and interpretation it is likely that some of them behave similarly. This potential collinearity makes it impossible to add all these variables in the regressions. Hence, we applied a Principal Component approach in order to comprise the eight indicators in the relevant components, thus minimizing the loss of information. The Principal Component Analysis (PCA) develops a composite index by defining a real valued function over the relevant variables objectively. The principle of this method lies in the fact that when different characteristics are observed about a set of events, the characteristic with higher variation explains a higher proportion of the variation in the dependent variable compared to a variable displaying less variation. Therefore, the issue is one of finding weights to be assigned to each of the concerned variables determined by the principle that the objective is to maximize the variation in the linear composite of these variables. In other words, this approach allows for identifying patterns in data, and expressing the data in such a way as to

Table 6.7 Impact of regulatory governance on performance of utilities

	Residential conn.per employee (1)	Energy sold per employee (2)	Distribut. losses (3)	Coverage (4)	Energy sold per conn. (5)	Duration of interrupt's (6)	Frequency of interrupt's (7)	OPEX per connection (in dollars) (8)	OPEX per MWH sold (in dollars) (9)	Avg resid. tariff (in dollars) (10)	Avg indust. tariff (in dollars) (11)	Cost recovery ratio (12)
Dummy transition of PSP	0.124*** (0.012)	1.159*** (0.014)	0.045*** (0.013)	−0.012*** (0.003)	0.054*** (0.005)	−0.010 (0.033)	0.031 (0.038)	−0.0269 (0.225)	−0.293 (0.227)	0.041** (0.018)	0.070*** (0.022)	−0.006 (0.060)
Dummy post-transition of PSP	0.062*** (0.009)	0.030*** (0.011)	−0.118*** (0.012)	0.001 (0.002)	−0.007 (0.005)	−0.276*** (0.024)	−0.332*** (0.023)	−0.213*** (0.036)	−0.179*** (0.044)	0.019 (0.012)	−0.027 (0.021)	0.194*** (0.050)
Regulatory governance index (ERGI)	0.236*** (0.013)	0.226*** (0.016)	−0.777*** (0.013)	0.005* (0.003)	−0.029*** (0.007)	−0.274*** (0.036)	−0.248*** (0.038)	−0.495*** (0.069)	−0.373*** (0.076)	0.154*** (0.021)	−0.074*** (0.028)	0.150*** (0.042)
Utility FE	Yes	Yes	Yes	Yes	Yes	Yes	Yes	Yes	Yes	Yes	Yes	Yes
Utility specific time trend	Yes	Yes	No	Yes	No	No	No	No	No	No	No	No

Observations	1859	1840	1983	1247	2337	1030	924	841	850	1655	831	660
Number of utilities	181	180	175	137	195	139	127	126	126	159	85	98

Notes:
Standard errors in parentheses
* significant at 10%; ** significant at 5%; ** significant at 1%

Table 6.8 Eigenvalues of factors

Component	Eigenvalue	Difference	Proportion	Cumulative
Factor 1	**3.75**	**2.63**	**0.47**	**0.47**
Factor 2	**1.12**	**0.09**	**0.14**	**0.61**
Factor 3	**1.03**	**0.25**	**0.13**	**0.74**
Factor 4	0.78	0.29	0.10	0.83
Factor 5	0.48	0.16	0.06	0.89
Factor 6	0.33	0.03	0.04	0.94
Factor 7	0.29	0.07	0.04	0.97
Factor 8	0.22		0.03	1.00

highlight their similarities and differences. Since patterns in data can be hard to find in data of high dimension, PCA may contribute in analyzing data. Furthermore, an additional advantage of PCA is that once you have found these patterns in the data, you may compress the data by reducing the dimensions, without much loss of information.

We use PCA to jointly take into account the information provided by our eight main governance indicators ratios (Table 6.8) and generate orthogonal indexes to measure regulatory agencies' governance. Factor scores were then calculated for each of the agencies. As a first step, we determine how many factors we may use in our analysis. Table 6.8 reports the estimated factors and their eigenvalues. Only those factors accounting for greater than 10 percent of the variance (eigenvalues >1) are kept in the analysis. As a result, only the first three factors are finally retained.

Among them, the first principal component factor (F1) accounts for 47 percent of the variance of the seven indexes. The other two component factors (F2 and F3) account for 14 and 13 percent of the variance respectively. The three factors together account for 74 percent of the total variance. These factors allow for computing the factor score coefficient matrix. To enhance these factors' interpretability, we use the varimax factor rotation method to minimize the number of variables that have high loadings on a factor. In other words, varimax rotation produces results which make it the most likely to identify each variable with a single factor. This approach greatly enhances our ability to make substantive interpretation of the main factors. Table 6.9 presents the factor loadings, where variables with large loadings (N > 0.4) for a given factor are highlighted in bold.

As seen in Table 6.9, Factor 1 reflects informal governance aspects in a regulatory agency, as it is correlated with informal autonomy,

Table 6.9 Factor loadings of indexes after varimax rotation

Variable	Factor 1	Factor 2	Factor 3	Unexplained
Tariff regulation index	−0.026	−0.085	**0.772**	0.120
Informal autonomy index	**0.480**	−0.113	0.032	0.541
Informal transparency index	0.370	0.288	0.022	0.281
Informal accountability index	**0.560**	−0.011	−0.109	0.384
Tools/capacities index	**0.561**	−0.037	0.062	0.261
Formal autonomy index	0.037	0.135	**0.621**	0.162
Formal transparency index	0.003	**0.655**	−0.040	0.183
Formal accountability index	−0.051	**0.670**	0.010	0.171

informal transparency, informal accountability, and tools and capacities. Nevertheless, good informal governance does not necessarily imply good overall performance; it may also be a manifestation of the agencies' behavior as to balance low formal governance. Factor 2 reflects formal aspects of regulatory governance and is highly correlated with formal transparency and formal accountability. Factor 3 reflects formal aspects of autonomy and the formal power of the agency to determine tariff's structure and level. This factor is highly correlated with the Tariff Regulatory index and the Formal Autonomy one.

We included these three factors in the models and the results are presented in Table 6.10.

As we did for the ERGI, the results may be better interpreted when we compute the impact on performance given an increase of one standard deviation for each factor. Standard deviations resulted in 1.51, 1.41 and 1.28 for each of the three principal components, respectively. Most of the coefficients for the three principal components resulted significant and with the expected signs in most of the cases; however, it seems that each of them has a distinct effect on each of the performance indicators. For instance, a standard deviation in the formal component has a higher effect on improving labor productivity by 15.9 percent and reducing frequency of interruptions and the residential tariffs by 13.8 and 19.0 percent, respectively. A standard deviation improvement in the third component that is related to formal autonomy and the attributions of the agency in terms of setting tariffs is associated with higher labor productivity by 11.4 percent and a 17.2 percent reduction in the average duration of interruptions. Furthermore, it produced a reduction in operation expenditure between 42.8 and 49.3 percent with consequent improvements in the cost recovery ratio. Finally, the first component resulted in less influence given that only three out of eleven coefficients resulted significant.

Table 6.10 Impact of regulatory governance on performance of utilities (principal component approach)

	Residential Conn.per Employee	Distribut. Losses	Coverage	Energy Sold per Conn.	Duration of interrupt's	Frequency of interrupt's	OPEX per Connection (in dollars)	OPEX per MWH sold (in dollars)	Avg Resid. Tariff (in dollars)	Avg Indust. Tariff (in dollars)	Cost Recovery Ratio
	(1)	(2)	(3)	(4)	(5)	(6)	(7)	(8)	(9)	(10)	(11)
Dummy Transition of PSP	0.122**	0.027**	−0.014***	0.059***	−0.043	0.046	−0.730*	−0.808**	0.147***	0.087***	0.068
	(0.012)	(0.013)	(0.003)	(0.004)	(0.037)	(0.044)	(0.397)	(0.400)	(0.019)	(0.021)	(0.062)
Dummy Post Transition of PSP	0.084***	−0.124***	0.002	−0.008	−0.358***	−0.366***	−0.193***	−0.137***	0.049***	−0.016	0.176***
	(0.008)	(0.013)	(0.002)	(0.005)	(0.025)	(0.024)	(0.039)	(0.049)	(0.013)	(0.021)	(0.053)
PCA 1 – Informal	0.001	−0.027***	−0.001	−0.048***	0.014	0.010	0.046	0.053	0.087***	0.010	−0.003
	(0.007)	(0.007)	(0.001)	(0.004)	(0.018)	(0.018)	(0.042)	(0.050)	(0.010)	(0.021)	(0.018)
PCA 2 - Formal	0.107***	−0.006	0.004*	0.037***	−0.024	−0.103***	0.050	0.092	−0.145***	−0.051***	−0.071*
	(0.008)	(0.006)	(0.002)	(0.004)	(0.026)	(0.028)	(0.084)	(0.085)	(0.014)	(0.016)	(0.037)
PCA 3 – Formal Autonomy and Tariffs	0.085***	−0.069***	0.012***	−0.009	−0.144***	−0.080	−0.405***	−0.039**	−0.036*	−0.030	0.266***
	(0.015)	(0.012)	(0.004)	(0.009)	(0.053)	(0.049)	(0.111)	(0.132)	(0.020)	(0.029)	(0.068)
Utility FE	Yes	Yes	Yes	Yes	Yes	Yes	Yes	Yes	Yes	Yes	Yes
Utility Specific Time trend	Yes	No	Yes	No	No	No	No	No	No	No	No
Observations	1782	1917	1190	2253	974	882	800	809	1596	820	619
Number of utilities	175	169	131	189	134	123	121	121	153	84	93

Notes:
Standard errors in parentheses. * significant at 10%; ** significant at 5%; ** significant at 1%

CONCLUSIONS

This chapter contributes to the literature that explores the link between regulatory governance and sector performance. We develop indexes of regulatory governance and using cross-country data about regulatory agencies and sector performance, we have shown that regulation matters and in particular that the governance structure of regulatory agencies matters significantly. We use two unique databases: (a) the World Bank's recently published Electricity Performance Database (World Bank, 2007) that contains detailed data for 26 countries and 250 utilities that represent 88 percent of the electricity connections in the Latin American and Caribbean region. The compiled data on the electricity distribution sector includes information on output, coverage, labor productivity, input, operating performance, service quality and tariffs; and (b) we have used also Electricity Regulatory Governance Database (Andres *et al.* (2007) for the development of the governance indexes. Based on an analytical framework to assess the governance of electricity agencies we designed a survey which was submitted to most of the regulatory agencies of the LAC region. The questionnaire was composed of 97 questions reflecting the four variables of agencies' governance and both formal and informal aspects of their functioning.

In assessing this relationship, we developed a methodology where we ran different models to explain the impacts of the change in ownership and different characteristics of the regulatory agency on the performance of the utilities. The results suggest that the mere existence of a regulatory agency, independent of the utilities' ownership has a significant impact on performance. Furthermore, after controlling for the existence of a regulatory agency, the ownership dummies are still significant and with the expected signs. We also proposed an experience measure in order to identify the gradual impact of the regulatory agency on utility performance. Our results confirm this hypothesis. In addition, this paper explores two different measures of governance; we used the ERGI, an aggregated measure of regulatory governance and then we decomposed the regulatory governance indexes into three main principal components related to informal and formal aspects of the agencies' governance, also considering the regulation of tariffs by agencies as an independent variable of their governance. The results suggest that governance matters and has significant impacts on performance when we simulated a standard deviation in each of these indexes.

In summary, we have shown that regulation matters for sector performance, on three aspects. We have shown that the existence of a regulatory agency matters, that the experience of the regulatory agency matters and that its governance matters as well. The results are consistent with the literature on the impact of private sector participation and show the relevance of the existence of a regulatory agency and its governance, defined as the agency's institutional design and structure that allows it to carry its functions as an independent regulator. Our results indicate a significant improvement in utility performance through the involvement of a regulatory agency even in the case of state owned enterprises. The results strongly support that the highest achievements are reached with the combination of private sector participation regulated through a regulatory agency that exhibits good governance.

ACKNOWLEDGEMENTS

Luis A. Andres, José Luis Guasch, and Sebastián Lopez are grateful to Daniel Benitez, Georgeta Dragoiu, Antonio Estache, Martin Rossi, and Tomas Serebrisky and the two anonymous refeeres for their comments and suggestions. They are also thankful to the participants at the Nice Regulatory Workshop for very useful comments. They are particularly indebted to Paulo Correa for sharing his data on Brazilian regulatory agencies and Mariam Dayoub and Aires da Conceicao for their assistance collecting the data in Brazil. Georgeta Dragoiu and Julio A. Gonzalez contributed in the collection of the performance data. The findings, interpretations and conclusions expressed herein are solely those of the authors and do not necessarily reflect the views of the Board of the Executive Directors of the World Bank or the governments they represent.

NOTES

1. This has been the overwhelming mechanism used by the literature on the subject to assess the independence and other attributes of regulatory agencies. Although, ideally, we would like to include the effectiveness of the different institutional arrangements on sector performance and on institutional quality outcomes, the cross-regional nature of our research and the limited resources to undertake this task convinced us of this approach as the most convenient.
2. Based on the information collected through the surveys submitted by countries, Andres et al. (2007b) designed a database composed of 46 electricity regulators (including both federal and national regulators).
3. Among other robust analysis the paper assigned different weights to the seven indexes. First they put double weight to the variables related to set and enforce tariffs. As many sector specialists argue, this is, per se, the main attribute of a regulatory agency. A second approach was based on the Principal Component Analysis approach. The methodology develops a composite index by defining a real valued function over the relevant variables objectively. The principle of this method lies in the fact that when different characteristics

are observed about a set of events, the characteristic with higher variation explains a higher proportion of the variation in the dependent variable compared to a variable with lesser variation in it. Therefore, the issue is one of finding weights to be given to each of the concerned variables determined on the principle that the objective is to maximize the variation in the linear composite of these variables. In other words, this approach allows for identifying patterns in data, and expressing the data in such a way as to highlight their similarities and differences.

4. We have performed a review of this arbitrary period definition with several country analysts, and this criteria seems to respond to most of the cases.
5. Note that there are some differences between when the agency was created (in general by law) with respect to the year when it was established. The governance data reported both dates. Despite this discrepancy, we selected the year when it was established, and ran similar specifications with the year of creation, and we obtained similar results.

REFERENCES

Andres, Luis, Vivien Foster, and J. Luis Guasch (2006), 'The impact of privatization on the performance of the infrastructure sector: the case of electricity distribution in Latin American countries', Policy Research Working Paper 3936, Washington, DC: World Bank.

Andres, Luis, J. Luis Guasch, Makhtar Dip, and Sebastian Lopez Azumendi (2007), 'Assessing the governance of electricity regulatory agencies in the Latin American and the Caribbean region: a benchmarking analysis', Policy Research Working Paper 4380, Washington, DC: World Bank,

Andres, Luis, J. Luis Guasch, Thomas Haven, and Vivien Foster (2008), *The Impact of private sector participation in infrastructure: Lights, Shadows, and the Road ahead*, Washington, DC: World Bank.

Aron, Janine (2000), *Growth and Institutions: A Review of the Evidence*, Washington, DC: The World Bank.

Bacon, R. W. and J. E. Besant-Jones (2001), 'Global electric power reform, privatization and liberalization of the electric power industry in developing countries', *Annual Review of Energy and the Environment*, **26**, 331–59.

Boardman, Anthony and Aidan R. Vining (1989), 'Ownership and performance in competitive environments: a comparison of the performance of private, mixed, and state-owned enterprises', *Journal of Law and Economics*, **32**, 1–33.

Brown Ashley C., J. Stern, B. Tenenbaum and D. Gencer (2006), *Handbook for Evaluating Infrastructure Regulatory Systems*, Washington DC: World Bank.

Chisari, Omar, Antonio Estache, and Carlos Romero (1997), 'Winners and losers from utility privatization in Argentina: lessons from a general equilibrium model', Policy Research Working Paper 1824, Washington, DC: World Bank.

Correa, Paulo, C. Pereira, B. Mueller and M. Melo (2006), *Regulatory Governance in Infrastructure Industries: Assessment and Measurement of Brazilian Regulators*, Washington DC: World Bank/Public-Private Infrastructure Advisory Facility.

Cubbin, John and J. Stern (2006), 'The impact of regulatory governance and privatization on electricity industry generation capacity in developing countries', *The World Bank Economic Review Advance Access*, Washington, DC.

Dussan, M. (1996), 'Electric Power Sector Reform in Latin America and the Caribbean', Working Papers Series IFM-104.

Estache, Antonio and Martin Rodriguez-Pardina (1998), 'Light and lightening at the end of the public tunnel: the reform of the electricity sector in the Southern Cone', World Bank Working Paper, May.

Estache, Antonio and Martin Rossi (2004), 'Have consumers benefited from the reforms in the electricity distribution sector in Latin America?' Unpublished manuscript, World Bank.

Estache, Antonio and Martin Rossi (2007) 'Regulatory agencies: impact on firm performance and consumer welfare', Unpublished manuscript, World Bank.

Frydman, Roman, Cheryl W. Gray, Marek Hessel and Andrzej Rapaczynski (1999), 'When does privatization work? The impact of private ownership on corporate performance in transition economies', *Quarterly Journal of Economics*, **114** (4), 1153–91.

Galal, Ahmed, Leroy Jones, Pankaj Tandon and Ingo Vogelsang (1994), *Welfare Consequences of Selling Public Enterprises*, Oxford: Oxford University Press.

Gilardi, Fabrizio (2002), 'Policy credibility and delegation to independent regulatory agencies: a comparative empirical analysis', *Journal of European Public Policy*, **9** (6), 873–93.

Gilardi, Fabrizio (2005), 'Evaluating independent regulators', in Fabrizio Gilardi *Designing Independent and Accountable Regulatory Authorities for High Quality Regulation*, Paris: Organization for Economic Cooperation and Development.

Guasch, J. Luis and Pablo Spiller (1999), *Managing the Regulatory Process: Design, Concepts, Issues and the Latin America and Caribbean Story*, Washington DC: World Bank and Caribbean Studies.

Gutierrez, Luis H. (2003), 'Regulatory governance in the Latin American telecommunications sector', Utilities Policies. Obtained at www.sciencedirect.com.

Halvorsen, R and R. Palmquist (1980), 'The interpretation of dummy variables in semi-logarithmic equations', *American Economic Review*, **70**, 474–5.

Heckman, James and Richard Robb (1985), 'Alternative methods of evaluating the impact of interventions', in James Heckman and Burton Singer (eds), *Longitudinal Analysis of Labor Market Data*, New York: Cambridge University Press, 156–245.

Johannsen, Katja Sander (2003), *Regulatory Independence in Theory and Practice – a Survey of Independent Energy Regulators in Eight European Countries*, Copenhagen: AKF.

Joskow, Paul (2003), 'Electricity sector restructuring and competition: lessons learned', *Cuadernos de Economía*, **40** (121), pp. 548–58.

La Porta, Rafael and Florencio López-de-Silanes (1999), 'Benefits of privatization – evidence from Mexico', *The Quarterly Journal of Economics*, **114** (4), 1193–242.

Laurin, Claude and Yves Bozec (2000), 'Privatization and productivity improvement: the case of Canadian National (CN)', working paper, Ecole des HEC, Montreal.

Maggetti, Martino (2005), *Towards a Framework to Assess the Informal Independence of Regulatory Agencies*, Lausanne: University of Lausanne.

Megginson, William, Robert Nash and Matthias van Randenborgh (1994), 'The financial and operating performance of newly privatized firms: an international empirical analysis', *Journal of Finance* **49**, 403–52.

Millan, J., E. Lora and Alejandro Micco (2001), *Sustainability of the Electricity Sector Reforms in Latin America*, Washington, DC/Santiago: Research Department, Inter-American Development Bank.

Oliveira, Gesner, E. Machado, L. Novaes, L. Martins, G. Ferreira, and C. Beatriz (2005), *Aspects of the Independence of regulatory Agencies and Competition Advocacy*, Rio de Janeiro: Getulio Vargas Foundation.

Organization for Economic Cooperation and Development (OECD) (2005), *OECD Guiding Principles for Regulatory Quality and Performance*, Paris.

Ramamurti, Ravi (1996), *Privatizing Monopolies: Lessons from the Telecommunications and Transport Sector in Latin America*, Baltimore, MD: Johns Hopkins University Press.

Rodrick, Dani (2004), *Getting Institutions Right*, Cambridge, MA: Harvard University.

Ros, Agustin (1999), 'Does ownership or competition matter? The effects of telecommunications Reform on the Network Expansion and Efficiency', *Journal of Regulatory Economics*, **15**, 65–92.

Ros, Agustin and A. Banerjee (2000), 'Telecommunications privatizations and tariff rebalancing: evidence from Latin America', *Telecommunications Policy*, **20**, 233–52.

Rossi, Martin (2004), 'Ownership and efficiency: evidence from Latin American electric utilities', Unpublished manuscript, University of Oxford.

Sirtaine, Sophie, Maria Elena Pinglo, Vivien Foster, and J. Luis Guasch (2004), *How Profitable are Private Infrastructure Concessions in Latin America? Empirical Evidence and Regulatory Implications*, Washington, DC: World Bank.

Stern, Jon and J. Cubbin (2005), 'Regulatory effectiveness: the impact of regulation and regulatory governance arrangements on electricity industry outcomes', World Bank Policy Research Working Paper 3536, Washington, DC.

Stern, Jon and S. Holder (1999), 'Regulatory governance: criteria for assessing the performance of regulatory systems: an application to infrastructure in developing countries of Asia', Regulation Initiative Discussion Paper Series Number 20.

World Bank (2007), *Benchmarking Analysis of the Electricity Distribution Sector in the Latin American and Caribbean Region*, Washington, DC: World Bank.

APPENDIX 6.1: LIST OF SELECTED VARIABLES OF PERFORMANCE

Name	Unit	Definition
Number of connections	Number	Total number of residential connections in the utility area
Energy sold	MWh	Total electricity sold per year
Average consumption	MWh	Energy sold per connection per year
Employees	Number	Total number of employees
Labor productivity (1)	Number	Ratio total connections per employee
Labor productivity (2)	MWh	Ratio energy sold per employee
OPEX	Dollars	OPEX (operation expenditures) of the distribution services per connection
OPEX per connection	Dollars	Ratio
OPEX per MWh sold	Dollar	Ratio
Distributional losses	%	Energy losses in distribution per year (due to technical losses and illegal connections)
Quality (1)	Hours/year	Average duration of interruptions per subscriber
Quality (2)	No./Year	Average frequency of interruptions per subscriber
Coverage	%	Number of residential subscribers per 100 households in the concession area (Residential coverage)
Average residential tariff	Dollars/MWh	
Average industrial tariff	Dollars/MWh	

APPENDIX 6.2: SELECTED CHARACTERISTICS OF LAC NATIONAL ELECTRICITY AGENCIES THAT SUBMITTED THE SURVEY

Name	Year	Legal status	Budget sources	Appeals' authority	Accountability	Staff number
Ente Nacional Regulador de la Electricidad (Argentina)	1993	Separate entity with autonomy from the line ministry	Regulation tax	Executive and Judicial reviews[a]	Executive and Congress	More than 100
Fair Trading Commission (Barbados)	2001	Separate entity with autonomy from the line ministry	Government budget and regulation tax	Judicial review	Executive and Congress	29
Superintendencia de Electricidad (Bolivia)	1996	Separate entity with autonomy from the line ministry	Regulation tax	Judicial review	Executive and Congress	68
Agencia Nacional de Energía Eléctrica (Brazil)	1997	Separate entity with autonomy from the line ministry	Regulation tax	Judicial review	Executive and Congress	765
Comisión de Regulación de Energía y Gas (Colombia)	1994	A separate entity with no autonomy from the line ministry	Regulation tax	Judicial review	Executive and Congress	From 51 to 100

Appendix 6.2 (continued)

Name	Year	Legal status	Budget sources	Appeals' authority	Accountability	Staff number
Superintendencia de Servicios Públicos (Colombia)	1994	A separate entity with autonomy from the line ministry	Government budget	Judicial review	Executive and Congress	305
Unidad Reguladora de Servicios Públicos (Costa Rica)	1996	Separate entity with autonomy from the line ministry	Regulation tax	Judicial review	Congress	167
Comisión Nacional de Energía (Chile)	1978	Separate entity with no autonomy from the line ministry	Government budget	Cuasi-judicial review (Autonomous Oversight Agency)	Government	44
Superintendencia de Electricidad y Combustibles (Chile)	1985	Separate entity with autonomy from the line ministry	Government budget	Cuasi-judicial review (Autonomous Oversight Agency)	Government	More than 100
Consejo Nacional de Electricidad (Ecuador)	1999	Separate entity with autonomy from the line ministry	Regulation tax	Judicial review	Government	100
Superintendencia de Electricidad (Republica Dominicana)	1998	Separate entity with autonomy from the line ministry	Regulation tax	Executive and Judicial reviews	Government and Congress	More than 100

Appendix 6.2 (continued)

Name	Year	Legal status	Budget sources	Appeals' authority	Accountability	Staff number
Superintendencia General de Electricidad y Telecomunicaciones (El Salvador)	1997	Separate entity with autonomy from the line ministry	Regulation tax	Judicial review	Government and Congress	106
Comisión Nacional de Energía Eléctrica (Guatemala)	1996	Separate entity with no autonomy from the line ministry	Regulation tax	Executive and Judicial reviews	Government and Congress	From 51 to 100
Comisión Nacional de Energía (Honduras)	1995	Separate entity with autonony from the line ministry	Government budget	Judicial review	Government and Congress	Fewer than 20
Office of Utilities Regulation (Jamaica)	1997	Separate entity with autonomy from the line ministry	No answer	Judicial review	Government and Congress	45
Comisión Reguladora de Energía (México)	1995	Separate entity with autonomy from the line ministry	Government budget	Judicial review	Government and Congress	130
Instituto Nicaragüense de Electricidad (Nicaragua)	1994	Separate entity with autonomy from the line ministry	Regulation tax	Judicial review	Government and Congress	200

Appendix 6.2 (continued)

Name	Year	Legal status	Budget sources	Appeals' authority	Accountability	Staff number
Autoridad Nacional de los Servicios Públicos (Panamá)	1996	Separate entity with autonomy from the line ministry	Regulation tax	Judicial review	Government	More than 100
Organismo Supervisor de la Inversión en Energía (Perú)	1996	Separate entity with autonomy from the line ministry	Regulation tax	Judicial review	Government and Congress	187
Regulated Industries Commission (Trinidad and Tobago)	2000	Separate entity with autonomy from the line ministry	Regulation tax	Judicial review	Government and Congress	Fewer than 20
Unidad Reguladora de Servicios de Energía y Agua (Uruguay)	2000	Separate entity with no autonomy from the line ministry	Regulation tax	Executive and Judicial review	Government and Congress	18

Note: Executive review generally involves the line minister or the President as the authorities in charge of reviewing an agency's decision. Judicial review implies the revision of the decision by a court.

7. Vertical relations and 'neutrality' in broadband communications: neither market nor hierarchy?

Howard A. Shelanski

INTRODUCTION

One of the most contentious debates in telecommunications policy involves the ability of network operators to negotiate vertical relationships with the providers of content and services ('applications') that flow over the operators' infrastructure. Network operators want the ability to manage traffic on their networks, ostensibly to protect against congestion, ensure network quality, and recover sufficient costs to fund continued network investment. As part of that traffic management, operators want to be able to strike different kinds of access agreements with different applications providers. The policy implication is a laissez-faire approach to vertical contracting in broadband markets. In contrast, applications providers typically want 'network neutrality': the ability to gain access to consumers without negotiating with intermediary network operators and without the possibility that an operator will discriminate in access quality against any particular provider's traffic.[1] The policy implication is that network operators should not be allowed to 'create different tiers of online service' by selling different levels of access at different prices to different providers of on-line content and services (Lessig and McChesney, 2006).

At the heart of the network neutrality debate is the question of whether the market for broadband communications can support both open applications competition and optimal levels of ongoing investment in network infrastructure. Most commentators agree that the general answer to that question is 'yes'. In the specifics, however, this positive consensus on potential results fractures into opposing positions on how those results can and should be achieved. On one side are those who argue that the affirmative answer to the question above is conditional upon the government's keeping out of the broadband market and leaving network owners to manage their networks as they deem necessary. On the other side are those whose affirmative answer to the general question is conditional upon the government's active regulation of the relationships between network owners and applications providers to ensure that the internet remains 'neutral'.

From the perspective of new institutional economics (NIE) there is something strange about this network neutrality debate. The central concern of NIE is governance and the comparative governance advantages of organizational alternatives like vertical integration, spot market transactions or long-term contracts. Thus, in the NIE framework the question of whether and how network owners should contract with applications providers would depend on the costs those vertical trading relationships might entail and which form of governance would maximize the joint value of trade for the network operator and applications provider. The network neutrality debate, however, has generally not been between the comparative virtues of different forms of governance, but between governance and non-governance; not between market versus hierarchical institutions to mediate exchange, but between unmediated access by applications providers and mediated access of any kind between the respective 'modules' of Internet applications and network transport.

One explanation for the current form of the debate stems from the structure of the last-mile network market – generally a duopoly – and the potential for network operators to exercise market power in any institutional setting, be it a spot market for the network capacity upstream providers need or some kind of more structured, long-term agreement between application providers and networks. Advocates of network neutrality regulation argue that given the market power of networks, the only solution is 'neutrality', free and unmediated access for any provider of on-line content and services. Anything else, they claim, will expose applications providers to inefficient hold-up and expropriation by network owners. The argument for neutrality implies that the concentrated network market makes both markets and hierarchies more prone to coercive exercise of market power than to efficient adaptation and coordination. Opponents of such regulation argue to the contrary that some hierarchical mediation of upstream network access is necessary to prevent network owners from having costs imposed on them, from being unable to strike efficient upstream agreements, and from being deterred from investing in improving the quality of their networks. As the debate has continued between those who argue that network neutrality regulation is necessary to preserve applications innovation and those who argue that such regulation would harm the growth and development of underlying network infrastructure, the United States Congress has been awash with legislative proposals from both perspectives. (Atkinson and Weiser, 2006).

Why such attention to network neutrality? The reason may lie in the fact that, although vertical issues have long been central to telephone regulation, the stakes for consumers have changed with the Internet. (Benjamin *et al.*, 2006). Only a few years ago, the principal value of the telephone network to consumers was person-to-person voice communication and the principal value of cable networks was video programming. Complementary, vertical services like voice mail or information services were comparably modest in importance. Now, those same networks deliver a vast universe of content and services through the Internet. Some such services, for example Internet telephony (VoIP) or video services, (IP-TV) may compete directly with the core services of the underlying networks. But most services are complements, not competitors, to the networks over which consumers reach the Internet, and there is enormous value in those complementary applications. Telephone and Cable networks have gone from wagging the tail to wagging the dog with respect to vertical services and their importance to consumers.

While the increasing value of the applications market gives rise to concern over vertical discrimination, we know from Oliver Williamson that it can simultaneously raise the potential benefits of vertical relationships between networks and applications providers depending on the attributes of the transactions at issue (Williamson, 1971, 1979). Indeed, for new and commercially risky applications in particular, vertical relationships can potentially reduce transaction costs and bring new products and services to market faster.

Not surprisingly, therefore, network neutrality regulation has both its advocates and opponents who speak in adamant terms about the consequences of either allowing network owners to discriminate among applications providers or barring them from doing so (Lessig, 2006; Owen, 2007; Yoo, 2005). Upon closer inspection, however, each side's arguments beg important questions to which answers are both empirically and theoretically elusive. Those open questions in turn weaken the basis for either the outright ban on discrimination sought by network neutrality advocates or the pure laissez-faire sought by its opponents.

This chapter will briefly examine several unanswered questions central to the network neutrality debate and discuss their implications for broadband policy. The first part of this chapter will examine the main claims made by each side of the network neutrality debate and discuss the unanswered questions upon which the merits of those arguments depend. The second part will analyze the policy implications of those unanswered questions, examine the balance of risks at issue in network neutrality regulation, and discuss how policy should account for those risks in the presence of incomplete information.

STRONG ASSUMPTIONS ABOUT REGULATING (OR NOT)

Proponents of network neutrality regulation contend that discriminatory network access terms will selectively impede applications providers' access to consumers and thereby chill innovation at the edge of the network (meaning innovation by those who use the network as a medium for providing their content and services to consumers), reducing the flow of new services and applications to the market. They contend that discrimination would force potential innovators either to buy a costly level of access or risk providing a second-class service with reduced priority to the conduits that reach consumers and, in turn, reduced chances for commercial success. Either choice imposes costs that will cause applications developers on the margin to engage in less innovation. Advocates thus argue that a level, or neutral, playing field for all applications providers is necessary to preserve the ability of intelligence at the 'edge' of the network to drive innovation and increase the welfare of consumers.

Arguments against network neutrality often rest on the similar, but diametrically opposed, proposition that investment and innovation will suffer unless network owners can recover costs imposed by high-volume applications. The innovation at issue here is not at the edge of the network, but at its 'core'. At issue is the need for capacity, reliability, and security for traffic moving across the network. Some network owners argue that the content and service providers whose applications generate the traffic should pay for the capacity to carry it to end users. From this perspective, applications providers impose costs on networks and should bear them accordingly, not shift them to network owners or subscribers. Network operators argue that they have no incentive or ability to exclude or reduce the appeal to consumers of any upstream applications, because those applications are what attract subscribers to their networks. They moreover note that some applications innovators on the edge of the network might be deterred not by discrimination, but by neutrality, because they will be unable to secure priority access from the network operator for services that need to run with a particular assured quality.

Each set of arguments above raises difficult empirical and theoretical questions, and each depends to some extent on the competitive dynamics of the network access market. The more networks there are in competition with each other for subscribers, the less easily can any individual network engage in inefficient discrimination against particular applications or applications providers. Consumers will choose networks that get them the content and services they want fast and reliably. Which side of the debate one credits will therefore depend at least in part on one's view of how competitive the market is and will be.

Discriminatory Access and Applications Innovation

Even assuming all applications innovation to be welfare improving, what basis is there for determining how much, if any, innovation deterrence would result from discrimination by platforms in the terms of access offered to applications providers? Two proponents of network neutrality regulation offer the following empirical motivation for their claim that non-neutrality would deter innovation:

> More than 60 percent of Web content is created by regular people, not corporations . . . Most of the great innovators in the history of the Internet started out in their garages with great ideas and little capital. This is no accident. Network neutrality protections minimized control by the network owners, maximized competition and invited outsiders in to innovate. Net neutrality guaranteed a free and competitive market for Internet content. The benefits are extraordinary and undeniable. (Lessig and McChesney, 2006)

Taking the above argument to be true, the fact that innovators thrived under a neutral regime does not itself tell us how many of those innovators would have been deterred had network operators offered a tiered set of offerings in which quality rose with price. The empirical observation that has motivated some to advocate network neutrality thus does not necessarily supply empirical support for the innovation deterrence argument on which that advocacy largely rests.

Nor is the logical or theoretical connection between neutrality and applications innovation so clear that the network neutrality advocates' innovation-deterrence argument should be accepted as a matter of reason. First, at least some applications providers may be deterred by the absence of a high-priority tier of access. Some services, for example video services, may need reduced latency to work well, and absence of an assured level of priority raises the risk that such services will fail to live up to their billing, hence deterring their introduction.

Second, there is no reason to assume that most services will in fact be harmed if they are transmitted with the base (that is lower) level of priority. Comparatively low-bandwidth applications may work perfectly well at lower tiers of access and their innovation might not depend on neutrality. Moreover, even if there is some quality effect, consumers have shown a willingness to tolerate slower interactions on the Internet in return for lower subscription prices. Success of an application therefore may not depend on purchasing a costlier tier of access from network operators, especially where there is some way to compensate consumers for any delays in service.

Third, even if neutrality was a causal factor in the explosion of innovation from the edge of the network in the first decade of the commercial Internet, that same environment need not be optimal for the next decade of a more mature Internet. It bears noting that in key areas of commerce, content and applications, the on-line world is populated by a handful of major players. The brand-name recognition, installed base of customers, and network externalities accumulated by established on-line players could present much greater obstacles in some lines of internet applications than would discriminatory access terms. Indeed, it is precisely the established players who fear non-neutrality because they may be natural, deep-pocket targets for aggressive access negotiation by network operators. Neutrality regulations would protect them from such pressure.

Neutrality may, however, also benefit established players in another way, this one less sympathetic or potentially beneficial for innovation: access quality may be an important way for new competition in some services to differentiate themselves from incumbents. Established applications providers have little interest in defending against entrants on new competitive dimensions. The 'neutral' status quo may therefore be of competitive advantage to applications incumbents while denying a competitive tool to new innovators from the edge.

Finally, platform competition was less developed during the early years of the commercial Internet. As the data discussed earlier show, few Americans (19 percent) even had Internet access at all from their homes in 1996, while today most have computers and a choice of broadband access providers. Even if neutrality was necessary to speed applications innovation under the early years of limited broadband availability and no choice of broadband providers, it is unclear that it would be in today's more competitive environment.

The arguments made above do not refute the possibility that non-neutrality will deter applications innovation. They do, however, show that there is little reason to presume such an effect for policy purposes and good reason to question whether non-neutrality will cause the severe harms that some network neutrality proponents suggest. The case for such harmful effects diminishes with increased network competition. Under duopoly, the case is ambiguous. As wireless platforms enter the market to compete against the cable and telephone networks, the ability of any network to discriminate inefficiently by artificially slowing selected traffic to sell priority declines because its rivals will have incentives to offer consumers greater assurance of fast content delivery.

Networks and Incentives to Discriminate

Consider next the incentives of network owners to engage in discrimination that harms innovation or consumer welfare. Opponents of network neutrality regulation have argued that network owners would have no incentive to discriminate against applications providers in a way that made network subscription less attractive to consumers. Underlying this claim is the idea that 'a monopolist – which, by definition, would have the ability to impede competition in adjacent markets – generally will have no incentive to do so' because it cannot enlarge its profits by doing so (Speta, 2000). Any reduction in value (or increase in price) of the upstream application will be met by a corresponding reduction in demand (or decrease in profits) for platform subscriptions, a phenomenon that Joseph Farrell and Philip Weiser have labeled 'internalizing complementary efficiencies' or 'ICE' (Farrell and Weiser, 2004).

Farrell and Weiser demonstrate, however, that while ICE often holds, under many conditions it does not. As Farrell explains, platform owners can often raise their profits by price discrimination, and even if one assumes the price discrimination itself to be efficient (which is not always the case), platform owners may discriminate against providers of complementary services in order to facilitate price discrimination (Farrell, 2006). Farrell illustrates his point through the simple example of a copy machine manufacturer that wishes to price discriminate by selling the copier at a low price and metering use through sale of repair services.[2] In order for repair services to be a metering mechanism for price discrimination, the copier manufacturer must receive revenues for all repairs done to its copiers. One way the manufacturer can do this is to withhold spare parts from independent repair firms and to do all the repairs itself, eliminating competition and reducing efficiency in the complementary repair market. Thus, the non-neutrality of the mechanism used to accomplish price discrimination can involve what Farrell has termed 'collateral-damage inefficiency' (Farrell, 2006). The important point is that whether or not the underlying price discrimination is itself efficient, that discrimination can be profitable for the manufacturer despite any collateral-damage inefficiency it might cause.

In theory the manufacturer could avoid this collateral damage through other means of metering. For example, instead of making repair services the metric, the manufacturer could make spare parts the metric and then meter usage of the copier through sales of spare parts to all providers of repair services. Copier owners would retain their choice of service providers and the most efficient service providers would remain able to compete for repair business. To the extent that more efficient metering mechanisms are harder to administer than preemption of competition in the complementary market, however, firms may opt for the latter despite the inefficiency.[3]

In the context of network neutrality, the pursuit of price discrimination could lead to harmful departures from neutrality toward upstream applications. While Farrell and Weiser (2006) show that platform owners may have incentives to discriminate inefficiently where the application competes with a core service of the platform (for example voice-over-IP for telephone networks or video-on-demand for cable networks), harm may still result even when the upstream application is not one that rivals the platform's main line of business. For example, one mechanism a cable network owner could use to price discriminate is to bundle Internet access with some application, say IP telephony. The network could offer consumers two choices: Internet access for $30 per month, or Internet access for $25 per month if the consumer also subscribes to the network operator for IP telephone service. To make this bundle profitable, the network operator not bound by network neutrality rules might discriminate in the terms of access it provides to rival IP telephone providers to put them at a competitive disadvantage. So long as the increased attractiveness of Internet subscriptions due to the $5 discount outweighs the decrease in attractiveness due to the reduced choice of IP telephone services, the network operator may find the collateral damage to the upstream applications market nonetheless to be profitable. The same scenario could hold for other means of price discrimination, say a phone company's metering of subscribers' Internet usage through video downloads or some other application susceptible to incremental charges.

This is not to say that there are no possible welfare benefits from the price discrimination described above. By using discrimination (whether through bundling, metering, or some other mechanism) to extract high surplus from one set of users, a network operator may enable another set of users to have access where they would not under a single-price regime. This is particularly so in the case for high-fixed-cost services like Internet access, where price discrimination might allow a network to offer some subscribers access at prices closer to marginal cost because it is recovering its fixed costs from other, higher-paying, customers. It is this very ambiguity in the welfare effects of price discrimination and in the incentives to discriminate inefficiently that is important. The welfare ambiguity means that any rule patently barring discrimination could have unintended, negative consequences because the conduct sought to be barred – price discrimination – is neither always bad nor always good.

Capacity, Efficient Priority Choices and Network Investment

A third set of questions in the network neutrality debate revolves around network capacity. If capacity is not scarce, then there is no need for networks to prioritize one provider's traffic over another and no need for investment in new capacity. Capacity thus implicates two important issues for the network neutrality debate. The first is whether upstream price discrimination is necessary to establish priority; the second is whether upstream price discrimination is necessary to recover the costs of investing in new capacity and network technology. The threshold question underlying both of these questions is whether capacity is scarce such that congestion will at least sometimes occur and require networks to prioritize one packet of information over another. If not, then it is hard to see what good could emerge from departures from neutrality, as such departures could be aimed neither at efficiently prioritizing traffic nor at efficiently recovering network investment.

There may be little agreement over the exact extent of current or future capacity constraints on broadband networks, but neither is there evidence that capacity is so plentiful that congestion, and hence the issue of priority, never arises. Indeed, one report argues that new capacity investment is necessary and that the market does not currently provide adequate incentives for network owners to make such investments (Deloitte and Touche, 2007). The head of television technology for one of the strongest advocates of network neutrality, Google, in a widely reported statement also emphasized the need for core investment when he said '[t]he Web infrastructure and even Google's [infrastructure] doesn't scale. It's not going to offer the quality of service that consumers expect'.[4] Given that capacity constraints cannot be assumed away in the network neutrality debate, the question becomes whether they can supply any justification for differentiating among applications providers in the terms of network access.

One rationale for allowing price discrimination is that it provides a basis for deciding which packet should take priority over another. This is exactly what raises concern among network neutrality advocates: new applications providers will have to either pay or sit in line. As discussed above, charging for priority may or may not have a significant negative impact on applications innovation. But if there really is a need to prioritize, it is important to examine the alternatives before ruling out price mechanisms. The most neutral alternative of random selection is unattractive and likely to serve consumers poorly. A spam e-mail is likely to be less valuable to either consumer or provider than a VoIP call or a paid music download. Random selection could lead the spam to be delivered first, however, benefiting no one except the provider of the lower-value service.

A more nuanced alternative is suggested by the definition of network neutrality at the beginning of this article: 'all *like* . . . content must be treated alike and move at the same speed' (Lessig and McChesney, 2006). Under a close reading of this definition, it might be fine for the network to prioritize VoIP over e-mail, so long as all VoIP were treated the same and all e-mail were treated the same. While such hierarchy of uses might be better than random prioritization, it still raises potential problems because it puts the network owner in the position of having to decide which uses or categories of content should be prioritized over others, which uses are 'like' other uses, and where innovative new uses should be placed in the priority queue. Defining a clear and administrable regulatory standard for 'like content' will prove difficult.

Creating a market for priority can alleviate the difficulties with random or 'like use' prioritization and reduce the allocative inefficiency that can result from those mechanisms. Network investment could become more efficient because firms with a desire for priority will capture direct private benefits (less delay for their packets) of their payments to the network operator. When the network owner or subscribers must bear the costs, the benefits are more diffuse, creating the potential for underinvestment. Moreover, to the extent price discrimination allows more highly valued information to move faster, it has the potential to increase the efficiency and consumer welfare of Internet activity. On the other hand, to the extent price discrimination is used in a targeted way as an anticompetitive strategy to raise the costs of particular applications providers it can be harmful. Again, the non-neutral strategy can have either (or both) positive and negative effects.

The next question related to capacity is whether recovery of capacity investment supplies a rationale for price discrimination toward applications providers. Networks receive revenues from subscribers, raising the question of why they would need to charge applications providers for access. There are several reasons why recovering network costs from subscribers might not be optimal. First, even though networks can and do charge subscribers different monthly fees for different Internet access speeds, that pricing mechanism may leave some subscribers who are willing to pay the cost of higher-speed access nonetheless unwilling to pay its price. Within each tier of access, there will be relatively high-usage subscribers and relatively low-usage subscribers. Because all subscribers to a given tier pay the same price, the latter may pay for more speed and capacity than they use while the former pay for less than they use. The subscription price that the relatively low-usage consumers pay is therefore above the costs they impose on the network. Were the subscription price for these users lower and more reflective of their actual usage, they would attract yet lower usage customers whose willingness to pay was above cost but not quite up to the existing monthly charge for the higher tier of access. To the extent payments from applications providers can ameliorate this potential inefficiency of consumer-side charges, charging those applications providers can be beneficial.

Second, even if subscription rates can be structured better to reflect each subscriber's actual usage, there may still be inefficiency in on-line consumption. One reason stems from the costs of trying out new, high-bandwidth content and applications. If consumers are paying the full costs of their usage, they may hesitate to try new services that would increase their costs. Some kind of transfer payment from the applications providers to consumers could overcome this inefficiency, although such compensation mechanisms might involve high transaction costs. If applications providers would be willing to pay more to networks in return for subscribers who have faster connections and are more willing to consume various content and services, then it might be more efficient, as well as more profitable, for networks to reduce subscription prices in conjunction with charging applications providers for different levels of access.

Finally, consumers and applications providers may have asymmetric valuations of their interactions. It may be more valuable for applications providers to have consumers use their services than it is for consumers to receive them. This is particularly true where the applications provider is paid by a third party – perhaps an advertiser or search listing – based on the number of people who visit the site. Any given consumer might find the experience worthless and merely 'click through' the site, but not so the applications provider, and presumably the advertisers or search listings, who have an interest in reducing the cost to subscribers of accessing their sites. If the network can only charge the consumer for network access, the joint surplus of consumers and applications providers might be lower than it would be if applications providers could pay to speed interactions with, and perhaps reduce prices to, consumers.

The above three reasons why it might not be efficient to charge only subscribers for use of network infrastructure do not resolve the question of whether price discrimination toward applications providers will improve consumer welfare or efficiency. They do show, however, that this issue is complex and that arguments for upstream price discrimination cannot be ignored just because networks charge subscribers. Internet platforms may well have the attribute of two-sided markets, in which charging end-users and applications providers can be more efficient than placing the charges on one side alone (Rochet and Tirole, 2006). Whether or not they do, and whether or not the gains from two-sided pricing offset possible costs, is beyond the scope of this chapter and an important topic for further research. For current purposes, however, the important point is that the question of the comparative costs and benefits of one-sided versus two-sided pricing is an open one that should not be assumed away on either side of the network neutrality debate.

COMPARATIVE RISKS OF ALTERNATIVE FORMS OF NON-NEUTRALITY

The previous section demonstrates that the effects of network non-neutrality toward applications providers is ambiguous, with some possibility that it could deter applications innovation but some possibility too that it could benefit, to varying degrees, network investment, applications competition and allocative efficiency. Conversely, mandatory neutrality could benefit applications innovation and prevent collateral inefficiencies due to anti-competitive vertical discrimination but could also reduce the efficiency of investment and the volume and nature of on-line transactions. In neither case, however, are the benefits either sufficiently sure or substantial to justify a policy that pursues one set of objectives (for example applications innovation) to the exclusion of others (for example network investment). There are too many open questions about the impact of either laissez-faire or a strict neutrality rule to make a persuasive case for either solution. Either choice is uncertain to achieve its intended objectives and likely to involve trade-offs and to entail a balance of risks with respect to other beneficial objectives.

This section argues that the policy choice need not be as stark as that between complete neutrality and unrestrained laissez-faire. Discrimination varies in its motivations and methods, and different kinds of network discrimination differ in the balance of risks they entail for networks, applications providers, and consumers. Regulation that restricts some forms of discrimination but not others might protect against the worst harms of non-neutrality without eliminating some of the investment and efficiency benefits that differentiated access terms for applications providers might allow.

Reasons for a Network to Discriminate

Several things might motivate a firm to discriminate in the terms it offers to customers or providers of complements. At the broadest level, a firm might discriminate because it must, due to scarcity. In the network context, a firm might be driven to sell priority because congestion requires packets to be dropped at times. In such a case, discrimination could take the weak form of granting priority to some packets only when the capacity constraint binds. An analogy might be a traffic lane that is reserved for eligible vehicles only at rush hour, but is open to general use at other times. This kind of discrimination is what Edward Felten calls 'minimal discrimination' (Felten, 2006).

Alternatively, a firm might sell priority because it can manipulate traffic, in either beneficial or harmful ways. The analogy here is to a special traffic lane that is reserved all the time, even at times when there would be no congestion were that lane open to use by all. The result could be to raise the probability of delay on the non-reserved lanes thus attracting customers who won't risk moving slowly and want an assurance of moving quickly at all times. This kind of discrimination is what Felten (2006) calls 'non-minimal' or 'delay' discrimination. Such discretionary prioritization is not necessarily inefficient, depending on the relative costs of delay to those users that incur the delay and those that pay to avoid it. It does, however, raise the prospect of inefficiency and anticompetitive manipulation. Even at this general level there are different risks of harm to competition and innovation. Discrimination driven by necessity that occurs only when capacity constraints bind runs less of a risk of harm than discrimination that is driven by market power and the ability to manipulate traffic.

Discrimination could be further motivated by a number of more specific forces that work in tandem with those motivations discussed above. For example, a network could discriminate against an applications provider as part of an anticompetitive strategy to harm an application or provider that the network does not like, perhaps to shift market share of a complement to the network operator. Alternatively, the network could discriminate because it realizes that some providers are willing to pay more if pushed to do so, thus shifting surplus from the applications provider to the network operator.[5] Or, the network could price discriminate to recover operating expenses or investment from those applications providers who cause the network to incur higher costs, thus shifting costs from the network operator to the applications provider. Again, each of these motivations entails different risks to competition and innovation, with raising rivals' costs being the most harmful motivation and cost-recovery being the most consonant with competition and innovation.

Methods of Network Discrimination

Next, consider alternative methods of discrimination. An important distinction is between targeted and non-targeted price discrimination. In broad terms, a network operator could select particular users or uses that it thinks should pay more for access and adopt policies that induce those firms to do so. For example, a network operator could set a higher price for all streaming video providers on the ground that such providers use a lot of platform capacity. The network could give other uses priority over the packets of any streaming video provider that fails to buy the higher level of access. Alternatively, the network could simply sell priority to whomever wants it, leaving each streaming video provider (or provider of any kind of any application) to decide for itself whether it is willing to have its packets delayed when there is congestion. The competitive risks vary for different kinds of targeted and non-targeted pricing.

Targeted and non-targeted pricing can also take several forms. A network operator could differentiate in its access pricing among specific users, particular kinds of use, or amounts of usage. The first, the targeting of specific users, would set prices depending on the identity of the provider whose traffic is moving over the network. Such categorization could simply be a proxy for use or usage. For example, if a network were to charge Acme Video, a hypothetical video-on-demand provider, a higher price for network access, it might do so not because Acme is Acme or because Acme provides video-on-demand, but because video-on-demand uses a lot of bandwidth and Acme happens to be a well-known provider that is easy to identify. On the other hand, the network operator might charge Acme the higher price either because Acme happens to be a rival in a particular complementary market or because the network operator knows Acme has deep pockets and will pay a lot not to have its traffic consigned to a slow lane. As discussed above, these latter two motivations may have little to do with cost recovery and carry some risk of anticompetitive harm or other allocative inefficiency.

Discrimination targeted at particular uses is potentially more neutral, although it is not necessarily better than discrimination by user. If higher prices are charged only based on whether a particular use is one that competes with a business of the network, then it may be anticompetitive. For discrimination by use to be better than discrimination by user, the categories must be chosen because they are reasonable proxies for costs imposed on the network rather than proxies for competition.

The most neutral of the three options for price discrimination is usage-based pricing; that is charging for the amount of traffic an applications provider does or expects to put on the network. Some forms of usage-based pricing blur the line between targeted and non-targeted price discrimination. For example, if a network operator were to meter traffic and, as congestion developed, turn some capacity into a priority 'lane' that any user could select for a fee, then the pricing would be non-targeted. If, however, the network operator mandated increasing fees as an applications provider crossed progressively higher thresholds of traffic volume, then the price discrimination would be targeting such high-volume users for higher access prices.

The most risky forms of price discrimination for competition and innovation therefore appear to be those where the network operator can target particular uses or users for higher prices. The least risky forms of price discrimination are those that charge for priority on a usage basis, where each applications provider can decide whether to purchase priority. While it may still be possible for pricing mechanisms to be designed to coerce particular applications providers to pay more, a posted menu of prices for priority based on usage raises fewer concerns than targeted pricing based on use or user.

The costs and benefits of price discrimination by networks to applications providers thus vary with two sets of factors: the motivation for price discrimination and the method by which it is accomplished. Charging for priority in the presence of capacity constraints and congestion is more likely to yield benefits than is selling priority in the absence of capacity constraints. The first can represent an efficient response to scarcity; the second runs the greater risk of being an inefficient exercise of market power. Next, charging for priority based solely on usage rather than setting terms that target particular uses or users is more likely to avoid anticompetitive uses of price discrimination. A basic taxonomy of network price discrimination, compared by level of anticompetitive risk, is summarized in Table 7.1.

Table 7.1 A simple taxonomy of price discrimination by networks

	Targeted pricing	Non-targeted pricing
Priority with capacity constraint	Moderate anticompetitive risk (??)	Lowest anticompetitive risk (best option)
Priority without capacity constraint	Highest anticompetitive risk (worst option)	Moderate anticompetitive risk (??)

The schema presented above suggests that not all discrimination need be equally harmful, in turn implying that the costs and benefits of network neutrality regulation will differ depending upon which kind of conduct it prohibits. To the extent there can be benefits to price discrimination itself, prohibiting even the comparably benign forms of discrimination might forego benefits in return for the prevention of less substantial harms. The next section addresses the implications of this possibility for regulatory policy.

Conclusion: Policy Alternatives Going Forward

The different motivations and methods of price discrimination raise the possibility of policy solutions that focus selectively on the most harmful kinds of discrimination without prohibiting other non-neutral conduct that could yield net benefits. Policy could regulate actions most likely to foreclose competition either among applications providers or between applications providers and the underlying network. Such regulation would not need to preemptively prohibit networks from offering a non-targeted menu of access tiers available to all applications providers regardless of their identity or type of service. This more selective focus is consistent with two commentators' recommendation for regulation that precludes network owners from discriminating among data packets routed on their networks based on the identity of users or uses (Frischmann and van Schewick, 2007). It reduces the risks of targeted discrimination without banning discrimination altogether, thereby preserving some of the potential benefits of upstream price discrimination by network operators. In terms of the chart displayed above, regulation would rule out the two left-hand quadrants. One might also try to rule out the lower right-hand quadrant because the priority there is discretionary rather than driven by physical capacity constraints. Capacity constraints may be hard to observe and monitor, however, so regulation might as a practical matter do better to focus more on the method (that is, pricing structure) than on the motivation (that is, existence or not of real capacity constraint) for price discrimination.

There are different ways in which departures from non-targeted pricing, and the associated hazards for competition, could be regulated. One alternative is to have a basic rule that prohibits outright blocking of any (legal) applications provider, coupled with a regime of *ex post* enforcement against price discrimination that can be demonstrated to be anticompetitive. The approach here is primarily an antitrust-style approach. It has the virtue of not prohibiting much conduct in advance of proven anticompetitive effects, but would involve the courts and enforcement agency in assessing the detailed terms of each individual deal that came before them. The no-blocking rule would mean that such an *ex post* regime would differ from general US antitrust law, which generally does not prohibit outright refusals to deal.[6] The focus of *ex post* enforcement would more likely be on whether the terms of trade were anticompetitive or not.

An alternative solution would be to impose some *ex ante* restraints on those terms of trade through a network-neutrality rule that imposes a light form of common carriage on the network operator. A modest rule might still allow networks to offer different access terms to applications providers but would require that those terms be transparent and available to all such providers. One promising proposal combines such an approach with *ex post* enforcement against any anticompetitive uses of price discrimination by a network. (Atkinson and Weiser, 2006). The devil is likely to be in the details for either of these approaches, and detailed exploration is beyond the scope of this brief chapter. The important point is that intermediate solutions exist that can dampen the worst potential harms of network access discrimination, without altogether banning all price-mediated prioritization of network traffic. In light of the open questions that each side of the debate raises, such intermediate solutions warrant further development.

Finally, the most essential long-run strategy to reduce the risks of anticompetitive discrimination raised by the advocates of network neutrality is to focus on horizontal competition rather than vertical regulation. If the competitive progress of the US telecommunications market can be maintained through effective radio-spectrum policy, network interconnection rules, and vigilant antitrust (particularly merger) enforcement, then network neutrality concerns will diminish. Congress and the FCC should therefore not lose track of longer-term structural solutions for improving competition and innovation in the broadband market, and should ensure that any interim regulation they impose will not remain in force as market conditions no longer justify them.

ACKNOWLEDGMENTS

This essay is based on the author's presentations at the Silicon Flatirons Digital Broadband Migration Conference, 19–20 February 2007, University of Colorado, Boulder, and at the conference on Deregulation or Re-Regulation: Institutional and Other Approaches, Nice, France, June 18–19, 2007.

NOTES

1. 'Network neutrality', while subject to varying definitions, can be summed up as the principle that 'all like Internet content must be treated alike and move at the same speed over the network. The owners of the Internet's wires cannot discriminate' (Lessig and McChesney, 2006).
2. Farrell does not use this example in his 2006 paper but did so in discussions with the author.
3. See, for example, *Eastman Kodak Co. v. Image Technical Services, Inc.*, 504 US 451, 478 (1992) (alleging vertical foreclosure by Kodak as a means to leverage profits).

4. Reuters, 'Google and cable firms warn of risks from Web TV', *USA Today*, 7 February 2007 (quoting Vincent Dureau), available at http://www.usatoday.com/tech/news/2007-02-07-google-web-tv_x.htm
5. Such arguments are sometimes framed as a claim that some applications providers are 'free riding' on network infrastructure because they make big profits in which network owners do not share. The argument is weak. Applications providers are no more free riding on network platforms than vice versa. Consumers do not purchase Internet access from network operators just to cruise the network; they subscribe to reach on-line content and services. Just as network operators do not share in the profits of such applications providers, nor do they share their subscription revenues with the applications providers that consumers pay to reach. Moreover, it should be noted that many applications providers fail, and while network operators may not share in the profits of the successful ones, nor do they share the investment risk and losses from applications ventures that fail. What may look like free riding to the platforms may look like portfolio skimming from the other side.
6. *Verizon Communications Inc. v. Law Offices of Curtis V. Trinko, LLP*, 540 US 398 (2004).

REFERENCES

Atkinson, Robert D. and Philip J. Weiser (2006), 'A "third way" on network neutrality', Washington, DC: Information Technology and Innovation Foundation (May) available at http://www.itif.org/files/netneutrality.pdf

Benjamin, S. Minor, Douglas G. Lichtman, Howard A. Shelanski and Philip J. Weiser (2006), *Telecommunications Law and Policy* (2nd edn.), Durham, NC: Carolina Academic Press.

Deloitte and Touche (2007), *Telecommunications Predictions: TMT Trends 2007-8*, http://www.deloitte.com/dtt/research/0,1015,sid%3D2245&cid%3D141753,00.html

Farrell, Joseph (2006), 'Open access arguments: why confidence is misplaced', in Thomas M. Lenard and Randolph J. May (eds), *Net Neutrality or Net Neutering: Should Broadband Internet Services Be Regulated?*, Washington, DC: Progress & Freedom Foundation.

Farrell, Joseph and Philip Weiser (2004), 'Modularity, vertical integration and open access policies: towards a convergence of antitrust and regulation in the internet age', *Harvard Journal of Law and Technology*, **17** (1), 85–135.

Felten, Edward (2006), 'Nuts and bolts of network neutrality', Practising Law Institute, 24th Annual Institute on Telecommunications Policy & Regulation, *PLI/PAT*, **887** (317): 326.

Frischmann, Brett and Barbara van Schewick (2007), 'Network neutrality and the economics of an information superhighway: a reply to Professor Yoo', *Jurimetrics*, **47**, 383.

Lessig, Lawrence, (2006), 'Hearing on "Net Neutrality" before the Senate', Committee on Commerce, Science, and Transportation, 109th Congress 54-60 (2006) available at http://www.lessig.org/blog/archives/ lessig_testimony_2.pdf (prepared statement of Lawrence Lessig, *et al.*).

Lessig, Lawrence and Robert W. McChesney (2006), 'No tolls on the Internet', *Washington Post*, 8 June, at A. 23, available at http://www.washingtonpost.com/wpdyn/content/article/ 2006/06/07/AR2006060702108.html.

Owen, Bruce (2007), 'The network neutrality debate: 25 years after *AT&T v. United States* and 120 years after the Act to Regulate Commerce, 20 January 2007', http://www.freestatefoundation.org/images/The_Net_Neutrality_Debate-Bruce_Owen.pdf.

Rochet, Jean-Charles and Jean Tirole (2006), 'Two- sided markets: a progress report', *RAND Journal of Economics*, **35** (3), 645–67, available at http://idei.fr/doc/wp/2005/2sided_markets.pdf.

Speta, James B. (2000), 'The vertical dimension of cable open access', *University of Colorado Law Review*, **71**, 975.

Williamson, Oliver E. (1971) 'The vertical integration of production: market failure considerations', *The American Economic Law Review* **61** (2), 112–23.

Williamson, Oliver E. (1979) 'Assessing vertical market restrictions: antitrust ramifications of the transaction cost approach', *University of Pennsylvania Law Review*, **127**, 953–93.

Yoo, Christopher (2005), 'Beyond network neutrality', *Harvard Journal of Law and Technology* **19** (1), 20–5.

8. Deregulation, efficiency and environmental performance: evidence from the electric utility industry

Magali A. Delmas, Michael V. Russo, Maria J. Montes-Sancho and Yesim Tokat

INTRODUCTION

Academics writing from the perspectives of economics, strategic management, and organization theory have devoted decades of research to how economic regulation and deregulation has impacted the behavior of firms. One stream of this literature focuses on how deregulation changes the scope of permissible activities and the economic incentives for incumbents and new entrants (for example, Bonardi, 2004; Fuentelsaz *et al.*, 2002; Haveman, 1993; Haveman *et al.*, 2001; Miller and Chen, 1994; Smith and Grimm, 1987). The second set of studies focuses on the impact of deregulation on economic performance (Berger and Mester, 2003; Corsi *et al.*, 1991; Grabosky *et al.*, 1994; Hao *et al.*, 2001, 2003; Isik and Hassan, 2003; Kankana *et al.*, 2001; Sturm and Williams, 2004; Tortosa-Ausina, 2002). The third set of studies analyzes the impact of deregulation on other attributes such as the quality of service or safety (Alexander, 1992; Auriol, 1998; Barnett and Higgins, 1989; Rhoades *et al.*, 2005; Rose, 1992; Tsuchiya, 2005).

The focus of many of these studies on a single indicator of performance fails to achieve comparative evaluation along several dimensions. But because deregulation involves economic, social and environmental dimensions, and because it is possible that there are trade-offs between these different dimensions of deregulation, studies need to use multiple indicators.

Furthermore, work to date has not expanded our knowledge about the ability of deregulation to affect the provision of public goods. Previous work has shown how private benefits accrue to customers and firms via deregulation-induced differentiation. This research has largely been restricted to dimensions that are typical of competition: markets served, products offered, prices charged, and so on. What has not been explored is whether or not benefits of a more public nature – like a cleaner environment – might also emerge following deregulation.

In this chapter, we compare the impact of deregulation of the US electric utility sector on two main dimensions of performance: productive efficiency and environmental performance. Productive efficiency, defined as the ability to obtain maximum output with given inputs (Farell, 1957), is an important measure of performance in the electric utility sector because there are constraints on inputs such as capital. For example in the US, high capital costs as well as lengthy permitting processes have limited the development of new power plants. Furthermore higher productivity can translate into price declines and better ability to compete in deregulated environments. In addition, because the electricity sector gives rise to significant environmental concerns, the effect of deregulation on environmental performance is of considerable interest. We therefore combine an efficiency perspective with a perspective related to the provision of public good. This approach has important policy implications as it allows the evaluation of deregulation performance in a more comprehensive manner.

We suggest that the deregulation process drove electric utilities to reconfigure some of their organization and resources and impacted their efficiency and environment performance. We find evidence that as deregulation in this industry was introduced, firms reduced their efficiency. We also find that firms reconfigured their productive assets to increase their generation of 'green' power.

In the next section, we describe briefly the process of deregulation in the US electric utility sector. Next, we develop hypotheses related to the impact of deregulation on efficiency and the provision of public good. We then describe our data and our empirical results. A concluding discussion follows.

DEREGULATION IN THE ELECTRIC POWER INDUSTRY

Historically, the US electric power industry generally consisted of vertically integrated utilities holding exclusive rights to serve retail customers within defined geographic areas. Deregulation as initiated in a number of American states spanning the country reassessed the propriety of monopoly franchises and liberalized these markets.

The birth of modern deregulation can be placed in 1978, when the Public Utility Regulatory Policies Act forced utilities to purchase electricity from private generators (Russo, 2001). This law set in motion a process that brought into question the concept of the utility monopoly and begat further deregulation. The Energy Policy Act of 1992, for example, allowed utilities and non-utilities to own independent power producers, and required utilities to provide transmission service for wholesale power transactions. But while these regulations facilitated the entry of independent power producers into the market, they did not allow competition at the retail level. Retail deregulation finally began in 1996, when the Federal Electric Regulatory Commission (FERC) issued Order 888, requiring utilities to open their transmission lines to competitors. Starting in 1998, New Hampshire, California, Pennsylvania, New York and Rhode Island launched pilot programs allowing competition (Joskow, 2000). Today, almost half of the states in the US have been through a deregulation process (see Figure 8.1).

Retail deregulation may well have potential long-term benefits in terms of reducing costs, promoting choice, and facilitating the development of

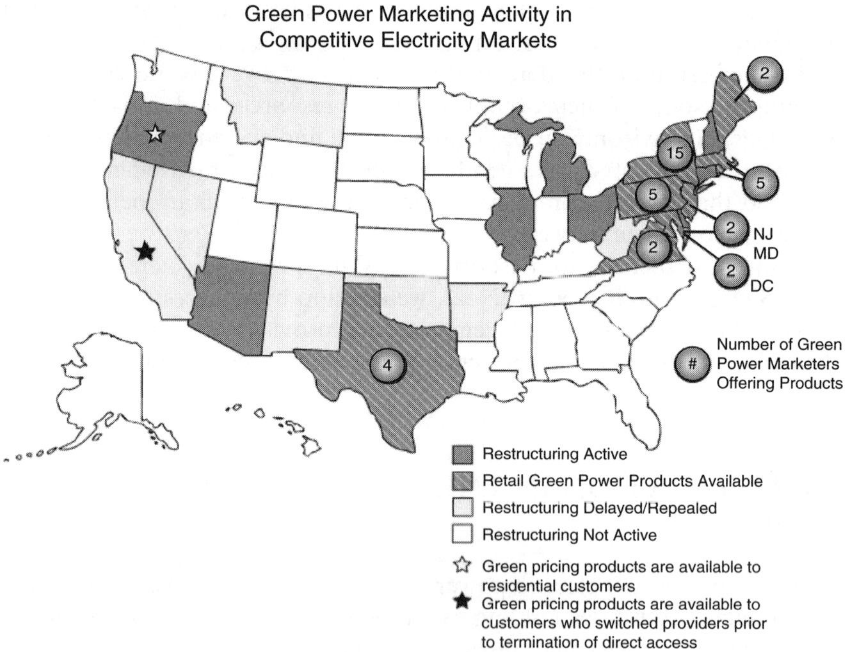

Source: Energy Information Administration and NREL (July 2004), http://www.eere.energy.gov/greenpower/resources/maps/images/marketing_map.gif, Accessed May 2005

Figure 8.1 Green power marketing activity in competitive electricity markets

renewable energy. We argue, however, that in the short term, the typical utility faces a very uncertain environment and significant transitory costs, which decrease its productive efficiency. First, a regulated environment is marked by several unique conditions, which are absent in a deregulated environment, creating a need by firms of time and resources to adapt to the new conditions. Second, when the process of deregulation is only partial, it may create a more complex environment for firms than would a completed deregulation process. On the more positive side, new competitive conditions stemming from deregulation can also facilitate differentiation strategies and the reconfiguration of existing resources, as seen for instance, with green power.

PARTIAL DEREGULATION AND ORGANIZATIONAL ADJUSTMENT

Deregulation is defined as the complete or partial elimination of regulation in a sector with the intent of improving economic performance (OECD, 1997: 11). While deregulation eliminates or reduces restrictions imposed on firm strategies (Gruca and Nath, 1994; Haveman *et al.*, 2001), it also brings some uncertainty regarding agency controls since the intermediary role of regulators between principal and agents diminishes (Kim and Prescott, 2005). Deregulation can bring lower programmability of managerial behavior and higher ambiguity in cause-effect relationships (Kim and Prescott, 2005). Consequently, organizations must adjust their governance structures.[1] Kole and Lehn in their study of airline deregulation observed several mechanisms that can be expected to change after deregulation, including ownership structure, executive compensation, and the composition and size of the board (Kole and Lehn, 1997).

Deregulation can take many forms, such as deregulation of market entry or exit; or deregulation of price control. It can be partial or complete, slow or fast. Kim and Prescott argued that both the form and speed of deregulation impact the speed of governance adaption (Kim and Prescott, 2005). Here, we take the argument further to argue that the scope of deregulation has an impact on firm efficiency. More precisely, we contend that partial deregulation has a negative impact on firm efficiency. Partial deregulation means that the process of deregulation is not completed. It might not be completed because regulators are still in the process of deregulating, or because regulators chose to open up to competition only part of the regulated sector. They might, for example, allow market entry but still regulate retail prices. We suggest below that both these partial forms of deregulation might have an impact on firm efficiency.

First, during the process of deregulation, firms will face the dual pressures of developing agency controls to address both deregulation and strategic choice (Kole and Lehn, 1997). This may entail some costly organizational redundancies. In the electric utility sector, Dyner and Larsen (2001) argue that the new conditions created by the deregulated environment require utilities to complement traditional planning models with new development strategies. As deregulation takes on its own momentum, electric utilities need to learn how to manage market risks due to wholesale price fluctuations. They can adopt, for example, new financial instruments such as weather derivatives, to hedge the risk of electricity price fluctuations due to weather conditions. Firms will in addition have to learn how to market their product, and will invest in marketing. Since sales may not increase in the short term (due to the time it takes to implement a system where customers can easily switch from one utility to another), firms may have to invest in new techniques without the benefits of increased market share. Furthermore, some firms that made capital investments during the regulatory period when the rate of return was regulated may not be able to recover these costs in a deregulated environment because the power rates necessary to pay for these plants may be too high to attract buyers in a competitive market. The 'stranded costs' produced by this phenomenon would be more difficult to recover with the advent of competition than under the previous regime of regulated monopoly (Baumol and Sidak, 1995).

Second, there are reasons to believe partial deregulation is associated with costs that can impede the economic benefits of deregulation (MacAvoy, 2007). As Joskow noted: 'electricity sector reforms have significant potential benefits but also carry the risk of significant potential costs if the reforms are implemented incompletely or incorrectly' (Joskow, 2008). Joskow holds that most of the deregulation experiences of the electric utility sector around the world have not followed the textbook liberalization model, and show the problems associated with incomplete or incorrect deregulation (Joskow, 2008). Competition is harder to foster in the electric utility sector than in most other sectors of the economy. Electricity generation is marked by high capital costs and constraints on building power plants that limit the number of players. These constraints on power plant construction limit competition as well as the flexibility of supply to respond to changes in demand (Borenstein and Bushnell, 2000). Furthermore, it is almost impossible to store electricity cost effectively after it is produced; so it has to be consumed immediately. Hence, entry into the market may be slow, bringing a risk of market power in the electricity trading market.

MacAvoy argues that only partial deregulation exists in the US, a mixture of oligopoly structure with direct price control with unsustainable costs associated with partial deregulation (MacAvoy, 2007). According to him 'restructuring has created extraordinary regulatory complexities, with an extremely high regulatory burden in pricing and service offerings' (MacAvoy, 2007: 36). In California, for instance, regulators protected consumers with retail price caps even though the wholesale power markets were not subject to price caps. The exercise of market power by suppliers resulted in high increases in the price of wholesale electricity (Joskow and Kahn, 2002).[2] Because retail prices were fixed, California utilities were limited in their ability to recover revenue and were forced into insolvency (Rossi, 2001–2002).

In conclusion, we expect that deregulation in the electric utility sector, because of its partial nature, will be associated with lower levels of productive efficiency. In the case of the electric utility sector, we expect an increase in the inputs necessary to generate and distribute electricity (wholesale prices, capital, labor, and distribution costs) without an associated increase in sales output.

Hypothesis 1: Deregulation in the US electric utility sector will be associated with lower levels of productive efficiency.

DEREGULATION AND ENVIRONMENTAL QUALITY

Prior to retail deregulation, electricity rates were set on a cost recovery and limited profit basis. Utilities recovered fuel costs through customer charges and were allowed to profit from investment in physical assets at a specific rate of return as set by each state public utility commission. Thus, electric utilities would comply with environmental regulation in certain knowledge of a return on investment to do so and having little incentive not to comply. How would these generators respond to deregulation?

One could argue that economic deregulation could lead to increased emissions because deregulation would force companies to bring their costs down by using cheaper but dirtier fossil fuels, like coal. We argue, however, that deregulation can lead to marketplace effects that reward firms for going beyond compliance to embrace cleaner generation. Consistent with other industries, as deregulation has unfolded in the electric generation industry, so has competitive heterogeneity. Some firms, such as Duke Power, stress low-cost power and focus on minimizing generation costs and, hence, prices to consumers. Differentiation also is possible, although it is difficult in this industry because there are few products as quintessentially commoditized as a kilowatt-hour.

One way to differentiate is by offering 'green power'. Differentiation of this kind, called 'environmental differentiation' consists of offering products that provide greater environmental benefits, or that impose smaller environmental costs, than similar products (Reinhardt, 1998). These products may be more costly than traditional products, but they allow a firm to command a price premium in the marketplace, or to capture additional market share. There is some evidence of willingness to pay for green power from renewable sources (Byrnes *et al.*, 1999). The amount of green power offered by electric utilities in the United States has increased rapidly in the last few years (Bird and Swezey, 2003; see Figure 8.1 for a geographic depiction of the availability of green products). These trends can make it attractive for electric utilities to use green power as a means of product differentiation (Lamarre, 1997). The number of customers participating in green pricing programs increased nearly fivefold between 1999 and 2003, to nearly 900 000 (Bird *et al.*, 2004; US Dept of Energy, 2004). Green power, however, has tended to cost more to generate, at least in the short term, than electricity from more conventional sources (Burtraw *et al.*, 2000). The consequence is a quintessential trade-off between the costs of differentiation and the potential profits from potential gains in market share.

Environmentally concerned consumers, who are generally better educated and enjoy higher incomes (Ottman, 1998), can be expected affect the electric utilities' performance and behavior – but only where deregulation has been set in motion. Where deregulation is underway and competition can be expected, we believe that environmental differentiation will take place. Customers who value green power will see the chance to purchase it and be more likely to do so.

Given that particular customer classes value green power, how can a company's resource mix (its portfolio of generating plants) change to respond to this segment of demand? Unlike textbook economic models, the resource-based view of heterogeneity of assets assumes that such a change is costly and requires new resources (Barney, 1991). This in turn necessitates new investments. Thus, if a firm follows this agenda, it will have to create or purchase the specific assets necessary to respond to the demands of customers. By reconfiguring its resources, it is in a better position to create value by successfully differentiating.

We therefore expect the firm to make investments to increase its renewable power generating assets in deregulated environment where its market shows sensitivity to environmental issues. In short, we hypothesize that differentiation strategies in the electric utility sector will appear along environmental lines under deregulation. We argue that under deregulation, firms will have an incentive to reconfigure resources in order to pursue environmental differentiation strategies. They will do this by increasing their investments in renewable energy generating resources. We therefore propose:

Hypothesis 2: Deregulation in the US electric utility sector will be associated with an increased provision of renewable energy.

EMPIRICAL EVIDENCE

To test our hypotheses on the effect of deregulation on productive efficiency and reduced emissions, we collected data for 128 investor-owned utilities from 1998 to 2001. Utilities in the sample represent 61 percent of US electricity production. To test Hypothesis 1, we ran a set of regressions using productive efficiency as a dependent variable (data from 1998–2001). To test Hypothesis 2, we ran a set of regressions using the change of percentages in the generation mix as a dependent variable (data from 1998–2000).[3]

Deregulation

Our deregulation variable takes the value of 1 if restructuring regulation has been enacted or a regulatory order has been issued, and 0 otherwise. Some firms are operating in several states and are therefore subject to different levels of deregulation as imposed by each of the states in which they are operating. In order to compensate for these differences, we weigh deregulation based on the percentage of electricity sold by each utility within the state.[4]

Because the process of deregulation is complex and varies across states, we also considered including additional variables account for the degree to which the firm is exposed to deregulation. Five stages can be included: (0) no activity; (1) commission or legislative investigation ongoing; (2) legislation orders pending; (3) comprehensive regulatory order issued; and (4) restructuring legislation enacted. We also considered including variables representing different types of deregulation such as whether: (a) divesture of generating assets is required; (b) there is price cap at the retail level; and (c) the recovery of stranded costs is allowed. Because we did not find significant differences in the results based on these various measures of deregulation and in order to simplify our presentation we decided not present these results in this chapter.[5]

A potential concern with our deregulation variable is that it may be statistically endogenous. It is possible that states choose to adopt deregulation in states where electric utilities have lower productive efficiency. A standard correction for this type of statistical endogeneity is instrumental variables. We therefore create an instrument variable to explain the deregulation choice of states. A valid instrument must be correlated with the explanatory variable but not with the error term in the explanatory equation. Our instrument variable is based on previous research that analyzes the factors that may influence the adoption of deregulation (Ando and Palmer, 1998). We use three variables to predict deregulation at the state level each year. The first is the retail price of electricity in the state,[6] the second represents the percentage of industrial sales within a state (source IEA), and the third represents the results at the 1996 presidential election at the state level.[7] This instrument variable is weighted by the percentage of electricity sold by each utility within the state.

Changes in Productive Efficiency

We estimate productivity using Data Envelopment Analysis (DEA) (Charnes *et al.*, 1978; Banker *et al.*, 1984). The DEA technique uses linear programming to convert multiple input and output measures into a single measure of relative productive efficiency for each observation. In this way, we construct a piecewise, linear industry best practice frontier using the observations in our sample over one year. If a utility in our sample is on this frontier, it is considered efficient and obtains a score of 1. If it is not on the frontier, its radial distance from the best practice frontier is a measure of the utility's inefficiency (efficiency scores are from 0 (less efficient) to 1 (most efficient).[8] Table 8.1 provides the descriptive statistics for the measures used to compute the measure of productive efficiency.

Because our efficiency score measures distance from industry best practice frontier for a specific year, it can be used only to compare firms within the same year but not across different years. Since efficiency scores have a truncated distribution, we use difference between maximum and minimum scores and interquartile range (difference between third and first quartiles) as measures of efficiency variation among competitors. Table 8.2 shows the median efficiency score, the difference between maximum and minimum efficiency scores, the interquartile range of efficiency scores for firms that serve exclusively regulated states (deregulation exposure = 0), exclusively deregulated states (deregulation exposure = 1), and both regulated and deregulated states (deregulation exposure between 0 and 1). Utilities serving deregulated states had greater efficiency variation in 1998 and 1999. However, this gap was closed in 2000 and 2001. We do not find any consistent pattern in the variation among competitors for regulated or deregulated environments. The results are therefore inconclusive based on these descriptive statistics.

Table 8.1 Descriptive statistics for measures used to compute efficiency

Variable	N	Mean	S.D.	Min	Max
Output factors					
Low-voltage sales (residential+commercial)	502	780 000	1 150 000	0	7 810 000
High-voltage sales (industrial)	502	222 000	263 000	0	1 530 000
Sales for resales	502	260 000	260 000	0	3 610 000
Inputs factors					
Labor cost	502	99 300	141 000	4	1 020 000
Plant value	502	3 910 000	5 000 000	9 737	34 100 000
Production expenses	502	702 000	901 000	5	7 150 000
Transmission expenses	502	19 700	26 800	25 200	205 000
Distribution expenses	502	42 000	59 100	0	411 000
Sales expenses	502	2 751	5 719	0	42 800
Administrative and general expenses	502	83 700	118 000	10	749 000
Electricity purchased from other sources	502	396 000	667 000	0	5 060 000

Note: The values are in thousand of dollars.

Table 8.2 Efficiency score variation among utilities in regulated and deregulated environments

Deregulation exposure[a]	Year	Median	Max-Min	Interquartile range	Number of utilities
0	1998	1.00	0.48	0.16	83
Between 0-1	1998	0.90	0.45	0.18	22
1	1998	0.81	0.76	0.33	74
0	1999	1.00	0.46	0.12	53
Between 0-1	1999	0.94	0.43	0.17	23
1	1999	0.95	0.77	0.30	104
0	2000	1.00	0.78	0.24	59
Between 0-1	2000	0.89	0.72	0.20	21
1	2000	0.92	0.67	0.28	92
0	2001	0.99	0.80	0.27	62
Between 0-1	2001	0.82	0.85	0.31	21
1	2001	0.95	0.75	0.29	93

Notes: Efficiency scores are between 0 and 1.

[a] The exposure of an electric utility to deregulation is based on the percentage of sales in a deregulated state.

Changes in Renewables

In the second set of models, our dependent variable represents the yearly changes in percentages of generation from renewable sources as a percentage of the electricity generated by a utility. Renewables included in the analyses are: wind, solar, geothermal, hydroelectric and biomass (plant-based fuel). This variable represents the difference between the percentages of renewable generation in two consecutive years.

We conducted some descriptive analyses, and compared the average percentage of electricity generated from renewables at the state level before and after retail deregulation. We use the *t*-test statistic with unequal variance to check whether there is a difference between deregulated and non-deregulated states. Table 8.3 provides the results of this analysis. This table shows that before 1998, there is no significant difference between states that did not implement deregulation from 1998 to 2000 and states that did implement deregulation from 1998 to 2000. After the beginning of the deregulation wave, deregulated states started to differ from non-deregulated states. There is a 10 percent significant difference between regulated and deregulated states for 'other renewables' (classified as wind, solar, geothermal, and biomass sources) in 1998, 1999 and 2000.

Control Variables

The control variables are divided into two main categories related to the nature of the competitive and political environment, and to the characteristics of utilities. Regarding the competitive and political environment, we include the following variables: (a) a variable representing the scores of the League of Conservation Voters (LCV) as a measure of the environmental sentiment of the people of a state;[9] (b) a variable representing the fragmentation of the market, created by dividing the total electricity sold in a state by the total number of utilities serving it, and then weighting the result by the specific states served; (c) a variable indicating whether the state has implemented Renewable Portfolio Standards requiring a percentage of generation in renewables; (d) a variable representing the level of toxic release emission in the state(s) where the utility is operating. Regarding the characteristics of utilities we include variables related to: (a) the size of the utility as measured by the total electricity sold in Mwh; (b) the average age of the plants belonging to the utility; (c) the proportion of residential sales; (d) the percentage of generation from coal; (e) research and development expenses as a percentage of total operational expenses; (f) whether or not the firm being analyzed is undergoing a merger with electric or gas utilities. The variables and their sources are described in Table 8.4.

Table 8.3 Average percentage of generation from renewables at the state level

		States that implemented deregulation during the period 1998–2000 (% of generation)	States that did not implement deregulation during the period 1998–2000 (% of generation)	T-test with unequal variance
Year 1997	Hydro	12.49	14.46	*0.28*
	Other renewables (wind, solar, geothermal, biomass sources)	0.48	0.10	*1.38*
Year 1998	Hydro	10.50	13.00	*0.41*
	Other renewables (wind, solar, geothermal, biomass sources)	3.72	1.23	*1.90**
Year 1999	Hydro	9.52	12.79	*0.53*
	Other renewables (wind, solar, geothermal, biomass sources)	3.68	1.35	*1.86**
Year 2000	Hydro	8.86	11.49	*0.47*
	Other renewables (wind, solar, geothermal, biomass sources)	3.47	1.40	*1.79**

Note: * 10% level of significance.

RESULTS

Table 8.5 presents the descriptive statistics and Table 8.6 the correlation table. Tables 8.7 and 8.8 present the regression results.

Deregulation and Productive Efficiency

Models A and B in Table 8.7 present the regression results with productive efficiency as a dependent variable. Because the distribution of the efficiency score is censored at 1, conventional regression methods cannot be used. We therefore use a Tobit regression model that assumes that the

Table 8.4 Description of the variables

Variables	Description	Source
Change in percentage of generation by renewables	The change in percentages of generation by renewables computes as a percentage of the electricity generated by a utility between two consecutive years. Percentage of renewables in the generation mix (wind, solar, geothermal, hydroelectric, and biomass).	EGRID
Productive efficiency	Annual Productive Efficiency Index (0–1) multiplied by 100. Obtained using Data Envelopment Analysis (DEA): *Output factors*: Low voltage (residential + commercial), industrial, sales for resale. *Input factors*: Labor cost, Plant value, production expenses, transmission Expenses, distribution expenses, sales expenses, administrative expenses, electricity purchased from other sources in dollars.	FERC, Form1
Deregulation	Dummy variable (0, 1). 1 if restructuring regulation has been enacted or a regulatory order has been issued and 0 otherwise. Weighted by percent of generation sold by utility in state (all subsequent variables are weighted by percent electricity sold for utilities that operate in multi states).	EIA
League of Conservation Voters (LCV)	Environmental scores of the members of the US House of Representatives and Senate (0–100) for each state. Weighted by total number of Congressional representatives in each state.	LCV
Fragmentation	Fragmentation of the market. Number of utilities that serve each state by the total quantity of electricity sold in the state. Weighted average of the fragmentations in the states served.	EIA
Renewables portfolio standard in place	State required a certain percentage of generation in renewables.	DSIRE
TRI / Area	Level of toxic release emissions in the states where the utility operates.	TRI
Residential proportion of customers	The proportion of residential sales divided by sales to ultimate consumers.	FERC, Form1

Table 8.4 (continued)

Variables	Description	Source
Percentage of generation from coal	Percentage of generation from coal (0–100).	EIA
Total electricity sales	Log total electricity sales in Mwh.	FERC, Form1
Research and Development	R&D expenses / total operational expenses.	FERC, Form1
Merger process	Merger with electric utility and merger with gas (diversification). Both variables are dummy variables.	EIA
Average plant age	Number of years since installation.	EIA

Table 8.5 Descriptive statistics

Variable	*N*	Mean	S.D.	Min	Max
Efficiency	502	92.07	11.32	52.90	100.00
Deregulation	502	0.47	0.48	0.00	1.00
IV	502	0.09	0.42	–0.90	0.93
Fragmentation	502	1.55	2.15	0.20	14.72
League of Conservation Voters (LCV) rating	502	43.03	23.16	0.00	96.67
Renewables portfolio standard	502	0.18	0.37	0.00	1.00
TRI /Area	502	1.17	1.04	0.00	4.02
Residential proportion of customers	502	0.29	0.13	0.00	0.53
Percentage of generation from coal	502	51.45	39.25	0.00	99.97
Total electricity sales (log scale)	502	16.12	1.60	8.76	19.02
Research and development (log scale)	502	0.69	0.76	0.00	4.22
Merger process with electric utility	502	0.24	0.43	0.00	1.00
Merger process with gas utility	502	0.11	0.32	0.00	1.00
Average plant age	502	31.95	12.91	2.00	91.00
Eastern interconnected system	502	0.79	0.40	0.00	1.00
Western interconnected system	502	0.13	0.34	0.00	1.00
Texas interconnected system	502	0.04	0.20	0.00	1.00

Note: These values are the descriptive statistics of 128 investor-owned utilities for the period 1998–2001.

Table 8.6 *Correlations of variables used in analysis*

	1	2	3	4	5	6	7	8	9	10	11	12	13	14	15	16	17
1. Efficiency	1.00																
2. Deregulation	−0.11*	1.00															
3. IV	−0.10*	0.34*	1.00														
4. Fragmentation	−0.14*	−0.29*	−0.08	1.00													
5. League of Conservation Voters (LCV) rating	0.05	0.35*	0.20*	−0.22*	1.00												
6. Renewables portfolio standard	−0.01	0.13*	0.05	−0.04	0.24*	1.00											
7. TRI /Area	0.12*	0.07	0.13*	−0.34*	0.02	−0.21*	1.00										
8. Residential proportion of customers	0.01	−0.02	−0.06	0.12*	−0.03	−0.09*	−0.17*	1.00									
9. Percentage of generation from coal	−0.04	−0.08	−0.01	−0.06	−0.22*	−0.14*	0.36*	−0.08	1.00								
10. Total electricity sales (log scale)	0.14*	−0.12*	−0.09*	−0.31*	−0.14*	−0.19*	0.24*	0.26*	0.37*	1.00							
11. Research and development (log scale)	0.02	0.01	0.04	−0.16*	0.11*	0.02	0.04	0.18*	0.07	0.32*	1.00						
12. Merger process with electric utility	−0.15*	0.18*	0.08	−0.12*	0.15*	0.19*	0.07	0.05	0.10*	0.16*	0.10*	1.00					

	1	2	3	4	5	6	7	8	9	10	11	12	13	14	15	16	17
13. Merger process with gas utility	0.10*	0.12*	0.11*	−0.13*	0.13*	0.02	0.00	0.08	−0.01	0.18*	0.14*	0.05	1.00				
14. Average plant age	0.04	−0.05	0.05	0.03	0.01	−0.02	0.08	−0.03	−0.14*	−0.11*	−0.09*	−0.13*	0.06	1.00			
15. Eastern interconnected system	−0.03	−0.03	0.06	−0.09*	0.17*	0.02	0.48*	−0.10*	0.18*	−0.02	0.12*	0.03	−0.11*	0.15*	1.00		
16. Western interconnected system	0.04	0.09*	−0.03	−0.09*	−0.09*	−0.13*	−0.39*	0.07	−0.07	0.10*	−0.11*	0.00	0.16*	−0.13*	−0.77*	1.00	
17. Texas interconnected system	0.00	0.06	0.16*	−0.09*	−0.11*	0.19*	−0.14*	−0.02	−0.04	0.06	−0.05	0.03	0.02	−0.10*	−0.40*	−0.08	1.00

Note: $N = 502$. *Correlations with an absolute value greater than 0.09 are significant the at 5% level.

Table 8.7 Tobit regression results – dependent variable: efficiency (1998–2001)

	(A)	(B)
Deregulation	−4.472	
	(2.179)*	
IV		−4.708
		(2.293)*
Fragmentation	−0.047	0.116
	(0.497)	(0.494)
League of Conservation Voters (LCV)	0.102	0.092
rating	(0.048)*	(0.046)*
Renewables portfolio standard	3.968	3.909
	(2.828)	(2.835)
TRI emissions / Area	5.491	5.586
	(1.298)**	(1.301)**
Residential proportion of customers	−10.854	−10.827
	(8.035)	(8.044)
Percentage of generation from coal	−0.121	−0.116
	(0.029)**	(0.029)**
Total electricity sales (log scale)	3.639	3.426
	(0.783)**	(0.775)**
Research and development (log scale)	−1.325	−1.136
	(1.350)	(1.349)
Merger process with electric utility	−9.164	−9.495
	(2.248)**	(2.237)**
Merger process with gas	2.168	2.341
	(3.224)	(3.213)
Average plant age	−0.074	−0.058
	(0.077)	(0.077)
Western interconnected system	7.148	6.833
	(3.400)*	(3.388)*
Texas interconnected system	1.386	2.683
	(5.054)	(5.156)
Year 1999	4.800	4.194
	(2.572)+	(2.548)
Year 2000	4.869	4.294
	(2.639)+	(2.615)
Year 2001	6.814	5.920
	(2.887)*	(2.858)*
Constant	44.303	47.190
	(12.003)**	(11.885)**
Observations	502	502

Notes: + Significant at 10%;* significant at 5%; ** significant at 1%.

distribution of the error term is normal and that explicitly takes limit and non-limit observations into account (Greene, 1997). In model A, we use only deregulation. In model B, we use the instrument variable (IV) instead of the deregulation variable.

Our regression analysis shows that the deregulation dummy is negative and significant. We find that the instrument for deregulation is also negative and has a statistically significant coefficient in Model B. These results confirm our first hypothesis, which states that deregulation had a negative effect on efficiency during the transitory period of 1998–2001.

Turning to the control variable, the variable fragmentation, representing the competitive environment is not significant. This could be explained by the fact that competition has not yet been really implemented. The variable that represents the size of utilities, measured in the amount of megawatt hours sold, is positive and significant. This shows that economies of scale play an important role in predicting efficiency and are consistent with previous findings (Roberts, 1986; Joskow, 2000; Kleit and Terrell, 2001). Our analysis shows that electric utilities which are in the process of merging with other utilities or independent power producers are less efficient than electric utilities that are not in the process of merging (the variable merger with electric utility is negative and significant). This may capture the cost that a firm faces during the merger process of two electricity-based entities. The coefficient, however, is not significant for the variable merger with gas utilities. The regression analysis reveals that the proportion of coal generation has a negative and significant impact on efficiency. This result is somewhat surprising. The variable average plant age is not significant. The geographical location of utilities also impacts efficiency. The dummy variable representing whether firms belong to the Western States is positive and significant.

Deregulation and Renewables

In Table 8.8, Model A and B, we performed a pooled ordinary least squares (OLS) estimation with robust-cluster variance estimator.[10] Model A presents the result with deregulation, Model B with the instrument variable.

Our pooled regression analysis shows that the variable representing deregulation is positive and significant. Thus Hypothesis 2, which ties deregulation to increases in renewables, is confirmed. The results presented in Model B with the instrument variable are nearly identical. Turning to control variables, the variable *LCV* representing the environmental concern of the state's populace is also positive and significant as can be expected. The variable representing the percentage of generation

Table 8.8 Pooled regression results – dependent variable: change in percentage of generation from renewables (1998–2000)

	(A)	(B)
Deregulation	4.034	
	(1.826)*	
IV		4.014
		(1.842)*
Fragmentation	0.262	0.131
	(0.425)	(0.425)
League of Conservation Voters	0.123	0.147
(LCV) rating	(0.046)**	(0.043)**
Renewables portfolio standard	0.209	–1.686
	(2.710)	(2.763)
TRI emissions / Area	−0.595	−1.099
	(0.956)	(0.987)
Residential proportion of customers	−2.789	−2.671
	(6.646)	(6.647)
Percentage of generation from coal	−0.068	−0.081
	(0.024)**	(0.023)**
Total electricity sales (log scale)	1.492	1.776
	(0.659)*	(0.648)**
Research and development (log scale)	−0.701	−1.156
	(1.093)	(1.093)
Merger process with electric utility	–4.953	–4.437
	(1.908)*	(1.906)*
Merger process with gas	–2.978	–3.978
	(3.521)	(3.516)
Average plant age	–0.158	–0.190
	(0.069)*	(0.070)**
Efficiency	−0.249	−0.256
	(0.085)**	(0.085)**
Western interconnected system	−2.979	−3.288
	(2.926)	(2.947)
Texas interconnected system	−3.111	−5.581
	(4.130)	(4.315)
Year 1999	2.878	2.139
	(1.562)+	(1.529)
Constant	12.197	11.420
	(11.538)	(11.518)
Observations	246	246
Adj. R-squared	0.21	0.21

Notes: Robust standard errors in parentheses. + Significant at 10%;* significant at 5%; ** significant at 1%.

from coal is negative and significant. Therefore, firms using a higher percentage of coal are less likely to invest in renewables than firms that rely more on nuclear power, natural gas or renewable resources. The variable representing the percentage of residential customers served is negative but not significant. The variable representing the size of utilities is positive and significant, as can be expected. The variable representing the age of the plants is also negative and significant, confirming that the older the generators of a given power company, the lower their investment in renewables. The variable representing whether a utility is merging with another electric utility is negative and significant, which may indicate that such utilities are reconfiguring their existing assets before investing in renewables. The variable representing the level of fragmentation of the market is positive but not significant. Likewise, the variables representing the dirtiness of the state and the existence of renewable portfolio standards are not significant.

CONCLUSION

The results are consistent with our hypotheses. They show that during the period studied, deregulation has a negative impact on efficiency and a positive impact on the provision of renewables, even after accounting for the effect of a dozen control variables. The negative effect of deregulation on efficiency provides an interesting result as it illustrates the costs of partial deregulation (without, however, proving that full regulation would produce greater efficiency). The findings related to the provision of renewables also support the notion that utilities began to shift their activities to reduce their environmental impacts following deregulation.

Our study has important policy implications. First, the effect of deregulation on performance is not unidirectional. There are positive and negative impacts. The main challenge is to compare such impacts, calculating the trade-off between productive efficiency and positive environmental outcomes that our study confirms arises as a consequence of deregulation. There is a need to develop evaluation tools that assign weights to these performance criteria. Confirming the importance of comparative evaluation along multiple performance dimensions, we find some interaction between production efficiency and environmental performance. Electric utilities that were less efficient were also those that invested less in renewables. This could support Rossi's argument that ensuring the provision of public goods, such as in the form of environmental protection, might not align with the objectives of deregulation, and may lead to dysfunctional power markets (1998–2001). Rossi explains how policies aiming threefold at: utility efficiency; the protection of consumers (say, through retail price caps); and at protecting the environment (through limitations, for example, on new power plant construction) could lead to a 'deregulation fiasco', which might be described as the consequences of accounting for the costs of externalities in a policy arena where protection of (the) public environmental and social good(s) is prioritized over private gain. Further research could tease out more precisely the relationship between efficiency and the provision of public good.

Second, partial deregulation might be associated with unanticipated effects. Policymakers may not have anticipated certain costs or effects on business strategies when they started the deregulation process. Further research should empirically assess the long-term impact of deregulation on efficiency and the provision of renewables in this sector when more data become available. This would allow the disentanglement of the costs associated with the process of deregulation, which are related to the adjustment period, from those associated with partial deregulation and that might be persistent.

While, our results show an increase in environmental product differentiation in electricity generation following deregulation, we still need to get a better understanding of electric utilities' rationale to undertake such strategies, especially in the context of partial deregulation. The impact of deregulation on the provision of renewable is significant, especially if we consider that deregulation in the US is associated with price caps that limit the benefits of increased prices from environmental differentiation strategies. Furthermore, the environmental differentiation literature argues that one way to create willingness to pay for public goods is to bundle them with private goods (Reinhardt, 1998). Many consumers, for example, are willing to pay a premium for non-toxic cleaners that directly benefit their health. Green electricity does not offer tangible private benefits because all kilowatt-hours are identical once they reach the consumer. Because, of these limitations, it is possible that electric utilities seek to address other stakeholders, in addition to consumers, when investing in renewables. These utilities might also attempt to anticipate potential environmental regulations or respond to pressures from environmental NGOs. Further research should provide a fuller understanding of the precise underlying mechanisms relating deregulation and utilities' environmental differentiation strategies.

Our study is not without limitations. As noted above, it measures costs related to the period of adjustment to deregulation. Research is needed to determine persistent costs. Although we focus on two main measures of performance, it would also be interesting to complement our study with additional performance variables. It would be interesting, for example, to test the effect of deregulation on the quality of service provided by electric utilities if an appropriate indicator for quality were identified. It would be instructive also to test the effect of electric utility deregulation on price in the electricity sector. Because the transmission and distribution components of prices remain regulated, however, this may not be feasible. Indeed, an analysis of prices could not, therefore, directly reflect utilities' strategies in response to deregulation. Additional research could study the impact of deregulation on emissions in the electric utility sector. Although changes in the generation portfolio have a direct impact on emissions, it is possible that deregulation has impacted abatement strategies that also impact emissions.

ACKNOWLEDGMENTS

This chapter builds on research performed by the authors and published in the *Strategic Management Journal* (Delmas and Tokat, 2005; Delmas *et al.*, 2007).

The authors acknowledge financial support from the following two sources: University of California Energy Institute grant #SB040035, 'Governance and emissions performance in the electric generation industry' and US Environmental Protection Agency Star Program grant #GR829687-01-0, 'Environmental Management Strategies and Corporate Performance: Identification and analysis of the motivators of regulated entities' environmental behavior and performance'.

NOTES

1. The potential for agency problems in firms in industries undergoing regulatory change is exacerbated as deregulation creates increased uncertainty regarding agency controls.
2. Prices in the summer of 2000 were nearly 500 percent higher than those during the same months in 1998 or 1999 (Joskow and Kahn, 2002).
3. Data for the second set of regressions was not available beyond 2000 for some of the variables.
4. This information was taken from the Energy Information Administration (EIA) publication *Sales and Electric Revenue*, Table A1: Electric Utilities Serving Ultimate Consumers in More Than One State.
5. Results are available upon request.
6. Since there could be some potential links between retail price, percentage of industrial sales, and efficiency, we also computed a variable instrument with only the presidential election variable. The sign and significance of this other variable instrument in our regressions is comparable to the one we present in this chapter. Results for this further variable are available upon request.
7. The regressions correctly predict the deregulation dummy for 70.6 percent to 78.4 percent of the cases, depending on the year of interest.

8. See Majumdar and Venkataraman (1998) and Coelli *et al.* (1998) for a good overview of the DEA technique.
9. The League of Conservation Voters (LCV), a US non-profit organization, produces a national environmental scorecard based on the environmental voting records of Congressional representatives. Each year, the LCV selects a set of environmental issues that constitute the 'environmental agenda' for the year (for example, tropical forest conservation, global climate change). The organization then creates and index based on the voting records of Congressional representatives for this environmental agenda.
10. We also ran a general least squares specification with random effects which generated nearly identical results.

REFERENCES

Alexander, D. L. (1992), 'Motor carrier deregulation and highway safety', *Southern Economic Journal*, **59** (1), 28–38.

Ando, Amy W. and Karen L. Palmer (1998), 'Getting on the map the political economy of state-level electricity restructuring', Discussion paper 98-19-REV, Washington, DC: Resources for the Future.

Auriol, E. (1998), 'Deregulation and quality', *International Journal of Industrial Organization*, **16**, 169–94.

Banker, R., A. Charnes and W. W. Cooper (1984), 'Some models for estimating technical and scale inefficiencies in data envelopment analysis', *Management Science*, **30** (9), 1078–92.

Barnett, A. and M. K. Higgins (1989), 'Airline safety: the last decade', *Management Science*, **35** (1), 1–21

Barney, J. (1991), 'Firm resources and sustained competitive advantage', *Journal of Management*, **17**, 99–120.

Baumol, W. J. and J. G. Sidak (1995), *Transmission Pricing and Stranded Costs in the Electric Power Industry*, Washington, DC: AEI Press.

Berger, A. N. and Mester, L. J. (2003), 'Explaining the dramatic changes in performance of US banks: Technological change, deregulation, and dynamic changes in competition', *Journal of Financial Intermediation*, **12**, 57–95.

Berry, D. M. and F. G. Mixon, Jr. (1999), 'Multiproduct outputs and scale economies in electric power production: some new estimates', *Review of Industrial Organization*, **15**, 65–76.

Bird, L. and B. Swezey (2003), *Green Power Marketing in the United States* (6th edn), Golden, CO: National Renewable Energy Laboratory.

Bird, L., B. Swezey and J. Aabakken (2004), *Utility Green Pricing Programs: Design, Implementation, and Consumer Response*, Golden, CO: National Renewable Energy Laboratory.

Bonardi, J. P. (2004), 'Global and political strategies in deregulated industries: the asymmetric behaviors of former monopolies', *Strategic Management Journal*, **25** (2), 101–20.

Borenstein, S. and B. J. Bushnell (2000), 'Electricity restructuring: deregulation or reregulation?', *Regulation*, **23** (2), 46–52.

Burtraw, D., K. Palmer and M. Heintzelman (2000), *Electric Restructuring: Consequences and Opportunities for the Environment*, Discussion Paper, Resources for the Future, Washington, DC.

Byrnes, B., C. Jones and S. Goodman (1999), 'Contingent valuation and real economic commitments: evidence from electric utility green pricing programmes', *Journal of Environmental Planning and Management*, **42** (2), 149–57.

Charnes, A., W. W. Cooper and E. Rhodes (1978), 'Measuring the efficiency of decision making units', *European Journal of Operational Research*, **2** (6), 429–44.

Coelli, T. D., S. P. Rao and G. E. Battese (1998), *An introduction to Efficiency and Productivity Analysis*, Boston, MA: Kluwer Academic Publisher.

Corsi, T. M., C. M. Grimm, K. G. Smith and R. D. Smith (1991), 'Deregulation, strategic change, and firm performance among LTL motor carriers', *Transportation Journal*, **31** (1), 4–14.

Delmas, M. and Y. Tokat (2005), 'Deregulation, efficiency and governance structures: the US electric utility sector', *Strategic Management Journal*, **26**, 441–60.

Delmas, M., M. Russo and M. Montes (2007), 'Deregulation and environmental differentiation in the electric utility industry', *Strategic Management Journal*, **28** (2), 189–209.

Dyner, I. and E. R. Larsen (2001), 'From planning to strategy in the electricity industry', *Energy Policy*, **29** (13), 1145–54.

Farrell, M. J. (1957), 'The measurement of productive efficiency', *Journal of the Royal Statistical Society*, Series A, **125** (3), 253–81.

Fuentelsaz, L., J. Gomez and Y. Polo (2002), 'Followers' entry timing: evidence from the Spanish banking sector after deregulation', *Strategic Management Journal*, **23** (3), 245–64.

Grabowski, R., N. Rangan and R. Rezvanian (1994), 'The effect of deregulation on the efficiency of US banking firms', *Journal of Economics and Business*, **46** (1), 39–54.

Greene, W. H. (1997), *Econometric Analysis*, Englewood Cliffs, NJ: Prentice-Hall.

Gruca, Thomas S. and Deepika Nath (1994), 'Regulatory change, constraints on adaptation and organizational failure: an empirical analysis of acute care hospitals', *Strategic Management Journal*, **15** (5), 345–63.

Hao, J., W. C. Hunter and W. K. Yang (2001), 'Deregulation and efficiency: the case of private Korean banks', *Journal of Economics and Business*, **53**, 237–54.

Haveman, H. A. (1993), 'Organizational size and change: Diversification in the savings and loan industry after deregulation', *Administrative Science Quarterly*, **38** (1), 20–51.

Haveman, H. A., M. V. Russo and A. D. Meyer (2001), 'Organizational environments in flux: the impact of regulatory punctuations on organizational domains, CEO succession, and performance', *Organization Science*, **12** (3), 253–73.

Isik, I. and M. K. Hassan (2003), 'Financial deregulation and total factor productivity change: an empirical study of the Turkish commercial banks', *Journal of Banking and Finance*, **27**, 1455–85.

Joskow, P. L. (1997), 'Restructuring, competition and regulatory reform in the US electricity sector', *Journal of Economic Perspectives*, **11** (3), 119–39.

Joskow, P. L. (1998), 'Electricity sectors in transition', *Energy Journal*, **19** (2), 25–52.

Joskow, P. L. (2000), 'Deregulation and Regulatory Reform in the US Electric Power Sector', Discussion Paper. MIT Prepared for the Brookings-AEI Conference on Deregulation in Network Industries, 9–10 December 1999.

Joskow, P. L. (2008), 'Lessons learned from electricity market liberalization', *Energy Journal*, Special issue, 9–12.

Joskow, P. L. and Edward Kahn (2002), 'A quantitative analysis of pricing behavior in California's wholesale electricity market during summer 2000', *Energy Journal*, **23** (4), 1–35.
Kankana, M., Subhash C. Ray and Stephen M. Miller (2001), 'Productivity growth in large US commercial banks: the initial post-deregulation experience', *Journal of Banking and Finance*, **25**, 913–39.
Kim, B. and J. E. Prescott (2005), 'Forms of deregulation, variations in speed of governance adaptation and performance', *Academy of Management Review*, **30** (2), 414–25.
Kleit, A. N. and D. Terrell (2001), 'Measuring potential efficiency gains from deregulation of electric generation: a Bayesian approach', *Review of Economics and Statistics*, **83** (3), 523–30.
Kole, Stacey R. and Kenneth Lehn (1997), 'Deregulation, the evolution of corporate governance structure, and survival', *American Economic Review Papers and Proceedings*, **87** (2), 421–5.
Lamarre, L. (1997), 'Utility customers go for the green', *EPRI Journal*, **22** (2), 6–15.
MacAvoy, P. W. (2007), *The Unsustainable Costs of Partial Deregulation*, New Haven, CT: Yale University Press.
Majumdar, S. K. and A. A. Marcus (2001), 'Rules versus discretion: the productivity consequences of flexible regulations', *Academy of Management Journal*, **44** (1), 170–9.
Majumdar, S. K. and S. Venkataraman (1998), 'Network effects and the adoption of new technology: evidence from the US telecommunications industry', *Strategic Management Journal*, **19** (11), 1045–62.
Miller, D. and M. J. Chen (1994), 'Sources and consequences of competitive inertia: A study of the US airline industry', *Administrative Science Quarterly*, **39** (1), 1–23.
OECD (1997), *Regulatory Reform: A Synthesis*, Paris: OECD.
Ottman, J. A. (1998), *Green Marketing: Opportunity for Innovation*, New York: NTC-McGraw-Hill.
Reinhardt, F. L. (1998), 'Environmental product differentiation: implications for corporate strategy', *California Management Review*, **40** (4), 43–73.
Rhoades, D. L., R. Reynolds, B. Waguespack and M. Willimans (2005), 'The effect of line maintenance activity on airline safety quality', *Journal of Air Transportation*, **10** (1), 58–71.
Roberts, M. J. (1986), 'Economies of density and size in the production and delivery of electric power', *Land Economics*, **62** (4), 378–87.
Rose, N. (1992), 'Fears of flying? Economic analysis of airline safety', *Journal of Economic Perspectives*, **6** (2), 75–94.
Rossi, J. (2001–2002), 'The electric deregulation fiasco: looking to regulatory federalism to promote a balance between markets and the provision of public goods', *Michigan Law Review*, **100**, 1768.
Russo, M. V. (2001), 'Institutions, exchange relations, and the emergence of new fields: Regulatory policies and independent power producing in America, 1978–1922', *Administrative Science Quarterly*, **46** (1), 57–86.
Russo, M. V. (2003), 'The emergence of sustainable industries: Building on natural capital', *Strategic Management Journal*, **24** (4), 317–31.
Russo, M. V. and P. A. Fouts (1997), 'A resource-based perspective on corpo-

rate environmental performance and profitability', *Academy of Management Journal*, **40** (3), 534–59.
Smith, G. K. and C. M. Grimm (1987), 'Environmental variation, strategic change and firm performance: a study of railroad deregulation', *Strategic Management Journal*, **8** (4), 363–76.
Sturm, J.-E. and B. Williams (2004), 'Foreign bank entry, deregulation and bank efficiency: lessons from the Australian experience', *Journal of Banking and Finance*, **28** (7), 1775–99.
Tedmon, C. S. and A. Roeder (1995), 'Technology as an enabling force in the global restructuring of the electric power industry – Technologies for the future global electrical power market: impact of deregulated markets', *The Electricity Journal*, **8** (10), 60–4.
Terry, J. C. and B. Yandle (1997), 'EPA'S toxic release inventory: stimulus and response', *Managerial and Decision Economics*, **18** (6), 433–11.
Thompson, H. G. Jr. (1997), 'Cost efficiency in power procurement and delivery service in the electric utility industry', *Land Economics*, **73** (3), 287–96.
Tortosa-Ausina, E. (2002), 'Exploring efficiency differences over time in the Spanish banking industry', *European Journal of Operational Research*, **139**, 643–64.
Tsuchiya, T. (2005), 'Utility deregulation and business ethics: More openness through gaming/simulation', *Simulation and Gaming*, **36** (1), 114–33
United States Department of Energy (2004), *Green Power Network: Buying Green Power*, http://www.eere.energy.gov/greenpower/buying/index.shtml, viewed 3 August 2004.
Wiser, R., M. Bolinger, E. Holt and B. Swezey (2001), *Forecasting the Growth of Green Power Markets in the United States*, Golden, CO: National Renewable Energy Laboratory.

9. The achievement of electricity competitive reforms: a governance structure problem?

Jean-Michel Glachant and Yannick Perez

INTRODUCTION

The competitive reform of electricity industries has recently experienced a surge of expansion worldwide, with over 200 new instances of sectorial deregulation between 1990 and 2008 (Glachant and Finon, 2003; World Bank, 2006; Sioshansi and Pfaffenberger, 2006; Glachant and Lévêque, 2009). Nonetheless, subsequent to the California electricity crisis (2000–2001), there has been a burgeoning dissatisfaction with regard to the limitations, and in some cases failures,[1] of these new ways of framing electricity industries (Kessides, 2004). We are witnessing a slowdown or, in some cases, a blocking of the reforms, as if the progression of competition policy in electricity industries had a cyclical component. This brings us to a deeper reflection on the nature of these processes. Previously, the unique characteristics of electricity industries appeared to set them apart from most other industries, deemed 'competitive'. These electricity industries notably feature: significant economies of scale or scope (extending to natural monopolies); far-reaching externalities (positive or negative) in production or consumption; and extensive vertical and horizontal integration (either under a single corporate umbrella or in the form of long-term *ad hoc* contracts). Within this very specific framework, the successful introduction of competitive mechanisms, substituting for administered regulation or internal corporate management hierarchies, along with the creation of open markets either up- or downstream of the formerly integrated networks, created disruptions and innovations in equal measure (Joskow and Schmalensee, 1983; Baumol and Sidak, 1994).

The purpose of this chapter is to propose tools for analyzing the process of the competitive transformation of electricity industries and to shed light on the difficulties encountered. The chapter is divided into three main sections. In the second section, we demonstrate that the launch of a competitive reform will not result in a credible industrial structure without the creation of a governance structure adapted to the new hybrid nature of the transactions. Thus, 'introduce competition only where this is readily feasible' is not a simple recipe for successful competitive reform. The borders between regulated and competitive activities are not always purely technical: they may originate from contingent decisions reflecting the 'modular' nature of electricity industries. In this context, the sequential character of decisions and interaction effects make it difficult, *ex ante*, to define a governance structure that is truly 'adept' at providing prolonged guidance to a lengthy process of competitive reform. Thus, the third section will examine how to build governance structures *ex ante* that will remain adaptable *ex post* to allow imperfections and failures in the competitive reforms to be corrected. Theoretically and empirically, the enormous requirement for successive 'coordinated adaptations' of the competitive reforms of electricity industries creates a recurring problem of multilateral bargaining to periodically redefine existing property rights and institutional arrangements. Thus, there exist 'veto players' in all institutional and industrial arrangements for piloting these competitive reforms. These veto players are agents with 'status quo' power over any subsequent changes to the reforms. The final section concludes.

HOW TO BUILD AN APPROPRIATE GOVERNANCE STRUCTURE?

The idea common to all economic analyses in favor of the competitive reforms is that the creation of markets within electricity industries presupposes preliminary acts of 'industrial surgery'. Prior to creating these markets or seeing them appear spontaneously, it is necessary to end the traditional vertical and horizontal integration of the incumbent monopolies. Thus, those links that will permanently be monopolistic must be separated from those with competitive potential with as much precision as possible. This cannot be accomplished overnight – it requires incremental experimentation with new procedures for segregating activities that have been integrated for decades. Thus, there is a transition period during which the new markets are weak and the incumbent monopolies remain quite strong. Consequently, a governance structure reflecting the competitive reform throughout this transition period is useful, even indispensable.

The duration of this transition period depends on many conditions, including the characteristics specific to each network industry. As early as 1985, O. Williamson foresaw that aviation[2] and roadways would be easier to reform along sustainable competitive lines than railways or electricity.

In fact, with regard to electricity reforms, which began in Great Britain in 1990, the architecture of competitive market design proved to be an unstable hodgepodge of market and non-market mechanisms (Newbery, 2000). In keeping with the principle of separating monopolistic activities from those that are potentially competitive,[3] the industry splintered into several distinct operational and transactional modules. However, the entire chain of all modules often required a more comprehensive and far-reaching governance structure than that provided by the initial competitive paradigm.[4] The electrical industry has proven itself unable to present a robust competitive market design that garners universal acceptance or, for that matter, that is capable of instantaneously and simultaneously coping with all the new problems having arisen as of the launch of the competitive process.

Thus, the building of competitive markets combines three dimensions:

1. the overall separation of potentially competitive activities from inherently monopolistic electricity activities (*unbundling*);
2. the segregation of all the operations and transactions of the industry into modules organized around various mechanisms for internal coordination (*modularity*); and
3. the implementation of the various modules in the chain to carry the competitive transactions (*sequentiallity*).

Unbundling and Boundaries

As emphasized by S. Littlechild (2006), the first British regulator and the inventor of the notion of the Price Cap as applied to telecoms, the principle of 'Competition where possible' is central to the reform of electricity industries and their transformation into vehicles for competitive markets. This type of division is expected to free competitive forces on one side of the new boundary and concentrate the regulatory activity in the electricity monopolies on the other side. However, the principle of unbundling assumes that there exists a 'natural' demarcation, clear and robust – by nature almost technical or at least technico-economic – between these two universes: the market for services and infrastructure monopolies. Sometimes this is true for roads and highways,[5] and it remains the case, though a little less unambiguously, in aviation[6] and telecom.[7] However, we generally consider that competitors to incumbent telecom operators have no difficulty duplicating their infrastructures and creating their own private grid, at least outside the 'copper' local loop.[8] The question is quite prickly in the case of electricity, because the service rendered is not storable[9] and there are no queues. Furthermore, the entire supply–demand equilibrium is a global phenomenon, common to the entire industry and extending beyond the ownership boundaries of dozens of different generators or sellers of electricity.[10]

In practice, it is not difficult to see why this issue of global equilibrium in electricity must be ensured by a third party with decision authority over all immediate and very short-term time horizons.[11] Thus, the transmission grid must directly administer very short-term imbalances between the consumption and generation of power (balancing management) and between the flows of current and line capacity (congestion management). We here observe that activities specific to the network monopoly are very strongly enmeshed with, and weakly separable from, all activities that are characteristic of the competitive links.

The very precise allocation of tasks and decision-making rights between competitive and monopolistic modules, as well as the detailed design of the interface mechanisms connecting these two module types, here continue to be central and decisive questions about the real nature of the competitive reforms: 'Where are the boundaries and who sets them?'.

Modular Boundaries Between Market and Non-market Activities

Boundaries between monopolistic activities and potentially competitive activities, like the boundaries between the firms themselves, between their respective tasks, and between their real or potential transactions and the corresponding markets, are thus not given once and for all prior to the launch of the competitive reform. Quite the opposite, these boundaries are primarily defined over the course of the long process of creating the reform. They are the result of segregating the industry into new operational modules. The competitive reform is thus a giant 'modularization' of the electricity industry, a giant industrial and transactional 'Lego set'.

According to Baldwin and Clark (2000): 'Modularity is a particular design structure, in which parameters and tasks are interdependent within modules and independent across them.' This technical definition of modularity is well suited to the new modularity of electricity industries. It nicely complements the work of Williamson and Joskow on '*technological separability*' that distinguishes between the technological constraints within non-separable clusters of tasks and a strong institutional constraint on the design of interfaces connecting task clusters that are technologically separable.[12] To Baldwin and Clark: 'The ideal of perfect modularity is full "plug and play" flexibility all along the value chain of the industry.' They then add, 'but in a complex design, there are often many levels of visible and hidden information'. Perfect modularity is thus not universal.[13] In the competitive reforms of electricity industries, the ideal of 'perfect modularity', the hermetic separation of task clusters having different natures, is far from universally implemented. The boundaries between modules split up by the competitive reforms remain porous to many leaks. Some modules retain interdependence between each other in their operational functioning, even if, of course, the interdependencies are stronger and more pervasive within the modules than between them. Thus, it is useful to bear in mind, as a sort of benchmark, how perfect modularity operating within a perfectly designed competitive reorganization of the chain of tasks within an electricity industry would look.

Perfect modularity would define 'independent task blocks', build 'clean impermeable interfaces', and separate 'hidden and visible information'. Three invaluable characteristics would result for the process of performing these tasks. First, perfect modularity would increase the potential for managing complex chains of operations. Second, perfect modularity would allow the various modules of a complex chain to operate in parallel with a certain degree of autonomy. Third, and finally, perfect modularity would make it easier to react to uncertainty, provided the uncertainty was confined to a single module.

We here recognize the motivation for separating the professions and tasks in the initial implementations of competitive reforms. However, we must acknowledge that market building often fails to reach that degree of perfect modularity in the competitive reforms. Conversely, actual modularity analysis of the competitive reforms of electricity industries frequently reveals nothing other than a flawed chain of imperfect modules and faulty interfaces. Porous borders and nonexclusive interfaces have been inserted between the monopolistic and competitive module clusters, as well as between the specific modules. At the same time, incomplete rules of operation have been imposed within the various modules. It follows that all of this modularity remains flawed, notably with numerous operational 'leaks' across modules. Thus, many direct dependencies persist in the operational functioning of a number of these modules, which are designated as externalities or incompleteness.

Three aspects of 'weak' modularity in electricity industries

The first aspect of the issue of weak modularity is the coexistence of fundamentally divergent alternatives in terms of how to create competitive wholesale markets. Chao and Peck (1996), Oren (1997) and Wilson (2002) have demonstrated that there are three different solutions to building and operating the structure of these electricity markets: compulsory organized multilateral markets (mandatory pools), voluntary organized multilateral markets (voluntary exchanges) or, last, markets that are exclusively bilateral ('OTC' markets).

The second aspect of weak modularity is the diversity of module

Table 9.1 An example of sub-modularity within the module 'monopoly transmission network'

English Transport System Operator (TSO)	American Independent System Operator (ISO)
Owns the assets and is a 'for profit' company	Does not own the assets and is a 'not for profit' entity
Plans and builds new lines	Does not plan or build new lines
Manages internal congestion with physical redispatching	Manages internal congestion with nodal pricing
Manages connections with other TSOs as boundary	Manages connections with other ISOs as new nodes
Prices access with regional 'postage stamp'	Prices access by calculating prices at each node
Charges new generator connection with shallow costs	Charges new generator connection with deep costs

Source: Rious *et al.* (2008).

organizations for monopolistic transmission activities. The pivotal architecture of electrical networks is the transmission grid, since this transports the energy generated by power plants over long distances and on a huge scale.[14] Comparing the typical organization of transmission in the competitive reforms of the United States (the Independent System Operator, or ISO) with its European analog (the Transmission System Operator, or TSO) immediately reveals the diversity of the Transmission modules put into place,[15] as Table 9.1 summarizes.

In England, the transmitter is a private firm that is listed on the stock exchange, owns its own transmission facilities, and plans and finances investments in the grid. It manages congestions with the physical method known as 'redispatching'. However, it does not transmit a direct price signal to the users of the grid who are liable to be at the source of this congestion. The cost of congestion is socialized across all grid users during periods of congestion.[16] A direct consequence of this method for managing congestion is the existence of a real border, both physical and price-based, that completely surrounds the zone administered by the transmitter. Furthermore, the transmitter charges the costs of transmission[17] in fees that are socialized[18] across a regional grid, with a dozen or more 'postage stamp prices' for generators and a similar number of other 'postage stamp prices' for consumers. Finally, the cost of new connections to the grid are also largely socialized, since the hook-up fee does not account for the cost of adapting the network upstream from the point of connection.[19]

In contrast, in the United States, most typically in the Pennsylvania, New Jersey, Maryland control zone (PJM), the transmitter is comprised of a club of electricity professionals. Thus, it functions as a cooperative, making no profits and distributing no dividends. This club does not own the transmission grid facilities, which remain the property of the incumbent operators. It is, however, their only operator. It is the System Operator (SO), and is distinct from the proprietor of the network, the Transmission Owner (TO). From the point of view of ownership of the network equipment, this System Operator is designed to be independent of the incumbents, making it an 'Independent SO', or ISO. This ISO neither plans nor finances investments on its grid. The users, generators and distributors, take the initiative of requesting modifications or extensions to the transmission grid, and then pay for them fully. This ISO manages congestion with an economic method known as 'nodal pricing', transmitting a direct and individualized price signal to each grid user liable to have an impact on congestion (by creating, exacerbating, or easing it). The cost of congestion is thus only borne by those who directly contribute to it, and only for as long as they do so, being calculated in very short time frames that are recomputed every ten minutes. Each of the thousands of nodes in the grid is handled independently, with a vast technical and economic program of costing congestion for each entry and exit node on the transmission system. That is why this pricing is called '*nodal*'. A direct consequence of this method for managing congestion is that no real border exists, either physical or price-based, around the zone administered by the transmitter. Its zone is nothing other than a collection of computation nodes. To the extent that adjacent transmitters practice the same nodal method of pricing and collaborate in its application, there are no real borders between neighboring transmission zones. This ISO does not charge users the other costs associated with transmission (notably the cost of infrastructures) – they are recovered through fees that are socialized across a local grid and administered by state Public Utilities Commissions, or PUCs. Finally, the costs of new connections to the transmission grid are not socialized. The hook-up fee imposes all the costs created by this connection, in terms of upstream development, on the new user (called 'Deep Cost' pricing).[20]

In conclusion, Rious *et al.* (2008) apply a systematic modular approach to the management of energy flows in electricity networks. Their paper subsumes the TSO's tasks into three modules comprising the core of transmission design: (a) short-term management of network externalities; (b) long-term management of network investment; and (c) coordinating cross-border trade with neighboring Transmission System Operators. They show that, for each of these three modules, three fundamentally different management modes are possible, yielding 27 options for organizing the basic functions of the TSO.[21]

A third, and final, aspect of the 'weak' nature of the organization of the modules in the competitive reforms of the electrical industry is found in the allocation of responsibilities and decision-making power within the regulatory functions (Green *et al.*, 2008; World Bank, 2006; Castalia Strategic Advisor, 2005; EDRD, 2004; Ocana, 2002; IEA, 2001).

Nearly every conceivable variant on the definition and allocation of regulatory functions has already been tried somewhere: Regulatory functions are shared between federal and local regulators (United States, Belgium); between the federal executive power, the association of local regulators, and representatives from local governments in a formula called 'Comitology' (European Union); between stakeholders who administer a mandatory pool and a strong regulator (England–Wales); between transmitters who own a voluntary exchange, stakeholders, and ministers from local governments (the Nord Pool of the four Scandinavian countries); between stakeholders[22] administering the ISO and a strong local regulator (Texas); between a weak or semi-weak regulator and the minister of energy (Spain and France); between a weak regulator and the transmitter (Sweden); self-regulation[23] by a national committee of stakeholders overseen by the competition watchdog and the courts (Germany).

This veritable patchwork of formulas has been characterized as 'regulatory modularization' by A. Midttun (2005). It is noteworthy that not one of these structures has proven able to provide adequate *ex ante* guarantees to simultaneously manage the classical risks of '*regulatory capture*'[24] and governmental opportunism (Holburn and Spiller, 2002), while effectively countering the exercise of market power by the dominant operators (Smeers, 2004).

In conclusion, we want to stress the fact that understanding all the dimensions and impacts of weak modularity in the electricity industry remains analytically problematic. This challenge is rendered more complex by the issue of choosing an appropriate sequence for key decisions. In fact, due to weak modularity, when a new module[25] appears, all modules that are already in place may need to react and adapt to the new situation. Thus, the order in which new modules appear, or are reconfigured and adapted, is of great importance.

Sequencing of Imperfect Modularity

Newbery (2000) stresses that the sequencing of the reform is critical. The sequencing of a reform is the way the reform agenda is decomposed into different steps to be undertaken at successive periods. This sequencing structures the behavior of stakeholders by the way it creates new interests and new rights over the various modules of activity and over the transactions that come into play between these modules. One of the most important consequences of this sequential modularity is that certain models of network industry reform, while working well under some circumstances and in some areas, are not easily transferable elsewhere.

Newbery (2002) emphasizes the importance of a robust reform strategy, which must include all of: the privatization process, the type of unbundling between monopolistic and competitive activities, the initial market design, the powers and functions of the sectorial regulator, and so on. According to Newbery:

> The logical sequence of events, some of which can happen simultaneously, is to first create the legislative and regulatory framework and institutions, and to restructure the state-owned Electricity Industry. Unbundling and corporatizing the generation companies, national grid, and distribution companies while they are still in public ownership can precede the legislation and setting up the regulatory agencies, but privatization cannot. Unbundling generation from transmission will require a restructuring of any contractual relationships between the two.

The interdependence of modules and changes at each step of a reform can be examined trough the analysis of institutional change developed by M. Aoki (2001). To Aoki, the explicit modification of some formal rules does not tell the entire story of institutional change. On the one hand, the influence of an institution on economic agents fundamentally relies on their 'shared beliefs'. It can only fully exercise its influence if agents buy into this influence. On the other hand, any particular institution is always party to a variety of interactions with related and complementary institutions.[26]

Any creation of new institutions occurs in a world that is already 'saturated' – populated with other institutions. Consequently, the compatibility and complementarity between the new institution and other, pre-existing institutions are fundamental objective characteristics that define the new institution.[27] Aoki (2001) specifically notes that the overlap of existing institutions affects the evolution and combination of their activities. The prior existence of 'given' institutions may facilitate, hamper or sidetrack the desired evolution and the actual consequences of the creation of new institutions.[28] This is why, in theory as much as in fact, the *ex ante* choice of a good competitive reform strategy for entire blocks of industry is more difficult than some optimists had prematurely announced. In fact what is called 'reform' is a set of interactions between the 'new' and the 'given' institutions. According to Rufin (2003):

> In these industries, the institutional framework plays such a crucial role that it provides an excellent setting for analyzing processes of institutional change.

INSTITUTIONAL REMEDY TO GOVERNANCE FAILURE?

Building a complete industrial and commercial chain of sufficiently competitive modules thus involves long stretches of time, always exceeding one decade. This is why the governance structure of the reform is as important as the initial design of the very first competitive modules (Saleth and Dinar, 2004; World Bank, 1995; Levy and Spiller, 1994 and 1996). Why, therefore, at the launch of these reforms, are new governance structures not defined that are more suited to their specific nature? Would they be more robust and reactive, and thus more conducive to prolonged adaptation of the industry and its chain of modules until it finally reached the stage of sustainable competitiveness?

This new way of thinking focuses on *ex post* guaranteeing the final goal of perfect modularity of network industries by the *ex ante* initial design of a perfect governance structure for the reforms. Unfortunately, this notion of perfect governance is plagued by numerous difficulties, not unlike the previous notion of perfect modularity.

Feasibility of Successive Governance Adaptations

Building a governance structure for reforms that is perfect in the long term essentially consists of defining and allocating the rights to future implementations of the reforms. This is how the governance structure is able, when the need arises, to define and allocate new rights. These new rights, which would obtain in the future and could be useful for steering the course of the reforms after the start-up period, might combine with pre-existing rights – already defined and allocated and protected by assorted institutional guarantees.

The institutional hurdle to implementing the new orientation encountered here is that all rights having existed for a long period are anchored in strong guarantees entrenched in their institutional environments. Thus, the notion of creating a perfect governance structure *ex ante* to steer the reforms over a long time horizon seems contradictory. Over the course of the long implementation of these reforms, the various stakeholders, whether private or public, and the new governance structure, can only sequentially uncover the exact character and relevance of the existing rights. Therefore, they can only intervene sequentially in the redefinition and reallocation of these rights in order to adapt the various modules of the industry and the markets[29] (Prosser, 2005). This is because, in North's (1990, 2005) view, we only discover the long-term properties of existing rights and institutional changes by a process of trial and error, and sometimes by blind chance.

For how could we design *ex ante* a potentially perfect structure that only allows modification of rights that significantly block adaptations that are truly required?

In Williamson's view, private economic agents are unable to create, *ex ante*, a perfect contract to frame their future relationship. And, similarly, according to North, public and private institutional agents are unable to build, *ex ante*, a perfect structure for reconfiguring industry modules and redefining the corresponding rights.

In real institutional change, the long-term governance structure of reforms can only act over the existing endowment of decision-making power and veto power (Glachant and Finon, 2000). This endowment is structured by the combination of rights entrenched in the arrangement of the various modules of the reform. Thus, the long-term governance structure of these reforms cannot be immutable throughout the sequential rearrangement of the chain of modules. Any after-the-fact reconfiguration that was not anticipated *ex ante* may yield unexpected configurations of decision-making and veto rights *ex post*. Such undesirable developments can then successfully anchor themselves in strong guarantees that are vigorously protected by the most fundamental elements of the institutional environment (political, executive and legal).

In practice, those who are piloting the competitive reforms cannot do all they would like in the long term to significantly reshuffle rights that have already been acquired, even when major adaptations that were not foreseen at the launch of the competitive reforms become imperative.[30] Institutional environments are inherently rigid, or semi-rigid, provisions that only rarely allow for a forcible redefinition of existing rights.

A Northian Analytical Framework

The normative content of the competitive reforms thus acts as a set of rules and rights that constrain the behavior of economic agents and allow conflicts arising from such constraints to be addressed. Levy and Spiller (1994) emphasize that the real content of these reforms depends on the functioning of other institutional provisions, such as the legislative, legal and executive framework specific to each country. Consequently, the institutional endowment of each country constitutes a unique context of guarantees and constraints that must be accounted for in the definition of the nature of the rules and governance structures of the reforms. Different solutions for the reform may be required in institutional situations that are durably divergent.[31]

There are few comprehensive comparative studies of transformations from old regulatory systems into new, pro-competitive regulatory systems.

Guasch and Spiller (1999) make a contribution that is central to electricity industries by analyzing failures in the legal system and their irrevocability. They present a model that analytically distinguishes between the notions of 'stability' of the new competitive rules and of 'consistency' with the nature of the institutional environment that prevailed at the launch of the reforms. In their analysis, the most stable institutional environments are characterized by the presence of numerous veto players, as they embody the principle of checks and balances. Veto players are actors, either individuals or groups, whose agreement is explicitly required for decision making in some fields of public policy. These veto powers are bolstered by the existence of administrative procedures that are quite strict and precisely define the procedures for modifying existing rules and rights, while providing for the right to appeal these changes to entirely independent courts of law.[32] The United States typifies that kind of institutional environment.[33]

Analytically, we then move on to environments classified as second best in terms of the stability of the competitive commitments. One of these second-best arrangements is found in another type of institutional environment, centralization. This is the case in Great Britain. Here, a strong protection of the rights of economic agents is ensured by a special regime of 'professional licenses' safeguarded by private law and regular courts of law. Of course, this second best cannot provide stability guarantees equal to those in the United States, as it lacks both the credibility of institutional checks and balances and the stability of the US administrative procedures.

Here, it is advocated that the introduction of a supreme, 'asymmetric' decision maker, endowed with the power to unilaterally modify existing rights and future rules, does not provide any greater long-term guarantee of the longevity of the reform's pro-competitive orientation. In this context, this analysis assumes rapid, non-modular and non-sequential initial construction of robust new competitive systems in electricity industries. Consequently, it can impute a high value to the stability of the initial arrangements. Essentially, it assumes that the initial arrangements are close enough to an *ex ante* perfect configuration that only minor adaptations will be required *ex post*.

However, were the initial configuration is less optimal, we would have needed to postulate the long-run necessity of making major *ex post* adaptations to the reforms, with a poor *ex ante* predictability of their future modalities. Thus, an institutional structure guaranteeing a great deal of stability *ex ante* could ultimately constitute a major obstacle to necessary adaptations to the unexpected, *ex post*.

A Framework to Adapting the Reforms

As showed by Macintyre (2003), Tsebellis (2002) and Perez (2002), we can opt for a more general analytical framework of the making of adaptive governance. This framework links adaptive governance of the reforms to the concentration of decision-making power. It sees the adaptation of governance as a process of institutional change among decision makers holding decision rights. The game they play is a type of 'veto play'. One key characteristic of that game lies in the number of such veto players. First the number of veto players constrains the possible discretionary behavior of each individual veto player. As the literature has amply demonstrated, an *ex ante* irrevocable commitment is necessary to guarantee the stability, and thus the credibility, of the competitive nature of the reforms (Levy and Spiller, 1994, 1996; Weingast, 1995). It is why constraining further discretionary behavior by spreading the decision rights just after the start of the reform contributes to building that credibility. However there is a second consequence. It leads to the paralysis of structures that are too decentralized with multiple veto players. This arises when accounting for all the *ex post* adaptation needs of the reforms that only appear over a lengthy period of time (Haggart, 2000; Macintyre, 2003).

According to Weingast (1995): 'government strong enough to protect property rights is also strong enough to confiscate the wealth of citizens'. Some institutional systems are sufficiently strong *ex ante* to modify the many rules impeding the establishment of new competitive regimes in electricity industries. Consequently, such systems should be sufficiently powerful to create robust new governance structures capable of administering a drawn out transition to the new competitive order. However, governments with that much power have little political incentive to curtail the exercise of their own power and enforce a neutral long-term policy of establishing a competitive regime in network industries. Such 'strong' governments typically have other political agendas, characterized by another structure of interests in their political systems.

At the other extremity of the institutional spectrum, 'Fragmentation and dispersal of power stemming from the interplay of constitutional structure and party system leads to policy delay, gridlock, and immobilism' (Tsebelis, 1995, 2002). 'Weak', or 'relatively weak', governments are clearly unable to vigorously undertake grandiose reform projects on a vast scale. They prove virtually powerless to correct their course if it later proves that errors were made at inception or if major adaptations to the unforeseen are required *ex post*. This is because veto players can easily block any *ex post* developments to the reforms.[34] Consequently, to understand how the competitive reforms work out over a long period of time, it is necessary to combine the usual notion of an *ex ante* 'institutional endowment', which provides the static environmental context for the reforms, with an analytical grid of veto players, as in Tsebelis (2002), to obtain *ex post* illumination of the evolution and adaptation. A comparative analysis of government policy and the political economy of reforming network industries must thus make room for an approach in terms of veto points and veto players. A number of domains of government policy can be studied in this framework, and the relevant literature is accumulating rapidly. One of the approaches can be found in Georges Tsebelis (1995, 2002) who, rather than explain a particular policy, seeks to provide a unified framework for a variety of problems and institutional systems.

Application of this analysis to typical institutional environments is the subject of a growing literature. For example, Holburn and Bergh (2004) demonstrate how to influence the decisions made by focusing lobbying efforts at the swing voter closest to one's particular preferences. Spiller and Liao (2008) assess the determinants of choices between three alternative instruments for influencing government decisions: disbursing funds (with, or without, corruption); revealing or manipulating information (this is lobbying proper); or litigation (*ex ante* or *ex post*). They show that the choice between these instruments depends upon their institutional effectiveness, and that this effectiveness is bounded by the structural characteristics of decision making in different institutional environments.[35]

The underlying idea – common to all approaches in terms of veto players – is simple. If certain actors, individuals or groups, have true veto power, and can thus stymie decision making by withholding their consent, they will use this power to advance their own agenda and interests. They will, in fact, block anything counter to their own interests. This is why the institution's receptiveness to competitive reforms that are adaptable in the long run will be a function of three variables: (a) the number of veto players; (b) the objective gap between the ideal preferences of the various veto players; and (c) the internal cohesiveness of each collective veto player.

An analysis in terms of veto players thus sheds new light on the implementation of competitive reforms in electricity industries. Raising the number of veto players tends to increase the stability of policy conducted in a given system, and cannot reduce it. A high level of policy stability reduces the importance of being able to set the decision-making agenda (a power that is typical, for example, of the European Council and the European Commission), since the individual responsible for setting the agenda will have a relatively small set of significantly different policies from which to select. This high degree of policy stability may also contribute to governmental instability in parliamentary systems, since governments will be less able to impose decisive results on the interest groups that support them. High policy stability may also lead some civil servants and bureaucrats to be much more active, or even activist. This is especially true in the case of independent authorities, such as sectorial regulators and judges, as well as for competition watchdogs, who act with the independence of judges. This situation can arise because of the inability of other institutions to coalesce and stake out strong preferences of their own or to block top bureaucrats from directly expressing their own preferences.

CONCLUSION

Neo-institutional analysis of the competitive reforms of electricity industries accounts for the decisive role of an institutional framework adapted to new transactions. Of course, it is the political reform process that defines an initial reorganization of property rights in these industries.

However, once this type of reform has been accepted, the crucial issue is the existence of a governance structure adapted to the transactional characteristics of these industries. We have identified three principal hurdles to the building of this adapted governance structure: where and when to introduce competitive mechanisms; how modularity organizes these various options of segregation and interface between competitive activities and network monopoly; and, finally, the profoundly sequential nature of the implementations of these reforms.

This is why the definition of a perfect governance structure presupposes an improbable perfect coincidence between the definition and allocation of new rights and their correlation with previously existing institutions and rights. The analysis in terms of veto players illuminates the difficulties adapting the initial design of the reforms in an institutional environment that will rarely tolerate several major reorganizations of the rights in effect. Thus, the need to adapt competitive reforms in the long run appears to be central to their analysis. In this case, the institutional environment appears as the ultimate support and constraint on reforms to electricity industries and on their potential to converge to a sustainable competitive framework.

NOTES

1. Such as: financial crises, corporate scandals (for example ENRON), stock market collapses, the California electricity crisis, numerous blackouts around the world, and severe alerts from antitrust authorities (including one from the European Union).
2. Aviation reorganized itself independently and durably – until the appearance of low cost airlines – on the 'Hub & Spokes' model with large airports and 'private'

interconnections between the flights of a single company or a pool of affiliated companies.
3. The design of the competitive electricity market remained heterogeneous and unstable, made up of many distinct industrial actors and transactional linkages, variously disassembled and reassembled and, sometimes, though not always, associated with competitive mechanisms or true markets.
4. We here recall the operational difficulties encountered by California's electricity markets between the summer of 2000 and the spring of 2001. We also think of the comprehensive redesign of the English system in 2002, leading to the closing of the Electricity Pool of England and Wales, which was mandatory for all generators and resellers as of the beginning of the reform on 1 April 1990.
5. Both are infrastructures that can easily be differentiated from taxis, buses and trucks.
6. Flight corridors and airport runways are clearly distinct from the airplanes chartered by airlines. However, it is also necessary to prescribe how these air routes and runways are to be allotted to the various users when the sum of all possible usage slots is less than the airlines' demand, in particular in the case of new entrants, and especially when these new entrants are 'low cost'. Are the airlines' large hubs private infrastructures with strictly controlled access, or are they private empires built on essential infrastructures freely accessible to all?
7. The issue is similar to that in the previous note.
8. Except for the local landline grid for which it must provide free access to competitors.
9. As in aviation.
10. It is as if all airlines operating in the same control space were obligated to continually equate the number of seats on all their airplanes to the exact number of passengers having boarded them!
11. From 'real time' to one or three hours before real time.
12. In other words, transactions arose in specific locations because designers created technologically separable interfaces that made transactions cost-effective at those points.
13. The plug and play image is helpful, compatibility between modules is not naturally given or cannot be seen as given without a huge work of harmonization, definition of standards and enforcement mechanisms to stabilize the design.
14. This component also underlies the spectacular 'blackouts' that have shaken up this industry on several occasions since the beginning of the twenty-first century (USA and Canada, Italy, Denmark, Germany and France, and so on).
15. Littlechild (2006) brings two aspects to the debate: he shows that, in Australia, merchant transmission companies have been allowed to compete with incumbent transmission monopolies for the building of new lines; while in Argentina transmission line expansion decisions have to be proposed, approved and paid for by market participants and not by the regulator or the regulated transmission company.
16. Via a half-hourly '*postage stamp*' price.
17. Especially the costs of infrastructures.
18. The fees are paid on average by all the users.
19. This method of pricing connections is called 'shallow cost'.
20. For a discussion of the economic consequences of the various methods of recovering connection costs in the electrical industry, see Hiroux (2004).
21. The paper also proposes a definition of a first-best TSO as the optimal combination of the three most efficient ways of performing the three tasks.
22. Another example is provided by Littlechild (2006) and the settlement of disputes organized in Florida. Instead of a traditional litigated process, settlements are often reached between utilities and the Public Council and/or users, and are typically approved by the regulator.
23. The basis of self-regulation is reciprocity: Individuals recognize the benefits they will derive from behaving in accordance with others' expectations. Such reciprocity may be reflected in individual agreements but, as standards of behaviour, will spread to other members of a group as property rights when the benefits of doing so exceed the costs of

defining those rights. The expectation is that such cost savings will be significant where the group is small enough for informal control – generally requiring continuing face-to-face interaction – but also where power is broadly dispersed.

24. Thus, proponents of the theory of capture demonstrate how repeated exchanges between the regulatory agency and the firms can culminate in collusion between them.
25. Or a new interface between modules.
26. For a detailed presentation of institutional change see Aoki (2001, chapters 9 and 10). For an overview, see Aoki (2004).
27. Aoki's central notion is that each institution generates incentives and manages information autonomously, which may make it difficult for economic agents to utilize and understand the enmeshing of complex institutions.
28. Working from a different analytical framework, Laffont (2005) arrives at the same conclusions regarding the difficulties in transferring regulatory institutions and policies from the developed countries to the developing world.
29. Prosser argues that the early legal structures adopted for UK utility regulation did have elements of a regulatory contract. However with the growth of competition and social regulation, a different model, that of a network of stakeholders, has largely replaced it.
30. As an example, Co_2 permits, renewable targets and different implementation of support mechanisms to foster Renewable Energies was not at the core of the EU Directive on liberalization in 1996, but come later in 2001 and 2008. For a discussion on this issue see Finon and Perez (2007).
31. Levy and Spiller (1994 and 1996) on telecommunications reform, Guasch and Spiller (1999) on reforms in various network industries in Latin America; Spiller and Savedoff (1999) on reforms in water distribution sectors; Spiller and Martorell (1996), Holburn and Spiller (2002) on electricity reform.
32. McCubbins *et al.* (1987, 1989).
33. A growing literature is starting to reconsider the assumptions used – like Rufin (2003), who identifies a 'Presidential Bias' in the Levy and Spiller framework.
34. See the quandary facing local and federal authorities during the California electricity crisis of 2000–2001.
35. For example, Congress (House of Representatives and Senate) is the key decision maker in the federal system of the United States, as is the President in France and the Prime Minister in England.

REFERENCES

Aoki, Masahiko (2001), *Towards a Comparative Institutional Analysis*, Cambridge, MA: Massachusetts Institute of Technology Press.

Baumol, J. William and J. Gregory Sidak (1994), *Toward Competition in Local Telephony*, Cambridge, MA: Massachusetts Institute of Technology Press.

Baldwin, Clariss and Kim Clark (2000), *Design Rules: the Power of Modularity*, Cambridge, MA: Massachusetts Institute of Technology Press.

Brousseau, Eric and Jean-Michel Glachant (eds) (2002), *The Economics of Contracts: Theories and Applications*, Cambridge: Cambridge University Press.

Brousseau, Eric and Jean-Michel Glachant (eds) (2008), *New Institutional Economics: A Guide book*, Cambridge: Cambridge University Press.

Castalia Strategic Advisor (2005), *Explanatory Notes on Key Topics in the Regulation of Water and Sanitation Services*, Washington, DC: World Bank.

Chao, H. and S. Peck (1996), 'A market mechanism for electric power transmission', *Journal of Regulatory Economics*, **10**, 25–59.

EBRD (European Bank for Reconstruction and Development) (2004), *Transition Report 2004: Infrastructure*, London: EBRD.
Finon, D. and Y. Perez (2007), 'Transactional efficiency and public promotion of environmental technologies: the case of renewable energies in the electric industry', *Ecological Economics*, **62**, 77–92.
Glachant, J.-M. and D. Finon (2000), 'Why do the European Union's electricity industries continue to differ? A new institutional analysis', in C. Menard (ed.), *Institutions, Contracts and Organizations*, Cheltenham, UK and Northampton, MA, USA: Edward Elgar, pp. 313–34.
Glachant, Jean-Michel and Dominique Finon (eds) (2003), *Competition in European Electricity Markets: A Cross Country Comparison*, Cheltenham, UK and Northampton, MA, USA: Edward Elgar.
Glachant, Jean-Michel and François Lévêque (2009), *European Union Electricity Internal Market: Towards an Achievement?* Cheltenham: Edward Elgar (forthcoming).
Glachant, J.-M., U. Dubois and Y. Perez (2008), 'Deregulating with no regulator: is Germany electricity transmission regime institutionally correct?', *Energy Policy* **36** (5), 1600–10.
Green, R., A. Lorenzoni, Y. Perez and M. Pollitt (2008), 'Benchmarking in the European Union, Working Paper University of Cambridge; also in J-M. Glachant and F. Lévêque (2008), *European Union Electricity Internal Market: towards an Achievement?* Cheltenham: Edward Elgar, (forthcoming).
Guash, J. Luis and Pablo T. Spiller (1999), *Managing the Regulatory Process: Design, concepts, Issues, and the Latin America and Caribbean Story*, Washington DC: The International Bank for Reconstruction and Development, the World Bank.
Haggard, S. (2000), 'Interest, institutions and policy reform', in A. O. Krueger (ed.), *Economic Policy Reform: The Second Stage*, Chicago, IL: Chicago University Press, pp. 21–61.
Hiroux, C. (2004), *Shallow Cost and Deep Cost, an assessment*, Working Paper GRJM, université Paris-Sud 11.
Holburn, Guy and Richard Van den Bergh (2004), 'Influencing agencies through pivotal political institutions', *Journal of law, Economics and organization*, **20** (20), 458–83.
Holburn, G. L. F. and P. T. Spiller (2002), 'Institutional or structural: lessons from international electricity sector reforms', in Eric Brousseau and Jean-Michel Glachant (eds), *The Economics of Contracts: Theories and Applications,* Cambridge: Cambridge University Press, pp. 463–502.
IEA (International Energy Agency) (2001), *Regulatory Institutions in Liberalised Electricity Markets*, Paris: AIE OCDE.
Joskow, Paul L. and Richard Schmalensee (1983), *Markets for Power*, Cambridge, MA: Massachusetts Institute of Technology Press.
Kessides, I. Nicolas (2004), *Reforming Infrastructure: Privatization, Regulation, and Competition*, A World Bank Policy Research Report, Washington, DC: World Bank and Oxford University Press.
Levy, B. and P. T. Spiller (1994), 'The institutional foundations of regulatory commitment: a comparative analysis of telecommunications regulation', *Journal of Law, Economics, and Organization*, **10** (2), 201–46.
Levy, Brian and Pablo T. Spiller (eds) (1996), *Regulations, Institutions and Commitment. Comparative Studies of Telecommunications*, Cambridge: Cambridge University Press.

Littlechild, S. (2006), 'Foreword', in F. P. Sioshansi and W. Pfaffenberger *Electricity Markets around the World*, Amsterdam: Elsevier.
Macintyre, Andrew (2003), *The Power of Institutions, Political Architecture and Governance*, Ithaca, NY: Cornell University Press.
McCubbins, M. D., R. G. Noll and B. R. Weingast (1987), 'Administrative procedures as instruments of political control', *Journal of Law, Economics and Organisation*, **3**, 243–77.
McCubbins, M. D., R. G. Noll and B. R. Weingast (1989), 'Structures and process, politics and policy: administrative procedures and the political control of agencies', *Virginia Law Review*, **75**, 431–82.
Midttun, Atle (2005), 'Deregulation: designs, learning and legitimacy', in John Gronewegen and Rolf Kunneke (eds), *Reform of Infrastructure Industries*, Cheltenham, UK and Northampton, MA, USA: Edward Elgar.
Newbery, David (2000), *Privatization, Restructuring, and Regulation of Network Utilities*, Cambridge, MA: Massachusetts Institute of Technology Press.
Newbery, D. (2002), 'Issues and options for restructuring electricity supply industries', DAE Working Paper WP 0210, University of Cambridge.
North, Douglass C. (1990), *Institutions, Institutional Change and Economic Performance*, Cambridge: Cambridge University Press.
North, Douglass C. (2005), *Understanding the Process of Economic Change*, Princeton Economic History of the Western World, Princeton, NJ: Princeton University Press.
Ocana, C. (2002), 'Trends in management of regulation: a comparison of energy regulators in member countries of the OECD', *International Journal of Regulation and Governance*, **3** (1), 13–32.
Oren, S. (1997), 'Economic inefficiency of passive transmission rights in congested electricity systems with competitive generation', *Energy Journal*, **1** (18), 63–83.
Ogus, A. (1995), 'Rethinking self-regulation', *Oxford Journal of Legal Studies*, **15**, 97–108.
Pagano, U. (2006), 'Legal position and institutional complementarities', in F. Cafiaggi, A. Nicita and U. Pagano, *Legal Orderings and Economic Institutions*, London and New York: Routledge.
Perez, Y. (2002), *L'analyse néo-institutionnelle des réformes électriques européennes*, Thèse de doctorat Université de Paris I Panthéon-Sorbonne.
Prosser, T. (2005), 'Regulatory contracts and stakeholder regulation', *Annals of Public and Cooperative Economics*, **76** (1), 35–57.
Rious, V., J-M. Glachant, Y. Perez and P. Desante (2008), 'The diversity of design of TSOs', Working Paper Cambridge and Working Paper MIT.
Rufin, Carlos (2003), *The Political Economy of Institutional Change in the Electricity Supply Industry*, Cheltenham: Edward Elgar.
Saleth, Maria and Ariel Dinar (2004), *Institutional Economics of Water: A Cross-Country Analysis of Institutions and Performance*, Washington, DC: World Bank Publications.
Sioshansi, Ferejhon P. and Wolfgang Pfaffenberger (eds) (2006), *Electricity Markets around the World*, Amsterdam: Elsevier.
Smeers, Y. (2004), 'TSO, electricity markets and market power', in '*European Regulatory TSO benchmarking conference*', Den Haag, May.
Spiller, P. T and S. Liao (2008), 'Buy, lobby or sue: interest groups' participation in policy making – a selective survey', in E. Brousseau and J.-M. Glachant,

New Institutional Economics: A Guidebook, Cambridge: Cambridge University Press.
Spiller, P. T. and L. V. Martorell (1996), 'How should it be done? Electricity regulation in Argentina, Brazil, Uruguay, and Chile', in R. J. Gilbert and E. P. Kahn (eds): *International Comparisons of Electricity Regulation*, Cambridge: Cambridge University Press, pp. 82–125.
Tsebelis, G. (1995), 'Decision making in political systems: veto players in presidentialism, parliamentarism, multicameralism and multipartism', *British Journal of Political Science*, **25** (3), 289–325.
Tsebelis, Georges (2002), *Veto Players. How Political Institutions Work?*, Princeton, NJ: Princeton University Press.
Weingast, B. R. (1995), 'The economic role of political institutions: market-preserving federalism and economic development', *Journal of Law, Economics and Organization*, **11** (1), 269–96.
Williamson, Oliver E. (1985), *The Economic Institutions of Capitalism*, New York: Free Press.
Williamson, Oliver E. (1996), *The Mechanisms of Governance*, Oxford: Oxford University Press.
Wilson, R. B. (2002), 'Architecture of electricity power market', *Econometrica*, **70** (4), 1299–340.
World Bank, (1995), *Bureaucrats in Business: The Economics and Politics of Government Ownership*, Oxford: Oxford University Press.
World Bank, (2006), *Handbook for Evaluating Infrastructure Regulatory Systems*, Washington, DC: World Bank Edition.

10. The US postal service

R. Richard Geddes

INTRODUCTION

Can the US Postal Service be characterized as a firm that was deregulated and is now moving toward re-regulation? To what extent can shifts in US postal policy be understood as a quest for economic efficiency? What theories can help us interpret the evolution of US postal policy, and how are they affected by changing political circumstances? Can those theories also help us understand what is likely to happen next in US postal policy? The purpose of this chapter is to help address this set of important questions.

The US Postal Service (USPS) operates within a unique, complex legal and political environment resulting from decades of institutional evolution. Postal policy has been liberalized, but the form of liberalization in the United States is unique. The USPS is clearly not an example of a firm that was deregulated and is now facing meaningful reregulation. Rather, its institutional evolution has been a slow, somewhat convoluted process of liberalization. That evolution is too nuanced, however, to be understood as a steady march toward economic efficiency. Rather, theories incorporating both efficiency and redistribution are necessary to understand US postal policy.

In this chapter, I first provide an overview of the current structure of the USPS to give a flavor for the unusual organizational arrangements involved. I review the major reorganization efforts that have affected postal policy in the United States. One salient aspect of postal organization is the degree of contracting out of mail preparation, known as worksharing. This overview suggests that US postal policy has become more liberal over time, even though major aspects of USPS organization inconsistent with a liberalized policy remain. It also shows that US postal reform has taken a course different from that in many other countries.

In the third section, I attempt to answer the second and third questions posed above: what theories can assist in understanding these changes, and how important are efficiency considerations in particular? Two theories of policy change are especially relevant. The first is the public-interest theory, or normative-analysis-as-positive-theory approach (NPT) which views government intervention as a way to correct market failure and improve social welfare. The main alternative is the private-interest theory, also called the economic theory, or ET. This approach portrays the regulatory process as one in which well-organized groups use state power to capture rents at the expense of more dispersed groups. If postal policy can be characterized as trending toward liberalization, then it is necessary to consider the predictions these theories generate regarding liberalization. In the third section, I find that the NPT does a poor job of explaining the change that has taken place or those elements that have been retained, but that the ET also provides unsatisfying answers to some aspects of US postal reform.

In the fourth section, I address the final two questions: To what extent are these changes the result of unique political circumstances, and what is likely to happen next in US postal policy. I there find that the evolution of US postal policy is too long and protracted to be explained by particular political circumstances. I also find that underlying economic forces are likely to compel the USPS to continue on its course of continued liberalization for the foreseeable future. Although some aspects of postal regulation were made more stringent by recent legislation, it is unlikely that the USPS will ever be substantially re-regulated. The fifth section summarizes and concludes.

THE CURRENT STRUCTURE OF THE US POSTAL SERVICE

Given the activity it undertakes, the USPS is an unusual organizational hybrid.[1] It is a business, providing a commercial service, but remains government owned. Although it offers services that face competition, its core activity is protected by a government-enforced monopoly. Many industries with organizational characteristics similar to the USPS have been deregulated or privatized, both in the United States and internationally. These industries share a network structure in that they have a distribution system of lines, pipes, or routes requiring the use of public rights-of-way, typically with strong physical linkages between component parts. Although other network industries in the United States, including airlines, telecommunications, oil, natural gas, electricity, trucking, cable television and railroads, among others, have all undergone substantial regulatory reform since the mid-1970s, US postal policy appears to have changed little.

Moreover, many other governments have substantially reformed their postal services. For example, New Zealand, Sweden and Finland abolished their postal monopolies as of 2002. Australia's monopoly is limited to four times the stamp price only,[2] and may be reduced to the stamp price itself. The European Union has limited all postal monopolies to five times the stamp price and is planning to eliminate them entirely.[3] Many postal services are also moving toward privatization. For example, the Dutch post is 60 percent privatized, while the German post is majority privately owned.

Although the USPS has not undergone similar major structural reform it has been liberalized in other more subtle ways over time. It has operated (or will be operating) under three main organizational regimes since the late 1960s which I characterize as direct Congressional control, under the 1970 Postal Reorganization Act, and under the 2006 Postal Accountability and Enhancement Act.[4]

Direct Congressional Control

Prior to 1970, the USPS was the Post Office Department. As a department of the federal government, Congress controlled almost every aspect of the Post Office's operations, a key aspect of which was rates (Tierney 1988: 10). In hearings before Congress, a wide array of mail users would argue against rate hikes, typically relying on emotional, anecdotal evidence (Tierney 1981: 105).[5] Congress was often loath to increase rates when confronted with stirring opposition coupled with little organized response from taxpayers who stood to lose from the large annual deficits that inadequate rate increases would bring. Moreover, delays in rate increases served organized mailers' interests. Delays in the 1967 rate increase, for example, collectively saved mailers $15 million each week.[6] Mailers were also effective at keeping second- and third-class mail rates low relative to first-class rates, which allowed them to benefit from the Post Office's monopoly, and thus from the relatively inelastic demand for first-class mail.[7]

Congress also benefited from the selection of postmasters. Although potentially helpful for their managerial skill and knowledge of local conditions, postmasters were instead often chosen for political patronage under an informal 'political advisor' system.[8] The system allowed members of Congress and occasionally local party officials to choose the local postmaster. Given the substantial fringe benefits, attractive retirement packages, and job security associated with a postmaster position, it is unsurprising that the jobs were used to generate political benefits.

Moreover, Congress mandated numerous details of labor arrangements, from wages to work assignments for particular positions. Postal unions became skillful at lobbying the members of Congress determining those arrangements. Unions exerted considerable political influence by virtue of their large size and broad geographic distribution across Congressional districts. Additionally, the Post Office Department was the single most unionized federal organization. About 90 percent of Post Office employees belonged to a union, versus 21 percent in other federal agencies.[9] Unions used their considerable influence to lobby for higher wages, improved benefits, and more job security.

The postal unions' success under this system was impressive. Only one postal pay bill was defeated in any House vote from 1955 to 1967 (Fenno, 1973: 246). When pushing through a pay bill, the unions obtained one of only two overrides of a presidential veto during the entire Eisenhower administration. Numerous statistical studies, discussed below, confirm that postal workers' pay exceeded that for other workers with similar education and experience. Both unions and large mailers thus emerged as powerful constituencies.

The political incentives created by this structure had unfortunate long-run fiscal consequences. Catering to large mailers' interests resulted in low revenues due to low rates, but complying with union interests necessitated high labor costs. Through a direct annual appropriation, taxpayers paid for the annual shortfall between revenues and costs. The real annual charge to the Treasury grew steadily. The Post Office deficit grew from $652 million in 1964 to $1.1 billion in 1967.

Several forces worked in concert to push the Post Office's structure to the breaking point. First, mail volumes were rising with economic growth. Second, although funding capital investment for postal delivery was rarely a top Congressional priority, budgets during the 1960s were particularly inadequate. Funding for the Vietnam War and President Johnson's Great Society programs took precedence. The result was limited (or nonexistent) capital investment and technological progress, which led to high costs. Mail was still sorted by hand, and post office buildings were often inadequate to handle improved mechanization. Floors were sometimes too weak to support heavy machinery, and ceilings were too low to allow large overhead conveyor networks. There was also an unusually high breakdown rate in the transportation fleet. The Post Office responded by hiring more workers but without capital improvements labor productivity remained low.

Changes in transportation modes also increased postal costs. Postal operations were designed to move mail by train, with large facilities located near train stations in downtown areas. During this period, however, railroads were declining in favor of trucks, which faced difficulty in reaching downtown locations.

The system reached a critical point in 1966 when the Chicago Post Office – at the time the world's largest – ceased to function. The backlog of mail exceeded 10 million pieces. That was far from an isolated incident however. A similar event occurred in Chicago in December 1963, when hundreds of thousands of Christmas parcels were delayed for months (President's Commission on Postal Organization 1968: 12).

The Postal Reorganization Act of 1970

An unusual confluence of interests supported reform. The Post Office itself was a major force in favor of reorganization, since it was promised enhanced modernization and independence. The business community supported reorganization, because it believed that reform would lead to better service and lower rates if improved management tools were applied. Indeed, the commission that Congress established to study the problem, known as the Kappel Commission, estimated that the Post Office could save at least 20 percent of postal costs per year if freed from political control and allowed to operate using prevailing business principles (President's Commission on Postal Organization 1968: 5–6). Large mailers valued the improved predictability and reduced variability of rates that reorganization promised. The main resistance to reorganization came from organized labor, which feared a decline in its hard-won Congressional influence and thus a reduction in power if collective bargaining with a continuing prohibition on strikes were adopted. Organized labor was compensated for its expected losses through a two-part pay raise agreement, and other concessions.

Congress also wanted the Post Office to become financially self-sustaining. It hoped that the imposition of a break-even constraint would strengthen the Post Office's incentives for cost efficiency and reduce its reliance on government subsidies. A break-even constraint would also place the cost of postal services onto mail users rather than taxpayers generally, which would distribute costs more fairly and provide economizing incentives.

Rationalization of the rate structure was envisioned. As the Kappel Commission noted, decades of political rate-setting resulted in an irrational rate structure. It was anticipated that setting rates in accordance with accepted principles of public utility pricing would enhance both the fairness and efficiency of postal rates (President's Commission on Postal Organization, 1968: 145–53).

The 1970 Act also reformed labor relations and working conditions. The Kappel Commission found that the hiring process was exceedingly slow, that senior appointments were politicized, that the promotion system stifled employee motivation, that employees received virtually no rewards for superior performance, that they received little training, and that working environments were often shoddy. It was hoped that independence from Congress would help address those problems.

Overall, the 1970 Act can be viewed as an important step toward liberalization. It moved away from direct taxpayer funding by requiring the USPS to become self-financing. It eliminated direct Congressional control over rates, granting the USPS substantial autonomy in rate-setting.[10] The act also granted the USPS more control over labor arrangements such as wages, working conditions and other managerial decisions. In these and other areas, the 1970 Act represents a step away from typical governmental organization and toward a more utility-like structure.

That structure remained essentially undisturbed for 35 years. The USPS has effectively met its break-even constraint over the long term, with the important exception of unfunded liabilities in the form of postretirement health costs, pension liabilities and workers' compensation.[11] The price of the basic first-class stamp has grown at roughly the rate of inflation. However, it eventually became clear that there were deficiencies in this structure. Rate proceedings were cumbersome. The powers of the Postal Rate Commission were inadequate to the task of regulating a government-owned monopoly. There were concerns about cross-subsidies from monopolistic to competitive products. Important modifications were implemented in the Postal Accountability and Enhancement Act of 2006, which I discuss below.

The Postal Accountability and Enhancement Act of 2006

Unlike the 1970 Act, there was no obvious crisis that precipitated the 2006 act (Public Law 109-435). Rather, the 2006 act reflects a lengthy process of deliberation and debate. Hearings were held by Congressman McHugh of New York and others for over a decade leading up to its passage. The 2006 Act is essentially two pieces of legislation wrapped into one. One is reform of the USPS' regulatory framework. The second is pension reform legislation. I discuss each in turn.

The 2006 Act implemented three main regulatory policy changes.[12] First, it granted the USPS the authority to change postage rates, within limits, without seeking prior regulatory approval. Under the 1970 Act, the USPS was required to submit proposed rate changes to the Postal Rate Commission prior to a rate change. The ensuing rate hearing often took many months. The 2006 Act divides USPS products into market dominant (meaning those where the delivery monopoly applies), and competitive products.[13] The USPS may increase prices in the market dominant category, provided that rates do not rise faster than the consumer price index.[14] For competitive products, the USPS may price as it wishes as long as each product covers its costs, and if all competitive products together make an appropriate contribution to USPS 'institutional' or overhead costs. One purpose of this arrangement is to avoid the cross-subsidization of competitive products with revenue from monopolized products. This change will also give the USPS more flexibility to set rates.

Second, the act created a new regulator with enlarged powers and a new name, the Postal Regulatory Commission. The Act required the new Commission to establish 'a modern system for regulating rates and classes' that meet a variety of objectives, such as enhancing incentives to reduce costs and increase efficiency, to create predictability and stability in rates, and to maintain financial stability.[15] The new Postal Regulatory Commission's powers include improved information-gathering authority (including subpoena power), the authority to control USPS service standards, control over new product offerings, and enhanced ability to prevent cross-subsidies from monopolistic to competitive products. The Postal Regulatory Commission is directed to issue regulations prohibiting unfair competition by the USPS. The new Commission also has the power to change which products fall into market dominant versus competitive categories 'by adding new products to the lists, removing products from the lists, or transferring products between lists'.[16] Also, the USPS is to be covered by the federal antitrust laws and is subject to commercial lawsuits.[17]

Third, the act limited the Postal Service's delivery monopoly to six times the stamp price. This creates a reserved area of monopoly power for the USPS. It may not introduce much competition, but this change does set the stage for gradually introducing competition by reducing the stamp price multiple over time. Additionally, it clearly defines the scope of the Postal Service's delivery monopoly, which had been a past concern.

Regarding pension reform, in 2003 Congress concluded that the formula used to determine the Postal Service's contribution to pensions for workers covered by the Civil Service Retirement System (CSRS) was flawed.[18] Congress retroactively changed that formula in the Postal Civil Service Retirement System Funding Reform Act of 2003.[19] That act had the effect of reducing the Postal Service's pension contributions, but it directed the annual savings be placed in an escrow account pending further legislative action. The 2003 act also shifted responsibility for increased CSRS pension payments for certain USPS retirees who had served in the military from the Treasury to the USPS. The effect of these two major changes was to reduce the Postal Service's annual pension contributions.

The 2006 act eliminated the escrow account and shifted the pension responsibility for the USPS employees with military service back to the Treasury. It also directed that the savings the USPS realized from its reduced pension contributions help pay down the Service's unfunded retiree health care liabilities.

These changes may not appear to represent a uniform movement toward liberalization. Similar to the 1970 Act, however, the 2006 Act moved USPS regulation a step closer to that of a public utility. The adoption of price cap regulation and enhanced regulatory authority mimics a public utility approach, as does the separation of monopolistic and competitive products. The elimination of sovereign immunity protection moves the USPS closer in legal structure to a private firm. The 2006 Act thus lays the groundwork for future privatization and de-monopolization.

There is however another important process that has also been operating for many years to liberalize the USPS: worksharing. Although it is used in a few other countries, worksharing has played a particularly important role in the liberalization of US postal policy.

Worksharing in the US Postal Service

Worksharing occurs when private mailers prepare the mail so as to lower costs to the USPS. Mailers in turn receive discounts for preparation. Worksharing takes many forms, including presorting, drop shipping,[20] bar coding, palletizing and containerizing the mail. The United States utilizes worksharing discounts more extensively than any other country.[21]

Unique institutional circumstances encouraged worksharing in the United States. Prior to the Postal Reorganization Act of 1970, and the creation of the Postal Rate Commission, mailers were able to produce mail in a presorted sequence due to computerization of mailing lists (Cohen *et al.*, 2001, 2001). Mailers petitioned the old Post Office to provide them with a discount for pre-sorting the mail but the Post Office refused.

After the 1970 Act, mailers again petitioned for discounts. Although the new Postal Service resisted the discounts, the 1970 law required that the newly created Postal Rate Commission approve product offerings. The Postal Service feared that its rates and classifications would be opposed by large mailers unless it included a presort discount. The USPS began offering discounts for pre-sorted first-class mail in 1976.

Inflation was high during the 1970s, so USPS costs were rising rapidly. It thus frequently requested higher rates to cover rising costs. There were a total of five postal rate cases during the 1970s, which provided opportunities for large mailers to air their concerns about higher rates. The USPS expanded worksharing discounts in response to that criticism. Worksharing was thus a way to ameliorate the impact of large rate increases on high-volume mailers. Also, mailers were able to bring compelling evidence before the Postal Rate Commission that the costs avoided by the USPS due to worksharing were substantial, which led to steeper worksharing discounts over time, in some cases over three times higher than the USPS wanted.

Worksharing has evolved into a large, complex schedule of rates that reflect the wide variety of ways that mailers can reduce costs. There are now about 250 distinct worksharing rates.[22] Most discounts relate to advertising material. It now includes virtually all mail classes. Mailers can now presort and drop ship mail at four different levels, the most refined being one of the 24 000 local delivery units (known as destination delivery units, or DDUs), where letter carriers depart on their routes.[23]

As noted, worksharing was introduced and expanded to provide mailers with an incentive to undertake mail preparation they can complete at lower cost than the USPS. However, it has the effect of moving production from the USPS to the private sector, and has therefore liberalized the US postal market without legislative action. This stands in contrast to postal liberalization in other countries, which required legislation. Some commentators suggest that worksharing may be more effective in liberalizing the postal market than de-monopolization.[24]

The amount of mail that is workshared in the United States has grown over time and is now significant. Figure 10A.1 in the appendix displays the percentage of first-class mail (which accounts for the majority of USPS revenue) that is now workshared.[25] That share was 12 percent in 1980, 33 percent in 1990, 47 percent in 2000 and 55 percent in 2006. The worksharing percentage is even greater in other mail classes. As of 2001, advertising mail was 96 percent workshared, periodicals were 94 percent workshared, while package services were 73 percent workshared (Cohen *et al.*, 2004: 16).

As might be expected from enhanced competition, worksharing has helped to lower USPS costs. According to one estimate, the cost reduction from all worksharing was $15 billion in 1999, or almost 25 percent of total USPS costs (Cohen, 2003: 19). This is at least partly due to the smaller workforce that is necessary when mail is workshared.

There are other signs that worksharing in the United States has liberalized the postal market. For example, one effect of presort discounts for first-class mail has been the development of third-party consolidators in many major US cities, which now produce about a third of all presorted first-class mail. These 'presort service bureaus' also barcode, sort, and often transport the mail for mailers who do not wish to do so.

Liberalization or Re-regulation?

Several aspects of this institutional evolution are noteworthy. It suggests a slow movement toward a more liberalized structure. Given the trend toward a public utility structure and worksharing, it cannot be characterized as deregulation and subsequent reregulation. The protracted nature of the reform process is also noteworthy. Postal liberalization in the United States was first examined in the late 1960s, and is ongoing today.[26] The hearings leading to the 2006 Act were begun in the early 1990s. In contrast, the deregulation of other industries, such as trucking and airlines, was essentially complete in several years. Maximum price regulation in the oil industry, for example, came and went in one decade.

Finally, postal services cannot be characterized as an industry with organized, politically powerful producers and weak consumers. Although employees are well organized through unionization, mailers are also organized through such groups as the Direct Marketing Association, Newspaper Association of America and the Parcel Shippers Association, among others. This is likely to have an important effect on the process of reform. Moving to the second and third questions addressed in this chapter: how then is structure and change in the USPS best understood? Below I examine several possible explanations, and assess their power in explaining US postal policy.

US POSTAL SERVICE ORGANIZATION: PUBLIC OR PRIVATE INTEREST?

There are two main approaches to the regulation of industry that help explain these changes. The first is a public-interest approach, also called Normative Analysis as Positive Theory, or NPT (Joskow and Noll, 1981). The NPT posits that regulation is supplied when it is normatively required (that is, in the public interest) to maximize social welfare. Here regulation corrects market failure, such as negative externalities or natural monopoly. Because there are no obvious, unusual negative externalities generated by postal delivery, this approach suggests a focus on correcting potential natural monopoly. The NPT implies that liberalization will occur when technological or demand characteristics change so as to eliminate this particular market failure (Peltzman, 1989: 18).

A second main approach focuses on the benefits intervention bestows on private parties. Intervention in a market here occurs in response to the demands of politically influential groups.[27] Economic rents, or wealth, are redistributed to politically powerful consumer and producer groups so as to maximize political support. This is sometimes referred to as the economic theory of regulation, or the ET. There are two main forces that can plausibly lead to liberalization under the ET: (a) if the difference between the regulated market equilibrium and the unregulated market equilibrium diminishes so that the political gain from intervention falls, and (b) if the wealth available for redistribution declines.

Postal Liberalization and Alternative Theories of Regulation

How well do these theories accord with the details of US postal liberalization? To be consistent with the NPT, either the demand or the technological characteristics of postal delivery would have to change so as to eliminate preexisting natural monopoly conditions. This raises the critical question of whether or not postal services were a natural monopoly prior to the 1970 Act. There is now a literature concluding that postal services are not, and never have been, a natural monopoly. Sidak and Spulber (1996: 43–55), for example, systematically analyze the various components of postal service, which include (a) contracting for long-distance transportation, (b) regional sortation and transportation, and (c) local pickup, sortation and delivery. They systematically demonstrate that none of these activities have natural monopoly characteristics.[28] Indeed, postal services are a paradigmatic case of a highly contestable market, and those types of delivery service that do not fall under the monopoly are competitive (Geddes 2003: 25).

An alternative public-interest explanation is sometimes offered, which is the desire to provide the same quality of delivery service (such as six-day-per week delivery) to all parts of the nation at a uniform price, known as 'universal service'. This justification suggests that a government-enforced monopoly is necessary in order to guarantee universal service. That is because private competitors would enter only on dense urban routes and 'skim the cream' that is necessary to cross-subsidize sparse, rural money-losing routes. If competition were allowed, it is argued, rural homeowners would not receive mail service.

As a public-interest justification, however, the universal service explanation for intervention is weak (Sidak and Spulber, 1996: 70–4, Geddes, 2003: 209–16). Moreover, for this concern to explain US postal policy under the NPT, reforms such as the 1970 Act should have weakened universal service provisions. Instead, universal service at uniform rates has been a particularly durable aspect of postal structure.

The ET offers an alternative approach to liberalization. It suggests a search for exogenous changes that resulted in the elimination of economic rents or changes in the unregulated market structure that reduce gains from intervention. Although there is no evidence of meaningful changes in the unregulated market structure (with low entry barriers it has always been quite competitive), the evidence is supportive of rent dissipation prior to the 1970 Act. As noted, because of restrictive work rules, lack of innovation, and other causes, organizational arrangements prior to 1970 became unwieldy, drastically increasing the cost of providing mail service as well as the direct subsidy, eventually leading to collapse.[29]

This appears to accord well with the ET, but a refinement by Becker is particularly relevant (Becker, 1983). Becker argues that deadweight losses act as a constraint on inefficient regulatory policies. Since neither winners nor losers in the redistributive process would oppose changes that reduced deadweight loss, Becker's approach suggests that the political process will tend toward efficient modes of redistribution. Such intervention-induced cost increases are particularly relevant for the 1970 postal reorganization. Peltzman provides a summary of Becker's approach that aligns closely with the 1970 reform:

> In Becker's framework the loss of rents (from cost increases) reduces the pressure for continued regulation of this industry relative to other industries, and the higher price increases the counter pressure from consumers. Suppose further that the cost increase has in fact been induced by regulation. Then the deadweight losses emphasized by Becker become especially important. There is now not only attenuated support for continued regulation but also the potential for major gains in political utility from deregulation. These would come from the elimination of the cost increase attributable to regulation. For a structurally competitive industry, the lower costs would translate into higher producer and consumer surplus in the short run and higher consumer surplus in the long run, thus raising the possibility that the coalition pushing for deregulation would include some producers. (Peltzman, 1989: 20-1)

This refinement of the ET is helpful for understanding postal reform. The 1970 Act was, by all accounts, driven by the inefficiencies of the pre-act structure, implying that the political benefits from deregulation were high. Also, as noted, the coalition for reform included producer interests in the form of the Post Office itself. The details of the 1970 reform thus accord well with the ET.[30]

The use of worksharing discounts is also consistent with the basic form of the ET as well as Becker's approach. Large mailers represent organized customers who would otherwise resist rate increases; their acquiescence can be obtained by blunting rate increases via discounts. Worksharing discounts also have an important efficiency component, however. To the extent that presorting and drop shipping are performed more efficiently by private firms than by the USPS (as suggested by the postal wage premium), then deadweight loss from the extant government-owned monopoly postal organization is reduced. This is also consistent with Becker's approach. Worksharing discounts have flourished even though they have been opposed by postal unions.

Both theories appear at a loss to explain the 2006 Act however. In contrast to 1970, there was no catastrophic increase in costs prior to 2006 that precipitated congressional action. Nor were there any dramatic decreases in demand that would diminish rents. Rather, as noted, the 2006 Act was the end result of a long period of deliberation and debate. The Becker contribution to the ET, with its emphasis on the efficiency-reducing aspects of reform, is here similarly unhelpful.[31] One might argue that worksharing discounts had the effect of reducing USPS revenue, which would reduce the rents available for redistribution to other parties and perhaps inspire added liberalization. Figure 10A.1 indicates however that worksharing has increased steadily since 1978, so this application of the ET has difficulty explaining the timing of the 2006 Act.

A separate literature may be helpful in understanding the 2006 reform. This approach evolved from work by Kenneth Arrow and emphasizes the essential indeterminacy of democratic political systems and how those systems evolve to address instability (Arrow, 1950). One implication of this literature is that much liberalization takes place without legislative action, as courts and regulatory bodies may interpret statutes in ways not envisioned by Congress. This approach suggests that legislative action will be reactive since Congress is forced to respond to circumstances that are changed by the regulator (Ferejohn and Shipan, 1989). This may help explain both the content and the ponderous pace of passage of the 2006 Act, as Congress felt compelled to address worksharing discounts and other policies that had grown under Postal Rate Commission oversight.

Theories of Regulation and Unchanging Postal Structures

Those aspects of postal structure left unchanged by liberalization in the United States may be as noteworthy as those that changed. Unlike postal liberalization in many other countries, US reform has focused on developing a utility-like structure while retaining the dual monopolies (over delivery and the use of the mailbox), government ownership, and uniform national rates (within particular weight/class categories). Any comprehensive theory of regulation/liberalization must address those aspects of USPS institutional structure that resist reform.

It is difficult to reconcile the retention of government ownership, monopoly power and uniform rates with the NPT's explanation of liberalization. Under the NPT, the retained features should help address natural monopoly problems. But such explanations are unsatisfying given the lack of evidence of natural monopoly in this industry. The ET however offers an explanation: those aspects of postal structure that are retained, although they may generate some deadweight loss, assist in the creation and distribution of economic rents to influential groups. Their retention, and the continuing political benefits from them, may also help explain the slow pace of reform in this industry.

A key prediction of the ET is that economic rents will in general be spread among several competing groups (including politically influential consumers, in this case large mailers) rather than being captured by only one constituency group, such as producers. Rent spreading among consumers, for example, manifests itself through prices that attenuate differences in marginal cost across consumer groups. In general, regulators are able to gain political benefits from reducing prices for some high-cost customers at the expense of other customers. The economic theory predicts that there will be a tendency for high-cost consumers (such as rural postal customers) to receive a relatively low price/marginal cost ratio, which constitutes a cross-subsidy from low-cost to high-cost consumers.[32] Keeping these predictions in mind, I now examine three persistent aspects of USPS structure, which are monopoly power, uniform rates and government ownership.

A defining aspect of the USPS is its delivery monopoly. Through the private express statutes of 1845, the USPS obtained a legal monopoly over most of first-class and a portion of Standard Mail. Legally enforced monopoly power is critical for the creation of economic rents. Without monopoly power, competitors would rapidly enter all sectors of the USPS market, and any super-normal profits would be eliminated. There would be no economic value left for redistribution.

The Postal Service defends its monopoly power. In 1970, Congress considered elimination of the monopoly as part of reorganization, and requested that the Board of Governors conduct a 'thorough reevaluation' of the restriction.[33] The Board recommended that the prohibition be retained. The Governor's defense of the monopoly was based partly on the theory of natural monopoly, and partly on the traditional justification of providing below-cost service to rural customers (Priest, 1975: 69).

The ET provides an explanation for the retention of monopoly power, since a number of well-organized groups benefit. The most important beneficiary may be organized labor, which receives rents in the form of high relative wages as documented by numerous empirical studies. For example, Smith (1976, 1977) finds that postal workers are paid more than their comparable private sector wage, as mandated by the 1970 act.[34] Similarly, Perloff and Wachter (1984) found that, in 1978, postal salaries were 21 percent higher than for similar workers in the private sector. Wachter and Perloff (1991) again found a postal wage premium of 21 percent using 1988 data, while Hirsch *et al.* (1999) found a wage premium of 28 percent.

Moving to rates, neither the 1970 nor the 2006 act disturbed the policy of uniform nationwide rates for each weight/class combination, regardless of distance or customer density.[35] For example, any letter weighing less than one ounce will currently be delivered first-class anywhere in the United States for 42 cents. To the extent that there are differences in the unit cost of serving rural versus urban customers, there is an intra-class cross-subsidy from urban to rural customers.

The desire to maintain these cross-subsidies through uniform rates and the monopoly power are intimately related. If private competitors entered on all routes where prices exceed cost the Postal Service would be left with only the least profitable customers. Stated differently, since profit-maximizing firms will compete until price equals cost, uniform rates would have to be abandoned if the private express statutes were repealed in the presence of cost differentials, and entry were allowed on all routes.

It is difficult to reconcile this policy with a public-interest approach. Aside from monopoly itself, the economic inefficiencies from cross-subsidy induced by uniform rates are well known.[36] Such rates result in over-consumption on high-cost routes and under-consumption on low-cost routes. The USPS has also offered a transaction cost justification. For example, Priest (1975: 72) states, 'The Governors further assert that with any varied pricing structure "regulatory red tape" will proliferate and the public will become confused.' And p. 70: 'The Postal Service must charge uniform rates. The Postal Service has found, according to the Governors, that it is only practicable to set rates "according to simple, published formulas of great generality."' Such justifications seem tenuous. Market forces, in the absence of monopoly prohibitions, would act to conserve on such transaction costs. If the reduction in confusion brought about by uniform rates actually offset higher costs due to sub-optimal pricing, then competitive private companies would adopt them. Moreover, given the availability of electronic mail, facsimile machines, lower long-distance telephone rates and plane fares, and lower cost overnight services, rural customers are unlikely to be isolated if asked to pay their true cost of delivery.

The ET provides an explanation for the endurance of the uniform rate. A uniform rate pricing structure is consistent with rent-redistribution within a class of mail. If costs are not constant across various customers within a class, then uniform rates create an intra-class cross-subsidy. As noted, politically effective rent distribution will tend to smooth or eliminate cost differences across customer groups. In the limit the regulator will totally ignore cost differences and set prices equal for different customer groups regardless of cost, as in the case of postal rates within a class. Additionally, since rural customers are a smaller numerical group, this is consistent with the prediction of rent-redistribution toward the politically effective group. Indeed, the Postal Service opposed elimination of uniform rates even though Congress in 1970 offered to pay it directly for any money lost on rural routes.

However, it is likely that monopoly power facilitates important cross-subsidies across classes of mail as well. Since it is difficult to measure the costs attributable to a particular class of mail,[37] it is hard to gauge the size of inter-class cross-subsidies. However, evidence reported in Geddes (1998) suggests that the 1970 act increased rates in heavily monopolized first-class mail and decreased them in competitive parcel post mail. This is consistent with greater inter-class cross-subsidy from monopolized to competitive classes. Overall, although the public-interest justification for monopoly power and uniform rates is unclear, the retention of those features is consistent with politically beneficial rent redistribution.

The final reform-resistant aspect of USPS structure is government ownership, which was unaffected by either act. This is noteworthy given that there has been successful privatization across a wide range of industries around the world, and in postal services in other countries. As with monopoly and uniform rates, the main public interest argument for retaining government ownership again appears to be universal service (Tierney, 1988: 32). This justification for government ownership raises the question of why universal service concerns cannot be addressed via contracts with private firms. The government could easily contract with a private firm to provide service to rural areas if so desired.[38]

Consistent with the ET, however, government ownership facilitates better control over rent spreading to various groups than does private ownership, particularly through the pricing structure (Peltzman, 1971: 146). When a firm is privately owned it focuses on profit-maximization as its objective, which essentially creates an agency problem in the redistribution of rents. That is, private firms are profit-seekers that naturally engage in profitable price-discrimination across customer classes, which undermines the political objective motivating both inter-class and intra-class cross-subsidies. As long as the USPS provides service to low-density customers, the political desire to cross-subsidize them and to cross-subsidize across mail classes will be more easily achieved through government ownership than private.

WHAT'S NEXT FOR US POSTAL SERVICES?

I here address the two final questions: Does US postal liberalization reflect changing political circumstances, and what is the likely future course of liberalization? Regarding the first, the pace of change in US postal services has been notoriously slow and deliberate. Although the details of any regulatory reform may reflect the political equilibrium at the time of passage, it is unlikely that particular political circumstances were the main driver of US postal reform. Congressional hearings prior to the 2006 Act absorbed a period of time when control of the House, Senate, and the Presidency all changed hands. The overall process of liberalization has spanned decades and numerous administrations as well as changes in congressional control. Nor does postal reform appear to be correlated with broad deregulatory movements in the United States. There was a strong movement toward deregulation of network industries, including trucking, railroads and airlines, in the late 1970s and early 1980s, but postal policy remained essentially unaffected. Additionally, the 2006 Act was passed not long after widespread dissatisfaction with deregulation of network industries was sowed by California's efforts to deregulate electricity. Worksharing has also displayed stable, continuous growth regardless of the political situation. It is thus unlikely that liberalization is attributable to changing political circumstances.

Regarding the future, it is likely that US postal liberalization will continue. One among several reasons is the rising use of electronic bill presentment and payment (EBPP). This is the process by which companies bill consumers and/or receive payments electronically, which reduces the need to send bills and checks though the mail. The major effect of EBPP on mail volume appears to be through bill payment, which was flat for many years but has begun to decline (Flynn, 2005: 2). There are signs that EBPP is growing in popularity. Between 2000 and 2003, for example, bills and statements from businesses to households grew at 3.3 percent per year, while first-class mail volumes declined. EBPP is distinct from electronic banking, which has a separate effect on mail volume. As customers become more comfortable with these alternative electronic methods of transacting, their usage rates will rise, negatively impacting mail volumes.

Also, the growing importance of advertising and business matter in the US mail stream affects postal liberalization. Advertising's share of total mail rose from 42 percent in 1987 to 48 percent in 2002. Advertising mail volume grew at 2.8 percent per year during that time, while non-advertising mail grew at 1.1 percent. Household-to-household or 'personal mail' declined from 5 percent to 3 percent of all mail during that time. The remainder is either business-to-household or household-to-business.

These developments are important because advertising material, which is normally sent as Standard Mail, has significantly higher demand elasticity than first-class mail (Geddes, 2005: 222). Advertisers have a variety of ways of reaching their customers. The shift toward advertising material suggests that mail volumes will be more sensitive to future rate increases, which will lead to more liberalization as the USPS seeks to meet its break-even requirement by cutting costs. Because advertising material is more heavily workshared, the shift will naturally lead directly to more private involvement in mail preparation. Also, because advertising material makes a small contribution to the Postal Service's overhead costs, this shift is likely to necessitate downsizing of the labor force if the break-even constraint is to be met. Finally, if other media (such as cable TV) offer a more cost effective way for advertisers to reach their customers, then there may be massive substitution out of direct mail marketing. These forces all suggest that postal liberalization is likely to continue.

SUMMARY AND CONCLUSIONS

The US Postal Service has undergone a long process of liberalization. Both the 1970 and the 2006 Acts moved the USPS toward a more businesslike, commercialized structure. Because it moves work into the private sector, worksharing in the United States has also played a significant role in liberalizing US postal services. There is no indication that postal services in the United States have been or will be reregulated.

Many of these developments are consistent with a private-interest theory of regulation, but one in which minimizing deadweight losses plays a vital role. There are many aspects of USPS organizational structure that were unaffected by either Act, including the delivery monopoly, government ownership and uniform rates. Those elements that are retained can best be understood as mechanisms for retaining and redistributing economic rents to politically influential groups, in particular organized labor. The best way to think about USPS institutional evolution may be as moving toward liberalization subject to the constraint that the loss of rents to both large mailers and employees is mitigated.

The process of liberalization of the USPS is likely to continue. Electronic alternatives to physical mail delivery are more commonplace, and consumers are more comfortable with their use. Advertisers have access to numerous alternatives.

NOTES

1. See the chapter by Sharon Oster and commentary by Henry Hansmann in Sidak (1994) for a detailed discussion of this organizational form.
2. This means that competitors are able to compete as long as they do not charge less than four times the prevailing stamp price, thus creating a reserved area of service for the incumbent.

3. After acrimonious discussion, the European Parliament determined that postal monopolies in all European Union countries must be abolished by the beginning of 2011. See http://www.freefairpost.com/pdf/Reuters_31.01.08.doc, visited 20 April 2008.
4. There were minor acts in intervening years but they did not institute major institutional changes.
5. These mailers were usually high-volume users such as advertisers.
6. *Wall Street Journal*, 20 September 1967, p. 3. This refers to 1967 dollars.
7. First-class mail is mainly personal letters, while second class is mostly periodicals and third class is mostly advertising material.
8. 'New Era Favors Career Postmasters', *Postal Life*, May 1969, p. 8.
9. See President's Commission on Postal Organization (1968), *Annex-Contractor Reports*, vol. 4, part 7, page 44. See also Priest (1994: 51) on high postal unionization rates.
10. See Geddes (2008) for a discussion of USPS autonomy in rate-setting under the 1970 act.
11. Those liabilities total about $72 billion. See Geddes (2005: 218, Table 1).
12. See Schuyler (2007) from which this discussion borrows.
13. The act lists first-class mail letters and sealed parcels; first-class mail cards; periodicals; standard mail; single-piece parcel post; media mail; bound printed matter; library mail; special services; and single-piece international mail, as market dominant products (39 USC 3621(a)(1)–(10)). The act lists priority mail, expedited mail, bulk parcel post, bulk international mail, and mailgrams as competitive products (39 USC 3631(a)(1)–(5)).
14. Under the new law, rates may be increased faster than the CPI in 'extraordinary and exceptional circumstances'.
15. 39 USC 3622(b).
16. 39 USC 3642(a). The Act, however, forbids the Postal Regulatory Commission from transferring a 'product covered by the postal monopoly' to the competitive products list (39 USC 3642(b)(2)).
17. That is, it will not benefit from sovereign immunity protections as it has in the past. Specifically, the act prohibits the USPS and other Federal agencies acting in concert with it or on its behalf, from engaging in conduct – with respect to any product not covered by the statutory postal monopoly – that constitutes an unfair method of competition. In addition, the act expressly prohibits the USPS from engaging in conduct that constitutes an unfair or deception act or practice. This latter change is important, as there have been concerns about the accuracy of USPS advertising in the past.
18. See Schuyler (2007: 3) from which this account borrows.
19. PL, 108–18.
20. Dropshipping refers to the mailer transporting the mail so that it enters the delivery process closer to its destination, thus bypassing USPS handling and transportation operations.
21. France has had worksharing discounts for many years. See Cohen *et al.* (2007). The Postal Service's system of discounts, however, is more extensive than La Poste's.
22. Ibid. These rates were typically the result of a rate case, where mailers, postal management, and unions all had input into a process overseen by the Postal Rate Commission. Because of their impact on work performed inside versus outside the USPS, these rates often generated intensive debate.
23. Those levels are the 21 regional bulk mail centers (BMCs), the 60 area distribution centers (ADCs), the 900 sectional center facilities (SCFs), and the 24 000 local delivery units (DDUs). It is currently not possible to drop ship First-class mail.
24. In his testimony before the President's Commission on the Postal Service, witness Robert H. Cohen stated that:

    > The United States letter monopoly is among the least liberal in the world because it is not subject to price or weight limitations. The US, however, allows worksharing, which has grown steadily and substantially over time. As a result, much of the value chain is now in the hands of mailers and third-party consolidators, and, due to worksharing, the US has the most liberalized postal market in the industrialized

world. Because even total liberalization of the monopoly may not be effective in creating postal competition (e.g. Sweden and New Zealand), worksharing may be a more effective way to introduce competition into a postal market.

25. First-class mail is also particularly important to the USPS because it makes a large contribution to USPS institutional or overhead costs, which are costs that cannot be attributed to any particular mail class. For example, it takes about three pieces of Standard Mail, which is mostly advertising, to make the same contribution to institutional costs as one piece of First-class mail. See Geddes (2005: 222).
26. This protracted process is evident in postal liberalization in many countries.
27. See Olson (1965), Stigler (1971), Peltzman (1976); and Becker (1983) among others.
28. Also see Geddes (2003: 216–20) for a discussion of why postal services are not naturally monopolistic. National security, rather than natural monopoly, was the originally reason for government intervention. See Priest (1975).
29. The focus here is on the use of the intervention in economic activity to redistribute wealth to politically effective groups. An alternative strand of the literature, developed by public choice scholars such as James Buchanan, William Niskanen, Gordon Tullock and others, emphasizes monopolization of the power of the state to extract rents for the benefit of political actors such as elected officials and bureaucrats. This approach may be most helpful in explaining postal policy prior to 1970, when Congress directly controlled the Post Office. The pre-1970 structure is also consistent with the ET in that two small, well-organized groups, large mailers and employees, were benefiting at the expense of diffuse poorly organized taxpayers who made up the annual deficit.
30. There is a sense in which the ET's focus on redistribution, and the NPT's focus on efficiency are unified by Becker's approach. For a refinement of this notion, see Keeler (1984).
31. The 2006 Act clearly reduced some inefficiencies in prior postal structure, such as cross-subsidies to competitive mail classes, but these are relatively minor compared to those addressed in 1970. Moreover, those inefficiencies likely existed for some time prior to the 2006 Act.
32. Peltzman (1989: 10–11) demonstrates this important result:

    > Suppose a regulated firm, X, sells to two customers, A and B. Suppose further that A and B have equal demands and equal political weight (that is, their utility enters the regulator's utility function in the same way), but that the marginal cost (MC) is higher for serving A than for serving B. Now recall the general result that X will not get maximum profits; for simplicity call this 'tax' on maximum profits, T, and assume it is fixed. Since X cares only about the size of T, not its distribution among A and B, and since A and B are politically equal, the regulator has only one remaining task: to make the price (P) to A and B (P_A and P_B), and thereby A's and B's consumer surplus, as nearly equal as possible, given T. The result will be a lower P_A/MC_A than P_B/MC_B. If T is big enough to permit it, the regulator will completely ignore the fact that $MC_A \neq MC_B$ and set $P_A = P_B$. While there are inevitable complications and ambiguities, this tendency for the high cost customer to get the low P/MC is common. It rests on the lack of any general connection between the cost differences and the political importance of the two buyers.

33. Postal Reorganization Act, sect. 7 (1970).
34. Specifically: 'It shall be the policy of the Postal Service to maintain compensation and benefits for all officers and employees on a standard of comparability to the compensation and benefits paid for comparable levels of work in the private sector of the economy' 39 USC § 1003 (a).
35. 39 USC § 3623(d) (1973). An exception is Parcel Post, which is priced according to zones.
36. See, for example, Coase (1947).
37. Miller (1985: 151) states, 'The existence of large common costs in enterprises like the

Postal Service makes it impossible to allocate total costs to individual services in a non-arbitrary manner.'

38. In a survey of the literature on state ownership by Andre Shleifer, the Postal Service was portrayed as a paradigmatic case of how contracting with private firms can address these concerns:

> A common argument for government ownership of the postal service is to enable the government to force the delivery of mail to sparsely populated areas, where it would be unprofitable to deliver it privately (Tierney, 1988). From a contractual perspective, this argument is weak. The government can always bind private companies that compete for a mail delivery concession to go wherever the government wants, or it can alternatively regulate these companies when entry is free. It cannot be so difficult to write the appropriate contract or regulation; after all, the government now tells the US Postal Service where it wants the mail to be delivered. (Shleifer, 1998: 136)

REFERENCES

Arrow, K. J. (1950), 'A difficulty in the concept of social welfare', *Journal of Political Economy*, **58** (4), 328–46.

Becker, G. S. (1983), 'A theory of competition among pressure groups for political influence', *Quarterly Journal of Economics*, **98**, 371–400.

Coase, R. H. (1947), 'The economics of uniform pricing systems', *Manchester School of Economics and Social Studies*, **15**, 139–56.

Cohen, Robert H. (2003), 'Testimony before the President's Commission on the Postal Service', www.prc.gov/pres_comm/cohen.pdf, accessed 21 April 2008.

Robert H. Cohen, William W. Ferguson, and Spyros S. Xenakis (1993), 'Rural delivery and the universal service obligation', in Michael A. Crew and Paul R. Kleindorfer (eds) *Regulation and the Nature of Postal and Delivery Services*, Boston, MA: Kluwer Academic Publishers.

Cohen, Robert H., William W. Ferguson, John D. Waller and Spyros S. Xenakis (2001), 'The impact of using worksharing to liberalize a postal market', in the Proceedings of Wissenschaftliches Institut für Kommunikationsdienste GmbH (WIK) 6th Köenigswinter Seminar on Postal Economics.

Cohen, Robert H., Matthew Robinson, Renee Sheehy, John Waller and Spyros Xenakis (2004), 'Postal regulation and worksharing in the US', in the Proceedings of Wissenschaftliches Institut für Kommunikationsdienste GmbH (WIK) 8th Köenigswinter Seminar on Regulating Postal Markets.

Cohen, Robert H., Per Jonsson, Matthew Robinson, Sten Selander, John Waller and Spyros Xenakis (2007), 'The impact of competitive entry into the Swedish postal market', paper presented at the 10th Königswinter Seminar on 'Postal Markets between Monopoly and Competition'.

Fenno, Richard F. (1973), *Congressmen in Committees,* Boston, MA, Little Brown.

Ferejohn, John and Charles Shipan (1989), 'Congress and telecommunications policy', in Paula R. Newberg (ed.), *New Directions in Telecommunications Policy*, Raleigh, NC: Duke University Press.

Flynn, Shawn P. (2005), 'Bill presentment & payment: electronic vs. mail', Pitney Bowes Background Paper No. 9.

Geddes, R. R. (1998), 'The economic effects of postal reorganization', *Journal of Regulatory Economics*, **13**, 139–56.
Geddes, R. R. (2003), *Saving the Mail: How to Solve the Problems of the US Postal Service*, Washington, DC: AEI Press.
Geddes, R. R. (2004), 'Timid steps toward postal reform', http://www.aei.org/publications/pubID.20964/pub_detail.asp, accessed 21 April 2008.
Geddes, R. R. (2005), 'Policy watch: reform of the US postal service', *Journal of Economic Perspectives*, **19** (3), 217–32.
Geddes, R. R. (2008), 'Pricing by state-owned enterprises: the case of postal services', *Managerial and Decision Economics*, **29** (7), 575–91.
Hirsch, B. T., M. L. Wachter and J. W. Gillula (1999), 'Postal service compensation and the comparability standard', *Research in Labor Economics*, **18**, 243–79.
Joskow, P. L. and R. Noll (1981), 'Regulation in theory and practice: an overview', in Gary Fromm (ed.), *Studies in Public Regulation*, Cambridge, MA, MIT Press.
Keeler, Theodore E. (1984), 'Theories of regulation and the deregulation movement', *Public Choice* **44**, 103–45.
Miller, J. (1985), 'End the postal monopoly', *Cato Journal*, **5**, 149–55.
Olson, Mancur (1965), *The Logic of Collective Action: Public Goods and the Theory of Groups*, Cambridge, MA, Harvard University Press.
Peltzman, S. (1971), 'Pricing in public and private enterprises: electric utilities in the United States', *Journal of Law and Economics*, **14** (1), 109–47.
Peltzman S. (1976), 'Toward a more general theory of regulation', *Journal of Law and Economics*, **19** (2), 211–40.
Peltzman, S. (1989), 'The economic theory of regulation after a decade of deregulation', in Martin N. Bailey and Clifford M. Winston (eds), Brookings Papers on Economic Activity: Microeconomics, pp. 1–59.
Perloff, J. M. and M. L. Watcher (1984), 'Wage comparability in the US Postal Service', *Industrial and Labor Relations Review*, **38** (1), 26–35.
President's Commission on Postal Organization (1968), *Towards Postal Excellence: The Report of the President's Commission on Postal Organization*, Washington, DC: US Government Printing Office.
Priest, George L. (1975), 'The history of the postal monopoly in the United States', *Journal of Law & Economics*, **18**, 33–80.
Priest, George L. (1994), 'Socialism and the postal monopoly', in J. Gregory Sidak (ed.) *Governing the Postal Service*, Washington, DC: AEI Press.
Schuyler, M. (2007), 'Congress delivers Postal Service legislation', Washington, DC: Institute for Research in the Economics of Taxation, IRET Congressional Advisory No. 216.
Shleifer, A. (1998), 'State versus private ownership', *Journal of Economic Perspectives*, **12** (4), 133–50.
Sidak, J. G. (1994), *Governing the Postal Service*, Washington, DC: AEI Press.
Sidak, J. G. and D. Spulber (1996), *Protecting Competition from the Postal Monopoly*, Washington, DC: The AEI Press.
Sidak, J. G. and D. Spulber (1998), *Deregulatory Takings and the Regulatory Contract*, Cambridge: Cambridge University Press.
Smith, S. P. (1976), 'Are postal workers over- or underpaid?' *Industrial Relations*, **15**, 68–176.
Smith S. P. (1977), *Equal Pay in the Public Sector: Fact or Fancy?* Princeton, NJ: Industrial Relations Section, Princeton University.

Stigler, G. J. (1971), 'The theory of economic regulation', *Bell Journal of Economics and Management Science*, **2**, 55–70.

Tierney, John T. (1981), *Postal Reorganization: Managing the Public's Business*, Boston, MA, Auburn House.

Tierney, John T. (1988), *The US Postal Service: Status and Prospects of a Public Enterprise*, Dover, MA, Auburn House.

Wachter, M. L. and J. M. Perloff (1991), 'A comparative analysis of wage premiums and industrial relations in the British Post Office and the United States Postal Service', in Michael A. Crew and Paul R. Kleindorfer (eds), *Competition and Innovation in Postal Services*, Boston, MA: Kluwer Academic Publishers.

APPENDIX

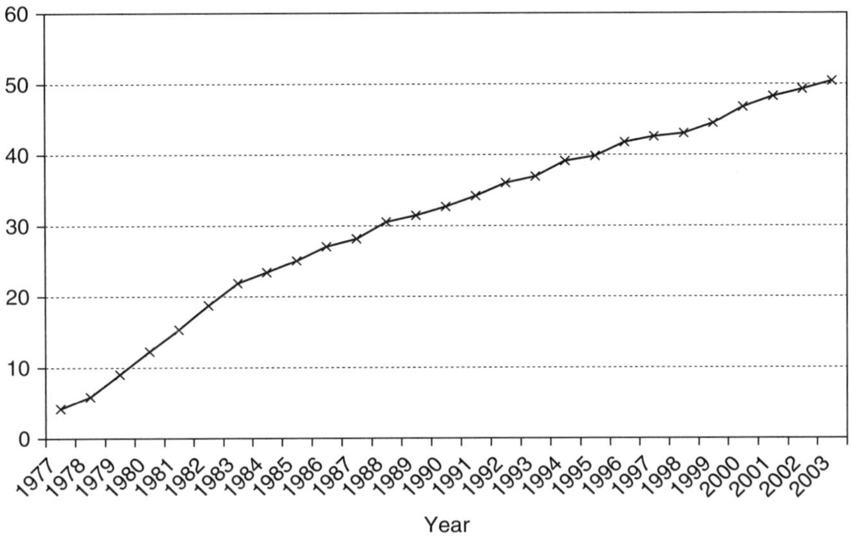

Figure 10A.1 Percentage of first-class mail volume that is workshared

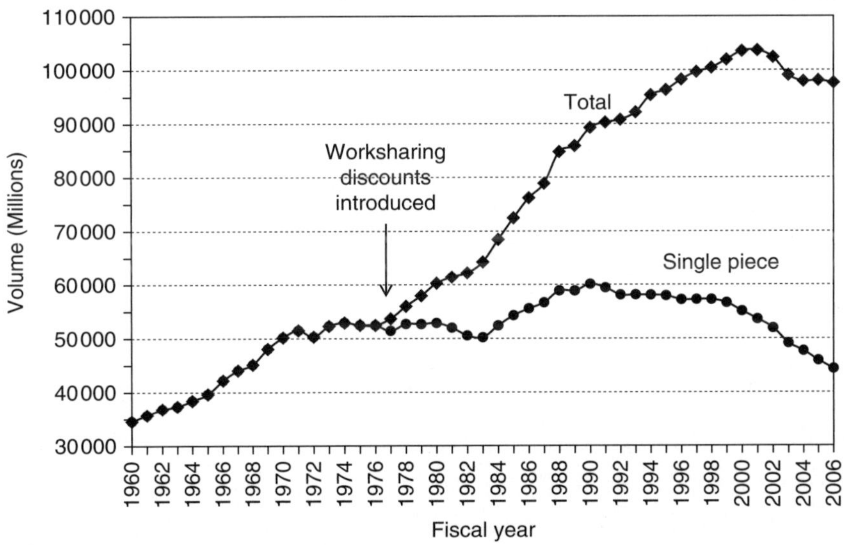

Figure 10A.2 First-class mail

PART III

Adaptation and changes

11. The Sarbanes–Oxley Act at a crossroads

Roberta Romano

INTRODUCTION

The history of US federal securities regulation can best be characterized as one of gradual expansion of regulatory scope within, in essence, a disclosure regime. The regulatory approach that the landmark federal legislation of the 1930s took is one of disclosure, in contrast to the then substantive regulatory approach of most states' securities laws, which prohibited the sale of securities not meeting state regulators's approval. The greatest expansion thereafter occurred in the 1960s, when stock traded in the over-the-counter market and cash tender offers were brought under the federal ambit.[1] But Congress periodically has revisited the scope of federal regulation, requiring, in the 1970s, public companies to maintain accurate books and records, in the wake of the revelation of US companies having made questionable payments to foreign officials,[2] and increasing the sanctions against insider trading in the 1980s, after a series of high-profile cases of insider trading involving hostile takeovers.[3]

By the 1990s, however, the regulatory imperative took another turn, as Congress focused on class actions and enacted legislation restricting private civil litigation for securities violations.[4] The Securities and Exchange Commission ('SEC'), by contrast, has consistently increased required disclosures, action it can undertake without the need for congressional authorization. The only instances in which the SEC has cut back on its regulatory reach have occurred where it has experienced competitive pressure from other regulatory jurisdictions, such as in adoption of shelf registration rules, that sought to curb the exodus of US debt offerings into the unregulated Eurobond market, or in limiting the disclosures required of foreign private issuers.

Following a number of spectacular corporate failures in 2001–2, Congress once again expanded the reach of federal regulation with the near unanimous enactment of the Sarbanes–Oxley Act ('SOX').[5] SOX increased the regulation of accounting firms as well as of issuers, by creating a new regulator for the accounting profession, the Public Company Accounting Oversight Board ('PCAOB'), and by imposing substantive governance mandates on public companies. The corporate governance requirements include management attestation of internal controls and financial statement accuracy, mandates regarding audit committee composition and functioning, forfeiture of CEO incentive compensation upon issuance of an accounting restatement, and prohibition of executive loans and the purchase of non-audit services from auditors. In addition, a small number of the provisions in SOX followed the conventional federal approach to securities regulation, by enhancing disclosure requirements and criminal penalties for securities violations.

After only a few years' post-enactment, however, widespread dissatisfaction has been expressed over the regulatory burden imposed by SOX. In particular, calls for rolling back the most burdensome provision of SOX have occurred with increased frequency, receiving the endorsement of prominent government and private commissions. The commissions' recommendations have been informed by a perceived weakening in the competitiveness of US capital markets and the disproportionate impact of SOX on smaller public firms. Their reports point, with varying degrees of emphasis, to a significant decrease in the number of new foreign listings and public offerings on US exchanges, and a commensurate increase in foreign delistings and domestic going private transactions, post-SOX.

The sea change in the perception of the value of SOX and the willingness to advance an agenda of lightening its regulatory burden is truly astounding given the overwhelming support for the legislation when enacted. SOX's advocates now find themselves increasingly in a politically defensive posture, having to justify and stave off attempts to dismantle, key components of the legislation. They are, of course, in a formidable defensive position, as it is a daunting task to adopt legislation: a supermajority – 60 Senate votes – is necessary for all practical purposes to alter the status quo. But the widespread criticism of SOX has, in fact, led the SEC to revisit its implementation, action in part taken no doubt preemptively to deflect efforts by members of Congress to revamp the legislation. Even in the midst of the subprime mortgage crisis and credit crunch of 2007–8, there has been neither a revival of praise for SOX nor backtracking by its critics.

The case history of the pushback on SOX is the subject of this chapter. The first section introduces the post-SOX policy debate concerning the statute, framed by four commissioned reports that call for alteration in SOX's implementation given its burdening of small firms and US capital markets. The second section of the chapter summarizes media and congressional responses to the critiques of SOX voiced in the reports. The rationale for this approach is that it facilitates gauging the political support for, and opposition to, revamping SOX and the form any congressional reform effort would take, as the media attempts to inform and shape the debate: an empirical political science literature has identified a connection between the saliency with which an issue is reported in the media and policy change. The chapter concludes with a prognosis of SOX's future.

POST-SOX PUSHBACK

Two key developments have framed the post-enactment debate over SOX. The first is the substantial expenditures firms have incurred to comply with section 404, which requires management to certify the adequacy of its internal controls and the outside auditor to attest to management's certification, and the disproportionately larger expected costs for smaller firms.[6] The second development involves capital market trends indicating a decline in the competitive position of the New York stock exchanges compared to foreign exchanges, particularly the London stock exchange. These developments have been the focus of four prominent commissioned reports.[7]

Pushback Related to Small Firm Costs

The Advisory Committee on Smaller Public Companies to the SEC ('SEC Advisory Committee') was established in early 2005 by then SEC Chairman William Donaldson, in response to complaints by small firms regarding the expenses that were being incurred in order to comply with SOX, and in particular, section 404. Its mission was to advise the SEC on how to assure that the costs of regulation for smaller companies would not be greater than the benefits. The committee held public hearings across the country, a decision that undoubtedly generated heightened awareness of and support for small firms's concerns. It issued an interim report in August 2005, whose recommendation to delay implementation of section 404 and real-time filing of periodic reports for small firms was adopted, and a final report in April 2006. The principal recommendation in its final report was to exempt small firms from section 404. The recommendation, which was not unanimous, would have exempted a far larger number of firms than the small firms for whom section 404 compliance was deferred: 78.5 versus 44 percent of public companies.

As a key rationale for the need for exemptive relief, the report emphasized that studies of section 404 compliance had found that actual expenditures were wildly in excess of the amount originally anticipated by the SEC to cover compliance (in the millions of dollars versus $91 000), and that even with a reduction in costs incurred in the second year of compliance, average expenditures were still considerable ($900 000 for smaller firms).[8] Compliance costs for smaller firms were expected to be higher and, of course, a much larger percentage of revenue. While not yet having to comply with section 404, audit fees had tripled from 2000–4 (before and after SOX) as a percentage of revenue for smaller public companies and, as the committee noted, best estimates of section 404 compliance costs placed external audit fees at only one-fourth to one-third of the total cost (Advisory Committee on Smaller Public Companies, 2006, p. 34).[9]

The SEC Advisory Committee further noted that SOX had introduced additional ongoing increased expenditures for smaller firms, that were insignificant for large firms, apart from internal controls. For example, small firms were less likely than large firms to have a sufficient number of independent directors to meet the stock exchange requirements adopted in conjunction with SOX along with SOX's audit committee mandate, and the expenses from an increased board size are recurring. A recent study by Linck *et al.* (2007) lends support to the Advisory Committee's contention, indicating that director compensation costs have risen dramatically, and disproportionately, for small firms post-SOX.

Besides documenting that small firms would bear far greater costs than large firms, the Committee further emphasized the disproportionate burden section 404 imposes on smaller firms because of their organizational structure, as well as more limited resources, personnel and revenue to offset implementation, compared to large firms. Transaction cost economics suggests that the cost of implementing a system of internal control is related to the trade-off between incentives and control that determines firm size (the degree of vertical integration of production) (for example, Williamson, 1975, 1985). Specifically, decisional authority is more concentrated in top management in smaller public companies, while their span of control is greater, and there are fewer personnel among whom tasks can be segregated to achieve internal controls than would be considered effective under the standard implementing section 404, which is geared to large organizations. Furthermore, features considered to be the hallmark of small compared to large firm operations – greater fluidity and flexibility of processes and individual tasks that are frequently shifted to meet changing business needs as a business grows – render SOX compliance difficult because such firms do not have static processes with well-defined boundaries that can be easily documented in an internal controls system. Accordingly, in the Committee's judgment, the 'one-size-fits-all' mentality embodied in the legislation and its implementation by the SEC was a profound misunderstanding of what internal controls would be appropriate for small firms.

By the time the Committee completed its study there was a new SEC Chairman, Christopher Cox, a former Republican congressman who had been a member of the conference committee that enacted SOX. Chairman Cox's response to the SEC Advisory Committee's recommendation was an announcement that the agency would not exempt small firms from the statute but that it would review the implementation of section 404 to reduce the regulatory burden imposed on all companies and delay yet again its implementation for small and foreign issuers (with the auditor attestation component being deferred one year further). The rationale for ignoring the committee's recommendation and instead postponing compliance for another year was that by then new guidance would be in place and the provision's regulatory burden would be reduced, making compliance 'doable' for smaller firms.

Pushback Related to Market Competitiveness

In contrast to the SEC Advisory Committee's focus on SOX's regulatory burden on smaller firms, the other three commissioned reports were directed at the impact of SOX on the global competitiveness of US firms and markets. The Committee on Capital Markets Regulation ('Paulson Committee') was a private group formed in September 2006 for the purpose of studying issues, and recommending policy changes, related to 'maintaining and improving the competitiveness of the US capital markets' (Committee on Capital Markets Regulation, 2006: vii). The group is often referred to as the 'Paulson Committee' because in the press release announcing its formation, Treasury Department Secretary Henry M. Paulson praised its creation and the committee's co-chair and director, a Harvard law professor, stated that Secretary Paulson had requested a November date for the committee's report so that the recommendations 'could be considered at post-election meetings of Congress' (Norris, 2006). Their working assumption no doubt was that the Republicans would continue to control Congress, which did not occur.

The committee's report presented data indicating that the competitive position of US capital markets has eroded: a decline in foreign company initial public offerings ('IPOs'), increase in foreign firms's private equity issues, increase in domestic going private transactions and in venture capital exits by private sales rather than IPOs and decline in the listing premium for cross-listed foreign firms. It identified several causes of the perceived decline in competitiveness, including litigation costs and not solely SOX. In contrast to the SEC Advisory Committee, the Paulson Committee did not recommend exemption of small firms from SOX. Instead, it recommended three modifications in section 404's implementation that would reduce its burden on all firms: a redefinition of materiality, increased guidance by the PCAOB for auditors so as to reduce their demands on management, and multi-year rotational testing for low-risk components of internal controls, which it thought would resolve the provision's compliance burdens.[10] As those suggested changes could be accomplished by SEC rule-making, it concluded that there was no need for legislative revision. By the time of the report's release, the Paulson Committee was aware not only of Chairman Cox's opposition to the SEC Advisory Committee's recommendations and legislative revision of SOX, but also of the new political reality in which the Democrats would be in control of Congress. Advocating that relaxation of SOX should be left to SEC rulemaking was regulatory relief that the Republican administration could accomplish on its own.

The Paulson Committee took a different tack to foreign firms' SOX compliance problems. It advocated exempting foreign firms from section 404 if they were subject to equivalent home-state regulation of internal controls. These firms' concern were of primary interest to the New York Stock Exchange ('NYSE'), which viewed SOX as adversely affecting its competitive position for foreign listings. The NYSE has long campaigned for permitting foreign issuers to be governed by home regulators in order to improve its market position against its principal competitor, the London Stock Exchange, because home rule would reduce the cost of those firms' listing in the United States (for example, Cochrane, 1994).

At approximately the same time that the Paulson Committee was being formed, Senator Charles Schumer and New York City Mayor Michael Bloomberg commissioned a study through the city's Economic Development Corporation from the consulting firm McKinsey and Co. to ascertain why foreign firms were increasingly raising capital outside of New York. McKinsey's study, released at a January 2007 media event attended by the Senator, Mayor and then New York Governor Eliot Spitzer, paralleled the Paulson Committee's report regarding the diagnosis of the problem and solution: it highlighted SOX and litigation as principal causes of the declining competitiveness of New York's stock markets and recommended modifications in the implementation of section 404 to provide clearer guidance, including a revised definition of materiality, and a 'top-down' (that is, management not auditor controlled) 'risk-based' approach.

The McKinsey study did differ in one respect from the Paulson Committee's report regarding the qualification offered for small firms' treatment: it recommended that the SEC consider permitting small firms to opt out of section 404 entirely (with disclosure of this choice to investors), if the agency's proposed guidance did not lower small firms' compliance costs, and not simply from the auditor attestation requirement. It also recommended that the agency consider exempting foreign firms that complied with foreign regulatory regimes receiving SEC approval, paralleling the Paulson Committee's position. No doubt, given its sponsorship by elected officials, the study was intended to advance an important political objective, to dramatize the relative deteriorating condition of a major contributor to New York's economy, and thereby mobilize support for concerted government action at the local, state and federal levels to rectify the situation.

The third reporting group studying US capital markets's competitiveness, the Commission on the Regulation of Capital Markets in the 21st Century ('Chamber Commission'), was created by the US Chamber of Commerce in February 2006. Although its report, issued in March 2007, voiced similar concerns to the other two reports, the recommendation on SOX differed in one important respect, an insistence on congressional action. It advocated legislation incorporating SOX into the Securities Exchange Act of 1934, in order to clarify that the SEC's exemptive power[11] was applicable to SOX's section 404. It advanced this approach as a mechanism to provide flexibility for the agency's implementation of SOX, so that it could vary section 404's requirements for differently sized public companies and exempt foreign firms. Advocacy of an approach permitting flexibility in small firms's regulation is consistent with the position the Chamber of Commerce took when SOX was moving through the legislative process: the Chamber lobbied at the time for differential treatment for small firms regarding provisions restricting auditor services (Romano, 2005: 1565).

To promote its agenda (which also advocated dramatic reorganization of the SEC), in conjunction with the report's release the Chamber held a summit, which was attended by SEC Chairman Cox and members of Congress. In a speech delivered at that meeting, Chairman Cox rejected the Chamber Commission's recommendation regarding SOX, stating: 'We don't need to change the law; we need to change the way the law is implemented, [and] the SEC has all the power and flexibility we need' (McTeague and Hill, 2007: 266). The key Democratic lawmakers present, Congressman Barney Frank and Senator Christopher Dodd, who chaired their chambers's committees with jurisdiction over the SEC, concurred with that judgment (McTeague and Hill, 2007).

THE MEDIA AND CONGRESS RESPOND TO SOX'S CONSEQUENCES

Corporate scandals can make good copy for the news media, and the media frenzy surrounding the 2001–2 corporate accounting scandals most surely helped fuel the political dynamic that produced SOX. One measure of gauging the political climate for revisiting SOX is the frequency of news coverage of the legislation's critiques, such as the concerns expressed in the commissioned reports over SOX's impact on small firms and market competitiveness. This approach is buttressed by a political science literature finding, across policy and geographical space, that legislators and agency officials respond to issues whose salience is heightened by the media.

The Relation Between the Media, Issue Saliency and Public Policy

A theoretical and empirical literature examining the relation between the media and government policies suggests that the media can and does influence policy outcomes by affecting the saliency of an issue. That thesis is derived from agency models in which citizen-principals are imperfectly informed about the actions of their agents (politicians and government officials). In the models's setup, the news media provides information that alters an issue's salience and thereby facilitates citizen monitoring, resulting in officials adopting policies that citizens prefer (Besley *et al.*, 2002). There are also models in which media publicity concerning elected officials' positions shifts the salient issues in an election, and thereby affects election outcomes, along with policy outcomes, as politicians focused on re-election adopt policies preferred by voters (Besley *et al.*, 2002). The functioning of the media in these models can be analogized to a Williamsonian governance mechanism that enables citizens to monitor whether politicians are fulfilling commitments, and thereby renders such commitments more credible (see generally Williamson, 1996).

Empirical studies bolster the models' plausibility, finding a significant correlation between issue saliency in the media (proxied by, for example, newspaper circulation or article word counts) and the implementation of government policies or election outcomes (for example, Besley and Burgess, 2002; Ferraz and Finan, 2007; Yates and Stroup, 2000). Moreover, the relation identified in the studies between issue salience and policy and election outcomes is robust controlling for factors known to affect outcomes.

Post-SOX Media Coverage

Media coverage post-SOX of the statute's impact was investigated through three lenses: reporting by leading national business journalists, regional and national newspapers.[12] Table 11.1 tracks the coverage of these three sources of the critiques of SOX regarding small firm costs and market competitiveness, along with the four commissioned reports, over time.

Table 11.1 Media coverage of SOX critiques, 1 December 2004 – 10 June 2007

	2004	2005	2006	2007
National business journalists				
Commissioned reports	0	1	17	4
Small firm costs	0	3	6	0
Market competitiveness+	0	8	15	5
Total SOX	2	18	32	7
Regional newspapers				
Commissioned reports	0	6	19	3
Small firm costs	0	7	21	2
Market competitiveness+	1	4	23	11
Total SOX	8	35	60	24
Enron references	38	1782	936	156
National newspapers				
Commissioned reports	3	16	50	23
Small firm costs	2	16	21	4
Market competitiveness	4	22	75	36
Total SOX	12	91	162	67
Enron references	86	1103	1328	322

Notes: National business journalists' are Alan Abelson, Holman Jenkins, Gretchen Morgenson, Alan Murray, Floyd Norris, Allan Sloan, and *Wall Street Journal* editorial page; 'Regional newspapers' are the *Birmingham News*, *Boston Globe*, *Houston Chronicle*, and *San Francisco Chronicle*; 'National newspapers' are the *New York Times*, *Wall Street Journal* and *Washington Post*, and their counts exclude articles by national business journalists tallied in the table, except for the counts in 'Enron references'. 'Commissioned reports' aggregates references to the Advisory Committee on Smaller Public Companies to the SEC, Committee on Capital Markets Regulation, Commission on the Regulation of Capital Markets in the 21st Century and their reports, and to the McKinsey & Co. study commissioned by Senator Charles Schumer and Mayor Michael Bloomberg. 'Small firm costs' tallies articles referring to SOX's impact on small firms' costs. 'Market competitiveness' includes articles referencing capital market competitiveness issues such as the number of initial public offerings, private placements, acquisitions of private firms rather than public offerings, going private transactions and stock market delistings. 'Total SOX' includes articles that had some reference to costs and/or benefits of SOX, or issues involving internal controls provision, obtained from the following Lexis searches: (a) for the newspapers: (sarbane w/5 oxley) or section 404 or (conflict of interest w/5 account! or audit!) or (option! w/5 executiv!) or (small w/3 business w/5 cost!) or (small w/3 company w/5 cost!) or accounting w/3 regulation) or (accounting w/3 legislation) or (transparency w/5 financial statement! (for the newspapers); and (b) for the journalists: journalist's name with 'byline or by' ('editorial' for *Wall Street Journal* editorials), and 'regulat! or legis!'. Articles referencing other SOX issues included in the search, such as accounting disclosure and analyst conflicts of interest, are excluded from the 'Total SOX' count. The counts for the specific topics do not add up to 'Total SOX' because some articles might reference more than one topic (which are double counted) and some articles included in 'Total SOX' discussed costs without referencing small firms in particular. Because the regional newspapers did not systematically include in Lexis wire stories or columns acquired from other newspapers, relevant articles by such

Table 11.1 (continued)

sources were further identified for *Boston Globe* and *San Francisco Chronicle* from equivalent searches kindly run in those newspapers' internal databases by Lisa Tuite and Richard Geiger, those respective newspapers' librarians, and for the *Birmingham News* and *Houston Chronicle*, by manually reading their business sections for the entire sample period. 'Enron references' are all articles, including letters to the editor, obtained from the Lexis search: 'enron and not enron field and not sports'. The tally includes many articles that have no connection to the Enron accounting scandal, for example, an article might include a reference to an individual who worked for Enron or analogize another entity's financial difficulties to Enron.

A central finding is that press coverage mentioning critiques of SOX has steadily increased, although it is trivial by comparison to coverage of the Enron scandal.[13] In addition, market competitiveness issues tend to receive far more attention than small firms' costs in all three news sources, although many of the untabulated stories (the 'Total SOX' line in the table) report on SOX compliance costs, an overlapping concern.[14]

An increase in reporting of criticism of SOX over time should not come as a surprise. The initial articles appeared two years after SOX's enactment, at about the time when large firms had to implement the internal controls attestation required by section 404. The steady increase in coverage of the SOX critiques over the surveyed period is consistent with both firms' continuing to find SOX compliance onerous, and the progression of commissioned reports identifying the burdens the statute was imposing on corporations and markets.

There is a key, marked difference in emphasis across the national journalists and national newspapers, and the regional newspapers' coverage of the two principal critiques of SOX, an adverse effect on capital market competitiveness and imposition of significant and disproportionate costs on small firms. Competitiveness is the object of far greater attention by the national journalists and national newspapers than small firm costs. By contrast, regional newspapers referred about equally to SOX's impact on small firms and on capital markets, and thus comparatively more frequently, to costs borne by small firms than the national press.[15] For all sources, however, references to small firm costs have dropped off in the first half of 2007.

A difference in perspective, informed by financial considerations, regarding what are the most important business issues to report between regional and national newspapers, would seem to provide a reasonably plausible and straightforward explanation for the observed difference in coverage. Small firm issues have a local dimension, as small firms typically comprise the largest number of businesses in a locality, and their issues would therefore be of greater interest to regional than national newspaper readers. Such a local connection would be encountered throughout the country, as small firms are ubiquitous. In support of this conjecture, there is no discernible difference in the relative coverage of small firm costs versus market competitiveness across the regional newspapers, indicating that a paper's geographic location did not affect coverage.[16] The significant difference in coverage across national and regional newspapers is consistent with industry trends regarding competition between national and regional newspapers, in which the latter increase their emphasis on local stories when a national paper enters their market (George and Waldfogel, 2006: 445–6).

A declining trend in IPOs or foreign listings is also, obviously, of particular importance to stock exchanges and the financial services industry, whose profitability is in no small part effected by such transactions. That financial sector is heavily concentrated in New York, where the national journalists' publishers and two of the three principal national newspapers are headquartered, providing a compelling, complementary explanation for competitiveness to be a particular focus of their attention. One in nine jobs in New York City is in the financial services industry and that sector generates over one-third of the city's business tax income and at 15 percent of its gross domestic product, is second only to real estate in importance (McKinsey and Co., 2007: 10). Editors and reporters for those newspapers would no doubt be attuned to this specific competitiveness issue.[17] Although not separately tabulated in the table, the non-New York based paper included in the national newspaper group, the *Washington Post*, published far fewer stories on market competitiveness than did either the *New York Times* ('NYT') or *Wall Street Journal* ('WSJ'), and had a lower ratio of competitiveness to small firm cost stories, paralleling the coverage of the regional papers. In fact, the *Washington Post*'s coverage of the critiques cannot be distinguished from that of the regional papers, whereas its reporting differs significantly (as does the regional newspapers's) from that of the NYT and WSJ on the SOX critiques.[18]

The news coverage of the four commissioned reports differed across the three media sources, typically tracking differences in emphasis accorded the SOX critiques. For example, although all newspapers reported on the SEC Advisory Committee, it was ignored by all national journalists save one. But nearly all of those journalists covered the Paulson Committee. This pattern parallels the journalists' overall lack of coverage of SOX's imposition of costs on small firms: they were more inclined to cover a committee whose report emphasized market competitiveness issues than one that focused on small firms. Similarly, the national newspapers provided more coverage to the McKinsey study than did the regional newspapers.[19]

The differential relative coverage of issues relating to the SOX critiques by regional and national newspapers has important ramifications for predicting how Congress, and hence the SEC, will respond to SOX, as well as for understanding recent congressional votes. Media impact studies of Indian state and Brazilian city elections imply that coverage by regional newspapers, as opposed to national newspapers, has electoral consequences (Besley and Burgess, 2002; Ferraz and Finan, 2007). The coverage differential in light of those studies would suggest that mitigating SOX's burden on small firms – the issue mentioned relatively more often by regional than national newspapers – has a higher likelihood of being front and center on Congress's agenda than resolving market competitiveness issues, than as might be inferred from examining solely the New York-based national newspapers. This would be particularly so as elections draw near, as legislators, to improve their electoral prospects, respond more attentively to constituents whose specific priorities are more often picked up in regional, not national, newspapers. This hypothesized behavior is, in fact, consistent with what we observe.

Congressional Efforts to Respond to the Critiques of SOX

There was no activity by legislators to loosen SOX's strictures until 2005, mirroring the media coverage of the SOX critiques. In the 109th Congress (2005–6), seven bills were introduced to reduce compliance and in the first six months of the 110th Congress (2007–8), eight such bills have been introduced. Paralleling the relative emphasis in coverage of the issues by the regional newspapers, compared to the national newspapers, most bills have focused on reducing the regulatory burden for small firms. Although the vast majority of bill sponsors and co-sponsors are Republicans, who are in the minority, their number is consequential.[20] Because cosponsorship is conventionally interpreted as a signal of legislative support (for example, Wilson and Young, 1997), this development is noteworthy. There has also been an uptick in hearings in which legislators have expressed concern over SOX (from a handful of hearings in 2004–5 to eight in 2006 and five in the first six months of 2007).

In addition to bill introductions and hearings, there have been three floor votes (two in the Senate and one in the House) which not only convey legislators' increasing unease with SOX's aftereffect, but also a shift in legislators' sentiment since SOX's virtually unanimous enactment. In April 2007, the Senate began consideration of a bill entitled the 'America Competes Act', which had broad bipartisan support: it authorized several billion dollars of spending on research in science and technology and on math and science teachers. Although the congressional leadership, no doubt, did not have SOX in its sights when advancing the legislation, it was packaged as an effort at 'maintaining competitiveness'. Senator Jim DeMint, a Republican from South Carolina and sponsor of a separate bill to exempt small firms from section 404 and revise implementation standards to reduce costs for complying issuers, introduced the small firm exemption as an amendment to the 'America Competes Act'.

A vote on the DeMint amendment was avoided by the Democratic majority by a strategic maneuver in which Senator Dodd, the banking committee chairman, supported by the committee's ranking member, Senator Richard Shelby, offered a competing amendment, that procedurally took precedence. It took the form of a resolution that consisted of a set of findings on SOX that: (a) it had enhanced corporate governance; (b) the SEC had determined it burdened small firms; and (c) the SEC Chairman had said the law did not have to be changed, and concluded with a sense of the Senate that exhorted the SEC and PCAOB to 'complete the promulgation of the final rules implementing section 404'.[21] The Dodd–Shelby amendment was adopted unanimously, and its sponsors then moved to table Senator DeMint's amendment, as inappropriate while the agency was working to come up with a fix for the problem. The maneuver succeeded, but over two-thirds of Republicans, constituting somewhat more than one-third of the Senators (35), voted against tabling the DeMint amendment.[22]

The procedural vote on the DeMint amendment is notable because it suggests that the core of the Republican party was willing to go on record in support of rolling back a significant chunk of SOX. With that vote, the legitimacy of a significant piece of SOX, in contrast to other landmark federal securities legislation such as the 1933 and 1934 Acts, has been put in question not just in academic circles but also in the political arena. Moreover, the Senate leadership apparently deemed a competing resolution of value for damping support for the DeMint amendment. The DeMint amendment would most certainly not have been enacted had there been no counter-proposal, as Senate voting procedures require a supermajority to stop debate by the cloture mechanism and Senator Dodd was dead set against revising SOX. The maneuver can therefore be understood to have offered two obvious advantages to Senator Dodd over a straight up or down vote on the DeMint amendment. It permitted him, and other colleagues, both to express empathy over SOX's impact on small firms and to reduce the possibility of having to exercise senatorial prerogative to block the amendment, or voting against it, and thereby being on record as opposed to revamping SOX. This behavior is consistent with the proposition that the political support for SOX has dramatically eroded. Indeed, converting a substantive vote into a procedural motion is a well-recognized Senate maneuver to avoid a controversial vote (Oleszek, 2007: 234).

A vote in the House of Representatives is of even greater consequence than that in the Senate. On 28 June 2007, the House passed the 2008 fiscal year appropriations bill for financial services and general government. That bill contained an amendment that prohibited the SEC from expending any of the appropriated funds on enforcing section 404 against small firms (the non-accelerated filers who would otherwise have to start complying with the section in 2008 because of the SEC's refusal to extend the postponed implementation for those firms beyond the current year). The amendment, offered by Representative Scott Garrett, a Republican from New Jersey, garnered bipartisan support as it was adopted by a vote of 267 to 154.[23]

Three factors plausibly explain the difference in voting support for revisiting SOX across the chambers. The House, the more frequently elected chamber, tends to be more closely attuned to concerns of the electorate than the Senate; the House vote was substantive and not procedural, so that the import of a negative vote would be more transparent to constituents rendering party discipline more difficult to enforce; and the provision upon which the House voted was more modest than the Senate's, as it called for a further delay in, rather than elimination of, SOX's application to small firms. Given the amendment's bipartisan support, it is not surprising that, in view of this vote, Chairman Cox, in testimony to the House Small Business Committee in December 2007, stated that he would propose postponing small firms' compliance with section 404's required auditor attestation on internal controls for an additional year to permit the agency's staff to undertake a study of the costs and benefits of section 404's implementation (Manickavasagam, 2007).[24]

PROGNOSIS ON SOX'S FUTURE

If history is a guide, Congress is typically unable to move rapidly to alter statutes regulating financial markets widely perceived to be flawed. It is instructive, for instance, that it took over 60 years to repeal the Glass–Steagall Act, which separated commercial and investment banking, although efforts were made to do so over the intervening decades. The law was only revamped in the aftermath of the banking debacle of the 1980s and awareness that the regulatory setup had contributed to the crisis and reduced competitiveness of US banks, with the accumulation of research indicating that banks' combined activities had not been responsible for the financial difficulties of the 1930s and that universal banking did not adversely affect the economies of the many nations permitting it (Barth *et al.*, 2000: 192).

Another pertinent illustration that is most apt as a template for prognostication on SOX involves the Foreign Corrupt Practices Act ('FCPA') of 1977, a statute with a regulatory objective similar to that of SOX, the adequacy of public companies' internal controls. Paralleling SOX, the FCPA was adopted with little opposition following an accounting scandal, the revelation that hundreds of firms had paid foreign officials hundreds of millions of dollars, not disclosed in their financial statements, in order to do business abroad (Fremantle and Katz, 1989: 755). The FCPA made illegal all but certain *de minimus* payments to foreign officials, including payments to third parties that ended up in government hands, imposed an accurate reporting and internal controls system requirement on public companies, and criminalized 'slush fund' disguised accounting as well as the payment of bribes.

Shortly after the FCPA was enacted, however, the business community began voicing concern over ambiguity in the statutory language regarding what constituted illegal conduct, and questions were raised about the cost of the new accounting requirements along with uncertainty in the scope of enforcement. Small firms were the most seriously disadvantaged by the statute: because they did not have the resources to operate abroad directly, small exporters used foreign agents and were therefore exposed to liability for actions by third parties whom they did not control. Efforts to revise the legislation began in earnest with the election of President Reagan, as improving US firms's global competitiveness was a core concern of his administration and revising the FCPA became a key feature in that agenda. The departing chairman of the SEC attempted to mitigate the objections to the FCPA by releasing a policy statement in January 1981 emphasizing 'reasonableness' in implementation and enforcement (SEC, 1981), a move strikingly replicated by the contemporary SEC's issuance of clarifying guidance on section 404's implementation. That effort failed, however, to resolve firms' perceived problems with the statute.

Immediately after taking office in 1981, the Reagan Administration began seeking congressional amendment of the FCPA, advocating not only redrafting to eliminate uncertainty but also repeal of criminal penalties.[25] Senator John Chaffee, who had introduced legislation to revise the FCPA prior to the election, reintroduced his bill in February 1981, which did not go as far as to eliminate criminal sanctions, and a similar bill was introduced simultaneously in the House. The Republican-controlled Senate passed that bill (by voice vote) in November 1981, but it stalled in the Democratic-controlled House (where a key legislator, the chairman of the subcommittee with jurisdiction, was unalterably opposed to tampering with the FCPA).

Bills to amend the statute to resolve business's concerns were introduced in each succeeding Congress (1983, 1985, 1987) with one approved again by the Senate only to be stalled in the House, and the revision was finally accomplished as an amendment to omnibus trade legislation in 1988 (Fremantle and Katz, 1989: 759). The amendment revised the FCPA's accounting and bribery provisions, addressing concerns regarding recordkeeping costs and third party payment liability, revisions that resolved difficulties the FCPA created for all firms but that were, as legislators noted in supporting the amendments, of especial importance to small firms.[26] Although the Republicans by then no longer controlled the Senate, support for recrafting the legislation was so overwhelming that the amendment could not be stopped by its few, albeit influential, Democratic opponents, who included the Senate banking committee chairman (a chief sponsor of the FCPA) and the former House subcommittee chairman who, after years of successfully bottling up the statute's amendment in the House, had recently been elected to the Senate.

If revision of SOX is not to take a similarly glacial course as that of the two illustrations, a major shift in the political environment would appear to be necessary. The recent congressional votes indicate that a substantial block of the Republican party is willing to revise a key provision of the statute, but not yet a majority of Democrats, and given the multiple veto points in the legislative process, the Republicans would not only need to retain the executive branch but also to recapture both chambers of Congress to ensure with substantial certainty that revising SOX moved up on the legislative agenda. Such a scenario would seem improbable given the political environment.[27] The Reagan administration did accomplish a revision of the FCPA under a Democratically controlled Congress but, as earlier mentioned, it took two terms to forge bipartisan support, along with a fortuitous event, the departure from the House to the Senate of a key Democrat who was said to have had single-handedly blocked the initiative in that chamber.

A key variable for predicting whether a significant revision could be accomplished without Republican political control is the state of the economy. Were the economy to deteriorate dramatically, if the downturn could be linked to SOX, then it could be politically perilous for legislators of any party to oppose SOX's revision, even though casual empiricism would suggest that congressional activity in response to economic declines or crises more often produces the precise opposite effect, an increase, not decrease, in regulation (Romano, 2005: 1591–4). However, drawing a link between SOX and an economic downturn, particularly issues of concern to voters in that context, such as deteriorating employment or wage levels or increasing inflation, would seem to be problematic, as those factors are not easily connected to the financial position of small firms and stock exchanges. There is no self-evident connection, for example, between SOX and the cascading credit crunch that has followed the subprime mortgage crisis, an absence of linkage that has a double-edged import: the crisis has not generated a backlash against the critiques of SOX, but it may well decelerate congressional effort to revise SOX by redirecting legislators' attention to banking issues.[28]

The most plausible scope of congressional action on SOX, absent Republican control of both the legislative and executive branches of the government, would seem to be a narrowly crafted elimination of the statute's applicability to the smallest firms. The number of Senators willing to support such a revision can be expected to increase if the SEC's interpretive guidance on section 404 does not have the agency's hoped for reduction in compliance costs for small firms.[29] That is, in my judgment, a probable scenario because much of the implementation problem involves external auditors's decisions (see, for example, Grundfest and Bochner, 2007), and auditors have been loath to cooperate in implementing a more flexible interpretation of the regulations. The accounting firms' comment letters to the SEC's proposed guidance, for instance, suggest that they might well not cooperate with the stated goal of a more flexible internal controls attestation process.[30] They would appear to prefer having employees follow mechanical rules and procedures rather than exercise judgment, especially when doing so would relax the audit standard, as implied by the revised guidance's suggestion that auditors use judgment and consider a firm's size and complexity.

No doubt, a primary reason for that cautious reaction is that accounting firms have adopted a decidedly risk averse approach to liability risk in response to the collapse of Arthur Andersen and the devastating financial losses sustained by that firm's members. But the firms have also been a principal beneficiary of section 404, and maintenance of the lucrative revenue stream from internal control audits under the existing standard may be an additional motivation for their resistance to the revised guidance. To the extent that such financial self-interest is a factor, if the revised guidance fails and a legislative move to exempt small firms from all of section 404 or the auditor attestation component materializes, then the threat to revenues might induce accounting firms to alter their approach to section 404 and reduce costs, similar to the SEC's accommodation to the House's appropriations bill amendment regarding section 404.

The politics of the issue also make small firm relief the most probable scenario for possible change to SOX. In addition to the influence on legislators of the constituent connection of small firms being numerous and located in all districts, evident in the relative coverage of regional newspapers of the

SOX critiques, public opinion in the United States has historically been decidedly more supportive of small rather than big business (Lipset and Schneider, 1987). For example, support levels persistently differ across opinion poll questions where the differences involve using the phrase 'big business' instead of 'business' or 'small business'. Rolling back regulation whose cost unduly burdens small firms would more easily resonate with the public than broad-based reform benefiting large firms and stock exchanges, and therefore is likely to be a politically more attractive position, which could be more credibly explained to constituents who might question the need for reform.[31] Of course, were the probability of enactment of regulatory relief for small firms to increase dramatically, then the SEC could well act preemptively and exempt small firms from part or all of section 404 in order to avoid the rebuke of a legislative directive, as illustrated by its action to delay further the applicability of section 404 to small firms following the House vote prohibiting agency expenditures to implement it.

All of this is not to say that the market competitiveness concerns raised by the reports of the Paulson Committee, McKinsey study and Chamber Commission with respect to SOX will necessarily be ignored by Congress.[32] The New York metropolitan area that is most adversely impacted by the issue has legislators in key congressional leadership positions. But the rubric of 'market competitiveness' issues is amenable to diverse SEC initiatives. The SEC, for instance, recently held a roundtable to explore the concept of 'selective mutual recognition' under which it would cede its regulatory jurisdiction to selected home country regulators of foreign firms listed on US exchanges (SEC, 2007b).[33] As Congress explicitly mandated that SOX apply to foreign firms, for such an initiative to work most effectively congressional action to revise SOX's language regarding foreign firms would presumably be necessary (whether undertaken on its own or at the behest of the agency).

Mutual recognition could be a dramatic development in SEC regulation, although the more selective – that is, the more the foreign regulatory regime must match that of the United States – the less meaningful the impact. If it resulted in specific SOX provisions being inapplicable to foreign issuers whose home regimes lacked the provisions, as is true of section 404, then there would surely be increased domestic political pressure for repeal of the provision for all US issuers to remove the asymmetry in regulation. That is because the competitive disadvantage of US firms compared to foreign firms would be exacerbated by such a policy, albeit the competitive position of US exchanges would be improved.

There are, of course, more US corporations than US stock exchanges. In this context, the foreign competitiveness issue would become more diffused across states: large domestic issuers, while perhaps not as ubiquitous as small public companies, are geographically spread out across the nation, compared to the stock exchanges and financial services industry voicing the current competitiveness concerns regarding SOX, which are concentrated in New York and a few other major urban areas. Moreover, US issuers might successfully reincorporate abroad and return as foreign cross-listed issuers to avoid SOX under a mutual recognition regime, and that would only further aggravate, rather than relieve, the stock exchanges' difficulties. Of course, this entire scenario is highly speculative, as it is not at all apparent that the concept of selective mutual recognition will ever go beyond the current Commission's drawing board.

CONCLUSION

As the post-SOX pushback illustrates, the critiques of SOX relating to adverse economic consequences for small firms and capital markets have gradually seeped into the political arena and have received increased media attention. This has resulted in several congressional votes conveying legislators's unease with the statute despite its virtually unanimous approval only a few years earlier. Readers of this chapter familiar with Oliver Williamson's seminal work on transaction cost economics would have had no difficulty anticipating the difficulties that are being experienced. Transaction cost economics emphasizes the importance of taking a microanalytic approach to firms and matching governance institutions to the specifics of organizational requirements and emphasizes that different forms of organization persist because they have different efficiency properties that determine their structure and form. From the perspective of transaction cost economics, SOX's mandate of uniform governance mechanisms for starkly different economic organizations is self-evidently wrong-headed, for a 'one-size-fits-all' regulatory setup is oblivious to the microanalytic context of organizational choice.

The US political system of separation of powers and checks and balances renders political power diffuse and the regulatory status quo, accordingly, quite difficult to recalibrate. Expansions of federal securities regulation have therefore occurred only sporadically, often after major business crises that focused public attention on firms and financial markets and galvanized legislators with reelection concerns to take action. Modification of poorly conceived securities regulation enacted in response to such crises has occurred even more episodically, taking many years to accomplish despite recognition in the academic and business community of the legislation's flaws. Consequently, despite the increasingly expressed dissatisfaction with SOX, absent a dramatic change in the political environment, it could well take considerable time before the statute's most severe shortcomings are adequately addressed.

ACKNOWLEDGMENTS

Oscar M. Ruebhausen Professor of Law, Yale Law School and Director, Yale Law School Center for the Study of Corporate Law, Research Associate, National Bureau of Economic Research, and Fellow, European Corporate Governance Institute. Gregory Ruben, YLS '08 provided superb research assistance. I have also benefited from helpful suggestions by Claude Menard and a referee.

NOTES

1. Securities Acts Amendments, Pub. L. No. 88-467, 78 Stat. 565 (1964); Williams Act, Pub. L. No. 90-439, 82 Stat. 454 (1968).
2. Foreign Corrupt Practices Act of 1977, Pub. L. No. 95-213, 91 Stat. 1494 (1977).
3. Insider Trading Sanctions Act, Pub. L. No. 98-376, 98 Stat. 1264 (1984); Insider Trading and Securities Fraud Enforcement Act, Pub. L. No. 101-704, 102 Stat. 4677 (1988).
4. Private Litigation Securities Reform Act, Pub. L. No. 104-67, 109 Stat. 737 (1995); Securities Litigation Uniform Standards Act, Pub. Law No. 105-353, 112 Stat. 3227 (1998).
5. Pub. L. No. 107-204, 116 Stat. 745 (2002). The Senate vote was unanimous; three members of the House voted against the legislation.
6. Compliance with the section has been postponed for the smallest of firms, those with a public float under $75 million ('non-accelerated filers' under 17 CFR. 240.12b-2).
7. In May 2007 the Financial Services Roundtable, the trade association for the largest financial services companies, created a fifth commission, as a follow-up to the issues raised by the three reports discussed in the text, with the objective of developing a 'competitiveness' regulatory agenda for the industry, and its report was issued in November 2007.
8. The SEC estimated that the average annual internal cost of compliance for section 404 would be $91 000 over the first three years in its 2003 regulatory release implementing the provision (Advisory Committee on Smaller Public Companies, 2006: 39). The compliance figures noted by the SEC Advisory Committee are from a study commissioned by the big four accounting firms. Sneller and Langendijk (2007) compile several studies' estimates of compliance costs along with an actual case study, all of which indicate stunning underestimation of the cost, by several orders of magnitude, by the SEC (whether one uses the SEC estimate they report of $34 300, or the $91 000 reported by the SEC Advisory Committee).
9. Several studies (for example, Eldridge and Kealey, 2005; Linck *et al.*, 2007; Sneller and Langendijk, 2007), along with surveys by the Financial Executives Institute and the law firm Foley and Lardner, have reported dramatic increases in audit fees, in addition to the SEC Advisory Committee's data derived from an SEC report. Throughout the period, the percentage of revenues that audit fees represent for smaller companies is much higher than it is for large companies.
10. It did add a caveat: if the SEC found, after adopting the report's proposed modifications, that compliance with section 404 was still too burdensome for small companies (firms that had not yet had to comply, and not those considered small under the more

expansive definition of the SEC Advisory Committee), then the committee recommended that the agency should seek legislation to exempt those firms from the auditor attestation requirement of the statute along with revision of management's required certification language, so that the language would accord with the lower level of certainty regarding internal controls that would accompany a lack of auditor attestation.

11. Section 36 of the 1934 Act, 15 USC §78mm. Some scholars contend that the SEC's exemptive authority is inapplicable to section 404 because Congress did not cast that provision as an amendment to the 1934 Act (for example, Cox, 2006).
12. The journalists and their newspapers for which searches were conducted are: Alan Abelson of Barrons, Holman Jenkins and Alan Murray of the *Wall Street Journal* ('WSJ'), Gretchen Morgenson and Floyd Norris of the *New York Times* ('NYT'), and Allan Sloan of *Newsweek*. The editorial page of the WSJ, the leading business newspaper, is also included in the individual journalist category, as it is a national editorial page that is thought not only to possess a distinctive editorial voice but also to wield clout. The tracked national newspapers are the NYT, WSJ and Washington Post. The four tracked regional papers are the *Birmingham News*, *Boston Globe*, *Houston Chronicle* and *San Francisco Chronicle*. Those newspapers were chosen to provide diverse geographical, as well as ideological, coverage. According to a measure of 'media slant' constructed from a comprehensive newspaper database by Gentzkow and Shapiro (2006), the Boston and San Francisco papers, along with the NYT and *Washington Post*, are on the left of the political spectrum and the Birmingham and Houston papers, along with the WSJ, are on the right. For a detailed discussion of the data see Romano (2008).
13. As indicated in Table 11.1, the 2007 entries are from slightly less than six months of coverage (through 10 June), compared to full years of coverage for 2005 and 2006, and the 2004 coverage is for only the month of December. To gauge the persistence of the relative salience of Enron, a search was conducted for news stories containing the word 'Enron'. The tally is crude because many of the identified stories had nothing to do with Enron's accounting scandal. The term has entered the vernacular so that an article might be discussing accounting problems at a company or school board and refer to the situation as being – or not being – another 'Enron'.
14. In addition, articles discussing the increased cost of IPOs due to SOX are counted as 'market competitiveness' and not 'small firm cost' stories, even though such costs principally affect small firms, on the rationale that the SEC Advisory Committee's report emphasized compliance, rather than IPO, costs as the critical problem for small firms while the other three reports that did not focus on small firm issues did discuss IPO costs, in relation to affecting adversely US stock markets' competitiveness. But as discussed in Romano (2008), the relative coverage of the two critiques remains the same when the count of 'market competitiveness' stories excludes potential small firm cost concern overlaps by including only articles that refer specifically to foreign firms or foreign capital markets.
15. A chi-square test of the cross-tabulation of article type (reference to small firm or market competitiveness criticisms of SOX) and newspaper type (national versus regional) was statistically significant at less than 1 percent.
16. A chi-square test of the cross-tabulation of article type against the four regional newspapers was insignificant. The similarity of coverage is not due to a simple syndication effect, whereby regional newspapers with limited resources and expertise in analyzing complex business issues directly reproduce the reporting of syndicated columnists. The regional newspaper business editors are, in fact, highly selective when republishing articles from wire services and other newspapers, and do not just replicate those sources' coverage. For example, the same search described in Table 11.1 for the Associated Press ('AP') identified 128 SOX-critique related stories, of which 31 concerned small firm costs and 75 concerned market competitiveness. The regional newspapers, however, not only published less than 10 percent of those AP articles, but also selected for republication far more small firm cost articles than market competitiveness ones, compared to their relative representation in that source (Romano, 2008).

17. For instance, slightly over half of the NYT's circulation is national, with the New York metropolitan area accounting for the rest. Because the WSJ is the leading financial newspaper, forgoing publishing when the stock exchange is closed, reporting on the stock exchange's financial condition would plausibly be expected to be of particular interest to its readers.
18. Cross-tabulations by type of critique (small firm costs or market competitiveness) of the national newspapers are significantly different, and the source is the *Washington Post* (see Romano, 2008). The cross-tabulation of those stories in the *Washington Post* versus the regional newspapers is, however, insignificant, whereas it is significant for the NYT and WSJ versus the regional newspapers, just as it was for the aggregate of the three national newspapers against the regional ones.
19. Cross-tabulations of the reports (tallying the four reports separately or grouping together the three reports focused on competitiveness) by newspaper type coverage (national versus regional) are not significant. There is, however, a significant difference in coverage when the national journalists are compared to national newspapers and the four reports are tallied separately, and when the national journalists are compared to regional newspapers and the three reports focused on competitiveness are grouped together.
20. Adjusting for overlapping sponsorship and cosponsorship across bills, 93 legislators signed on to the eight bills introduced in 2007, with a high of 52 cosponsors (48 being Republicans) on a House bill delaying section 404's implementation for small firms.
21. Section 5002, America Competes Act, S. 761, 110th Cong., 1st. Sess, as amended 24 April 2007. The bill passed the Senate but an alternative bill that originated in the House was enacted.
22. One Democrat voted against tabling the motion.
23. All but one Republican voted for the amendment (eight not voting) along with 74 Democrats, which is almost one-third of the party's caucus.
24. The amendment was dropped in conference and, as is common with appropriations legislation (Kirst, 1969), in the accompanying explanatory statement, the Chairman's decision to postpone the section's implementation to small firms was approvingly noted, along with instructions to the agency to take small firms' concerns into account (US House of Representatives, 2008). The Chairman fulfilled his pledge in February 2008, as the agency noticed a year-long extension of the deferred application of section 404 to small firms (SEC, 2008).
25. In contrast to his predecessor, John Shad, the Reagan administration's nominee for SEC chairman, supported congressional legislation to revise the statute (Gerth, 1981: D6).
26. See, for example, 134 Cong. Rec. S 10654 (3 August 1988) (remarks of Sen. Sanford) ('the bill brings some much needed clarification to the operation of the Foreign Corrupt Practices Act. This clarification is essential if companies, particularly small businesses, are to behave competitively, but legally, in foreign markets.'); id. at 10585 (2 August 1988) (remarks of Sen. Dixon) ('The only thing that is added [by the conference report regarding the FCPA] is greater clarity. The only thing missing is the chilling effect that currently prevents many small businesses from even attempting to do business overseas).
27. For instance, the common political wisdom in the spring of 2008 is that the Democrats will retain, if not increase, their control of the Senate, because there are more Republican seats up for election, and many are thought to be contestable, along with their control of the House.
28. Policy change appears to be importantly related to legislators's 'selective attention', because of the limits on the capacity of human cognitive processes that permit us to 'attend to only limited elements of the environment at any given time' (Jones and Baumgartner, 2005: 16). The reform proposals variously mentioned have been directed at regulation of the residential mortgage lending process or provision of financial assistance to homeowners and banks. In addition, the Treasury Department's blueprint for financial regulation reform that would consolidate myriad regulatory agencies and

rearrange them into a limited number of agencies defined by regulatory function, is another source of diversion for legislators away from focusing on SOX. Although it was released in the midst of the subprime mortgage meltdown, the administration indicated that it was not directed at alleviating the crisis, but meant to serve as the starting point for future consideration of regulatory reform, not only because it had been in the works for a long time, but also, no doubt, because it was being advanced at the end of the administration's term of office. Indeed the core of the plan broadly mirrors the financial services industry's advocacy of a far more simplified regulatory regime in order to enhance competitiveness, change more comprehensive in its implications than any of the bills put forth with regard to revising SOX.

29. It is not at all apparent that supporters of revision could reach the magic number of 60 Senators, as the deference to the SEC expressed in the Dodd–Shelby amendment might have been an example of symbolic politics for some legislators, through which they could express sympathy to constituents regarding small firms's plight without intending to act.
30. In the comment letters, the firms persistently objected to proposed modifications to loosen audit standards, and advocated that the SEC conform its proposed definitions to more restrictive PCAOB definitions (see SEC, 2007a). It should further be noted that accounting members of the SEC Advisory Committee were also the dissenters from its recommendation to exempt small firms.
31. In his landmark study of Congress, Richard Fenno notes that for the vast majority of votes, legislators are not constrained by constituent preferences and can vote 'as they wish,' provided that they can satisfactorily explain their votes to constituents (Fenno, 1978: 151). In addition, recasting the issue in terms of small firm costs instead of accounting fraud or investor protection shifts the legislative debate to a new venue – the House and Senate small business committees rather than the committees with jurisdiction over the SEC – a move to which political scientists studying policy change assign crucial importance for legislative success as an issue's existing venues typically represent vested interests and are resistant to altering the status quo (Jones and Baumgartner, 2005: 5).
32. The America Competes Act also included a resolution, sponsored by Senators Schumer and Mike Crapo and added to the bill by unanimous consent, expressing the sense of the Senate that US capital markets were losing their 'competitive edge', referencing the McKinsey study (section 5007, S.761, American Competes Act, supra note 19). It both urged state and federal regulators not to 'impose regulatory costs that are disproportionate to their benefits' and to ensure regulation protected investors. The ambiguously-phrased sentiment, paralleling that of the Dodd–Shelby amendment, suggests it was an exercise of symbolic politics, in which legislators expressed empathy for constituents' problems without having to take any concrete steps to alleviate them.
33. The SEC also just abandoned the requirement that foreign firms reconcile their financial statements with US accounting principles, as long as the firms comply with international accounting standards (Marcy, 2007). Although this action does not alleviate the costs of those issuers's SOX compliance, it undoubtedly will improve US stock markets' relative competitive position, as the substantial expense entailed in reconciliation has long been considered an important reason why small foreign firms do not list on US exchanges (for example, Cochrane, 1994).

REFERENCES

Advisory Committee on Smaller Public Companies to the US Securities and Exchange Commission (2006), *Final Report*, http://www.sec.gov/info/smallbus/acspc/acspc-finalreport.pdf.

Barth, J. R., R. D. Brumbaugh, Jr. and J. A. Wilcox (2000), 'Policy watch: the repeal of Glass-Steagall and the advent of broad banking', *Journal of Economic Perspectives*, **14** (2), 191–204.

Besley, T. and R. Burgess (2002), 'The political economy of government responsiveness: theory and evidence from India', *Quarterly Journal of Economics*, **117** (4), 1415–51.

Besley, T., R. Burgess and A. Prat (2002), 'Mass media and Political accountability', in *The Right to Tell: The Role of Mass Media in Economic Development*, (Washington, DC: World Bank), pp. 45–60, http://miranda.worldbank.catchword.org/vl=1110093/cl=14/nw=1/fm=docpdf/rpsv/bk/wb/9780821352038/v1n1/s1/p11.

Cochrane, J. L. (1994), 'Are US regulatory requirements for foreign firms appropriate?' *Fordham International Law Journal*, **17** (5), S58–S67.

Cox, J. D. (2006), 'Comment letter in response to SEC Release 33-8666', http://www.sec.gov/rules/other/265-23/26523-309.pdf

Committee on Capital Markets Regulation (2006), *Interim Report*, http://www.capmktsreg.org/pdfs/11.30Committee_Interim_ReportREV2.pdf

Eldridge, S. W. and B. T. Kealey (2005), 'SOX costs: auditor attestation under Section 404,' http://papers.ssrn.com/sol3/papers.cfm?abstract_id=743285

Fenno, Jr., R. F. (1978), *Home Style: House Members in Their Districts*, London, and Glenview, IL: Scott, Foresman & Co.

Ferraz, C. and F. Finan (2007), 'Exposing corrupt politicians: the effect of Brazil's publicly released audits on electoral outcomes', IZA Discussion Paper No. 2836, http://www.iza.org/index_html?lang=en&mainframe=http%3A//www.iza.org/en/webcontent/personnel/photos/index_html%3Fkey%3D3028&topSelect=personnel&subSelect=fellows

Fremantle, A. and S. Katz (1989), 'The foreign corrupt practices act amendments of 1989', *International Lawyer*, **23** (3), 755–67.

Gentzkow, M. and J. M. Shapiro (2006), 'What drives media slant? Evidence from US daily newspapers', http://faculty.chicagogsb.edu/matthew.gentzkow/biasmeas052507.pdf

George, L. M. and J. Waldfogel (2006), 'The *New York Times* and the market for local newspapers', *American Economic Review*, **96** (1), 435–47.

Gerth, J. (1981), 'Shad: ease regulations', *Washington Post*, D6 (6 April).

Grundfest, J. A. and S. E. Bochner (2007), 'Fixing 404', *Michigan Law Review*, **105** (8), 1643–76.

Jones, B. D. and F. R. Baumgartner (2005), *The Politics of Attention How Government Prioritizes Problems*, London and Chicago, IL: University of Chicago Press.

Kirst, M. W. (1969), *Government Without Passing Laws*, Chapel Hill, CA: University of North Carolina Press.

Linck, J. S., J. M. Netter and T. Yang (2007), 'The effects and unintended consequences of the Sarbanes-Oxley Act, and its era, on the supply and demand for directors', AFA 2006 Boston Meetings Paper, http://papers.ssrn.com/sol3/papers.cfm?abstract_id=902665

Lipset, S. M. and W. Schneider (1987), *The Confidence Gap: Business, Labor, and Government in the Public Mind* (rev. edn.), Baltimore, MD: Johns Hopkins University Press.

Manickavasagam, M. (2007), 'SEC chair mulls proposing further delay for small company Section 404 compliance', *BNA Corporate Accountability Report*, **5** (48), 1226 (14 December).

Marcy, S. (2007), 'SEC ends GAAP reconciliation for reports meeting IASB-issued IFRS', *BNA Corporate Accountability Report*, **5** (45), 1134 (16 November).

McKinsey and Co. (2007), *Sustaining New York's and the US' Global Financial Services Leadership*, http://www.senate.gov/~schumer/SchumerWebsite/pressroom/special_reports/2007/NY_REPORT%20_FINAL.pdf

McTeague, R. and R. Hill (2007), 'Cox opposes call for SOX exemptions: Dodd says market concerns are premature', *BNA Corporate Accountability Report*, **5** (11), 266 (16 March).

Norris, F. (2006), 'Panel of executives and academics to consider regulation and competitiveness', *New York Times* C3 (13 September).

Oleszek, W. J. (2007), *Congressional Procedures and the Policy Process* (7th edn), Washington, DC: CQ Press.

Romano, R. (2005), 'The Sarbanes–Oxley Act and the making of quack corporate governance', *Yale Law Journal*, **114** (7), 1521–611.

Romano, R. (2008), 'The uncertain future of the Sarbanes–Oxley Act' (manuscript); forthcoming, *Yale Journal on Regulation*.

Sneller, L. and H. Langendijk (2007), 'Sarbanes Oxley Section 404 costs of compliance: a case study', *Corporate Governance*, **15** (2), 101–11.

US House of Representatives Appropriations Committee (2008), Consolidated Appropriations Act, Division D-Financial Services and General Government Appropriations Act, Comm. Print on H.R. 2764, Pub.L. 110-161, http://frwebgate.access.gpo.gov/cgi-bin/getdoc.cgi?dbname=110_cong_house_committee_prints&docid=f:39564d.pdf.

US Securities and Exchange Commission (1981), 'Foreign Corrupt Practices Act of 1977', *Federal Register*, **46** (26), 11544 (9 February).

US Securities and Exchange Commission (SEC) (2007a), 'Comments on the proposed interpretation: proposed rule on management's report on internal control over financial reporting', http://www.sec.gov/rules/proposed/2007/s72406commsumm.pdf.

US Securities and Exchange Commission (SEC) (2007b), 'SEC announces roundtable discussion regarding mutual recognition', Press Release 2007-105, http://www.sec.gov/news/press/2007/2007-105.htm (24 May).

US Securities and Exchange Commission (SEC) (2008), internal control over financial reporting in Exchange Act periodic reports of non-accelerated filers, Proposed Rule', 79 *Federal Register*, **79**, 7450 (7 February).

Williamson, O. E. (1975), *Markets and Hierarchies: Analysis and Antitrust Implications*, London: Collier Macmillan Publishers and New York: Free Press.

Williamson, O. E. (1985), *The Economic Institutions of Capitalism*, London: Collier Macmillan Publishers and New York: Free Press.

Williamson, O. E. (1996), *The Mechanisms of Governance*, Oxford and New York: Oxford University Press.

Wilson, R. K. and C. D. Young (1997), 'Cosponsorship in the US Congress', *Legislative Studies Quarterly*, **22** (1), 25–43.

Yates, A. J. and R. L. Stroup (2000), 'Media coverage and EPA pesticide decisions', *Public Choice*, **102** (3/4), 297–312.

12. Information asymmetries and regulatory rate-making: case study evidence from Commonwealth Edison and Duke Energy rate reviews

Adam Fremeth and Guy L. F. Holburn

INTRODUCTION

Since Baron and Myerson (1982) a large theoretical literature has explored the impact of asymmetric information on the design of optimal regulatory policies for natural monopolies (Armstrong and Sappington, 2007; Laffont and Tirole, 1993). A central insight from this research is that regulators who are uninformed about firm costs or market demand conditions can maximize social welfare by offering pricing structures that effectively pay informational rents to the firm. These induce the firm to truthfully reveal true costs or market demand. Subsequent models have built on Baron and Myerson by adopting alternative assumptions on dimensions such as the firm's technology, regulatory policy instruments and commitment abilities. Despite these theoretical extensions, there has been little empirical assessment of the relationship between asymmetric information and regulated rates.

In this chapter we conduct a qualitative investigation of the relationship between regulators' knowledge of regulated firms and their policy decisions. While directly observing the extent of regulatory knowledge presents a measurement challenge for researchers, we instead identify mechanisms through which information about regulated entities is revealed to external parties, including regulators. We focus our attention on three types of mechanism: the first considers the development of tacit knowledge through a regulator's prior experience in office in the task of administering regulatory policies; the second is the publication of codified knowledge about a firm in the form of other agency, or judicial, rules or orders. Greater first-hand regulatory experience and greater amounts of external information both reduce information asymmetries and the evidentiary barriers to regulators implementing new policies, increasing their incidence. Third, organized interest groups, such as consumers or NGOs, can provide information which, if credible, can establish the evidentiary basis for a policy decision.

We consider evidence for our hypotheses in the context of two in-depth case studies of rate changes implemented for two major investor-owned electric utilities in the United States, Commonwealth Edison and Duke Energy.

ASYMMETRIC INFORMATION, EVIDENCE AND REGULATORY POLICY

In the canonical principal-agent formulation of regulatory policy-making under conditions of asymmetric information, the degree of information asymmetry between firms and regulators is assumed to be a fixed constant. An alternative assumption, however, is that agencies differ in their knowledge and understanding of the firms they regulate, depending on factors such as staff experience and learning from prior monitoring activities. Agencies may also vary in their willingness to expend effort in the acquisition of expertise and information (Bawn, 1995; Aghion and Tirole, 1997; Bendor and Meirowitz, 2004; Stephenson, 2007).

We contend that one impact of differing regulatory information asymmetries on the policy-making process is to affect the costs to the regulator of collating evidence to support a policy decision. A common administrative requirement is that regulators base their decisions on documented evidence presented during quasi-judicial hearings. In the US, utility regulators must specify 'findings of fact' after formal hearings which form the basis for establishing rates. Obtaining supportive evidence, however, can be a costly exercise for regulators who wish to initiate new policies. Regulators who are less well informed about the firm, and thus about policy alternatives and consequences, find it more difficult to justify a change in policy since it takes longer to collect and analyze data, and to consult with other parties. Well informed agencies are better able to identify and assess the impact of alternative policies on firms and external parties, and hence to collate supporting evidence for their decisions at relatively low cost.

There are two implications for policy-making. First, agencies with better information will be more likely to initiate policy changes since the costs of obtaining the necessary evidence to justify the change will be lower. In the pharmaceutical industry, for example, more experienced FDA regulators have a greater tendency to detect non-compliant manufacturing processes during inspections, and hence to impose sanctions (Macher *et al.*, 2008). Conversely, more poorly informed agencies will be less likely to identify firms that are out of compliance. If they do so, they will incur greater costs of obtaining sufficient evidence to justify a change in policy. Without evidence, the agency would be at risk of being overturned by the courts on procedural grounds. Courts have often deferred to regulatory agencies on matters of substance though are more willing to overturn on procedural grounds (Studness, 1992). Section 706 of the Administrative Procedure Act (APA) enables federal courts to 'set aside agency action, findings, and conclusions found to be arbitrary, capricious, [or] an abuse of discretion'. Federal judicial precedent has established that an agency demonstrate it has 'examine[d] the relevant data and articulate[d] a satisfactory explanation for its action, including a rational connection between the facts found and the choice made' (*State Farm v. Motor Vehicles Manufacturers' Association*, 463 US 29 (1983)). Similar 'hard look' provisions exist for state-level agencies.

Second, more expert agencies will be better positioned to block firm-initiated policy proposals. When regulated firms present evidence to support a new policy – for example, the authorization of a new pharmaceutical drug, new utility rates or a new technical standard – agencies with a deeper understanding of the firms or industries will be more able to identify biases in their arguments and to assess the validity of their claims, thereby providing the grounds for denial. Less expert agencies, on the other hand, will have a higher cost of countering the evidentiary basis of such proposals, increasing the probability of acceptance.

In the next section we develop this thesis in greater depth in the context of changes to regulated rates in the utilities sector.

UTILITY RATE-MAKING IN THE UNITED STATES

In the United States, regulatory policies in the utilities sector are primarily designed and implemented by state-level independent agencies, Public Utility Commissions (PUCs). PUC mandates are broadly defined: federal legal precedent establishes that PUCs must set rates that enable utilities to earn a 'fair and reasonable' return on 'used and useful' assets (Lesser, 2002; Howe, 1985), though methodologies for assessing such criteria are not specified. Rates are determined through periodic rate reviews which can be initiated at any point by the PUC or by the utility. Upon initiation of a rate review, a series of public hearings is held where the utility, PUC staff and any admitted interest groups present arguments and information supporting their positions about justifiable allowed rates-of-return, operating costs and assets to be included in the rate base (Hyman, 2000).

At the end of this process, which may extend up to a year or more in duration, PUC commissioners make a majority decision on the rates that final consumers are obliged to pay. Depending on the commissioners' assessment of utility costs and the allowed rate of return, rates may increase or decrease as compared to the status quo.

Utilities have an incentive to initiate rate reviews if they expect that the PUC will establish the allowed rate of return at a level above the actual level the utility is currently earning. Since rates are otherwise fixed, the actual earned rate of return on assets decreases as the utility's operating and investment costs increase, all else equal. Historically, utilities have thus tended to initiate reviews after periods when costs have risen, for instance after the construction of new infrastructure facilities, in order to obtain higher rates and profits (Joskow, 1974). PUCs, on the other hand, have an incentive to trigger rate reviews if they consider actual earned profits to be above the level determined by the target allowed rate of return. In this case, a rate review would lead to a reduction in rates and profits for the utility.

Information asymmetries between the utility and PUC affect the initiation decisions of each party. For the PUC, it is difficult to observe accurately the utility's earned rate of return at any point in time and hence whether a rate reduction is justified. Better informed PUCs are more likely to identify, and be able to document, whether a utility is over-earning, and hence to implement rate reductions. More astute PUCs are also better able to assess the validity of any utility claims that they are under-earning and that rate increases are required. Anticipating greater levels of scrutiny and an increased probability of denial, utilities will be less likely to initiate reviews that call for rate increases when PUCs have better information about the utility. In general, then, we predict that conditions of reduced information asymmetries will be correlated with more rate reductions and fewer rate increases. We now identify several natural sources of information heterogeneity among regulators in order to develop specific hypotheses about factors affecting the incidence of utility rate increases and decreases.

Regulatory Resources

One source of regulator knowledge about utility costs, operations and market conditions is direct regulatory experience (Macher *et al.*, 2008). As regulatory commissioners and staff accumulate more experience over time through monitoring and evaluation activities, they develop deeper knowledge about specific regulated entities. Some of this knowledge exists tacitly within agency personnel; other aspects become codified and transmitted through documented analyses and reports. Agencies with relatively greater financial resources are also able to devote more resources to overseeing each regulated firm, thereby contributing to the stock of organizational knowledge.

With greater experience and resources, regulators become more adept at understanding utility true costs, profits and managerial capabilities, as well as the impact of exogenous events – such as changes in weather patterns, regional economic growth, environmental standards or financial market conditions – on utility earnings. All else equal, then, regulators with greater human and financial resources will be better able to identify when rate reductions are justified and to provide the necessary evidence during a rate review; and to challenge utility requests for rate increases.

External Information

Information on utility costs and operations can originate from sources other than an agency's own experience and oversight activities. In the electric utility sector, federal agencies such as the Nuclear Regulatory Commission (NRC) or the Environmental Protection Agency monitor selected aspects of utility performance and have the authority to punish violations. The NRC, for instance, can impose financial penalties, ranging from \$75 000 for security breaches to \$450 000 for technical violations requiring a plant shutdown (Feinstein, 1989). Information revealed by independent agencies can shape Public Utility Commission beliefs about utility costs and management prudence. Similarly, for utilities that operate in multiple states, other PUC rate determinations can also yield valuable information about corporate management practices and abilities (Lyon and Mayo, 2005). Both types of information assist PUCs in justifying rate reductions or in countering utility claims that costs have risen and that rates should be increased.

Interest Group Opposition

Organized interest groups also have an incentive to provide credible information to PUCs on regulated firms and regulatory policy consequences in order to influence policy outcomes (Grossman and Helpman, 2001). State administrative procedure acts generally grant authority to major interested parties, such as large industrial consumers or consumer advocates, to have standing in public rate hearings (De Figueiredo and Van den Bergh, 2004; Holburn and Van den Bergh, 2006). Standing provides interest groups with the chance to access utility informational filings, to present arguments and evidence regarding policy and to challenge utility claims. Interest groups can also petition PUCs to initiate rate investigations or rate reductions though PUCs need not comply with such requests.

We argue that interest group opposition is more effective at limiting the incidence of rate increases than at promoting rate decreases. Due to informational asymmetries regarding utility costs, it is difficult for interest groups to independently obtain and provide evidence to a PUC that would justify a reduction in rates. Interest groups do not have authority to access utility records or management accounts in the same ways than do PUCs. Imperfect information about utility costs thus makes it difficult for interest groups to credibly petition the PUC to initiate a rate review with the purpose of ultimately reducing rates. However, lobbying for intervener status during utility-triggered rate reviews – which then provides access to utility information – is less costly. When a utility initiates a rate review it makes available to the PUC and interested parties the informational basis of its claim for a rate increase. This documentation can provide the basis for interest groups to more carefully scrutinize utility operations and to formulate counter arguments. Anticipating such behavior, utilities will be less likely to request rate increases in adverse environments, including those characterized by strong interest group competition.

In summary, we anticipate that regulators are more likely to implement rate decreases and less likely to implement rate increases when they are endowed with greater amounts of experience, resources and external information. Furthermore, we predict a differential effect from interest group and political opposition as we expect a reduction in the incidence of rate increases but a smaller effect on the incidence of rate decreases.

COMMONWEALTH EDISON AND DUKE ENERGY RATE REVIEWS

We now consider our predictions in the empirical context of two case studies of recent reviews of the regulated rates of US electric utilities, one involving a rate increase, the other a decrease. One case involves an increase to rates ordered by the Illinois Commerce Commission (ICC) in 2006 for Commonwealth Edison (ComEd), while the other is a rate decrease ordered in 2003 by the South Carolina Public Service Commission (SCPSC) for Duke Energy (Duke). While these two rate cases are not necessarily typical of rate reviews in general, the contrast of the preceding events, and of the informational environment, between a rate increase and decrease are informative.

Between 2003 and 2005, ComEd, the largest electric utility in Illinois, had made substantial investments in its transmission and distribution networks in response to worsening reliability performance,[1] notably rising frequency and duration of service interruptions.[2] The claimed value of this investment was more than $2 billion, a substantial increase above the existing ICC-approved rate base that had been valued at $3.6 billion in the firm's previous rate case in 2003. Consequently, the financial rate of return that the firm earned on its assets had fallen below the 8.99 percent level previously authorized by the ICC in 2003.

Having made these investments, ComEd had an incentive to reveal its increased costs to the ICC in order to obtain financial recovery. In August 2005 it filed for an annual rate revenue increase of $345 million. Since the burden of proof lay with ComEd to justify the proposed change in policy, it provided a substantial amount of documented evidence that supported its claim. The initial filing contained over 600 pages of evidence covering more than 100 cost issues. After almost a year of administrative hearings and analysis, during which the ICC and other parties considered ComEd's original and additional evidence, the ICC deemed that an increase in rates was justified, though not by the full amount that ComEd had requested.[3]

By contrast, utilities do not typically have an incentive outside normal reporting procedures to voluntarily reveal reductions in costs or increased earned rates of return, which would then motivate regulators to reduce rates and allowed profits. The burden of proof thus rests with regulatory agencies to document excessive earnings though, in the presence of asymmetric information, this can be a costly and uncertain exercise. Agencies also typically operate under fixed budgets that are determined annually through political budgeting procedures, implying the existence of opportunity costs associated with earnings investigations.

The circumstances surrounding the decision of the South Carolina Public Service Commission to reduce Duke's annual rates by $30 million in 2003 illustrates differences in the mechanisms through which information is revealed in rate reductions. Prior to the 2003 rate case, Duke had been embroiled in a 15-month investigation of its accounting practices. According to a whistleblower, Barron Stone, a senior business analyst within the accounting department at Duke, and later confirmed by an independent audit by Grant Thornton, the firm had used unorthodox accounting practices to intentionally underreport its income by $124 million from 1998 to 2000. Duke had allegedly included expenses from its unregulated retail operations in its regulated accounts and had additionally not correctly reported $84 million of insurance rebates on its nuclear power plants. Such accounting maneuvers enabled Duke to effectively boost its regulated profits significantly above the level permitted by the SCPSC. These remained undetected by the SCPSC for almost a three-year period.[4] Duke eventually settled the case with the SCPSC, a condition of which involved implementing more transparent accounting policies. These in turn enabled the SCPSC to identify over-earning in 2003: the commission staff had determined in a quarterly financial report dated 31 March 2003 that the firm had earned an excessive amount of revenue due to an increased demand for energy during colder than average winter temperatures. Duke had surpassed its allowed operating revenues by $41 million and earned a return on equity of 14.25 percent rather than the regulated target of 12.25 percent which had been set in a prior rate case. The executive director of the SCPSC had called this over-earning 'unprecedented in the recent past for an electric utility'. In an effort to avoid a full rate investigation that would have examined many more cost issues, Duke accepted the SCPSC's order and agreed to reduce its rates by $30 million and to write down $16 million of long term debt. This would effectively reduce its return on equity to 12.03 percent.

The contrast in the origin of information that motivated these rate changes is clear. In Illinois, extensive information on cost increases was purposively documented by ComEd for the ICC. In South Carolina, however, an exogenous signal – in the form of an internal whistleblower – alerted the regulatory authority to hitherto undetected excess profits several years beforehand.

Regulatory Resources

The ability of regulatory agencies to assess true utility profitability varies with their experience and resources. Public utility commissions that are well funded, and that have experienced and knowledgeable commissioners and staff are partly able to mitigate their informational disadvantage. As a result, commissions that are rich in such resources cannot only more effectively deliberate utility requests for rate increases but also identify circumstances that justify a rate decrease. In the period 1980–2000, there were approximately 950 electric utility rate increases implemented by PUCs, and approximately 220 rate decreases. Our analysis of average PUC commissioner experience, as gauged by time in office, is consistent with our expectations about the greater amount of PUC commissioner experience required to successfully implement a decrease compared to an increase: we find that in the typical rate increase, the average commissioner in a PUC had 3.38 years of experience in office, whereas the equivalent number is 4.10 years for rate decreases.[5]

Consistent with this general pattern, Duke's 2003 rate decrease was ordered by a relatively experienced regulatory body. The SCPSC is headed by seven commissioners who are elected by the General Assembly of South Carolina for four year terms. In 2003 these commissioners had on average over five years of experience in that role, greater than the historic national average. In fact, Commissioner William Saunders had sat on the PSC for over ten years, enabling newer members to benefit from his experience. In addition, the executive director of the SCPSC, Gary Walsh, had 30 years of experience in the organization, providing him with an intimate understanding of Duke's operations even though Duke had not had a formal rate review for more than a decade.

The stock of organizational experience thus allowed the commission to develop a relatively nuanced understanding of the three electricity firms that they regulated and to identify circumstances that might warrant a rate reduction. Indeed, in 1998 the SCPSC ordered a rate cut for South Carolina Electric and Gas (SCE&G) which had exceeded its return target by 1.04 percent. Five of the seven commissioners that ordered the Duke decrease in 2003 had also participated in the 1998 SCE&G rate case.[6]

Unlike the SCPSC, the Illinois Commerce Commission had a relatively inexperienced set of commissioners with, on average, less than three years in office at the time of ComEd's rate case in 2006. The most experienced was Kevin Wright, appointed by the prior governor, George Ryan, in September 2002. However, the commissioners were supported by a well funded and professionally staffed organization. The ICC operated with an annual budget of $125 million and had almost 300 employees, placing it in the top 20 percent among state public utility commissions as ranked by budget. Furthermore, ComEd's previous rate case from a mere two years earlier allowed three of the five commissioners and the commission staff to have a deeper understanding of ComEd's operations.[7,8]

The familiarity of the commission staff with ComEd's position allowed it to develop a rebuttal to some of the evidence presented by the firm. The staff responded to over 60 issues in a 77-page document and provided as much information as ComEd in its recommendation on the appropriate rate of return.[9] The firm had its allowed rate of return decreased by almost a full percentage point from the 2003 ruling.[10] In addition, the staff focused on rebutting ComEd's attempt to include an $853 million pension asset within its allowed rate base. The staff argued, with the support of expert witness testimony, that this action was unnecessary to support the firm's current bond rating status and that it would more appropriately be included within the firm's unregulated operations. Again the ICC ruled in accordance with the staff on this issue, ordering the rate base to be set at $665 million below ComEd's request.

External Information

In addition to the tacit knowledge that accumulates through experience in an organization and its employees, an understanding of regulated entities can be shaped by external information and evidentiary sources. Both the Duke and ComEd cases illustrate how such evidence can influence the decisions of a regulatory commission.

Duke operates as a regulated utility in North Carolina, where it serves 1.7 million customers, as well as in South Carolina, where it has 600 000 customers. As a result of the federal and state investigations initiated in response to claims of accounting improprieties at Duke in 2002, Duke reached an $18.25 million settlement in its largest state, North Carolina. The settlement imposed strict rules on Duke which required the firm to meet with the regulatory staff of the NCUC every quarter and to discuss operations and accounting procedures, and for Duke's senior officers to certify all financial documents filed with the commission. Not surprisingly, the South Carolina PSC had closely monitored events in North Carolina. Based on the evidence that emerged initially from the events triggered in Duke's North Carolina business, it too negotiated a financial settlement with Duke that reduced rates, as well as new operational monitoring procedures.

ComEd's rate case in Illinois coincided with extensive public deliberation about a proposed merger between Exelon, ComEd's parent company, and Public Service Enterprise Group (PSEG). The $17 billion merger would have created the largest utility in the country, though regulatory hurdles and interest group pressures ultimately ended negotiations between the companies in September 2006. As part of the original merger filings to both state and federal regulators, a significant body of evidence had been revealed concerning the appropriate return on equity that ComEd would require in order to attract investors. The Consumers Utility Board (CUB), which acts as the public advocate in Illinois, along with the support of the city of Chicago and Cook County, had used some of this information when establishing its position in the 2006 rate case.[11] In particular, these interest groups used the stock valuations for the merger which were conducted by three major investment banks (Morgan Stanley, JP Morgan, and Lehman Brothers) and which indicated that a 7.75 percent return on equity would be appropriate for ComEd. This was substantially below the returns allowed by public utility commissions in other states and also below the 11.0 percent that ComEd had requested. With its limited budget, the CUB leveraged this secondary evidence to build a case that the traditional valuation techniques, including the capital asset pricing model and the discounted cash flow model, were overly subjective and led to inflated return figures. Adopting the recommendations of investment banks represented a novel approach to the regulatory review process and industry publications took note of this strategy.[12] Although the ICC did not adopt the CUB position, it selected a return on equity of 10.04 percent that was still substantially below the firm's demand and even below that recommended by the ICC staff. The language of the final order explicitly commented on the CUB's methodology and noted that in future such evidence could continue to complement traditional valuation techniques. Thus, as with the case of Duke Energy in South Carolina, it appears that evidence on utility operations emanating from external sources played an important role in rate case outcomes.

Interest Group and Political Opposition

Information on utility operations and on policy effects may also be conveyed by organized interest groups who choose to participate in administrative hearings. Interest groups can oppose or support utilities by presenting information on policy alternatives and consequences during administrative proceedings that agencies must account for in their ultimate rulings or orders. The ComEd rate case illustrates how, by initiating formal policy reviews, firms can expose themselves to interest group and political opposition which, in the absence of a review, may pose less of a threat to the firm. In 2005, when ComEd initiated proceedings with the ICC, electricity policy had already become a salient political issue as the state was undertaking restructuring of the power generation market. Public debates over the merits of uniform wholesale power auctions, which ComEd supported, had focused on concerns that rates could rise by more than 15 percent.[13] As a result, ComEd's transmission and distribution rate case attracted significant attention. In the political arena, Rod Blagojevich, the Democrat governor of Illinois, had taken a strong public stand against ComEd's rate request. Blagojevich had written to the ICC stating that rate increases should be avoided and that he was prepared to dismiss any commissioner who supported an increase, despite the absence of a clear legal basis for doing so.[14] Since his election to office in 2003, Blagojevich had appointed four out of the five ICC commissioners, including the chairman, Charles Box (see Table 12.1).

Although the ICC has a legally independent status as a regulatory agency, its policy decisions are monitored by the state legislature, which has responsibility for establishing budgets, conducting hearings and which, additionally, can enact legislation to modify agency rulings. The political environment of the state house and senate thus also has the ability to shape ICC decisions. In 2005, both chambers of the legislature were dominated by Democrats. For the first time in five election cycles the Democrat party had sizable majorities in the house and senate (see Table 12.2). Traditionally, the Democrat party had tended to favor consumer over shareholder interests, as compared to Republicans. Democrat control then of the executive, legislature and ICC did not augur favorably for ComEd.[15]

Table 12.1 ICC Commissioners in 2005–6

Commissioner	Political affiliation	Prior profession	Start of term	Expiry of term	Appointed by
Charles Box	Democrat	Mayor	January 2006	January 2009	Rod Blagojevich
Robert Lieberman	Democrat	CEO of Center for Neighbor-hood Technology	February 2005	January 2010	Rod Blagojevich
Lula Ford	Democrat	Teacher	January 2003	January 2008	Rod Blagojevich
Erin O'Connell-Diaz	Republican	Administrative Law Judge at ICC	April 2003	January 2008	Rod Blagojevich
Kevin Wright	Independent	Political staffer	September 2002	January 2007	George Ryan

Table 12.2 Political party control of Illinois House of Representatives and Senate

Election Year	House		Senate	
	Democrats	Republicans	Democrats	Republicans
2006	66	52	37	22
2004	64	53	31	27
2002	64	54	32	26
2000	62	56	27	32
1998	60	58	28	31

In addition to a political environment that appeared to be stacked against it, ComEd opened a Pandora's Box of organized interest group opposition when it launched its rate case. Thirty-three parties registered as intervenors in the rate case, enabling them to obtain ComEd's evidence and testimony and to present their own arguments during administrative hearings (see Table 12.3 for a full list). The most active participants were the Attorney General, the Citizens Utility Board (which was supported by the city of Chicago and Cook County), and Illinois Industrial Energy Consumers (IIEC). These groups selectively challenged specific elements of ComEd's filing. The CUB, for instance, dedicated part of its budget to engage the services of an expert witness who, on the basis of an alternative method of analysis, argued for a smaller rate of return and a significant

Table 12.3 Intervenors in the 2006 Commonwealth Edison rate case

Attorney General of the State of Illinois	Downers Grove Sanitary District
BlueStar Energy Services, Inc.	Dynegy Inc.
Building Owners and Managers Association of Chicago	Illinois Association of Wastewater Agencies
Castwell Products, Inc.	Ford Motor Company
Chicago Transit Authority	Corn Products International, Inc.
Caterpillar Inc.	Merchandise Mart Properties, Inc.
Abbott Laboratories, Inc.	Sterling Steel Company, LLC
Citgo Petroleum Corporation	Daimler Chrysler, Inc.
Citizens Utility Board	ISG Riverdale, Inc.
City of Chicago Community Action for Fair Utility Practice	MidAmerican Energy Company
Constellation Energy Commodities Group, Inc.	Midwest Generation EME, LLC
Constellation NewEnergy, Inc.	Northeast Illinois Regional Commuter Railroad Corporation, d/b/a Metra
The Cook County State's Attorney's Office	Peoples Energy Services Corporation
United States Department of Energy	University of Illinois
Direct Energy Services, LLC	Thermal Chicago Corporation
Illinois Industrial Energy Consumers	Coalition of Energy Suppliers

reduction to the return on equity. The IIEC adopted a similar strategy, advocating a return on equity of 9.9 percent and a capital structure that favored debt. The Attorney General's office supported many of the arguments of the ICC staff and CUB but devoted considerable attention to arguing against including certain pension fund monies in the rate base. The staff of the ICC was required to respond to all issues presented by ComEd but developed a particularly strong challenge to the size of the firm's rate base and its operating expenses. Tables 12.4 and 12.5 illustrate the differences between these parties' positions on the allowed rate of return, rate base, operating expenses and the final order made by the ICC.

The final ICC order on 26 July 2006 barely improved ComEd's financial position. Whereas ComEd had originally requested a revenue increase of \$345 million, the ICC permitted only an \$8 million adjustment. Although utilities rarely receive the full amount of their requests in rate reviews, the magnitude of the difference in ComEd's is unusual. During the 1980s and 1990s, U.S. electric utilities received, on average, 58 percent of their requested revenue increases.[16,17] It is instructive to examine more closely the three components of the ICC decision – the allowed rate of return, the rate base and operating expenses – in order to understand the basis of the ruling.

Table 12.4 Commonwealth Edison rate case: policy positions

	ComEd	CUB	ICC Staff	Final Order: ICC Commissioners[a]
Rate of return	8.94%	6.69%	7.86%	8.01%
• Return on equity	11.0%	7.75%	10.19%	10.04%
• Return on debt	6.50%	6.23%	6.48%	6.48%
• Debt ratio	45.8%	62.8%	62.8%	57.14%
Rate base ($'000)	$6 186 933	$5 946 592	$5 301 687	$5 521 350
Operating revenues ($'000)	$1 923 215	$1 733 090	$1 598 847	$1 585 997
Revenue increase ($'000)	$337 218	$155 534	$21 181	$8331

Note: [a] Illinois Commerce Commission, *No. 05-0597: Final Order* (Springfield, Illinois: Illinois Commerce Commission, 26 July. 2006) 306.

Table 12.5 Commonwealth Edison rate case: historical comparison

	2003 rate case order	2004 test year[a]	ComEd Requested increase to 2004 test year	2006 ICC final order	Difference between final order and test year
Revenues ($'000)	$1 507 636	$1 577 686	$345 529	$1 585 997	$8311
Operating expenses ($'000)	$1 237 297	$1 235 546	$139 102	$1 238 885	$3339
Rate of Return	8.99%	7.07%	1.87%	8.01%	0.94%
Rate Base ($'000)	$3 616 663	$6 185 134	$1799	$5 521 350	($663 784)

Note: [a] The test year is a period of measurement for a recent and representative consecutive 12-month period consisting of a full year of operations that a PUC uses to establish rates for a future period. The period is jointly determined by the PUC and the focal utility and is commonly the first stage of a rate case. The PUC collects operational data for this period to be used in the deliberations of the rate case. The test year is used to examine earned returns compared to either previously authorized earnings levels (based on approved rates of return) or compared to requested earnings levels (based on requested or recommended rates of return).

First, public utility commissions have some discretion to select their preferred rates of return since legislative acts and judicial precedent do not specify particular methodologies for calculating them.[18] The ICC's ruling on the allowed return on equity was significantly below that requested by ComEd, and was even lower than that recommended by the staff of the ICC. In fact, compared to public utility commission rulings in other states,

Table 12.6 Return on equity rulings for electric utilities in 2006

Utility	Regulating state	Authorized ROE
Jersey Central Power & Light Co.	New Jersey	9.55
Kansas Gas & Electric Co.	Kansas	10.00
Pacific Power & Light Co.	Oregon	10.00
Commonwealth Edison Co.	Illinois	10.04
Maine Public Service Co.	Maine	10.20
Cincinnati Gas & Electric Co.	Ohio	10.29
Interstate Power & Light Co.	Minnesota	10.39
Avista Corp.	Washington	10.40
Interstate Power & Light Co.	Iowa	10.40
Kentucky Power Co.	Kentucky	10.50
Northern States Power Co.	Minnesota	10.54
Sierra Pacific Power Co.	Nevada	10.60
Entergy Gulf States	Louisiana	10.65
Oklahoma Gas & Electric Co.	Oklahoma	10.75
Upper Penninsula Power Co.	Michigan	10.75
San Diego Gas & Electric Co.	California	10.79
Detroit Edison Co.	Michigan	11.00
Madison Gas & Electric Co.	Wisconsin	11.00
Northern States Power Co. – WI	Wisconsin	11.00
Wisconsin Public Service Corp.	Wisconsin	11.00
Consumers Energy Co.	Michigan	11.15
Wisconsin Electric Power Co.	Wisconsin	11.20
CLECO Power LLC	Louisiana	11.25
Pacific Gas & Electric Co.	California	11.35
Southern California Edison Co.	California	11.60
Florida Power & Light Co.	Florida	11.75
Progress Energy Florida	Florida	11.75

the return on equity of 10.04 percent was one of the lowest allowed in 2006 (see Table 12.6). This provides evidence of greater weight being placed by the ICC on consumer over shareholder interests.

Second, the ICC's decision on the allowed rate base also demonstrates how regulatory discretion can be utilized when competing claims are both supported by evidence. A substantial component of ComEd's proposed increase to the rate base consisted of a pension asset valued at $853 million. ComEd testified that they had chosen to 'fully fund' its portion of Exelon's, ComEd's parent company, pension plan in an effort to improve their credit rating. According to the firm, the net result would save ratepayers approximately $30 million in reduced annual pension expenses and that shareholders should be compensated for this investment. The ICC, however, chose to completely disallow this asset, referring to the staff's argument that funding the pension asset at that time was unnecessary.

Third, the ICC drastically cut much of ComEd's requested operating expense increase. For instance, ComEd had sought a raise of $84 million in 'Administrative and General' costs since its last rate case, which represented a 55 percent increase. The firm had argued that the operations of the organization had changed significantly since generation assets had been transferred to Exelon and that many of the firm's activities had now been restructured. The ICC ruled, however, that ComEd had not met the required evidentiary standard to prove that its proposed A&G expenses were prudent and reasonable. The commission ruled close to the staff's position by permitting only a $17 million increase in this line item.[19]

It is hard to discern objectively the quality of the arguments that ComEd and other parties made during the hearings on these and other cost items, and hence to determine objectively whether ICC rulings were 'just'. However, it is unlikely that ComEd's position was groundless: presenting frivolous or unsupported arguments would expose the utility to better evidenced counter arguments from opposing groups, and would undermine the utility's credibility in future rate cases (perhaps inviting more intense monitoring and scrutiny by the ICC). However, while the ICC ruled in favor of ComEd on a variety of sub-issues during the course of the rate case, the organized interest group opposition that ComEd confronted on many of the components provided an evidentiary basis for the ICC to justify its decision – enabling the ICC to exercise a degree of discretion. On other issues, the ICC was able to claim that ComEd had not provided sufficient information to make its proposal credible. Given the nature of the broader policy environment in which electricity policy was becoming highly politicized at the time of the rate case, it is less surprising that ComEd failed to achieve a significant earnings improvement.

In contrast to ComEd's rate case in Illinois, adverse interest group or political forces did not appear to be a factor in Duke's 2003 rate change in South Carolina. Indeed, although the SCPSC cut Duke's rate revenue, it nonetheless permitted the utility to still earn a relatively generous return on equity. The SCPSC set this at 12.03 percent, which was within the top 25 percent of electric utility ROE rulings in the country during 2003, ranging from 9.5 percent to 12.75 percent (see Table 12.7). The overall political environment was also relatively benign, with Republican control of the legislature and Republican-appointed PSC commissioners (see Tables 12.8 and 12.9).

As already noted, organized interest group opposition was not responsible for triggering the prior accounting investigation and ultimate rate reduction. In fact, following the SCPSC's determination that Duke had overearned, Elliot Elam, the consumer advocate in South Carolina, had requested a

Table 12.7 Return on equity rulings for electric utilities in 2003

Utility	Regulating state	Authorized ROE
Jersey Central Power & Light	New Jersey	9.5
Public Service Electric & Gas	New Jersey	9.75
Rockland Electric Co.	New Jersey	9.75
Maine Public Service Co.	Maine	10.25
United Illuminating Co.	Connecticut	10.45
Pacific Power & Light	Oregon	10.5
Aquila Inc.	Colorado	10.75
Public Service Co. of Colorado	Colorado	10.75
PacifiCorp	Wyoming	10.75
San Diego Gas & Electric Co.	California	10.9
Sierra Pacific Power Co.	California	10.9
Kentucky Power Co.	Kentucky	11
Central Vermont Public Service Corp.	Vermont	11
ENTERGY Gulf States, Inc.	Louisiana	11.1
Interstate Power & Light Co.	Iowa	11.11
Pacific Gas & Electric Co.	California	11.2
Empire District Electric Co.	Oklahoma	11.27
Southern California Edison Co.	California	11.6
Commonwealth Edison Co.	Illinois	11.72
Duke Power	South Carolina	12.03
Cleco Power LLC	Louisiana	12.25
Madison Gas & Electric Co.	Wisconsin	12.3
South Carolina Electric & Gas	South Carolina	12.45
Orange & Rockland Utilities Inc.	New York	12.75

comprehensive examination of Duke's rates, which would have included a full investigation of the rate base, as well as the appropriate rate of return and operating expenses. However, unable to provide specific new evidence about the reasonableness of the firm's costs, such claims were dismissed by the PSC. While the PSC had the authority to launch a full rate review of its own accord, this would have been a costly exercise, especially for a relatively small commission with 90 staff and wide range of regulatory responsibilities.

CONCLUSION

The general argument we advance here is that the extent of information asymmetries between regulators, interest groups and regulated firms affects the administrative costs of policy-making. By relaxing the traditional assumption in principal-agent models of policy-making that *ex ante*

Table 12.8 SCPSC Commissioners in 2003

Commissioner	Political affiliation	Prior profession	Start of term	Expiry of term	Majority of general assembly at election
Mignon Clyburn	Democrat	Journalist	July 1998	Present	Republican
William Saunders	Democrat	Broadcaster	March 1994	March 2004	Democrat
James Blake Atkins	Democrat	Scientist	February 2000	March 2004	Republican
Randy Mitchell	Democrat	Judge	July 1998	Present	Republican
H. Clay Carruth	Undisclosed	Lawyer	July 1998	March 2004	Republican
Nick Theodore	Democrat	Lt. Governor	July 2002	March 2004	Republican
C. Robert Moseley	Republican	Banker	July 1998	Present	Republican

Table 12.9 Political party control of South Carolina House of Representatives and Senate

Election year	House		Senate	
	Democrats	Republicans	Democrats	Republicans
2002	51	74	21	25
2000	54	70	22	24
1998	59	64	24	22
1996	53	70	26	20
1992	72	50	32	14

information asymmetries are a non-varying constant, we explore various mechanisms through which regulators can become more informed about utility costs and profitability. Such information can come in the form of tacit knowledge or codified knowledge sources. Factors such as prior regulatory experience, agency resources, external agency rulings and interest group monitoring can all lower the costs of rate-making, thereby enabling regulators to adjust policy in response to external shocks and to block firm-initiated proposals. Regulated firms also act strategically by not requesting favorable policy changes when the decision costs to the regulator of denying or substantially modifying such requests are lower.

Our prediction that greater information asymmetries increase the rents accruing to regulated firms – in the form of higher rates – is similar to the predictions of Baron and Myerson's (1982) model. However, an important difference is in the mechanism through which this rent transfer occurs. While Baron and Myerson anticipated that uninformed regulators should design a menu of rate options, either at or above utility costs, we argue that the administrative cost to external parties of obtaining evidence on the true state of utility costs creates rate 'stickiness'; regulators find it costly to identify instances when utility costs have fallen, and then to obtain supporting evidence, thereby lending a bias towards status quo rates that benefits utilities during periods of cost deflation.

One policy implication of our analysis is that public utility commissions can reduce the extent of information asymmetries by implementing organizational structures, practices and policies that are designed to capture and share experiential knowledge within the commission. Levels of tacit knowledge, for instance, may be increased by seeking to retain more experienced commissioners and staff, or by explicitly encouraging knowledge sharing with less experienced personnel. Commissions that have typically witnessed rapid turnover in commissioners may be able to partly compensate by adopting measures that reward stability of employment in senior appointed staff members, such as executive directors. A second implication is that administrative measures that reduce informational asymmetries and monitoring costs – for example by providing public access to utility information to a large number of affected parties – will decrease the utility's informational advantage. Although there are likely to be additional administrative costs associated with conducting hearings with more intervenors, there should be benefits from more information provided to the commission.

In our two case studies we present some preliminary evidence that is consistent with our expectation that richer informational environments will exert downward pressure on regulatory rate decisions. Nonetheless, an important limiting factor that weakens our ability to make causal inferences is in the inability to directly observe the extent of regulatory knowledge. Future research might also broaden the empirical scope to include a statistical examination of our predictions regarding rate changes for a larger population of electric utilities.

NOTES

1. Reliability problems came to the forefront for ComEd when in the summer of 1999 power failures left many parts of Chicago without electricity for multiple days and closed the commodity exchanges and courthouses.
2. Illinois Commerce Commission, No. 05-0597: Executive Summary (Springfield, IL: Illinois Commerce Commission, 30 August 2005), 1–2.

3. ComEd was also allowed to recover $8 million of administrative costs it had incurred to conduct the rate review. Illinois Commerce Commission, No. 05-0597: Order (Springfield, IL: Illinois Commerce Commission, 26 July 2006), 45–50.
4. Stan Choe, 'Duke Energy settles accounting case with North Carolina Utilities Commission', *Charlotte Observer*, 30 October 2002.
5. A t-test of means identifies that this difference is statistically significant at the 1 percent level ($t = 3.817$).
6. Stan Choe, 'High profits at Duke Power may prompt rate cut for South Carolina customers', *Charlotte Observer*, 15 July 2003.
7. Commissioners Hurley and Ford voted on the 2003 decision, and Commissioner O'Connell-Diaz was the Administrative Law Judge on the case at that time.
8. Illinois Commerce Commission Docket 01-0423.
9. Illinois Commerce Commission, No. 05-0597: Summary of Positions of the Staff of the Illinois Commerce Commission (Springfield, IL: Illinois Commerce Commission, 4 May 2006).
10. Philip S. Cross, 'Regulators trust, but verify', *Public Utilities Fortnightly*, November 2006.
11. Illinois Commerce Commission, No. 05-0597: The Statement of positions of the Citizens Utility Board, the Cook County state's attorney's office, and the City of Chicago (Springfield, IL: Illinois Commerce Commission, 4 May 2006).
12. Philip S. Cross, 'Regulators trust, but verify', *Public Utilities Fortnightly*, November 2006.
13. Arthur Laffer and Patrick Giordano, 'Exelon Rex', *Wall Street Journal*, 1 December 2005.
14. Robert Manor, 'ComEd bankruptcy warning sounded', *Chicago Tribune*, 29 September 2005. In fact, this was not an idle threat as soon after he apparently forced the current chair of the commission, Edward C. Hurley, to resign in what Blagojevich referred to as a decision that was 'being made for all of the right reasons'. The governor then attempted to install in his place Marty Cohen, the executive director of the consumer advocacy office, the Citizen's Utility Board. While the Senate rejected the governor's proposal, the vote against the confirmation was only narrowly passed with a three vote majority (31–28).
15. ComEd had in fact sought to develop some political support in an otherwise hostile political environment. In particular, it had courted Emil Jones Jr., the Illinois senate president. Jones had raised 14 percent of his 2005 campaign contributions at a 'Buffet-by-the-Pool' event hosted at the home of ComEd CEO, Frank Clark. At least $78 000 of the $127 000 raised at this 5 June 2005 fundraiser was contributed by executives or board members at ComEd or its parent company, Exelon. Jones subsequently confronted Blagojevich when he tried to appoint the consumer advocate to the ICC. See Greg Hinz and Steve Daniels, 'ComEd's juice sparks high-powered ally' *Crain's Chicago Business*, 29 August 2005.
16. ComEd had been relatively more successful in its previous rate cases. Through the 1980s and 1990s ComEd had been on par with the rest of the industry in receiving, on average, approximately 60 percent of the total amount of revenue increase requested over eight rate cases.
17. These figures were calculated by the authors using data from all major electric utility rate cases that resulted in rate increases during the 1980s and 1990s, totaling 947 cases.
18. As the New Mexico Public Utility Commission commented about its discretionary powers, '*[there is] a zone of reasonableness between confiscation [of utility assets] and extortion [of consumers] in which the Commission has great discretion in setting just and reasonable rates*' (New Mexico PUC Brief, Supreme Court Case No. 24,148, *PNM Gas Services v. NMPUC*, 1998).
19. ComEd appealed the order and provided detailed evidence upon rehearing supporting a further increase to its G&A expense. The ICC's rehearing order on 20 December 2006 increased this allowed expense by a further $50 million. The majority of this increase was in wage and salaries and restructuring allocations that were related to the firm's recent organizational restructuring.

REFERENCES

Aghion, P. and J. Tirole (1997), 'Formal and real authority in organizations', *Journal of Political Economy*, **105**, 1–29.

Armstrong M. and D. E. M. Sappington (2007), 'Recent developments in the theory of regulation', in M. Armstrong and R. Porter (eds), *Handbook of Industrial Organization (Vol. 3)*, Amsterdam: North-Holland.

Baron, D. P. and R. B. Myerson (1982), 'Regulating a monopolist with unknown costs', *Econometrica*, **50**, 911–30.

Bawn, K. (1995), 'Political control versus expertise: Congressional choices about administrative procedures', *American Political Science Review*, **89**, 62–73.

Bendor, J. and A. Meirowitz (2004), 'Spatial models of delegation', *American Political Science Review*, **98**, 293–310.

De Figueiredo, R. J. and R. G. Vanden Bergh (2004), 'The political economy of state-level administrative procedure acts', *Journal of Law and Economics*, **47**, 569–88.

Feinstein, J. S. (1989), 'The safety regulation of US nuclear power plants: violations, inspections, and abnormal occurrences', *Journal of Political Economy*, **97**, 115–54.

Grossman, G. M. and Helpman, E. (2001), *Special Interest Politics*, Boston, MA: MIT Press.

Holburn, G. L. F. and R. G. Vanden Bergh (2006), 'Consumer capture of regulatory institutions: the creation of public utility consumer advocates in the United States', *Public Choice*, **126**, 45–73.

Howe, S. (1985), 'The used and useful standard: What should the criteria be?' *Public Utilities Fortnightly*, 7 February.

Hyman, L. S. (2000), *America's Electric Utilities: Past, Present and Future*, Arlington, VA: Public Utilities Reports.

Joskow, P. L. (1974), 'Inflation and environmental concern: structural change in the process of public utility price regulation', *Journal of Law and Economics*, **17**, 291–327.

Laffont, J. J. and J. Tirole (1993), *A Theory of Incentives in Regulation and Procurement*, Boston, MA: MIT Press.

Lesser, J. A. (2002), 'The used and useful test: Implications for a restructured electric industry', *Energy Law Journal*, **23**, 349–82.

Lyon, T. P. and J. W. Mayo (2005), 'Regulatory opportunism and investment behavior: evidence from the US electric utility industry', *RAND Journal of Economics*, **36**, 628–44.

Macher, J. T., J. M. Mayo and J. A. Nickerson (2008), 'Exploring the information asymmetry gap: evidence from FDA regulation', unpublished manuscript.

Stephenson, M. C. (2007), 'Bureaucratic decision costs and endogenous agency expertise', *Journal of Law, Economics, and Organization*, **23**, 469–98.

Studness, C. M. (1992), 'Implications of imprudence and deregulation for utility financial policy', *Public Utilities Fortnightly*, 1 May.

13. Adaptation in long-term exchange relations: evidence from electricity marketing contracts

Dean V. Williamson

INTRODUCTION

This research takes up an old, enduring question about what contracting parties can achieve in a long-term contract that they cannot achieve by a sequence of short-term contracts.[1] In the environment examined here, the action depends on the role of renegotiation in enabling contracting parties to adapt terms of exchange over time to changing conditions.[2] As a matter of course, short-term contracts enable parties to renegotiate and adapt terms of exchange after a short term (Myers, 1977: 158; Williamson, 1971: 116). Thus, if adaptation over the long term is important, why would parties ever commit to long terms? One part of the answer advanced here depends on 'friction': long-term contracts allow parties to program fewer, rather than more, costly instances of renegotiation. A familiar trade-off obtains between enabling flexibility in contractual relations and the costs of supporting that flexibility: a sequence of short-term contracts may afford greater flexibility, but programming a sequence of short-term contracts also entails programming a sequence of costly renegotiations (Masten and Crocker, 1985; Crocker and Masten, 1988).

Managing trade-offs between flexibility and renegotiation suggests that 'efficient adaptation' can be an interesting economic problem (Crocker and Masten, 1991), but that is just one consideration in a much larger contracting problem. The first-order action pertains to investment incentives (Williamson, 1971: 116). In the environment examined here, adaptation may involve expanding, withdrawing, or tuning up production capacity over the course of (possibly) long-term exchange. A difficulty is that one party's decision to expand, withdraw, or tune up capacity can diminish the payoffs of counterparties joined in long-term contracts. Thus, the prospect of changing production capacity might induce demands by counterparties to either adjust other terms of contract in response to changes in capacity or to circumscribe any one party's plans to change capacity. Specifically, counterparties might demand safeguards in long-term contracts in the form of provisions that enable them to impose renegotiation in response to other parties' proposals to expand, withdraw, or tune up capacity. Alternatively, they might demand shorter-term contracts. We thus come full circle. Contract duration is one instrument parties can use for containing the frequency of costly renegotiations, but renegotiation itself constitutes an instrument parties may use for adapting terms of contract as well as production capacity over the course of long-term exchange – which in turn may affect the duration of contracts and the incentives of parties to invest in production capacity in the first place. Either way, contract duration now involves trade-offs: longer terms increase the prospect of unprogrammable demands to adapt contracts to changing circumstances, but shorter terms amount to programming a higher frequency of costly renegotiations.

In this chapter I examine an environment in which contract duration constitutes but one of four dimensions of contract that parties use for managing adaptation over the course of long term exchange. I examine an environment in which parties tailor: (a) contract duration; (b) veto provisions; (c) risk-sharing schemes; and (d) financial structure (debt or equity) to support investment in production capacity. Like Crocker and Masten (1988), this chapter accommodates the prospect that there can be important interactions between contract duration and other mechanisms parties use to enable adaptation. I borrow from Williamson (1988) the hypothesis that debt financing requires fewer costly monitoring mechanisms than equity financing.[3] With this hypothesis in hand, one can craft an organic explanation of, among other things, the role of both programmed and unprogrammed renegotiation in enabling parties to adapt terms of contract over the course of long-term exchange and the prevalence of debt over equity in the financing of highly redeployable assets.

The environment I examine is not specific to electricity generation but is inspired by problems parties encounter in mobilizing investment in electricity generation capacity. Firms that develop generation facilities (hereafter, 'generators') tell a compelling but incomplete story about how they organize the financing of specific generation capacity. They line up long-term contracts with electricity 'marketers'. Marketers trade electricity on wholesale electricity markets, and they often secure 'dispatch rights' from generators – rights to make real-time demands for electricity generation as well as demands to cease generation. In return, marketers compensate generators according to two-part schemes. The variable part of the scheme compensates generators for their operating costs and generators extract profits through the fixed part of the scheme. Marketers end up bearing risk for generators, and generators turn around and appeal to prospective creditors ('the bank') for loans to finance the construction or acquisition of electricity generation capacity. Indeed, generators report that they need to line up two-part compensation in order to motivate creditors to finance investment in generation capacity that can support timely dispatch demands.[4]

After parties have committed to a contract, the prospect of adding, withdrawing or tuning up capacity can pose an interesting problem. Changing capacity can affect the vertical rent that the parties share, but not the incentives of the generator. If the generator has already secured its share of the rent by means of a two-part compensation scheme, it may perceive private benefits to expanding capacity. A problem is that bringing new capacity online can complicate the efforts of the marketer to commercialize capacity that is already under contract.[5] At the very least, a marketer might be compelled to demand adjustment of the fixed part of the two-part compensation scheme. Anticipating this, the parties might craft contracts that enable them jointly to internalize the effects of changing capacity. One way to do this would be to allow each party to veto proposals by the other to expand capacity. The point is not that a party would veto a proposal but that veto provisions enable parties to impose renegotiation when and if the counterparty proposes a change in capacity.

One hazard that veto provisions pose is that the antitrust authorities might take an interest in what is going on, and, indeed, it was this kind of interest that motivated this study. But the bigger point is that the generators' pose an incomplete rationale for contracts that involve the combination of: (a) long terms; (b) two-part compensation; (c) debt financing; and (d) veto provisions. If adapting terms of contract is so important, why not commit to a short-term, because, as a matter of course, a short-term contract enables renegotiation (and, thus, adaptation) after a short term? Alternatively, if two-part compensation induces the generator to over-invest in production capacity, why not dispense with two-part compensation, as contracting parties sometimes do, and impose something like linear pricing, that is, a price per kilowatt-hour? Finally, what is so special about fobbing off all of the market risk on marketers to support debt financing, because fobbing off risks on another party does not make risks disappear?

One might be tempted to suggest that electricity generation firms are risk-averse and that marketing firms are better equipped to deal with risk. Risk-aversion is, however, too facile a hypothesis, and it becomes interesting to pose the alternative hypothesis that these multi-billion dollar firms are risk-neutral. I put risk-aversion aside and characterize an environment in which it can nonetheless be efficient for parties to impose all market risk on the marketer. I present a simple, largely reduced-form model that features interactions between the four dimensions of contract. That in itself is not interesting. What is interesting is that the modeling exercise suggests a simple narrative about how electricity marketing contracts work, and it provides stark predictions about patterns that should emerge in contract data. I examine a dataset of 101 electricity marketing contracts and find that these patterns actually obtain.

The principal propositions pertain to patterns of complementarity and substitution between the four dimensions of contract. One proposition is that veto provisions and contract duration complement each other in that long terms increase the prospect of unprogrammed demands for adaptation, and veto provisions allow parties to impose renegotiation as a way of addressing unprogrammed demands. At the same time, short-term contracts tend not to feature veto provisions, because short terms afford parties the option of renegotiating after a short term. A second proposition is that veto provisions and two-part compensation complement each other. Dispensing with two-part compensation (and thus imposing some risk on generators) induces generators to internalize some of the rent-diminishing effects (if any) of proposals to expand capacity. Having internalized such effects, the contracting parties might be able to dispense with veto provisions. In contrast, imposing two-part compensation creates demand for schemes, such as veto provisions, that enable parties to impose renegotiation.

The propositions and empirical results are also interesting, because they are relevant to antitrust analysis. The results suggest that veto provisions enable contracting parties to maximize the private benefits (the 'vertical rent') that they collectively perceive. In instances in which a single marketer contracts with more than one competing generator, then one can easily suggest that generators themselves use veto provisions as a way of committing to restrict investment in production capacity going forward. Restricting capacity constitutes a robust means of committing to restrain output and raise wholesale electricity prices. Now consider the case of a marketer contracting with a single generator. Again, veto provisions enable the parties to maximize the vertical rent, but it would be difficult to suggest how maximizing the vertical rent is anticompetitive. Rather veto provisions enable the parties to induce no less investment going forward than the generator would pursue were it responsible for marketing its own output. Indeed, were the antitrust authorities to bar parties from imposing veto provisions in their contracts, generators might have more difficulty mobilizing investment in which they end up underinvesting in capacity or even foregoing investment entirely.

The remainder of the chapter proceeds in three parts. The first part lays out a simple model of a contracting problem in which contract duration, veto provisions, risk-sharing and financial structure are endogenous. The model is not specific to electricity marketing but rather subsumes the generator's and marketer's contracting problem in a more general framework. The advantage of the generalized framework is that it can accommodate analysis in environments that feature either highly-redeployable assets or assets that are highly relationship-specific. The results demonstrate patterns of complementarity and substitution between contract duration, veto provisions, risk-sharing and financial structure. The second part of the paper describes the structure of electricity marketing contracts and presents empirical results. The last part concludes.

MODEL AND HYPOTHESES

Even though the model is not specific to electricity marketing, I will refer to the two contracting parties as the 'generator' and the 'marketer'. The two risk-neutral parties craft a contract that extends over an interval of duration $T \geq 0$. Parties contribute assets that may or may not be highly redeployable outside of their specific relationship. The generator contributes production assets that involve significant sunk costs. The marketer contributes complementary assets or capabilities, and the parties produce in as many as two states. In the initial state, the parties anticipate a continuous and stationary stream of payoffs $z(t)$ with $\mathrm{E}[z(t)] = z$. The state may change in that at any time $t^* \in [0, T]$ the stream of payoffs may change. I am agnostic on how the payoffs change, but I characterize the change by a continuation value $S(t^*) = S$. One can, for example, understand the continuation value as the expected 'salvage' value. Realizing the continuation value entails either redeploying assets or adding, withdrawing or tuning up capacity as well as adapting the terms of contract. I am agnostic on how parties respond to the change in states, but I do suggest that implementing a cost-effective response may involve some dissipation of surplus. The extent of rent-dissipation will depend partly on how parties design their contract.

Terms of contract include contract duration T and three binary choices. First, parties decide whether or not to impose the residual claim on the marketer, in which case the generator receives a fixed payoff at every $t < t^*$. I pose the alternative as 'sharing risk', although the alternative could entail imposing the residual claim on the generator. Second, the parties decide whether or not to impose a veto provision in the contract. Specifically, they decide whether or not to impose a provision according to which either party might veto the proposal of the other to add, withdraw or tune up the generator's production capacity. Hence, a contract is a quadruple (s, v, d, T) with

$$T = \text{Contract duration}$$

$$s = \begin{cases} 1 & \text{marketer bears all risk} \\ 0 & \text{generator bears some risk} \end{cases}$$

$$v = \begin{cases} 1 & \text{Veto provision included} \\ 0 & \text{No veto provision} \end{cases}$$

$$d = \begin{cases} 1 & \text{Debt financing} \\ 0 & \text{Equity financing} \end{cases}$$

Parameters

Parties can use the veto provision to impose renegotiation over the terms of contract and over the prospect of adding, withdrawing or tuning up production capacity. The interpretation is that renegotiation forces the parties to realize adjustments in capacity, including the prospect of liquidation, that maximize the vertical rent. The adjustments the parties have to make may be unprogrammable which renders them noncontractible. Thus, renegotiation may serve the purpose of enabling the parties to realize rent-maximizing adjustments. The key point is that renegotiation may itself entail some dissipation of rent, which I indicate by the parameter R. Failure to realize the vertical rent invites some dissipation of rents, which I indicate as a tax of proportion δ of the continuation value S. Meanwhile, imposing a risky stream of payoffs on the generator raises the (instantaneous) auditing/monitoring costs of outside investors by increment m.

The Monitoring Hypothesis

I justify this characterization of monitoring costs as follows: the marketer may have its hand in a broad portfolio of projects with any number of generators. Pooling streams from different projects amounts to pooling risks, but pooling risks may make it more difficult for outside investors to disentangle and monitor streams thus creating demands for costly auditing schemes. The generator, however, may separately incorporate each of its production projects.[6] In the language of Hansmann and Kraakman (2000), the generator may be able to 'partition assets' across separately incorporated entities so that outside investors may forgo the costs of disentangling any one project's streams from those of other projects. But risky streams still require monitoring, because generators might cheat investors by misrepresenting their payoffs. However, relieving the generator of project-specific risk relieves outside investors of having to bear incremental monitoring and auditing costs (Williamson, 2005). Thus, imposing the residual claims on the marketer still enables risk pooling, but it also enables parties to economize on auditing and monitoring costs; investors need only concentrate the lens of costly auditing and monitoring on the marketer.

I indicate K as the sunk costs of instituting a mechanism to monitor the generator's payoffs,[7] and I indicate c as the instantaneous marginal cost of producing instantaneous output z. I indicate ρ as a discount rate and λ as a hazard rate reflecting the instantaneous likelihood of the state reverting to the continuation state. Next, I indicate γ as the instantaneous rate at which the cost of producing output increases.[8]

Finally, I indicate $\alpha \in [0, 1]$ as the proportion of the vertical rent that is relationship-specific – that is, α indicates 'asset-specificity', the degree to which assets committed to the relationship cannot be redeployed without dissipating value. One can appeal to asset-specificity to characterize tradeoffs between debt and equity financing of the sort anticipated in Williamson (1988). The purpose here, however, is to demonstrate the robustness of patterns of complementarity and substitution across degrees of asset-specificity.

To recap, the parameters of the system are:

z = Instantaneous income at time $t \in [0, T]$
c = Instantaneous cost of producing z
m = Instantaneous monitoring costs
K = Cost of instituting monitoring mechanism
R = Dissipation due to renegotiation
S = Continuation value
δ = Dissipation, proportional to the continuation value S, that results from distorted investment incentives
ρ = Discount rate
α = Degree of asset-specificity
γ = Rate of cost appreciation
λ = Hazard rate

Given a 'contingency' occurs at time t^*, the parties at time $t = 0$ perceive a discounted vertical rent V:

$$V(t^*; T) = \int_0^{t^*} (z - ce^{\gamma t} - (1 - sd)\alpha^d m)e^{-\rho t}dt + [S - vR]e^{-\rho t^*}$$
$$- [d\alpha + (1 - v)s\delta]S(e^{\rho(T-t^*)} - 1) \qquad (13.1)$$

While this expression appears to be complex, its interpretation is straightforward. Contracting parties would realize an (expected) vertical rent

$$V(t^*;T) = \int_0^{t^*} (z - ce^{\gamma t})e^{-\rho t}dt + Se^{-\rho t^*} \qquad (13.2)$$

but for a series of negative deviations from the vertical rent that depend on how parties structure their financing and design their contract. The interpretation is that imposing veto provisions ($v = 1$) allows the parties to avoid the (discounted) rent dissipation δS that occurs at time t^*, but setting $v = 1$ forces them to bear the (discounted) renegotiation tax R.[9] Parties secure the (discounted) continuation value S, and they secure the expected stream of payments z through time t^* less the costs of producing that stream. Finally, imposing risk on the generator ($s = 0$) forces the parties to bear incremental monitoring costs m, but imposing risk forces the generator to internalize the effects of inefficient investment at time t^*, thus enabling the parties to avoid the tax δS. In contrast, relieving the generator of risk and imposing the residual claim on the marketer enables the parties to avoid incremental monitoring costs but introduces the prospect of distorted investment at time t^*. Note, that either imposing the veto or imposing risk on the generator allows the parties to avoid the tax δS.

Asset-specificity enters V in two places. First, parties perceive monitoring costs $\alpha^d m$. Thus, in the absence of other remedies, parties perceive monitoring costs m under equity financing ($d = 0$) but perceive lower monitoring costs αm under debt financing ($d = 1$). The difficulty with debt, however, is that it frustrates efforts to 'work things out' (Williamson, 1988) and salvage relationship-specific value in the event the stream of payoffs revert to the continuation payoffs. Specifically, parties perceive a tax $d\alpha S$ proportional to the continuation value S.[10] The advantage of equity – indeed, the entire purpose of equity in this environment – is to allow parties to avoid the rent dissipation αS that attends ventures featuring some degree of relationship-specific value.

If one lets $F(t^*; \cdot)$ indicate the probability of an unprogrammable contingency occurring by time t^* – with corresponding probability mass function $f(t^*; \cdot)$ – and if one lets EV indicate the expectation of V, then one can characterize the parties expected payoff at time $t = 0$ as:

$$E\pi = EV - (1 - sd)\alpha^d K = \int_0^T V(t^*; T)f(t^*; \cdot)dt^* + (1 - F(T; \cdot))V(T; T) - (1 - sd)\alpha^d K \qquad (13.3)$$

Note that imposing $s = 1$ (the marketer bears all risk) and $d = 1$ also allows the parties to avoid the up-front sunk costs K of instituting a monitoring mechanism.

Now, if one lets λ indicate the hazard rate, then the density function corresponds to the exponential density $f(t; \lambda) = \lambda e^{-\lambda t}$ and $(1 - F(t; \lambda)) = e^{-\lambda t}$. Economic modelers often use the Poisson distribution to model the number of unprogrammed events that may occur within a given interval of time, but the exponential distribution constitutes the reverse side of the coin; it constitutes a way of modeling the time that lapses until the next contingency occurs. In the environment explored here, we are interested in the time it takes for a single event, the realization of the continuation value, to occur.

With exponential hazards in hand, we have:

$$E\pi(s, v, d, T) = \left[\frac{z - (1 - sd)\alpha^d m}{\rho + \lambda}\right](1 - e^{-(\rho+\lambda)T})$$
$$+\left[\frac{c}{\gamma - \rho - \lambda}\right](1 - e^{(\gamma-\rho-\lambda)T}) - (1 - sd)\alpha^d K$$
$$+\left[\frac{S - vR}{\rho + \lambda}\right](\lambda + \rho e^{-(\rho+\lambda)T})$$
$$-\left[\frac{d\alpha + (1 - v)s\delta}{\rho + \lambda}\right]S[\rho(e^{-\lambda T} - 1) + \lambda(e^{\rho T} - 1)] \tag{13.4}$$

This last expression for the expected vertical rent $E\pi(s, v, d, T)$ yields complementarity and substitutability results. These six results are the pairwise interactions that obtain between the four dimensions of contract s, v, d, and T.

Proposition: Given $\alpha, \delta, \rho, K, R, S$ are each greater than zero, then

1. v and T are strict complements
2. v and s are strict complements
3. v and d are weakly substitutes and complements
4. s and d are strict complements
5. s and T are not complements, but, given $\alpha m = 0$, s and T are weakly substitutes

6. d and T may be neither complements nor substitutes, but for low degrees of asset-specificity (low α) and $m > 0$, d and T may be complements

Proof: One can prove each item by characterizing whether or not the function $E\pi(s, v, d, T)$ has increasing or decreasing differences in each of the six possible pairs of inputs (Topkis 1998: 42). I demonstrate the results for items (13.1) and (13.5):

One can conclude that v and T are complements if the function $E\pi(s, v, d, T)$ exhibits increasing differences in v and T. The function $E\pi(s, v, d, T)$ exhibits increasing differences if, for all $T_1 > T_0$,

$$E\pi(s, 1, d, T_1) - E\pi(s, 0, d, T_1) \geq E\pi(s, 1, d, T_0) - E\pi(s, 0, d, T_0) \tag{13.5}$$

It is sufficient to show that $E\pi(s, 1, d, T) - E\pi(s, 0, d, T)$ is increasing in T or, the same thing, that $\partial/\partial T\{E\pi(s, 1, d, T) - E\pi(s, 0, d, T)\} \geq 0$.

This last expression yields

$$R\rho e^{-(\rho+\lambda)T} + \left(\frac{\lambda\rho}{\rho + \lambda}\right)s\delta S(e^{\rho T} - e^{-\lambda T}) \geq 0$$

which holds for any R and ρ both greater than zero.

By similar calculations, one can show that s and T are not complements and may be substitutes. One can conclude that s and T are substitutes if the function $E\pi(s, v, d, T)$ exhibits decreasing differences in s and T – that is, if $\partial/\partial T\{E\pi(1, v, d, T) - E\pi(0, v, d, T)\} \leq 0$. This last condition yields $d\alpha^d me^{-(\rho+\lambda)T} - (\lambda\rho/\rho + \lambda)(1 - v)\delta S(e^{\rho T} - e^{-\lambda T}) \leq 0$, which fails if $d = v = 1$ and $m > 0$. This condition is satisfied if $\alpha m = 0$.

The model itself does not immediately lend itself to hypothesis testing, but it does suggest that one should interpret the optimal choice of contract duration (T), risk-bearing (s), veto provisions (v), and financial structure (d) as functions of each other. In what follows, I pose the hypothesis that one can approximate the joint selection of T, s, v and d by a system of linear equations:

$$\begin{aligned}
\ln T &= \alpha_T + \beta_{Ts}s + \beta_{Tv}v + \beta_{Td}d + \gamma_T W_T \\
s &= \alpha_s + \beta_{sT}\ln T + \beta_{sv}v + \beta_{sd}d + \gamma_s W_s \\
v &= \alpha_v + \beta_{vT}\ln T + \beta_{vs}s + \beta_{vd}d + \gamma_v W_v \\
d &= \alpha_d + \beta_{dT}\ln T + \beta_{ds}s + \beta_{dv}v + \gamma_d W_d
\end{aligned} \tag{13.6}$$

where W_T, W_s, W_v and W_d indicate vectors of predetermined variables with corresponding vectors of coefficients $\gamma_T, \gamma_s, \gamma_v$ and γ_d. See Appendix 13.1 for details.

Let $E\pi = \max_{s,v,d,T} E\pi(s, v, d, T; \cdot)$ indicate the value function. The inputs T and v are Edgeworth complements if $(\partial^2 E\pi)/(\partial T \partial v) > 0$ which implies $\partial T/\partial v > 0$ and $\partial v/\partial T > 0$. In this linear version of the model featured in Appendix 13.1, the hypothesis that contract duration T and veto provisions v are complements amounts to

$$\frac{\partial^2 E\pi}{\partial T \partial v} = \frac{B^{Tv}}{T} = \frac{\rho_T \beta^{Tv}}{T} > 0$$

where ρ_T is a constant of proportionality. While it is not possible to estimate ρ_T, the test of complementarity amounts to a test of the hypothesis

$$\frac{\partial T}{\partial v} = -\left(\frac{\dfrac{\partial^2 E\pi}{\partial T \partial v}}{\dfrac{\partial^2 E\pi}{\partial T^2}}\right) = T\beta_{Tv} > 0$$

or simply $\beta_{Tv} > 0$.

Similarly

$$\frac{\partial v}{\partial T} = -\left(\frac{\dfrac{\partial^2 E\pi}{\partial T \partial v}}{\dfrac{\partial^2 E\pi}{\partial v^2}}\right) = \frac{\beta_{vT}}{T} > 0 \text{ implies } \beta_{vT} > 0$$

Similar calculations, which I state without proof, yield the following: The complementarity of two-part risk-sharing s and veto provisions v implies $\beta_{sv} > 0$ and $\beta_{vs} > 0$; the complementarity of two-part risk-sharing s and debt d implies $\beta_{sd} > 0$ and $\beta_{ds} > 0$.

Hypotheses

The Proposition indicates six qualitative patterns one should observe in the contract data. The patterns are the pair-wise interactions that obtain between the four dimensions of contract. All of these pair-wise interactions depend on the parameters of the system, but three of these interactions constitute patterns of complementarity that obtain across almost all parameter settings. Specifically, the Proposition suggests that veto provisions and contract duration should complement each other across all degrees of asset-specificity so long as the discount rate is non-zero and the costs of renegotiation are non-zero. In contrast, debt financing and contract duration are not complements in general, but they do complement each other for low-degrees of asset-specificity. Meanwhile, two-part compensation and veto provisions generally complement each other, and two-part compensation and debt financing generally complement each other.

It is these three more general results that I pose as hypotheses. I will, however, limit estimation to a system of three equations that excludes a fourth 'debt' equation, because the data indicate little evidence of variation in the financial structure of electricity generating projects.[11]

H1: Contract duration T and veto provisions v are complements. Within the context of the linear model, this amounts to $\beta_{Tv} > 0$ and $\beta_{vT} > 0$.
That is, allowing parties to impose unprogrammed renegotiation allows them to reduce the frequency of programmed renegotiation. Also, imposing the residual claim on marketers increases the prospect of distorted investment; neutralizing the prospect of unprogrammed renegotiation induces parties to increase the frequency of programmed renegotiation by imposing a shorter term.

H2: Two-part risk-sharing s and veto provisions v are complements. Within the context of the linear model, this amounts to $\beta_{sv} > 0$ and $\beta_{vs} > 0$.

H3: Two-part risk-sharing s and debt d are complements. Within the context of the linear model, this amounts to $\beta_{sd} > 0$ and $\beta_{ds} > 0$.

Since estimation excludes a 'debt' equation, I will not be able to test hypothesis H3, but I include the hypothesis for completeness. The discussion of results will focus on hypotheses H1 and H2.

DATA AND ESTIMATION

I work out of a dataset of 101 electricity marketing contracts that contracting parties recognize either as 'power sales agreements', 'tolling agreements', or 'power purchase agreements'. These contracts join an entity that owns and operates generating assets and an energy marketer who acquires rights to dispatch electricity from the generating assets. Sixty-nine of the contracts were acquired from the publicly posted filings parties made to the Federal Energy Regulatory Commission ('FERC').[12] The 69 contracts exclude other contracts filed with the FERC that the FERC partially or completely withheld from public view. Even so, I managed to extract one withheld contract from one generator's filing to the Securities and Exchange Commission. The remaining 31 contracts derive from filings parties made to the Justice Department in connection with antitrust investigations. Each of these 31 contracts correspond to filings at the FERC that the FERC opted to withhold partially or completely from public view.

Are the data representative of electricity marketing relationships? I suggest that a dataset restricted to the 69 filings publicly posted at the FERC is not representative and that the expanded dataset of 101 contracts is representative. Most notably, the full dataset includes 23 contracts that I interpret as veto provisions. Thirteen of these 23 veto provisions show up in the contracts excluded from the publicly-posted set of 69 contracts. That is, those 69 contracts only include ten of the 23 contracts that feature veto provisions. Here is where the data gathering capabilities of the Antitrust Division of the US Department of Justice come into play. The Division acquired contracts, including the 31 contracts not publicly posted at the FERC, by exercising its subpoena powers as part of an antitrust investigation. Specifically, the Division issued 'Civil Investigative Demands' (CID's) to entities that were subject to investigation as well as to entities excluded from investigation. The entire purpose of the compulsory CID process was to develop a representative dataset of contracts. Indeed, I find that a researcher forced to restrict analysis to the 69 publicly posted contracts would not yield all of the hypothesized results. That researcher would miss some of the most important action in electricity marketing contracts. That action includes the fact that duration of contracts that include veto provisions tend to be double that of contracts that exclude such provisions. In contrast, analysis extended to full (if not large) dataset of 101 contracts yields robust and affirmative results.

Electricity marketing contracts often pertain to transactions between corporate affiliates or to transactions that are not specific to generating units. So, for example, one energy marketer might commit to deliver some volume of electricity to another marketer at some node in the electricity transmission grid, but such a transaction may not specify a source of generation. In contrast, all of the contracts in the dataset involve specific generating assets. At the same time, corporate subsidiaries like Duke Energy Marketing may market electricity for other Duke subsidiaries that manage generation assets.[13] A few such contracts are featured in the dataset.

In Table 13.1 I distinguish the duration of contracts (in years) and the generation capacity placed under contracts (in megawatts [MW]) by type of generation. I distinguish generation by six types of fuel: gas-fired generation ('Gas'), nuclear, coal-fired generation ('Coal'), oil, wind-driven generation ('Wind'), and all other ('Other'). 'Other' includes projects that burn waste from fiber products mills. Much gas-fired generation

Table 13.1 Duration of contracts and generation capacity

	Gas[a]	Nuclear	Coal[a]	Oil[a]	Other Fuel	Wind	All Capacity
Observations	79	4	11	7	5	6	101
Contract duration (years)							
Mean	12.39	9.18	5.69	4.07	5.04	14.87	11.59
Std. Deviation	7.98	4.49	2.74	1.22	3.01	8.19	1.79
Minimum	0.22	30.40	2.92	2.50	2.18	2.45	0.22
Maximum	28.19	13.00	11.81	5.17	10.00	26.08	28.19
Generation capacity (MW)							
Mean	635.62	909.30	1592.60	2350.71	27.50	81.75	599.61
Std. Deviation	961.51	559.55	2012.08	2177.80	16.93	109.89	909.57
Minimum	27.00	500.00	20.00	292.00	6.50	5.00	5.00
Maximum	5645.00	1730.00	5645.00	5645.00	52.00	300.00	5645.00

Note: [a] The columns do not partition the data set. Rather, some contracts feature distinct generating units fired by natural gas, coal, or oil. Such contracts are double or triple counted in the columns 'Gas', 'Coal' and 'Oil'.

constitutes capacity that responds to marginal demands whereas nuclear and coal-fired generation is suited to serve 'baseload' demands.[14] Baseload capacity generates electricity at the lowest marginal costs (lowest cost per MW). It is thus well suited to serving the 'baseload' demand. The optimal program for baseload capacity is to fire it up and let it run indefinitely. In contrast, marginal capacity operates at higher marginal costs. Baseload capacity would seem to dominate marginal capacity, but marginal capacity is better suited to economically 'ramping up' and responding to fluctuations in demand. Generators reserve it to serve peaks in demand that might, for example, attend the hottest hours of a hot day during which everyone turns on the air conditioning. Wind-driven generation is hybrid in that it does not easily fit into a marginal/baseload dichotomy. To begin with, it is less well suited to responding to peak demands, because the wind is not subject to generators' control.

Table 13.1 indicates the 101 contracts feature an average duration of 11.59 years, although the shortest ran about two weeks, and the longest ran 28.19 years. Contracts that included baseload capacity (nuclear and coal), tended to feature short terms whereas those that included gas-fired generation averaged 12.39 years in duration, and those pertaining to wind-driven generation averaged 14.87 years. On average, each contract covered 599.61 MW of generation capacity. Contracts pertaining to wind-driven

Table 13.2 Distribution of veto provisions and risk-sharing provisions across types of generation capacity

		Gas[a]	Nuclear	Coal[a]	Oil[a]	Other fuel	Wind	All capacity
Marketer bears risk	**(s = 1)**	**62**	**1**	**6**	**5**	**1**	–	**66**
Veto provision	(v = 1)	21	–	–	–	–	–	21
Parties share risk	**(s = 0)**	**17**	**3**	**5**	**2**	**4**	**6**	**35**
Veto provision	(v = 1)	–	–	–	–	–	2	2
Total Contracts		**79**	**4**	**11**	**7**	**5**	**6**	**101**

Note: [a] The columns do not partition the data set. Rather, some contracts feature distinct generating units fired by natural gas, coal, or oil. Such contracts are double or triple counted in the columns 'Gas', 'Coal' and 'Oil'.

generation or 'Other' generation covered, on average, 81.75 MW and 71.58 MW respectively. Contracts that included gas-fired generation averaged 635.62 MW per contract.

Seventy-nine of the 101 contracts included gas-fired generation. Twenty-one of these 80 contracts featured provisions that allow at least one party, the marketer, to impose renegotiation (see Table 13.2). I count all 21 provisions as *de facto* 'veto provisions', but, strictly speaking, only eight of these 21 provisions are *de jure* veto provisions. The 15 other provisions are composed of rights-of-first-refusal or 'first-offer'. A generator may, for example, propose an expansion of generation capacity. A right-of-first-refusal gives the incumbent marketer an opportunity to evaluate the proposal and, more importantly, to hold up the prospect of the generator contracting with a different marketer. For example, the marketer Williams Marketing Energy & Trading maintains rights of first-offer, but no veto rights, in its 20-year contract with the generator Cleco Evangeline.[15] In another 20-year contract, the marketer Coral Power, LLC maintains the right to veto 'upgrades' of generating units that the generator Baconton Power, LLC might propose. The parties agree to make 'equitable adjustments' to the two-part compensation scheme in the event they proceed with such upgrades.[16] A 15-year contract between Williams and the generator AES Southland features an explicit veto in that both parties reserve the right to veto proposals by the other to expand or withdraw capacity.[17]

Only two other contracts, both pertaining to Wind, featured veto provisions. The two Wind contracts both feature explicit veto provision, probably because wind-driven generation tends to rely on subsidies to be economical. Parties may not be too keen to invest heavily in long-lived assets only to find subsidies taken away in the future.

Overall, 66 of the 101 contracts imposed the residual claim on marketers ($s = 1$). Sixty-two of the 66 contracts pertained to gas-fired generation. Of the 21 non-gas contracts, only four imposed the residual claim on marketers. This is not surprising. Sometimes marketers share risk with generators ($s = 0$) by compensating them according to linear schemes; they pay fixed fees per unit output, usually a kilowatt-hour. Meanwhile, marginal generation, by virtue of being marginal, is more subject to variation in dispatch demands. A combination of variation in dispatch and linear compensation yields variation in compensation whereas schemes that impose the residual claim on marketers yield fixed streams to generators. In contrast, baseload capacity generally features little variation in dispatch, thus the combination of baseload capacity and linear compensation tends to yield streams that are subject to little or no variation. Wind is a little different in that generators do not control all dimensions of the technology; they cannot 'ramp up' if the wind is inadequate. Wind tends to feature linear compensation which, in turn, implies some variation in the stream of payments marketers yield to generators.

Identification Strategy

The modeling exercise suggests that contract duration (T), the structure of compensation (s), veto provisions (v), and financial structure (d) are jointly determined. As a matter of theory I have posed a linearized system of four equations, one equation for each of the four endogenous variables. As a matter of practice I estimate a system of three equations, because there is no evidence that financial structure deviates from some form of debt. I apply both single-equation methods and simultaneous equation methods to a linearized system, and I apply single-equation methods to a non-linear formulation. While all of the estimation methods yield consistent results, I only report those from the simultaneous estimation of the linearized system.

The model does not provide explicit guidance about how one might identify structural coefficients in the system of equations, but the arguments that motivated the model – arguments about types of friction and hazards – do suggest an 'identification strategy'. My strategy is to assign covariates to at least one of three sets of 'shifters' (instrumental variables) and to assign one set of shifters to each of three equations in the system. The first set of shifters is designed to reflect contracting parties' demands for adaptation that are induced by the actions of parties external to the contracting relationship. Third parties might, for example, expand their own production capacity or expand or withdraw transmission capacity. Such actions may induce congestion on transmission networks, thus diminishing the capacity of the contracting parties to commercialize their own production. Such actions may also diminish the rent the contracting parties had expected to realize going forward. The second set of shifters reflect both demands for time-sensitive dispatch as well as the technical feasibility of serving demands for timely dispatch. The third set of shifters reflect marketers' sensitivity to generator opportunism. A generator might, for example, develop a generation project in a geographic area that is poorly suited to accommodating further expansion of generation capacity. Urban areas may, for example, feature little in the way of sites at which a generator could develop new capacity. Thus constrained, a generator may not be situated to opportunistically expand capacity, and the marketer may be able to dispense with veto provisions.

I argue that contract duration is an important instrument for accommodating the hazards posed by third parties. Accordingly, I will assign the first set of shifters to a 'contract duration equation'. Next, I argue that both demands for variable dispatch the technical feasibility of variable dispatch shift demand for two-part compensation. Accordingly, I assign the second set of shifters to a 'compensation equation'. Finally, I note that the entire theoretical exercise is predicated on the argument that veto provisions are designed to accommodate hazards posed within the contracting relationship itself. Accordingly, I assign the last set of shifters to a 'veto equation'.

Many of the shifters are themselves endogenous in that they depend on initial decisions to invest in generation facilities. These decisions include decisions over the location of generation facilities and over types of generation technologies. I maintain the hypothesis that decisions over contractual form do not feedback into decisions to develop or acquire generation facilities. The principal argument of the chapter is that dissipation of the vertical rent varies over different types of contracts, but I suggest that variation in dissipation is not so great as to frustrate wholesale investment or to induce a decision, say, to supplant a project to develop a gas-fired generation facility in a highly populated area with an alternative project to develop a coal-fired plant in a sparsely populated area.

I now indicate 18 variables that I apply to estimation of the system of three equations, and I then indicate the assignment of covariates to the three sets of 'shifters':

Dependent variables

1. Term	The duration of term of the contract, excluding options to extend.
2. TwoPart	A binary indication that the risk-bearing scheme assigns the residual claim to the marketer ($s = 1$) by means of a two-part

scheme. Two-part schemes usually render a fixed fee to the generator and a set of payments that cover its marginal costs. Almost all other sharing rules are linear ($s = 0$).

3. Veto — A binary indication that the contract features a veto provision ($v = 1$).

Explanatory variables

4. New — A binary indication that the contract covers new generation capacity.
5. Capacity factor — A means of identifying marginal capacity from capacity subject to more regular dispatch. I gather from the Energy Information Agency (EIA) of the Department of Energy annual indications of the proportion of time capacity under contract was dispatched. I take the average of time dispatched over the years 1996 through 2002.[18]
6. County capacity factor — The proportion of time all capacity in the county was dispatched in a year.[19]
7. PopsPerMW — Another means of distinguishing marginal capacity from baseload capacity. The ratio of county population to nominal capacity (MW) under contract. It constitutes a proxy for marginal generation since large, baseload generation plants are often located outside of populated areas and small, and 'peaking' units tend to be located within load pockets which themselves tend to be located within densely populated areas.[20]
8. SubstationsPerArea — An indication of local transmission capacity; the number of substations per unit area (square kilometer) in a county.[21]
9. Gas turbine — A binary indication that the contract includes gas-fired generation that includes 'jet engine' type peaking units.[22]
10. Combined cycle — A binary indication that the contract covers combined cycle units.[23]
11. Combustion engine — A binary indication that the contract covers units powered by an internal combustion engine.[24]

12.	Steam turbine	A binary indication that the contract covers units driven by steam turbines.[25]
13.	Wind	A binary indication that the contract features wind-driven generation capacity.
14.	Population density	Population per unit area (square kilometer) of the county in which the generating units are situated.[26]
15.	MW	Generation capacity (MW) under contract.
16.	FERC	A binary indication that the contract was filed with the FERC, and the FERC opted to make the contract available to the public.
17.	Retail	A binary indication that the 'marketer' is a retail distributor of electricity or is an end user.[27]
18.	CountyMWPerArea:	The ratio of county-wide capacity (MW) to unit area (square kilometer) in a county.[28]

Shifters Reflecting Demands for Adaptation

I use the variables New, Capacity Factor, County Capacity Factor, PopsPerMW and SubstationsPerArea (variables 4 through 8) to reflect different types of demand for adaptation. Insofar as 'New' reflects the expected economic life of generating units, then it reflects programmable opportunities to salvage assets. The variables Capacity Factor and PopsPerMW constitute means for distinguishing marginal generation capacity, capacity that intendedly serves marginal demands, from inframarginal generation capacity ('baseload' capacity) that is subject to more regular demands (the 'baseload').

I include these variables to control for the prospect that marginal capacity may be more susceptible to three types of hazards and may, in turn, be subject to unprogrammable demands for adaptation. The hazards are: (a) the unprogrammable prospect of being crowded out by new capacity and knocked 'out of the money'; (b) transmission congestion that may attend peaking demands for electricity; and (c) higher monitoring costs that can attend generation capacity that is more subject to variable dispatch demands. I illustrate the crowding-out hazard in Figure 13.1. Consider a market institution under which the marginal cost of marginal capacity imposes a uniform wholesale price. Adding inframarginal capacity may shift the supply curve from S_0 to S_1. Capacity located at B_0 gets displaced to B_1. In demand state D a price of P_0 would have prevailed, and capacity

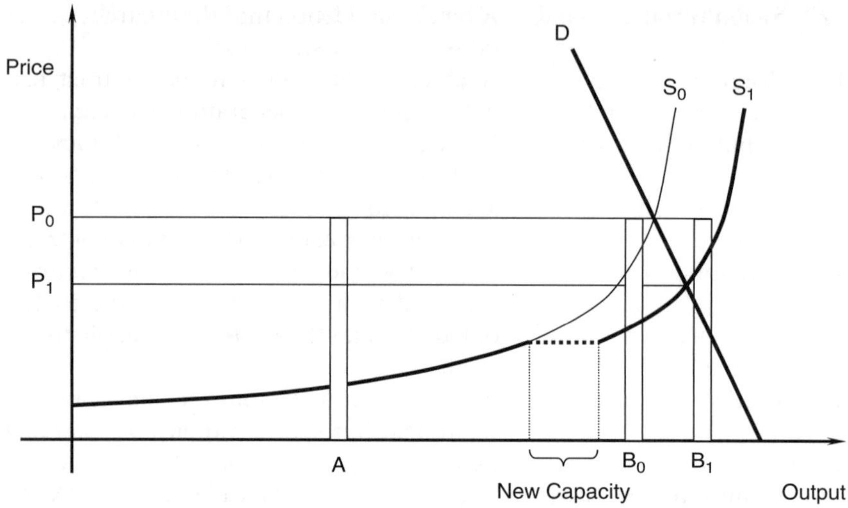

Figure 13.1 The crowding-out hazard

at B_0 would have been 'in the money' – the marketer would have been able to realize a positive price-cost margin were it to exercise its option to dispatch electricity. After the addition of new capacity, a lower price of P_1 obtains, in which case the capacity at B_1 get knocked 'out of the money.' (The parties lose marginal revenue at a rate equal to the cross-hatched rectangle above B_1.) Meanwhile, the capacity at A remains in the money, but the marginal review diminishes by $P_0 - P_1 > 0$. (The parties lose marginal revenue at a rate equal to the cross-hatched rectangle above A.) The margin still gives the contracting parties some capacity to service underlying debt obligations in demand state D, but the parties responsible for managing capacity displaced to B_1 lose all capacity to service debt in demand states like D.

The hazards attending transmission congestion also require some comment. Transmission constraints are interesting, because they can frustrate a marketer's demands for timely dispatch.[29] Even so, while marginal capacity might be more susceptible to congestion hazards, generators accommodate the prospect of congestion by judiciously locating marginal capacity inside 'load pockets' – that is, inside the areas that generate the peaking demands that induce congestion. I use the variable PopsPerMW to control for prospect that generators judiciously site marginal generation inside load centers. I use SubstationsPerArea to reflect the density of local transmission networks.

Shifters Reflecting Demand and Supply for Time-sensitive Dispatch

I use the variables Gas Turbine, Combined Cycle, Combustion engine, Steam Turbine, Wind and MW to control for the technological feasibility of time-sensitive dispatch, and I use Population Density to control for aspects of the demand for timely dispatch. The technology variables provide ways of distinguishing capacity that can technically accommodate dispatch demands from capacity that is less amenable to timely dispatch. Again, the important idea is that marginal generation can involve greater monitoring costs. Absent remedies such as two-part compensation, parties might have to engage more efforts to monitor and audit the streams of revenues that derive from the irregular dispatch of marginal units. It is reasonable, then, to expect that generating units that can accommodate dispatch demands, such as gas turbine units, will tend to align with two-part compensation. In contrast, combined cycle units feature heat recovery systems which allow them to be more fuel-efficient but may be less amenable to ramping up quickly to respond to dispatch demands. Generators might even dedicate such units to serving base load demands, especially in areas in which regulators favor gas-fired generation over other types of generation (for example, coal) that contribute to emissions of nitrous oxide and sulfur dioxide. Wind-driven generation may be less amenable to timely dispatch in that it depends on an external factor, the wind, beyond generator's control thus limiting the capacity of wind-driven generation to ramp-up to serve peaking demands. Meanwhile, MW reflects upper bounds on the capacity that could be available for dispatch.

Shifters Reflecting Demands for Veto Provisions

Finally, I use FERC and Retail in conjunction with CountyMWPerArea (variables 16 through 18) to capture aspects of demand for contract renegotiation. I use FERC to capture hidden attributes of transactions that the FERC may have systematically used to inform its decision to publicly post contracts. I use Retail to control for the prospect that retail end-users and distributors may present generators with less volatile demands and may thus pose fewer contracting hazards. I use CountyMWPerArea to control for the prospect that certain geographic areas may be more densely endowed with generation capacity and may thus be less amenable to supporting further expansion of generation capacity. A generator may simply not be able to secure new 'greenfield' sites or even 'brownfield' sites for new generation projects, in which case a marketer would be less pressed to secure veto rights in a contract.[30]

Methods of Estimation

I simultaneously estimate equations that correspond to a linear version of the model

$$\text{LogTerm}_i = \alpha_T + \beta_{Ts}\text{TwoPart}_i + \beta_{Tvi}\text{Veto}_i + \gamma_T W_{Ti} + \varepsilon_{Ti}$$

$$\text{TwoPart}_i = \alpha_s + \beta_{sT}\text{LogTerm}_i + \beta_{sv}\text{Veto}_i + \gamma_s W_{si} + \varepsilon_{si}$$

$$\text{Veto}_i = \alpha_v + \beta_{vT}\text{LogTerm}_i + \beta_{vs}\text{TwoPart}_i + \gamma_v W_{vi} + \varepsilon_{vi}$$

where $i = 1, \ldots N$, W_{Ti} and W_{vi} are vectors of variables that reflect programmable or unprogrammable demands for adaptation, W_{si} includes variables that reflect the feasibility of timely dispatch, and the error terms ε_{Ti}, ε_{si} and ε_{vi} indicate potentially non-normal processes.

The theoretical model implies that contract duration (Term), TwoPart and Veto are jointly determined, which in turn implies that the equations should be estimated by methods that accommodate endogeneity of the regressors. In Table 13.3 I present results from applying three-stage least squares (3SLS) with bootstrapped standard errors to the linearized model.[31]

Appealing to 3SLS amounts to applying the linear probability model which in turn may induce heteroskedastistic residuals. Bootstrap methods can be applied to three-stage least squares estimation (Freedman and Peters, 1984; MacKinnon, 2002), and bootstrapping data directly ('pairs' bootstrap), in contrast to bootstrapping residuals from the original estimation, constitutes a method of generating standard errors and confidence intervals that are robust to heteroskedasticity (MacKinnon, 2006: 9; Johnston and Dinardo, 1997: 369). It also constitutes a method of accommodating error processes that may be non-normal. Nevitt and Hancock (2001) further observe that the bootstrap provides an alternative and often superior means of generating standard errors with small datasets featuring data that may be non-normal.

Results

The two results correspond to hypotheses H1 and H2.

Result 1: Contract duration and veto provisions are complements.

The results reported in Table 13.3 indicate $\beta_{Tv} = 1.4187$ and $\beta_{vT} = 0.1989$, both statistically significant at the 5 percent level with or without bootstrapped standard errors. Results from estimation by

Table 13.3 Results obtained from applying three-stage least squares with bootstrapped standard errors to the linearized model

Explanatory Variables	Dependent Variables		
	LogTerm	TwoPart	Veto
LogTerm		**−0.0205**	**0.1989****
		0.1719	0.0801
TwoPart	**−0.5738**		**0.3796****
	0.3883		0.1524
Veto	**1.4187****	**0.8358****	
	0.6956	0.3677	
New	**0.5904****		
	0.2285		
Capacity factor	**0.3595**		
	0.4710		
County capacity factor	**0.0848**		
	0.4694		
Log PopsPerMW	**−0.1385****		
	0.0623		
Log SubstationsPerArea	**0.1833***		
	0.0975		
Generating turbine		**0.1989***	
		0.1059	
Combustion turbine		**0.2137**	
		0.1818	
Combined cycle		**0.1964***	
		0.1027	
Steam turbine		**−0.1249**	
		0.1225	
Wind		**−0.4172****	
		0.1908	
Log population density		**6.05E-03**	
		2.88E-02	
Log capacity (MW)		**−7.11E-04**	
		4.85E-02	
FERC			**−0.1006**
			0.0756
Retail			**−0.0655**
			0.0720
Log CountyMWPerArea			**−0.0425***
			0.0252
Constant	**3.3906*****	**0.3425**	**−0.3812****
	0.8451	0.3473	0.1877

Note: The notations ***, **, and * respectively indicate 1%, 5% and 10% levels of significance.

OLS and 2SLS, with or without bootstrapped standard errors, and by Two-stage Conditional Maximum Likelihood (2SCML)[32] are consistent and statistically significant.

Result 2: Two-part risk-sharing and veto provisions are complements. The results indicate $\beta_{sv} = 0.8358$ and $\beta_{vs} = 0.3796$, both statistically significant at the 5 percent level with or without bootstrapped standard errors. Results from estimation by OLS and 2SLS, with or without bootstrapped standard errors, and by 2SCML are consistent and statistically significant.

Discussion

The results suggest that, other things equal, long terms of contract and veto provisions tend to cluster together and two-part compensation veto provisions tend to cluster together. A more ambitious interpretation would be that long terms, veto provisions, and two-part compensation all tend to cluster together.[33] Sure enough, contracts that feature both veto provisions and two-part compensation tend to feature longer terms than all those of all other contracts. Twenty-three contracts feature both veto provisions and two-part compensation, and the average duration of these contracts exceeds 18 years whereas the duration of the other 78 contracts averages less than ten years. The second regression result is also consistent with another simple interpretation: contracting parties might address the prospect of a generator's incentives to overinvest in generation capacity by either imposing a veto provision or denying two-part compensation. More pointedly: contracting parties should not need to impose both veto provisions and market risk on the generator. It turns out that, with the exception of two contracts featuring wind-driven generation, no contracts that impose market risk on the generator also impose veto provisions.

The results are interesting, because they are consistent with the hypothesis that the problem of adapting relationships over the course of long-term exchange is an important determinant of contract form. The regression results are robust across diverse methods of estimation, but one might be concerned that the results are sensitive to the choice of instruments. I suggest, however, that one can have some confidence in the instruments (the three sets of 'shifters') in that they themselves yield sensible results. For example, contracts for the marketing of smaller generation units located in densely populated areas tend to feature shorter terms. (The coefficient on the log of PopsPerMW is negative and significant.) It was suggested that such generation facilities would be more susceptible to being knocked 'out of the money' by competitive investment and that that, in turn, would induce contracting parties to impose more flexibility in their contracts by imposing shorter terms. At the same time, the results indicate that variables reflecting demands for two-part compensation do, in fact, indicate greater dependence on two-part compensation. For example, the coefficients on the variables Generating Turbine and Wind are respectively positive and negative. Finally, variables reflecting diminished demand for veto provisions indicate diminished demand. For example, contracts featuring generation located in counties more densely endowed with generation capacity are less likely to feature veto provisions. (The coefficient on the log of CountyMWPerArea is negative and significant.)

CONCLUSION

Why would one party (labeled the 'generator,' say) yield to a second party (the 'marketer') the right to veto decisions as important as investment decisions that the generator might make at any point over a long interval of time? It seems natural to suggest that the two parties together have committed to a scheme to restrain investment in production capacity, all in a larger effort to restrain competition. The hypothesis is incomplete, however, insofar as the two parties themselves are not competitors in some market. Alternatively, the hypothesis would be much more compelling were one to find that the marketer maintains contractual relations with more than one competing generator. In such a context, veto provisions in long-term contracts may enable competing generators to commit to restraining investment in production capacity, all in a larger effort to restrain competition between each other.

In this chapter I develop an alternative 'efficient adaptation' hypothesis. In some contexts one might understand veto provisions as mechanisms parties use to facilitate contract adjustment over the course of long-term exchange. To understand this hypothesis and to operationalize tests of the hypothesis, one cannot focus on veto provisions in isolation but must characterize interactions with other dimensions of contract. I examine an environment in which there exist important interactions between four dimensions of contract: veto provisions, financial structure, contract duration and profit-sharing. Efficient adaptation suggests pair-wise interactions between these four dimensions of contract. The evidence examined here yields patterns that are consistent with efficient adaptation being an important economic problem. These patterns are also consistent with friction and distorted investment incentives rather than asset-specificity and hold-up problems being the principal drivers of the action in the environment examined.

ACKNOWLEDGMENTS

The paper derives from a larger project titled 'Adaptation and the financial structure of long-term exchange relations'. I thank Scott Masten and seminar participants at The George Washington University, the Antitrust Division, the Haas School of Business at Berkeley, and the 2006 International Industrial Organization Conference for helpful comments and questions on earlier work. I also thank the participants of the conference 'Deregulation or re-regulation: institutional and other approaches' organized in June, 2007 by Claude Menard and Michel Ghertman. Finally, I thank two anonymous referees and Claude Menard for many helpful comments and suggestions. The usual disclaimer applies. Additionally, the views expressed in this paper do not reflect official policy of the United States Department of Justice.

NOTES

1. See, for example, Fudenberg *et al.*, 1990 and Williamson, 1991: 172–6 on sequential short-term contracting.
2. The idea that renegotiation could serve an efficiency-enhancing purpose illuminates deep questions about how and why contracts would be 'incomplete'. (Maskin and Tirole 1999 pose many of these question.) A complete contracting framework admits no role for renegotation and contract duration. I put such questions aside, make a traditional appeal to incompleteness and work out implications for contract design from there.
3. The discussion of Hansmann and Kraakman (2000: 399-401) on monitoring and 'asset-partitioning' is apposite. See also Williamson (2005).
4. For example, Black Hills Corporation reported that 'We aim to secure long-term power sales contracts in conjunction with project financing. This enables us to minimize our liability and to design a debt repayment schedule to closely match the term of the power sales contracts so that at the end of the contract term, the debt has largely been repaid.' (See page 10 of the SEC Form 10-K for the year ending 31 December 2001.) Similarly, AES Ironwood, LLC reported that 'Each monthly payment by [our marketer] Williams Energy will consist of a total fixed payment, a fuel conversion payment and a start-up payment. The total fixed payment, which is payable regardless of facility dispatch by Williams . . . is anticipated to be sufficient to cover our debt service and fixed operating and maintenance costs and to provide us a return on equity.' (See page 6 of the AES Ironwood SEC form 10-K for the year ending 31 December 2001.)
5. For example, output from new capacity can induce congestion on transmission networks thus complicating transmission of electricity from capacity under contract. Output from new capacity may also depress prices in wholesale markets or knock existing capacity 'out of the money'. More on this below.
6. In the electricity generation context, generators uniformly incorporate generating projects in distinct production LLCs.
7. The sunk costs are important, and the appeal to them is consistent with the framework of Williamson (1988).
8. Imposing > 0 may seem artificial, but it constitutes a simple way of securing the second-order conditions for an interior solution of the optimal contract duration. The key

point, however, is that there are any number of isomorphic ways to secure an interior solution. For example, the term constitutes an indirect way of modeling depreciation of production capacity. I suggest that imposing constitutes little loss of generality and does not otherwise constitute an interesting, instructive assumption.

9. Note that the rent dissipation that attends distorted investment at time t^* is diminishing with time. This is not an important assumption.
10. The rent dissipation that attends failure to 'work things out' is also diminishing with time.
11. Some contracts make explicit reference to underlying credit agreements. Others indicate 'lenders' in the background, and yet others indicate both underlying credit agreements and lenders. No contracts make explicit reference to equity financing, although some generating projects are organized by clusters of investors who likely make nominal equity infusions, yet even these investors explicitly line up debt financing. Finally, I note that even generators that are affiliated with their marketers depend on debt financing. Duke Energy, for example, maintains both a marketing subsidiary and generating subsidiaries. Duke sets up each generating project as an LLC responsible for organizing its own financing.
12. The FERC stopped requiring marketers to file contracts in 2002. The dataset features every contract I could identify in all available filings.
13. Duke Energy Corporation owns or leases generation in California through four wholly-owned subsidiaries. These four subsidiaries maintain marketing contracts with Duke Energy Marketing. See the Duke Energy filing with the FERC dated 25 June 1998 at docket # ER98-2680-002, the FERC filing dated 31 December 1998 at docket # ER99-1199, and the Duke Energy Corporation SEC filing 10-K for the year 1999.
14. Not all gas-fired generation capacity operates at the margin. 'Jet engine type' generators constitute capacity that is suited to serving 'peaking' demands, because they are amenable to serving dispatch demands on short notice. 'Combined cycle' gas-fired generation may less amenable to dispatch demands but is more efficient than peaking generators, because they include systems to recover the heat that jet engines dissipate.
15. See the FERC filing dated 30 June 2000 at docket # ER00-3058-001.
16. See page 46 of the Baconton filing dated 10 July 2000 at docket # ER00-3096.
17. See page 2 of the Williams/AES agreement filed 7 May 2001 at docket # ER98-2184-006.
18. A few sites had not been equipped to dispatch electricity before 2002. I accommodate the missing data by indicating the 'capacity factor' as the average capacity factor of all other data.
19. Source: EIA.
20. Sources: Census Bureau and the contracts themselves. The variable constitutes a compact way of distinguishing small units in the hinterlands and large units that feed baseload demand from small unit inside load pockets. For example, some small units outside of load pockets constitute the joint product or 'cogeneration' of facilities that burn waste, including wood chips, at dumps or lumber mills located outside of densely populated areas.
21. Source: EIA.
22. Sources: The contracts themselves and the EIA. Corresponds to EIA nomenclature 'GT'.
23. Sources: The contracts themselves and the EIA. Corresponds to EIA nomenclatures 'CC', 'CA' and 'CS'.
24. Sources: The contracts themselves and the EIA. Corresponds to EIA nomenclature 'IC'.
25. Sources: The contracts themselves and the EIA. Corresponds to EIA nomenclature 'ST'. Steam turbines may be fired by gas, coal, oil, other fuel, and heat from a nuclear generator.
26. Source: Census Bureau.
27. For example, I feature the California Department of Water Resources as an end-user in one contract.

28. Sources: EIA and Census Bureau.
29. See, for example, Chapter 3 of 'The changing structure of the electric power industry: selected issues, 1998' by the Energy Information Agency at http://www.eia.doe.gov/cneaf/electricity/chg_str_issu/chg_str_iss_rpt/toc.html. 'Congestion in the transmission system occurs when a transmission line reaches its transmitting capacity, limiting the system operator from dispatching additional power from a specific generator. Congestion may be caused by generation or power grid outages, increases in energy demand, or loop flow problems. When congestion occurs, the transmission system operator may have a number of options it can use to solve the problem. For example, it can curtail power from certain generators, or it can dispatch another generator outside the congested area to supply power. Curtailment of power from a generator may be referred to as redispatch, and the use of another generator to supply power is called out-of-merit dispatch.' Transmission constraints can also frustrate competitors' efforts to dispatch electricity.
30. Generators might yet be able to expand capacity on existing sites.
31. The results are also robust to various single-equation methods. I also estimated the equations by OLS, two-stage least squares (with and without bootstrapped standard errors), and the two-stage conditional maximum likelihood method (2SCML) of Rivers and Vuong (1988). 2SCML involves including three new generated variables, 'LogTerm Residuals', 'TwoPart Residuals' and 'Veto Residuals' to single-equation estimation of the contract duration equation and to estimation of probits for TwoPart and Veto. The residuals derive from ordinary least squares regression of reduced-form equations – that is, from separately regressing LogTerm, TwoPart and Veto on all of the exogenous variables featured in the system. Applying 2SCML to the duration equation yields the same coefficient estimates that one would obtain from two-stage least squares and yields virtually the same standard errors (Davidson and MacKinnon, 1993: 240). As Petrin and Train (2003) observe, 2SCML constitutes an application of the 'control function' approach to probit models. It is a single equation method that accommodates continuous endogenous explanatory variables and provides simple Hausman-like 'endogeneity tests' (Hausman, 1978) of both continuous and discrete explanatory variables (Rivers and Vuong, 1998: 358; Wooldridge, 2002: 474). The tests amount to tests of the significance of the coefficients assigned to the generated variables LogTerm Residuals, TwoPart Residuals, and Veto Residuals.
32. Estimation by 2SCML also provides only weak evidence of the exogeneity of LogTerm, TwoPart and Binary with respect to each other. The upshot is that the coefficient estimates themselves and standard errors estimated by 2SCML may only be correct up to a scale factor. Even so, the t-ratios cancel the scale factors out and can be interpreted. See Wooldridge (2002): 474.
33. One reason the interpretation would be ambitious is that both the Proposition and the regression results suggest that long terms of contract and two-part compensation might tend to be substitutes for each other in environments featuring highly redeployable assets such as electricity generation facilities.

REFERENCES

Crocker, K. and S. Masten (1988), 'Mitigating contractual hazards: options and contract length', *RAND Journal of Economics*, **19** (3), 327–43.

Crocker, K. and S. Masten (1991), 'Pretia ex machina? Prices and process in long-term contracts', *Journal of Law and Economics*, **34** (1), 64–99.

Crocker, K. and K. Reynolds (1993), 'The efficiency of incomplete contracts: an empirical analysis of air force engine procurement', *RAND Journal of Economics*, **24** (1), 126–46.

Davidson, Russell and James G. MacKinnon (1993), *Estimation and Inference in Econometrics*, New York: Oxford University Press.
Freedman, D. and S. Peters (1984), 'Bootstrapping an econometric model: some empirical results', *Journal of Business and Economic Statistics*, **2** (2), 150–8.
Fudenberg, D., B. Holmstrom and P. Milgrom (1990), 'Short-term contract and long-term agency relationships', *Journal of Economic Theory*, **51** (1), 1–31.
Hansmann, H. and R. Kraakman (2000), 'The essential role of organization law', *Yale Law Journal*, **110** (3), 387–440.
Hausman, J. (1978), 'Specification tests in econometrics', *Econometrica*, **46** (6), 1251–72.
Johnston, Jack and John Dinardo (1997), *Econometric Methods*, 4th edn, New York: McGraw-Hill.
MacKinnon, J (2002), 'Bootstrap inference in econometrics', *Canadian Journal of Economics*, **35** (4), 615–45.
MacKinnon, J. (2006), 'Bootstrap methods in econometrics', Queen's Economics Department Working Paper 1028.
Maskin, E. and J. Tirole (1999), 'Unforeseen contingencies and incomplete contracts', *Review of Economic Studies*, **66** (1), 83–114.
Masten, S. and K. Crocker (1985), 'Efficient adaptation in long-term contracts: take-or-pay provisions for natural gas', *American Economic Review*, **75** (5), 1083–93.
Myers, S. (1977), 'Determinants of corporate borrowing', *Journal of Financial Economics*, **5** (2), 147–75.
Nevitt, J. and G. Hancock (2001), 'Performance of bootstrapping approaches to model test statistics and parameter standard error estimation in structural equation modeling', *Structural Equation Modeling*, **8** (3), 353–77.
Petrin, A. and K. Train (2003), 'Omitted product attributes in discrete choice models', NBER Working Paper 9452.
Rivers, D. and Q. Vuong (1988), 'Limited information estimators and exogeneity tests for simultaneous probit models', *Journal of Econometrics*, **39** (3), 347–66.
Topkis, Donald M. (1998), *Supermodularity and Complementarity*, Princeton, NJ: Princeton University Press.
Williamson, D. (2005), 'The financial structure of Commercial Revolution: Financing long-distance trade in Venice 1190–1220 and Venetian Crete 1303–1400', mimeo.
Williamson, O. (1971), 'The vertical integration of production: market failure considerations', *American Economic Review*, **61** (2), 112–23.
Williamson, O. (1988), 'Corporate finance and corporate governance', *Journal of Finance*, **43** (3), 567–91.
Williamson, O. (1991), 'Economic institutions: Spontaneous and intentional governance', *Journal of Law, Economics and Organization*, **7** (Spring), 159–87.
Wooldridge, Jeffery M. (2002), *Econometric Analysis of Cross Section and Panel Data*, Cambridge, MA: MIT Press.

APPENDIX 13.1

I interpret s, v, and d as continuous variables, and I pose the joint payoff (the vertical rent) of representative contracting parties as:

$$E\pi = k + \rho_T(\ln T)\left(\alpha_T - \frac{\ln T}{2}\right) + \rho_s s\left(\alpha_s - \frac{s}{2}\right)$$
$$+ \rho_v v\left(\alpha_v - \frac{v}{2}\right) + \rho_d d\left(\alpha_d - \frac{d}{2}\right)$$
$$+ \rho_T(\ln T)\gamma_T W_T + s\rho_s\gamma_s W_s + v\rho_v\gamma_v W_v + d\rho_d\gamma_d W_d$$
$$+ B^{Ts}(\ln T)s + B^{Tv}(\ln T)v + B^{Td}(\ln T)d$$
$$+ B^{sv}sv + B^{sd}sd + B^{vd}vd \qquad (13A.1)$$

where W_T, W_s, W_v and W_d indicate vectors of predetermined variables with corresponding vectors of coefficients $\gamma_T, \gamma_s, \gamma_v$ and γ_d, k is a constant, and ρ_T, ρ_s, ρ_v and ρ_d indicate constants each greater than zero. If one lets $B^{sT} = \rho_T\beta_{Ts} = \rho_s\beta_{sT}$, $B^{Tv} = \rho_T\beta_{Tv} = \rho_v\beta_{vT}$, $B^{Td} = \rho_T\beta_{Td} = \rho_d\beta_{dT}$, $B^{sv} = \rho_s\beta_{sv} = \rho_v\beta_{vs}$, $B^{sd} = \rho_s\beta_{sd} = \rho_d\beta_{ds}$ and $B^{vd} = \rho_v\beta_{vd} = \rho_d\beta_{dv}$ indicate cross-equation restrictions, then optimization yields a system of four equations:

$$\begin{aligned} \ln T &= \alpha_T + \beta_{Ts}s + \beta_{Tv}v + \beta_{Td}d + \gamma_T W_T \\ s &= \alpha_s + \beta_{sT}\ln T + \beta_{sv}v + \beta_{sd}d + \gamma_s W_s \\ v &= \alpha_v + \beta_{vT}\ln T + \beta_{vs}s + \beta_{vd}d + \gamma_v W_v \\ d &= \alpha_d + \beta_{dT}\ln T + \beta_{ds}s + \beta_{dv}v + \gamma_d W_d \end{aligned} \qquad (13A.2)$$

The cross-equation restrictions reduce to four restrictions $\beta_{Tv}\beta_{vs}\beta_{sT} = \beta_{Ts}\beta_{sv}\beta_{vT}$, $\beta_{Tv}\beta_{vd}\beta_{dT} = \beta_{Td}\beta_{dv}\beta_{vT}$, $\beta_{Td}\beta_{ds}\beta_{sT} = \beta_{Ts}\beta_{sd}\beta_{dT}$ and $\beta_{sv}\beta_{vd}\beta_{ds} = \beta_{sd}\beta_{dv}\beta_{vs}$. The estimated results do not deviate from these restrictions with statistical significance.

APPENDIX 13.2 CONTRACTS DERIVED FROM FILINGS TO THE FERC

Marketer	Generator	FERC Docket # or SEC filing
Alliant Energy	Minergy Neenah	ER00-89
Ameren Energy Marketing, Dynegy Power Marketing, LG&E Energy Marketing	Midwest Electric Power Inc.	ER00-3353-001
Aquila Energy Marketing Corporation and UtiliCorp United Inc.	Elwood Energy II LLC	ER01-2270
Aquila Energy Marketing Corporation and UtiliCorp United Inc.	Elwood Energy III LLC	ER01-2681
Aquila Power Corporation and Utilicorp United Inc.	LSP Energy LP	ER00-3539
Attala Energy Company LLC	Attala Generating Company LLC	ER02-2165
Avista Energy	Rathdrum Power	ER02-216, ER01-2862
Central Illinois Light Company	AES Medina Valley Cogen	ER01-788
Central Illinois Light Company	Altorfer	ER01-1758
CinCap Duke Trenton	Duke Vermillion	ER01-2335
Commonwealth Edison Company (Coal Stations Agreement)	Midwest Generation LLC	ER00-1378
Commonwealth Edison Company (Collins Station Agreement)	Midwest Generation LLC	ER00-1378
Commonwealth Edison Company (Peaking Stations Agreement)	Midwest Generation LLC	ER00-1378
Commonwealth Edison Company	Midwest Generation LLC	ER02-289
Consolidated Edison Company of NY	Entergy Nuclear Indian Point 2 LLC	ER01-1721-001
Constellation Power Source Inc.	Calvert Cliffs Nuclear Power Plant Inc.	ER02-445
Constellation Power Source Inc.	Carr Street Generating Station	Orion Power Holdings 2000 10-K
Constellation Power Source Inc.	Deseret Generation & Transmission Cooperative	ER02-339

Appendix 13.2 (continued)

Marketer	Generator	FERC Docket # or SEC filing
Coral Energy	Tenaska Gateway Partners	ER01-2903
Coral Power LLC	Baconton Power LLC	ER00-3096
Coral Power LLC	WFEC Genco LLC	ER01-1481
CPN Pleasant Hill LLC	MEP Pleasant Hill LLC & MEP Pleasant Hill Operating LLC	ER01-905
Dominion Nuclear Marketing I and Dominion Nuclear Marketing II	Pleasants Energy LLC	ER02-698
Duke Energy Corporation	Rockingham Power LLC	ER00-2984-001
Duke Energy Trading and Marketing LLC	Bridgeport Energy LLC	ER01-2352
Duke Energy Trading and Marketing LLC	Casco Bay	ER01-216
Duke Energy Trading and Marketing LLC	Duke Energy Moss Landing LLC	ER02-1662
Edison Mission Marketing and Trading Company	Harbor Cogeneration	ER99-4018
El Paso Energy Marketing Company	Berkshire Power Company LLC	ER00-498
El Paso Power Services Company	Cordova Energy Company LLC	ER01-2595
Engage US LP	Elwood Energy LLC	ER99-4100
Exelon	Kincaid Generation	ER01-2274
Exelon	University Park Energy	ER01-2725
Exelon Generation Company LLC	AmerGen Energy Company LLC	ER02-786
Exelon Generation Company LLC	Elwood Energy	ER01-1975
Exelon Generation Company LLC	Southeast Chicago Energy Project LLC	ER02-2017
Florida Power & Light Company	DeSoto County Generating Company LLC	ER02-1446

Appendix 13.2 (continued)

Marketer	Generator	FERC Docket # or SEC filing
Holy Cross Energy and Public Service Company of Colorado	Public Service Company of Colorado	ER02-8
LG&E Energy Marketing Inc.	LG&E Power Monroe LLC	ER02-902
MidAmerican	Cordova Energy Company	ER00-1967
Mirant Americas Energy Marketing LP	Commonwealth Chesapeake Company LLC	ER00-3703, ER02-1537
Mirant Americas Energy Marketing LP	Mirant Chalker Point LLC	ER01-2974
Mirant Americas Energy Marketing LP	Mirant Mid-Atlantic LLC	ER01-2981
Mirant Americas Energy Marketing LP	Mirant Peaker LLC	ER01-2975
Mirant Americas Energy Marketing LP	Mirant Zeeland LLC	ER01-2479
Morgan Stanley Capital Group Inc.	South Eastern Electric Development Corporation	ER99-3654
Municipal Energy Agency of Nebraska	Black Hills Power Inc.	ER01-2577
Niagara Mohawk Energy Marketing	Black River Power LLC	ER00-2044
Niagra Mohawk Power Corporation	Constellation Nuclear LLC	ER01-1654
NRG Power Marketing Inc.	NEO California Power LLC	ER02-1700
NRG Power Marketing Inc.	NRG Energy Center Dover	ER02-1698
Pacificorp	FPL Energy Vansycle	ER01-838
Pacificorp	Rock River I	ER01-2742
PECO Energy Company	AmerGen Energy Company LLC	ER00-1806
PG&E Energy Trading Power LP	DTE Georgetown	ER00-3054
PG&E Energy Trading Power LP	Lake Road Generating Company LP	ER02-2130

Appendix 13.2 (continued)

Marketer	Generator	FERC Docket # or SEC filing
Public Service Company of Colorado	Indeck Colorado LLC (Arapahoe Station)	ER00-1952
Public Service Company of Colorado	Indeck Colorado LLC (Valmont Station)	ER00-1952
Public Service Company of New Mexico	Delta Person Limited LP	ER01-138
Public Service Electric & Gas	Cedar Brakes IV	ER01-2765
Select Energy Inc.	Northeast Generation Company	ER00-953
Sempra Energy Trading Corporation	Ogden Martin Systems of Union Inc.	ER00-1155
Sempra Energy Trading Corporation	Sunbury Generation	ER00-357
The California Department of Water Resources	Pacificorp Power Marketing	ER01-2685
Virginia Electric and Power Company	Doswell Limited Partnership	ER01-1182
Virginia Electric and Power Company	LSP Energy LP	ER00-3539
Williams Energy Marketing & Trading Company	AES Alamitos LLC AES Huntington Beach LLC AES Redondo Beach LLC	ER98-2184, ER98-2185, ER98-2186
Williams Energy Marketing and Trading Company	Cleco Evangeline LLC	ER00-3058-001
Wisconsin Electric Power Company	Badger Windpower LLC	ER01-1071
Wisconsin Power and Light Company	Northern Iowa Windpower	ER02-192
WPS Energy Services	Northeast Empire LP	ER01-2568
Yampa Valley Electric Association	Public Service Company of Colorado	ER01-1814

The Parameters of the System are

z = Instantaneous income at time $t \in [0, T]$
c = Instantaneous cost of producing z
m = Instantaneous monitoring costs
K = Cost of instituting monitoring mechanism
R = Dissipation due to renegotiation
S = Continuation value
δ = Dissipation, proportional to the continuation value S, that results from distorted investment incentives
ρ = Discount rate
α = Degree of asset-specificity
γ = Rate of cost appreciation
λ = Hazard rate

Other Variables and Symbols are

t	B^{Ts}	α_T	β_{Ts}	β_{Tv}	β_{Td}	γ_T	ρ_T
t^*	B^{Tv}	α_s	β_{sT}	β_{sv}	β_{sd}	γ_s	ρ_s
T	B^{Td}	α_v	β_{vT}	β_{vs}	β_{vd}	γ_v	ρ_v
s	B^{sv}	α_d	β_{dT}	β_{ds}	β_{dv}	γ_d	ρ_d
v	B^{sd}						
m	B^{vd}						
π	ε_{vi}						
T_0	ε_{si}						
T_1	ε_{Ti}						

Various Expressions Include

$$V(t^*; T) = \int_0^{t^*} (z - ce^{\gamma t} - (1 - sd)\alpha^d m)e^{-\rho t}dt + [S - vR]e^{-\rho t^*}$$
$$- [d\alpha + (1 - v)s\delta]S(e^{\rho(T - t^*)} - 1)$$

$$V(t^*; T) = \int_0^{t^*} (z - ce^{\gamma t})e^{-\rho t}dt + Se^{-\rho t^*}$$

$$E\pi = EV - (1 - sd)\alpha^d K = \int_0^{T} V(t^*; T)f(t^*; \cdot)dt^*$$
$$+ (1 - F(T; \cdot))\, V(T; T) - (1 - sd)\alpha^d K$$

$$f(t;\lambda) = \lambda e^{-\lambda t}$$

$$(1 - F(t;\lambda)) = e^{-\lambda t}$$

$$E\pi(s, v, d, T) = \left[\frac{z - (1 - sd)\alpha^d m}{\rho + \lambda}\right](1 - e^{-(\rho+\lambda)T})$$

$$+ \left[\frac{c}{\gamma - \rho - \lambda}\right](1 - e^{(\gamma-\rho-\lambda)T}) - (1 - sd)\alpha^d K$$

$$+ \left[\frac{S - vR}{\rho + \lambda}\right](\lambda + \rho e^{-(\rho+\lambda)T})$$

$$- \left[\frac{d\alpha + (1 - v)s\delta}{\rho + \lambda}\right]S[\rho(e^{-\lambda T} - 1) + \lambda(e^{\rho T} - 1)]$$

$$E\pi(s, 1, d, T_1) - E\pi(s, 0, d, T_1) \geq E\pi(s, 1, d, T_0) - E\pi(s, 0, d, T_0)$$

$$E\pi(s, 1, d, T) - E\pi(s, 0, d, T)$$

$$\frac{\partial}{\partial T}\{E\pi(s, 1, d, T) - E\pi(s, 0, d, T)\} \geq 0$$

$$R\rho e^{-(\rho+\lambda)T} + \left(\frac{\lambda\rho}{\rho + \lambda}\right)s\delta S(e^{\rho T} - e^{-\lambda T}) \geq 0$$

$$E\pi(s, v, d, T)$$

$$\frac{\partial}{\partial T}\{E\pi(1, v, d, T) - E\pi(0, v, d, T)\} \leq 0$$

$$d\alpha^d m e^{-(\rho+\lambda)T} - \left(\frac{\lambda\rho}{\rho + \lambda}\right)(1 - v)\delta S(e^{\rho T} - e^{-\lambda T}) \leq 0$$

$$\begin{aligned}
\ln T &= \alpha_T + \beta_{Ts}s + \beta_{Tv}v + \beta_{Td}d + \gamma_T W_T \\
s &= \alpha_s + \beta_{sT}\ln T + \beta_{sv}v + \beta_{sd}d + \gamma_s W_s \\
v &= \alpha_v + \beta_{vT}\ln T + \beta_{vs}s + \beta_{vd}d + \gamma_v W_v \\
d &= \alpha_d + \beta_{dT}\ln T + \beta_{ds}s + \beta_{dv}v + \gamma_d W_d
\end{aligned}$$

$$E\pi = \max_{s, v, d, T} E\pi(s, v, d, T; \cdot)$$

$$\frac{\partial^2 E\pi}{\partial T \partial v} > 0$$

$$\frac{\partial T}{\partial v} > 0$$

$$\frac{\partial v}{\partial T} > 0$$

$$\frac{\partial^2 E\pi}{\partial T \partial v} = \frac{B^{Tv}}{T} = \frac{\rho_T \beta^{Tv}}{T} > 0$$

$$\frac{\partial T}{\partial v} = -\left(\frac{\dfrac{\partial^2 E\pi}{\partial T \partial v}}{\dfrac{\partial^2 E\pi}{\partial T^2}} \right) = T\beta_{Tv} > 0$$

$$\frac{\partial v}{\partial T} = -\left(\frac{\dfrac{\partial^2 E\pi}{\partial T \partial v}}{\dfrac{\partial^2 E\pi}{\partial v^2}} \right) = \frac{\beta_{vT}}{T} > 0$$

$$\text{LogTerm}_i = \alpha_T + \beta_{Ts}\text{TwoPart}_i + \beta_{Tvi}\text{Veto}_i + \gamma_T W_{Ti} + \varepsilon_{Ti}$$

$$\text{TwoPart}_i = \alpha_s + \beta_{sT}\text{LogTerm}_i + \beta_{sv}\text{Veto}_i + \gamma_s W_{si} + \varepsilon_{si}$$

$$\text{Veto}_i = \alpha_v + \beta_{vT}\text{LogTerm}_i + \beta_{vs}\text{TwoPart}_i + \gamma_v W_{vi} + \varepsilon_{vi}$$

$$\begin{aligned} E\pi = {} & k + \rho_T(\ln T)\left(\alpha_T - \frac{\ln T}{2}\right) + \rho_s s\left(\alpha_s - \frac{s}{2}\right) \\ & + \rho_v v\left(\alpha_v - \frac{v}{2}\right) + \rho_d d\left(\alpha_d - \frac{d}{2}\right) \\ & + \rho_T(\ln T)\gamma_T W_T + s\rho_s\gamma_s W_s + v\rho_v\gamma_v W_v + d\rho_d\gamma_d W_d \\ & + B^{Ts}(\ln T)s + B^{Tv}(\ln T)v + B^{Td}(\ln T)d \\ & + B^{sv}sv + B^{sd}sd + B^{vd}vd \end{aligned}$$

$$B^{sT} = \rho_T\beta_{Ts} = \rho_s\beta_{sT}$$

$$B^{Tv} = \rho_T\beta_{Tv} = \rho_v\beta_{vT}$$

$$B^{Td} = \rho_T\beta_{Td} = \rho_d\beta_{dT}$$

$$B^{sv} = \rho_s\beta_{sv} = \rho_v\beta_{vs}$$

$$B^{sd} = \rho_s\beta_{sd} = \rho_d\beta_{ds}$$

$$B^{vd} = \rho_v\beta_{vd} = \rho_d\beta_{dv}$$

$$\beta_{Tv}\beta_{vs}\beta_{sT} = \beta_{Ts}\beta_{sv}\beta_{vT}$$

$$\beta_{Tv}\beta_{vd}\beta_{dT} = \beta_{Td}\beta_{dv}\beta_{vT}$$

$$\beta_{Td}\beta_{ds}\beta_{sT} = \beta_{Ts}\beta_{sd}\beta_{dT}$$

$$\beta_{sv}\beta_{vd}\beta_{ds} = \beta_{sd}\beta_{dv}\beta_{vs}$$

14. Why and how should new industries with high consumer switching costs be regulated?: The case of broadband Internet in France

Jackie Krafft and Evens Salies

INTRODUCTION

This chapter deals with the recent debate on the impact of deregulation in the info-communications industry, including new arguments promoting re-regulation based on institutional and other approaches (Richards, Foster and Kiedrowski, 2006; Alleman, 2005). While most contributions on the subject focus on wholesale markets, retail price control and access prices, we explore the question of regulation/deregulation by addressing the role played by the costs levied on consumers for switching between Internet service providers (hereafter ISP) and their Internet connection technologies (see Farrell and Klemperer, 2007, for a most comprehensive survey of consumer switching costs). Empirical and econometric evidence on the retail markets of several network industries that have been opened up to competition and where buyers and sellers are bound by contracts, suggests that there are also significant consumer switching costs in these markets. In some new info-communications industries, such as broadband Internet, these costs are likely to be especially high when firms practise subscription pricing, develop their own networks and supply specific assets such as modems. This raises the question of the current processes of regulation and competition in Europe as the most profitable means of market functioning, since these processes largely ignore the issue of consumer switching costs.

As we shall see, our definition of switching costs for a customer wanting to change ISP takes account of the existence of relationship-specific investments by consumers *á la* Williamson (1985).[1] Relying on the recent literature on consumer switching costs allows us to distinguish between costs created endogenously by companies to render consumers 'captive' and costs that are more exogenous, such as the costs involved in the search for an alternative ISP or the costs related to changing technologies on switching. The effects of these costs on the decision by firms to sell differentiated products is well understood (see for example Gerlach 2004). Some economic studies show the impact of those costs on consumers' choices of ISP, and their innovative Internet connection technologies. Gans and King (2001), for example, examined similar issues in relation to local number portability, showing that the costs customers face in changing phone numbers can be reduced by market regulation. The present chapter, from a policy perspective, emphasizes that the existence of consumer switching costs in new industries reinforces the importance of competition and regulation policies co-existing while playing different roles.

Our objective in this chapter is to study the impact of high consumer switching costs in the broadband Internet retail market, and the role of European regulation and competition policies. Broadband in Europe has two characteristics. First, there has been good take up by consumers, but technological inertia has favoured dominance by a single technology, Digital Subscriber Line (hereafter DSL). This contrasts with the situations in the USA where cable is privileged, and in Asia where highly advanced technologies such as Fibre To The Home (FTTH) is widespread (Fransman, 2006). Second, in France, Germany and Italy, DSL, the broadband technology offered by the incumbent, is also dominant in related markets (fixed and mobile telephony); however, in a number of leading countries in the broadband domain (UK, Sweden) the incumbent's market share has been eroded by new entrants. In the former group of countries, prices are still high and the ongoing processes of regulation and competition do not seem to be driving a downward trend. This is problematic since the emergence of the innovation 'broadband Internet' in Europe was expected to promote effective competition among technologies and among firms, resulting in lower prices.

In the second section we discuss broadband Internet regulation in Europe. In the third section we highlight the consequences of the regulation process in the French case, and compare it with the situation in the other OECD countries. Broadband in France is an example of persistent dominance of the incumbent (France Telecom), which is the leader in DSL technologies, despite the high prices it charges to consumers. In the fourth section we try to explain this situation as being based on the high switching costs that exist at consumer level – an area that so far has been neglected and which has prevented the regulation and competition policies that are in place from producing the outcomes expected in terms of diversity of technologies and firms, and lower prices. The fifth section sets out some of the reasons for the ineffectiveness of competition and regulation policies in such a context. In the sixth section we argue that French retail broadband Internet markets may need a new form of regulation that will counter these effects, and especially the costs induced by firms' anticompetitive practices, for example, misinformation and unnecessarily lengthy minimum subscription periods. We do not argue for the elimination of switching costs; our objective is to show that consumer switching costs intrinsic to Internet connection technologies (defined by Klemperer (1995) and Herk (1993) as social or real consumer switching costs) may be so high that any additional artificial costs must be avoided. Obviously, any actions taken to reduce switching costs are the responsibility of the relevant institutions, and the benefits to society should outweigh their costs (including the costs of any actions). We need accurate measures of switching costs and levels of market intervention. The final section provides our conclusions.

REGULATORY FRAMEWORKS IN EUROPE: DIRECTIVES 97/33/EC ON INTERCONNECTION AND 02/58/EC ON ELECTRONIC COMMUNICATIONS

In a number of European countries, including France, at the beginning of the broadband era regulators hoped that 'infrastructural' or 'full facilities-based' competition would emerge and speed broadband diffusion (Fransman, 2006; Krafft, 2006; Krafft and Salies, 2008). Implementation of Directive 97/33/EC (1998-2002) essentially encouraged the emergence in Europe of new technologies developed by newcomers, which it was hoped would supersede incumbency advantages. The fact that these new technologies might require substantial upfront costs was not understood by the regulators or the newcomers themselves and, at the time, ample funding was obtainable from the stock market (Fransman, 2004; Krafft, 2004). For most new entrant firms, the strategy adopted to develop a network was to obtain from the regulator a licence to operate at local or regional level, for instance in large urban centres, with the intention of expanding to the national level in the future. This first step did not produce the expected results. First, demand for broadband was smaller than had been expected. At the end of 2002, demand had stagnated and operators entering in the two or three years after that were unable to develop their business strategies. Second, the financial crash that occurred in early 2000 questioned the viability of newcomers that were reliant on the stock market or bank loans to finance their infrastructure projects, resulting in bankruptcy or exit from the market for many. This first period of regulation demonstrated that competition was ultimately very limited, mainly due to a context in which regulation imposed only weak requirements on incumbents (Fransman, 2006; Krafft, 2006; Krafft and Salies, 2008).

At the technical level, the regulatory framework focused predominantly on *ex ante* price control. Three specific measures were put in place. Control of Retail Prices (CRP) was considered necessary in contexts where the historical operators exercised market power at the retail level. This required a consumer protection function. Second, governments typically imposed a universal service obligation (USO) requiring the historical telecommunications operator to provide service to all parts of their national territories at a uniform price, despite the presence of significant cost differences. Third, control of access prices (CAP) was necessary, with charges for interconnection based on the principles of transparency and cost orientation.

These measures were not exempt from criticism. CRP in practice often led to a situation where, under monopoly conditions, tariffs were seriously unbalanced with respect to cost; results related to USO were debatable – new firms entering the market without this obligation had strong incentives to focus on low cost, profitable customers, putting the incumbent at a disadvantage. And in relation to CAP, 'cost orientation' was much too vague a phrase to avoid the levying of excessive interconnection charges (see Cave, 2004).

The criticisms and the difficulties involved in implementation of the regulation combined with the fact that, over time, the info-communications market with its high degree of technological and market convergence was becoming increasingly competitive, resulted in the introduction of the EC Directive (02/58/EC) for a common regulatory framework on electronic communications and services. It is only since its implementation in 2002 that European regulators have been focusing on a stronger source of infrastructural competition, known as 'local loop unbundling', or LLU. LLU is a regulatory process requiring the incumbent's exchange lines and network to be physically disconnected, to enable connection to the network of a new entrant. This allows the new entrant to install equipment at the incumbent's local exchange, and to use the incumbent's local loop to provide services directly to consumers. A major benefit of LLU is that it enables a degree of facilities-based competition since it gives the new entrant a significant degree of control over the local access network. However, it also means that the incumbent's incentive to invest in upgrading the local loop might be diminished as a result of the regulation that gives low price access to its network by competitors. Thus, a key issue is to define a regulated access price that is sufficiently high to give the incumbent a reasonable rate of return on its investment in the local loop, and sufficiently low to give new entrants an incentive to engage in innovative competition with the incumbent. LLU has helped to create favourable conditions for the emergence of a more diversified offering and for price reductions, encouraging greater take up of broadband Internet. However, it has also provided a greater incentive for new entrants to restrict their services to those mandated by the incumbent. At this stage of greater maturity of broadband, regulation has imposed strong requirements on the incumbent, but also has encouraged increasing technological lock-in to DSL on the side of competitors. LLU has encouraged intra-platform competition rather than competition among technologies since, ultimately, the new entrants have found it less costly to adopt DSL than to diffuse alternative technologies.

The EC Directive (02/58/EC) has promoted predominance of competition law over regulation in which market definition and dominance are central. Market definition involves application of the Hypothetical Monopolist Test and identifies the smallest set of goods and services, which, were a firm to gain control over them, would allow that firm to raise prices by 5 per cent to 10 per cent, over a sustained period, usually 12 months. A firm's ability to force through a price increase obviously depends on the extent to which customers can substitute the good or service in question (demand substitution) and the extent to which other firms can (rapidly) adapt their existing productive capacity to enhance supply (supply substitution). In terms of demand substitution, the existence of consumer costs for switching between services has been shown to be central to price setting criteria in industries where buyers and sellers are bound by contracts. In the case of broadband, consumers have to bear the transaction costs when subscribing to an ISP, and the Internet services they offer are not (perceived as) identical. Dominance occurs at the level of the individual firm, and colluding firms. Single firm dominance is based on the calculation of a Lerner index as a proxy for market power, with additional reference to market share, relative position of competitors, existence of new entrants, power of suppliers and buyers.

What was intended by the European directives implemented in 1997 and 2002, was a decisive contest between the incumbent's choice of technology (for example DSL) and the alternative technologies (such as cable or Wifi) supported by new entrants, providing high quality packages at cheaper prices. In the case of broadband Internet in France, one firm, France Telecom, continues to dominate the market in terms of shares of customers served, and technology supplied, namely DSL, and at prices that are high compared with other countries.

BROADBAND IN FRANCE VERSUS EUROPE AND THE OECD COUNTRIES

Figure 14.1 depicts the incumbent market shares in the OECD countries. We plotted the values for 2004 and 2007 in order to evaluate the outcomes of the two regulatory frameworks implemented in Europe. It can be seen that in France, the market share of the incumbent is high, and slowly decreasing despite the implementation of these directives.

In France in 2004 the incumbent France Telecom was ranked first for market share (47.2 per cent), ahead of providers of the same technology AOL (7.5 per cent), Neuf telecom (7.0 per cent), Alice (6.0 per cent), Tele 2 (4.7 per cent), Cegetel (3.9 per cent) and Club Internet (3.3 per cent). The market share of Iliad/Free, the sole Wifi provider, was 16.9 per cent (for a detailed presentation of broadband in France and Europe, see Krafft and Salies, 2008). Based on OECD data (www.oecd.org/sti/ict/broadband), in 2006, and despite the introduction of the regulatory framework designed to stimulate competition, the market positions of the major actors had not

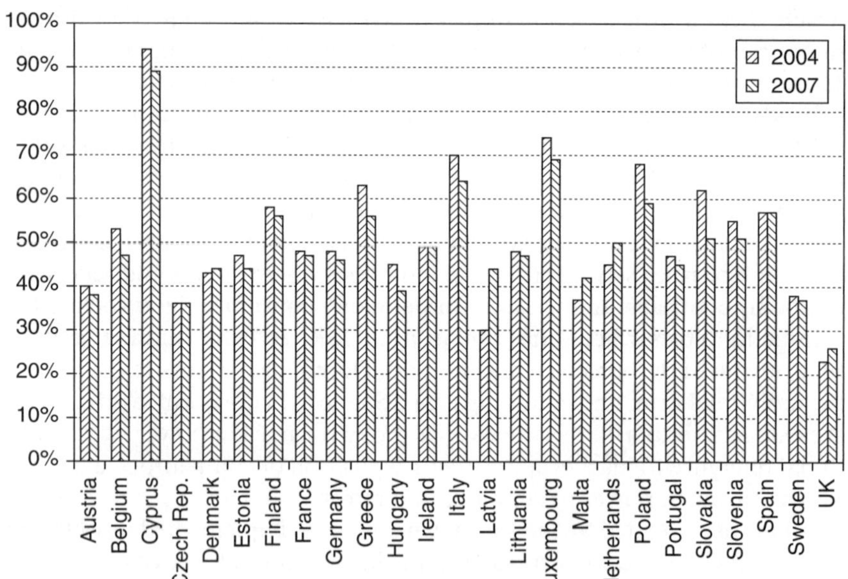

Source: elaboration from European Competitive Telecommunications Association, www.ectaportal.com.

Figure 14.1 Incumbent market shares in Europe and OECD countries in 2004 and 2007

evolved significantly. Other sources show that France Telecom's dominance has increased over time. In December 2006, Xitimonitor (www.Xitimonitor.com) estimated France Telecom's market share at 48.6 per cent, followed by Iliad/Free (20.3 per cent), Neuf (10.1 per cent), Alice (5.4 per cent), Club Internet (4.6 per cent), Noos (4.1 per cent), Aol (4.0 per cent) and Tele 2 (1.2 per cent). It should be noted, that in 2008, Neuf and Club-internet merged to form one group whose market share reached almost 19 per cent.

If we look at a breakdown of the technologies used for broadband access in the European and OECD countries in 2004 and 2007 (Figure 14.2), we can see that France (unlike the UK, the US, Japan and Korea) relies massively on DSL, and that this technology has been contested very little over time by the emergence of alternative technologies such as cable and Fibre/Lan.

Finally, in terms of price, in France prices are high compared to other OECD countries, and not decreasing (Figure 14.3).

The implementation of current regulation and competition processes in Europe – and particularly in France – has major implications for innovative industries such as broadband Internet. The move towards more competition policy and less regulation in Directive 02/58/EC has been somewhat problematic. For instance, it can be seen that anti-competitive decisions have never by themselves had the outcomes they were intended to produce. At the end of November 2001, France Telecom had 90 per cent of the French market for Asynchronous DSL (ADSL) Internet access. On 21 December 2001 the EC issued France Telecom with a Statement of Objections on the grounds that preliminary DSL Internet access services were currently being charged at below cost. The EC finally adopted a decision against France Telecom (16 July 2003) for abuse of its dominant position in the form of predatory pricing for ADSL-based Internet access services to the general public. This accusation of anti-competitive practice against France Telecom is a specific example of the application of the new regulatory framework to a market whose share was high, enabling the imposition of predatory prices.

INCUMBENT'S MARKET POWER AND CONSUMER SWITCHING COSTS

In the network industries, such as Internet, mobile telephony, energy, the opening of retail markets to competition has not always been accompanied by high switching costs. The economics literature points out that consumers have to pay different costs to initiate new relationships with their alternative retailers, some of which are related to firms' strategies for

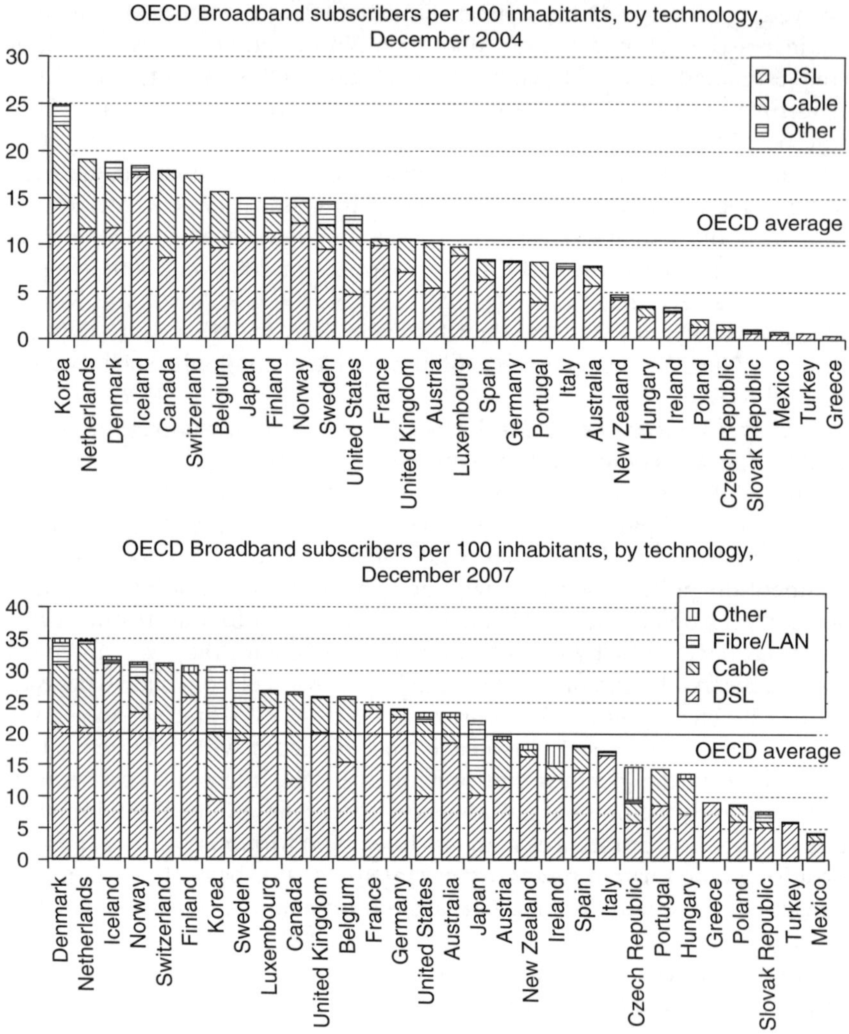

Source: OECD, www.oecd.org.

Figure 14.2 Breakdown of technologies used for broadband access in European countries in 2004 and 2007

keeping consumers captive. Before turning to consumer switching costs for broadband Internet we first discuss the effects that the existence of these costs has for the behaviour of firms selling homogeneous or differentiated products, regardless of how these costs are perceived (before switching)

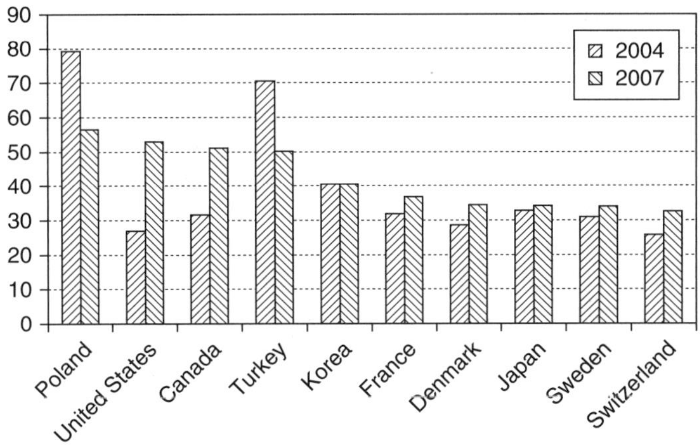

Source: our elaboration from OECD data.

Figure 14.3 Broadband average monthly subscription price, 2004 and 2007 (US$ PPP)

or paid (after switching).[2] Although this has been acknowledged, more empirical work is needed.

In residential broadband markets, the new user or the switcher is faced with transaction costs. Unless e-mail portability is allowed, the transaction costs involved in changing ISP include the consumer changing his or her e-mail address, and can be measured in terms of the time involved. Search costs are involved in finding out which ISPs operate in the local area, and which is offering the most advantageous package based on a consumer's particular needs.[3]

This particular cost, which involves comparison and selection of providers, may be small since there are comparison sites on the web that offer this service free of charge. The availability of certain technologies will depend on the location, which is a key determinant of availability (Papacharissi and Zaks, 2006). For some technologies, for example DSL, the quality degrades with the distance from the central switching office. Transaction costs also include return of a rented modem to the original ISP and the renting of identical (or other) equipment from the new provider. Switching requires customers to replace their current Internet connection devices. For example, to switch from France Telecom (Wanadoo) to Club-Internet requires a new modem, even though both services are DSL; each ISP has its own individual modems, which, without expert knowledge, are not interchangeable between Internet services. This non-redeployment implies another transaction cost.[4]

When real switching costs exist, firms may find it profitable to lock consumers in even further by creating endogenous switching costs. The most obvious type of lock-in device is the inclusion of a modem with the provision of service, which makes the customer believe it is not possible to redeploy a modem from another ISP. It is non-trivial to determine whether non-redeployment of modems creates switching costs that are exogenous (intrinsic to the commodity itself) or endogenous (induced by a firm's marketing strategy). It is likely that the negative effect of this artificial lock-in on customer migration is even stronger when 'bought-in' customers are misinformed about the technologies that are available, and how they work. Mayo and Cullum (2006) use the expression 'barriers to switching' in the context of competitive and innovative (non-mature) market structures. Artificial lock in can take the form of binding terms in the contractual relationship linking the customer and the firm, for example an extended minimum subscription period and notice conditions for customers wanting to terminate their contract. In some cases, consumers have to pay quite high cancellation fees (in 2005, up to €96 with some providers of broadband Internet in France). A report published in June 2006 indicates that the average minimum subscription period is three years.

The effect of subscription pricing combined with non-redeployment deters broadband Internet customers dissatisfied with poor service due to congested networks, from switching to an alternative ISP. Herk (1993) points to a similar situation in the context of cellular telephony. Though firms have good reasons for wanting to develop long-term relationships with their customers, including recouping their acquisition costs (broadcast advertising, door-to-door selling, and so on), artificial switching costs created by contractual conditions add to the consumer's reluctance to switch to an alternative IPS, and especially if this involves a different connection technology. Furthermore, practices aimed at artificially increasing the duration of the relationship may not increase customer satisfaction, but may highlight the need to provide services to consumers for long periods of time and for constant usage (Bolton, 1998).

In the particular context of the broadband industries, there is a specific cost involved in switching between different technologies, for example from DSL to Cable. For instance, the consumer has to learn how to use the new technology – a 'learning cost' (see for example Chen and Hitt, 2006).[5] These different technologies may involve both different connection speeds and very different connect devices (note for example, the differences between Cable and DSL technologies). Therefore, a consumer already using one type of modem may consider an alternative as both functionally and qualitatively different, and thus perceive this as a cost for switching to this alternative technology. Though the availability of some Internet services offered to broadband consumers may vary in terms of types of modems, the primary function of ISPs is to allow access to the Internet, which makes providers very substitutable in this respect. Thus, once a provider has achieved a large customer base, there is no incentive for it to invest in one of the alternative technologies being offered by competitors (see Krafft and Salies, 2008). A competitor offering an alternative technology knows that it may not be easy to attract the incumbent's customers as they would be obliged to learn how to use the new technology. Though the high levels of switching costs may act as barriers to entry (see also McAfee *et al.*, 2004), announcements by an innovating new entrant firm may facilitate its entry (see Gerlach, 2004, for a theoretical demonstration in the case of vertical differentiation).

In the first quarter of 2005, there were 28 ISPs in France, nine of which had a market share of more than 1 per cent and were retailing broadband Internet connection for domestic consumers: Alice+Tiscali, AOL, Cegetel, Club-internet, France Telecom, Illiad/Free, Neuf, Noos, Tele 2. The choice of Noos and Iliad/Free is relevant to demonstrate the potential influence of technology-related learning costs. AOL is also an interesting case because it is the oldest established firm among the competitors to France Telecom, in the French broadband market. Tele 2, Cegetel and Club are minor players in the DSL market thus we would expect the switching costs for their customers to be small. We ranked these nine firms according to their market share, from highest to lowest (see Figure 14.4). Across firms, prices and market share were generally positively related. France Telecom has the highest average prices and the highest market share; the second largest firm, AOL, charges the second highest prices (magnitude of the correlation coefficient between annual fees and market share is 0.66). We looked at these nine providers (presented in Table 14.1) in terms of the average price for the different speeds available. It would have been more accurate to consider a single download speed, but this would have meant excluding several suppliers from our analysis. The speed that corresponds to the highest number of providers (5) is 16 Mb; however, France Telecom does not have a 16 Mb offering and we wanted to include the incumbent in our analysis.[6] We arbitrarily consider the case of customers who receive a modem from their selected provider and remain a customer for one year. This has some implications for the computed tariffs. Some providers levy a cancellation fee at the end of a 12-month subscription period, and these fees have been included in our analysis. Analysing only customers with more than one year subscription would (inconveniently) necessitate having to account for changes in tariffs (some tariffs change after the initial 12-month subscription period) and to make assumptions about how consumers discount the future.

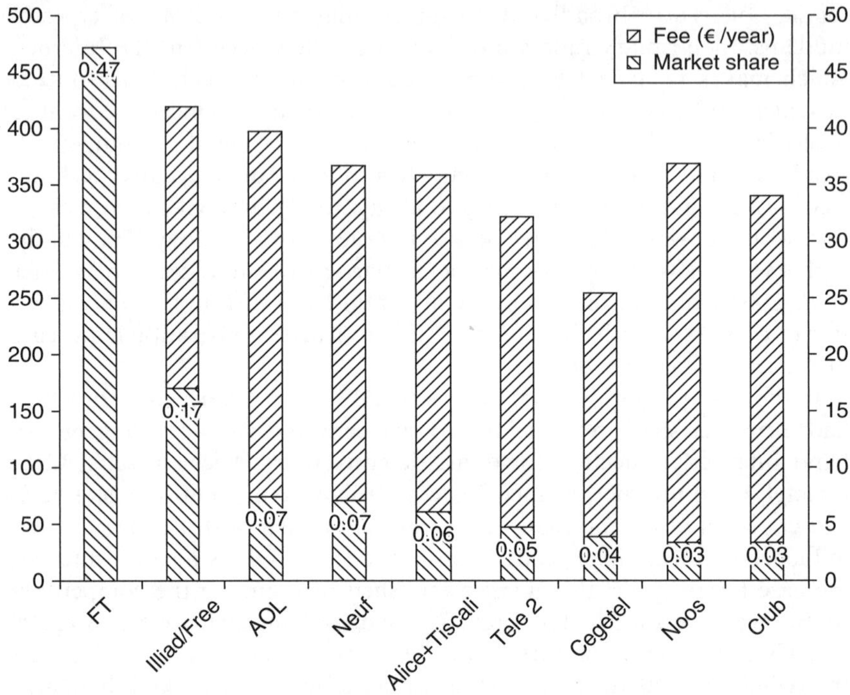

Figure 14.4 Prices and providers' market share

Figure 14.4 shows that the broadband Internet industry is characteristic of an industry with consumer switching costs. Interestingly, the largest and second-largest broadband providers are those that charge the highest prices on average, and whose customers incur the highest switching costs. Switching cost theory provides a nice explanation for this. Newcomers tend to enter with introductory offers or discounts (see Chen, 1997) to undercut larger firms already present in the market, in order to grab not only these firms' customers, but also new customers. For example, the France Telecom's 18 Mb offering is priced at €29.90 for the first three months, after which it is €39.90.[7] This is referred to in the literature as 'bargain-then-ripoff' pricing: firms increase their prices once customers are locked-in. Once captured, customers develop brand loyalty even where entrant firms are concerned, which allows these firms to increase their charges at some future date. Firms, thus, have an obvious interest in competing for market share when consumers show inertia, as current market share is an important determinant of future profits (Klemperer, 1995: 520).

Our calculation of switching costs uses Shy's (2002) measures. The

Table 14.1 Internet offers and values of switching costs in euros

Technology	Provider[a]	Market share (%)	Annual fee	Switching costs	
				From France Telecom	To France Telecom
DSL	France Telecom[a]	47.21	439.80		
DSL/Wifi	Iliad/Free	16.93	419.88	328.95	96.19
DSL	AOL	7.47	397.70	385.45	18.01
DSL	Neuf	6.99	367.80	392.33	−15.23
DSL	Alice+Tiscali	6.02	359.40	399.12	−30.61
DSL	Tele 2	4.77	322.20	410.23	−77.24
DSL	Cegetel	3.88	254.80	420.45	−151.60
Cable	Noos	3.36	368.70	415.30	−41.87
DSL	Club-Internet	3.34	340.80	417.29	−69.95

Note: [a] France Telecom's fee is made up as follows 36.00 + 12 × 1/2 [29.90 + (29.9 × 3/12 + 39.90 × 9/12)], where the average is taken across the 8 Mb offer (29.90) and 18 Mb offer (37.40 = (29.9 × 3/12 + 39.90 × 9/12)).

model assumes that firms set prices. Each firm considers whether to undercut one, and only one, competing firm at a time. The generic model is thus restricted to a description of competition between two firms. Two firms a and b sell a homogeneous service to N consumers. There are $N_\alpha > 0$ brand a-oriented consumers (type α) and $N_\beta > 0$ brand b-oriented consumers (type β), with $N \equiv N_\alpha + N_\beta$. Type α consumers incur a net cost s_{ab} of switching to firm b while type β consumers incur a net cost s_{ba} of switching to a. The model solution (see Shy, 2002) leads to the following measures of switching costs for type α customers ($s_{ab} = T_a - N_\beta T_b / N$) and type β customers ($s_{ba} = T_b - N_\alpha T_a / N$), where T_a is firm a's price and T_b is that of firm b. Shy's model is applied to old users and does not distinguish between old and new adopters. For a distinction between old and new users, the reader is referred to Farrell and Shapiro (1988).

The use of the concept of net switching costs in Shy's model requires recourse to the concept of added-value introduced by Green (2000). Net switching cost is the difference between the gross costs of switching, whose elements were defined at the beginning of this section, and an added-value (the positive extra utility that customers attach to the target firm). This added-value depends, for example, on the likelihood that the target firm will survive.

Switching costs are set out in Table 14.1 based on Shy's (2002) methodology. Our calculations of customer switching costs reach high values, up to the level of an annual fee. For example, the highest switching cost calculated is €420.45, which is only slightly below France Telecom's average price (€439.80). This means that a typical France Telecom customer who wants to switch to Cegetel stands to save €185 (439.80 – 254.80), but would incur switching costs of €420.45 (see Table 14.1). Cegetel's customers, in their turn, incur a negative perceived cost from switching to France Telecom of –€151.6, which is interpreted as a disutility of staying with Cegetel (or as a willingness to switch to France Telecom), but the price differential (the monetary gain from switching) is actually too low to induce switching. The negative costs of switching support the observation that the incumbent is likely to win back lost customers, but this disutility is insufficient to induce Cegetel's customers to make the switch to France Telecom. France Telecom's annual fee (switching cost inclusive) €439.8 + (– €151.6) = €288.2 is still larger than the price charged by Cegetel of €254.8. It would seem likely, therefore, that Cegetel or Tele2 would exit the market because of failure to lock in new customers. As a response to this market pressure, in August 2005 Neuf and Cegetel merged.

Switching between France Telecom and Iliad/Free must incur different types of switching costs since these firms supplied almost functionally identical products over the period studied. Our results show that the costs of switching from Iliad/Free are quite high while the costs of switching from Neuf and other smaller firms to Iliad/Free are comparatively small. There may be several reasons why Iliad/Free's customers seem to be locked in to a significant extent. First, the Wifi technology may be creating a particular attachment to Iliad/Free. Also, we believe that customers that chose Iliad/Free made their choice on the basis of its high-speed offering. Iliad/Free won 130 000 new consumers in the third quarter of 2005 by offering not only an alternative technology, but also services that were cheaper and higher speed.

Switching costs are also likely to induce ISPs that supply more than one technology to take advantage of the technology that has been more widely adopted. The effects of switching costs on the diffusion of alternative technologies to DSL in broadband retail, is demonstrated by the decision of France Telecom in March 2005, to sell its cable business to an American investor, Cinven,. The higher subscription price for Cable (along with the lower corresponding share of consumers) than DSL in the first quarter of 2004 provides support for France Telecom's attempt to attract consumers to take up its then dominant DSL technology. However, this may also reflect the different costs of switching between those technologies. Given the performance of Cable relative to DSL, in our view France Telecom's decision was an attempt to attract and lock in all its new consumers to DSL while discouraging its Cable customers from remaining with that technology.[8] At that time, France Telecom had around 2 million DSL customers, but only some 80 000 on Cable.[9] The annual charge for DSL was priced at €440 and for Cable €540 (all options inclusive in both cases).[10] We measured the switching costs using the methodology in Krafft and Salies (2008). Based on the above prices and market shares, the switching costs from DSL to Cable can be estimated at €440–80 000 × €540/2 080 000 = €419 and €540–2 000 000 × €440/2 080 000 = €117 from Cable to DSL. Here, we are not considering switching between two brands (two firms), but between two technologies within one brand. If the firm wants to maintain its customer bases for both technologies then, in a sense, it is playing a strategic game with itself. We assume that the firm has already recovered some of the fixed costs involved in acquiring its customers, and can focus on sales maximization. In this case, the price offered in one market/technology to a consumer covers the marginal costs involved in serving this customer. Introducing these marginal costs and dealing with retail margins rather than retail prices would affect the results qualitatively, only in the case that the costs involved in providing the two technologies differed significantly. This is a subject for future research.

Following Green's (2000) model, these costs should be interpreted as net values. Green's theoretical model considers the concept of 'added value' from buying an alternative product such that the cost of switching becomes a net rather than a gross cost. Given the existence of technological switching costs, we would argue that perhaps regulators and competition commissions should have operated differently, for example, by subsidising France Telecom to enhance its cable technology. There is clearly a role for the regulator in preventing the potential effect of technological switching costs on the adoption of cable. This suggestion is in line with Waterson (2003: 146) who suggests that in some sectors the regulatory authorities should set quality standards as an essential means to encourage consumers to switch. Assuming it would be sensible to subsidize DSL consumers to switch to Cable, this raises the question of how the regulator could identify those consumers who actually want to do so, and to subsidize their switching preferably in such a way as to be costless for the taxpayer.

The evidence for the broadband Internet retail market shows that the effects of consumer switching costs may be substantial, which favours the dominance of ex-monopolies (or of firms already owning a large market share) and, therefore, their technology (technological inertia). Consequently, the market may drive promising firms to exit or to consolidate with dominant firms and select older/less innovative technologies (Krafft and Salies, 2008). This indicates that the ongoing process of regulation policy needs continuous revision to produce the desired results in terms of competition between firms, technologies and prices.

LIMIT TO TODAY'S REGULATION AND COMPETITION POLICY IN INNOVATIVE INDUSTRIES WHEN CONSUMERS HAVE SWITCHING COSTS

The fact that the EC directives have not had the desired results has provoked increasing debate about whether competition policy should replace regulation, or whether their continued co-existence is necessary. The former seems to be the dominant thesis. For instance, Shelanski (2005) and Waverman (2006) provide a list of critics of the conventional monopoly regulation in the US and suggest that it would be appropriate to shift from a regime of *a priori* rules governing incumbent-firm conduct to a regime of *ex post* competition law enforcement. Alleman and Rappoport (2005) and Cave (2006) emphasize the fact that policy makers misread (recent) economic theory including dynamic and game theoretic models and are thus using an inappropriate background regulatory model. Finally, all these contributions point to the prohibitive cost of regulation as a major reason for deregulation, although no definition or evaluation of this cost is provided.

The co-existence thesis in this context appears to be an exception, although with strong proponents (Papacharissi and Zaks, 2006) for the continuance of regulation in the specific field of broadband where the development of innovation is considered a major issue. Stelzer (2006), in a collection of essays prepared for the UK Office of Communications (Ofcom), provides a list of regulation and competition rules to stimulate research and development and innovation in the info-communications industry. In the same collection, and focusing on the consumer agenda, Mayo and Cullum (2006), stress that pro-active regulatory action should be reinforced to sweep away the barriers to consumers' switching between companies and to promote informed choice. This would include enabling consumers to share their experiences of different companies, which would benefit firms delivering good products and providing high service standards, and penalize those that do not. More generally, they advocate for publication of information on performance within a co-regulation model that involves consumers' associations. In this view, and in contrast to the views developed by Stelzer and Mayo and Cullum, the potential gains of re-regulation are seen as being substantial compared with the costs. However, elaborating a strict benefit-cost test is always difficult in a situation where uncertainties in the estimates can be significant and hard to quantify (Hahn, 1998; Harrington *et al.*, 2000). Even in the most straightforward *ex post* calculation, the definition of baselines is somewhat arbitrary, and depends on the analysts' subjective views of what would have happened in the absence of regulation. In other words, estimates of regulatory costs cannot escape being hypothetical to some degree.

While these contributions emphasize innovation and the emergence of new industries on the one hand, and the existence of consumer switching costs on the other, they do not address their coexistence in a context where the industry is new and characterized by high switching costs. The reason that we would support co-existence is that since high consumer switching costs do exist and can be measured in new industries, such as broadband, purely deregulated situations – even when based on strong competition policy principles – may lead to inefficient outcomes for several reasons. First, firms are indeed heterogeneous as they are differentiated by the costs of switching between functionally different products (for example Cable and DSL modems are different connection technologies: DSL comes with a free do-it-yourself installation kit whilst Cable requires a professional installer). Even in the DSL consumer market where technologies can be considered to be functionally identical products, each ISP provides its own modem, which is not redeployable in the sense of Williamson (see pp. 333–41 above). Second, if regulation and competition policies ignore switching costs, then a reluctance by consumers to switch suppliers can lead to sub-competitive outcomes (see Waterson (2003) for evidence in several retail markets, including non-innovative ones). The incentive to announce innovation may be reduced, yet truthful information about products is pro-competitive and should be encouraged by the regulator. Further measures to stimulate competition may not bring more innovation, affecting productive efficiency in the short run (exit of potentially efficient competitors), and dynamic efficiency in the longer run (elimination of higher quality/cheaper price emergent offers). Furthermore, *ex post* – competition policy – sanctions often occur too late, and the long run evolution of the industry may be affected since inefficient outcomes may persist after an anti-competitive decision (see pp. 333–41 above).

The implementation of the framework in Directive 02/58/EC, which sees competition law replacing (supposedly inefficient) regulatory rules, reveals that there are some important deficiencies in this replacement process. To resolve these, we need to explore how competition laws can co-exist with regulatory rules that are not exclusively centred on *ex ante* price control. In our view, rules dedicated to informing consumers *ex ante* on what they obtain when they subscribe to a broadband service and, more, crucially what costs and barriers they will face if they want to switch providers, are elements necessary to restore efficiency in the current framework. Competition policy should be oriented more towards decreasing consumer switching costs – not necessarily the priority currently.

REGULATION AND COMPETITION IN INNOVATIVE INDUSTRIES WITH SWITCHING COSTS

Regulation policy, by definition, applies to specific sectors, whose structure is such that competitive forces cannot be expected to operate efficiently. Regulation policy is generally considered as being distinct from competition policy, which traditionally applies to mature industries or to industries whose structural conditions are compatible with the normal functioning of competition (Motta, 2004: xviii). Regulation involves assessment over time of competitors' behaviours, while competition policy operates *ex post*, and normally proceeds from institutions, regulators and the regulatory rules applying to specific industries (emergent, in transition, innovative), and is designed to nurture the development of these industries over time. The propositions that follow support the coexistence of regulation and competition policies since broadband is not a mature industry and needs ongoing assessment of both technological and market developments by a regulatory authority. The competition authority should focus on reducing the barriers to switching.

In the current regulation and competition framework within Europe, the role of the regulator is to select and regulate monopoly/oligopoly providers, especially in the fields of infrastructure provision, investment, access and pricing, operation (Quality of Service), horizontal and vertical interconnection, universal access/service provision. We would argue that regulators need to regulate, *ex ante* and over time, the introduction of innovative products from new entrants and their adoption by consumers. This is a difficult area – especially if consumers are reluctant to switch even though they would gain extra utility from doing so. One issue that should be considered is what sort of regulation would be most appropriate to facilitate consumers switching to firms providing alternative and potentially the most efficient technologies, where efficiency is measured in terms of connection speed, and depends on geographical location. In a new regulatory framework that takes account of consumer switching costs, the role of the regulator, based on its inherent industry expertise (which competition authorities do not have),[11] would be to deliver all *ex ante* information including quantitative and qualitative aspects, that might influence the choice of consumers. It would also be responsible for selecting providers on the basis of the fitness of their offerings to the needs of consumers, and to enabling consumers to switch providers should they want to do so. Restoring a strong role to the regulation authorities would involve, in terms of consumer switching costs, consideration *ex ante* and over time of whether a new competitor's failure to attract new consumers is due to its cost inefficiency, or because its product is not so attractive, and not because consumers have become locked into their current supplier. This would require consumers to be well informed about the alternative technologies

This would leave room for both consumer associations and the regulator's office to co-exist. The responsibility of the consumer association would be to build expertise in comparing competing firms, and to provide customers with clear and accessible information on the different offerings available. Currently, this task is generally done by private businesses, and the information is often dispersed and not easily usable, requiring consumers to spend considerable time and effort collecting and synthesizing the information. The information available is also not necessarily reliable since independence between these businesses and the broadband providers cannot be guaranteed.[12] Although the regulatory authorities may not have the in-house resources required to take on this job, it could direct consumers to the best sources of comparative information. To reduce search costs for consumers, the authorities could provide guidelines and a comparative overview of the technical feasibilities of different offers. The regulator should *ex ante* provide ongoing information on what consumers obtain for the price of the subscription in terms of speeds and services; what are the average delays involved in getting access to services; what are the average delays faced by consumers in moving to a new supplier; what are the technical and geographical requirements to access. Here, consumers should be made aware that because of technical and/or geographical problems, broadband speeds could reduce from an advertised 20 MB (which is what the consumer is paying for) to 512 KB (what the consumer actually gets), leading to the unavailability of a number of applications. The guidelines should also provide a comparative overview of service quality to limit cognitive costs on the consumer's side:[13] based on quantitative criteria (availability – proportion of the population with access to broadband if they want it; penetration – proportion of the population with a broadband connection; capacity and speed; price; bugs, average length of breakdowns, number of complaints) and qualitative criteria (quality of access and goodness of fit with user needs), the regulator should diffuse the experiences of consumers with the technologies available and provide information about their reliability. Specific attention should be devoted to after sales services. Also based on quantitative information (price and response to customer service) and qualitative criteria (quality of customer service, goodness of fit with user needs), expert advice should be available to consumers on the effectiveness of customer and after sales services, and helplines – all of which vary greatly.[14] A comparative overview of subscription costs should be provided that highlights any costs to consumers from being locked into contracts. Information should be provided about the delays involved in closing accounts and opening new ones, whether e-mail portability is available, cancellation penalties. Special mention should also be devoted to the issue of the notice period, which was reduced to ten days in France through the application of Chatel's law on 3 January 2008.

In terms of competition policy, unlike Motta (2004: 81) it is our view that they should necessarily prevent artificial lock in by firms. As suggested in Farrell and Klemperer (2007: 41–3), policy intervention to reduce switching costs may be appropriate in the case of artificial lock in. Also, announcement of an innovative product may require advertising, a cost that perhaps should be shared or entirely borne by the incumbent rather than the new entrants alone. When advertising is costly, incumbents have a first mover advantage *vis-à-vis* small consumers when only the large consumer segment has been opened to competition. Advertising aimed at large consumers may capture the attention of small consumers. On the basis of the guidelines to switching provided by the regulatory authorities, if switching costs are prohibitive and persistent over time, competition authorities may decide that artificial switching costs are operating and make decisions forbidding anti-competitive behaviour from broadband operators. The measure of switching costs would act as an indicator of important barriers to consumers' ability to adopt the technology they prefer or to change suppliers easily. Presumably, the more clear information is provided by the regulator about the evolution of switching costs and, thus, existence of potential barriers to switching, the less frequently will competition policy be required to intervene. Making the technology more transparent may be important, but this should not preclude information that adopting a new technology may involve sunk costs for most consumers. Firms may have to subsidize those costs to attract customers. Therefore, too low switching costs may discourage firms from subsidizing these costs since they cannot be certain that they will keep their consumer base. This might induce them to favour technologies that require less learning, and possibly involve lower levels of innovation.

CONCLUSION

This chapter looked at consumer switching costs in the broadband industry, often overlooked in the debate on deregulation versus regulation or re-regulation. Our investigation of the French case shows that these costs are high and this is having an impact on the move towards deregulation. In our view, a new form of regulation is needed in order to assess and diffuse all the information involved in switching costs. Competition policy should intervene in cases where switching costs continue to be prohibitive, and where it is possible that artificial switching costs may exist.

In terms of future research, in the literature competition is increasingly considered as a process, which implies that so-called market imperfections, such as switching costs, may become useful devices for ensuring the coordination that facilitates the innovation process. According to this view, regulation policy must determine why and when switching costs are to be condemned (or not). Regulation policy should be used to enable a restructuring of the industry and the emergence of a new market structure. The existence of such a structure in the long run may require some market imperfections, among which, technological switching costs or, more generally, transaction costs, are a means to prevent too fast a change in the organization of the industry. Artificial switching costs created by the contracts between ISPs and consumers must be eliminated: they penalize consumers who want to switch between different ISPs, and promote lock in.

ACKNOWLEDGEMENT

We are grateful to two anonymous referees. We also thank Michel Ghertman for his insightful comments and participants at the 2007 conference held in Nice in honour of Oliver Williamson, for valuable comments on an earlier draft. The comments of Jean-Luc Gaffard, Jacques Laurent Ravix and GREDEG working paper seminar participants at the University of Nice – Sophia Antipolis are also acknowledged.

NOTES

1. Reference to Williamson's (1975, 1985) relationship-specific investments by customers is not new in the literature on consumer switching costs. As far as we know, Farrell and Shapiro (1988) is the first paper to make this connection in a model of dynamic competition (see Farrell and Klemperer, 2007: 1973).
2. Note that the distinction between 'perceived' and 'paid' switching costs will be clear from the context.
3. These types of transaction costs can also be described as 'shopping costs'. Note that, unlike Chen and Hitt (2006), we do not distinguish between search and transaction costs; we assume the former are included in the latter, which include the costs to consumers of using the market, in Coase's sense.
4. We thank Michel Ghertman for his suggestion to deepen the comparison between switching costs *à la* Klemperer and redeployment costs *à la* Williamson.
5. This cost is not necessarily related to 'learning to use new brands', as in Klemperer (1995: 517) because in our case, products are not necessarily functionally identical.
6. We do not weigh prices when calculating the annual fee, which implicitly assumes that consumers are distributed uniformly across the different speeds on offer from each firm.
7. This price excludes the cost of the modem.

8. As it is the number of services associated with Cable that is more important we consider the products to be differentiated.
9. See the website of the French regulator: http://www.art-telecom.fr/fileadmin/reprise/publications/c-publique/anmarch-detail051004.pdf, accessed May 2007.
10. These prices are exclusive of cancellation fees.
11. Note that the regulator is industry specific while competition laws are by nature general in their competence.
12. Some inquiries into the independence of price comparators are currently underway by the French Ministry of the Economy, Finance and Industry. See http://www.dgccrf.minefi.gouv.fr, accessed June 2008.
13. These costs refer to people's desire to reduce the psychic 'cost' of exposure to information inconsistent with staying with one's current ISP. For example, one would not search for alternative ISPs' offers to avoid the discomfort of learning that there are cheaper offers with similar quality level. Cognitive costs are likely to increase with brand reputation and experience with one's current supplier.
14. The Chatel law eliminates any incentive for providers to charge extra fees per minute to customers who call from their fixed line (the average price was €0.34 /minute before the law).

REFERENCES

Alleman, J. (2005), 'Dynamic solutions to policy failures. Overview and Introduction', *Communications and Strategies*, **60** (4), 11–13.

Alleman, J. and P. Rappoport (2005), 'Regulatory failure: time for a new paradigm', *Communications and Strategies*, **60** (4), 105–21.

Arcep (2008), http://www.arcep.fr/fileadmin/reprise/communiques/lettre/pdf/lettre59-page23-loi-chatel.pdf.

Arcep (2006), Modèle réglementaire de coût des FAI – Notice explicative, http://www.arcep.fr/fileadmin/reprise/dossiers/internet/quest-consult-coutfai-avril06.pdf, June.

Bolton, R. (1998), 'A dynamic model of the duration of the customer's relationship with a continuous service provider: the role of satisfaction', *Marketing Science*, **17** (1), 45–65.

Buigues, P. (2004), 'The competition policy approach', in P. Buigues and P. Rey (eds), *The Economics of Antitrust and Regulation in Telecommunications*, Cheltenham, UK and Northampton, MA, USA: Edward Elgar.

Cave, J. (2006), 'Market-based alternatives or complements to regulation', in E. Richards, R. Foster and T. Kiedrowski (eds), *Communications: The Next decade, A collection of Essays Prepared for the UK Office of Communication*, Ofcom.

Cave, M. (2004), 'Economic aspects of the new regulatory regime for electronic communications services', in P. Buigues and P. Rey (eds) *The Economics of Antitrust and Regulation in Telecommunications*, Cheltenham, UK and Northampton, MA, USA: Edward Elgar.

Chen, P. and L. Hitt (2006), 'Information technology and switching costs', in T. Hendershott (ed.), *Handbook on Economics and Information Systems* (Vol.1), Amsterdam: Elsevier, pp. 437–70.

Chen, Y. (1997), 'Paying customers to switch', *Journal of Economics and Management Strategy*, **6** (4), 877–97.

Directive 97/33/EC of the European Parliament and of the Council of June 97 on interconnection in telecommunications with regard to ensuring universal service and interoperability through application of the principles of Open Network Provision.
Directive 02/58/EC of the European Parliament and of the Council of July 2002 concerning the processing of personal data and the protection of privacy in the electronic communications sector.
Farrell, J. and P. Klemperer (2007), 'Coordination and lock-in: competition with switching costs and network effects', in M. Armstrong and R. Porter *Handbook of Industrial Organization*, Vol. 3, Ch. 31, pp. 1968–2072, Amsterdam: North-Holland, http://www.nuff.ox.ac.uk/users/klemperer/Farrell_KlempererWP.pdf.
Farrell, J. and C. Shapiro (1988), 'Dynamic competition with switching costs', *RAND Journal of Economics*, **19** (1), 123–37.
Fransman, M. (2004), 'The telecoms boom and bust 1996–2003 and the role of financial markets', *Journal of Evolutionary Economics*, **14** (4), 369–406.
Fransman, M. (ed.) (2006), *Global Broadband Battles: Why the US and Europe lag while Asia leads*, Stanford, CA: Stanford University Press.
Gans, J. and S. King (2001), 'Regulating private infrastructure investment: optimal pricing for access to essential facilities', *Journal of Regulatory Economics*, **20** (2), 167–89.
Gerlach, H.A. (2004), 'Announcement, entry, and preemption when consumers have switching costs', *RAND Journal of Economics*, **35** (1), 184–202.
Green, R. (2000), 'Can competition replace regulation for small utility customers?' Centre for Economic Policy Research, discussion paper 2046, http://www.cepr.org
Hahn, R. (1998), 'Government analysis of the benefits and costs of regulation', *Journal of Economic Perspective*, **12** (4), 201–10.
Harrington, W., R. Morgenstern and P. Nelson (2000), 'On the accuracy of regulatory cost estimates', *Journal of Policy Analysis and Management*, **19** (2), 297–322.
Herk, L. F. (1993), 'Consumer choice and Cournot behaviour in capacity-constrained duopoly competition', *RAND Journal of Economics*, **24** (3), 399–417.
Klemperer, P. (1987), 'The competitiveness of markets with switching costs', *RAND Journal of Economics*, **18** (1), 138–50.
Klemperer, P. (1995), 'Competition when consumers have switching costs: an overview with applications to industrial organization, macroeconomics, and international trade', *Review of Economic Studies*, **62** (4), 515–39.
Knittel, C. (1997), 'Interstate long distance rates: search costs, switching costs, and market power', *Review of Industrial Organization*, **12**, 519–36.
Krafft, J. (2004), 'Entry, exit and knowledge: evidence from a cluster in the info-communications industry', *Research Policy*, **33** (10), 1687–706.
Krafft, J. (2006), 'Emergence and growth of Broadband in the French Info-communications system of innovation', in M. Fransman (ed.), *Global Broadband Battles: Why the US and Europe Lag while Asia Leads*, Stanford, CA: Stanford University Press.
Krafft, J. and E. Salies (2008), 'The diffusion of ADSL and costs of switching Internet providers in the broadband industry: evidence from the French case', *Research Policy*, **37** (4), 706–19.
Mayo, E. and P. Cullum (2006), 'The consumer agenda on regulation', in E. Richards, R. Foster and T. Kiedrowski (eds), *Communications: The Next*

Decade, a Collection of Essays Prepared for the UK Office of Communication, Ofcom.
McAfee, R. P., H. M. Mialon and M. A. Williams (2004), 'What is a barrier to entry', *American Economic Review (AEA Papers and Proceedings)*, **94** (2), 461–5.
Motta, M. (2004), *Competition Policy – Theory and Practice*, Cambridge: Cambridge University Press.
Papacharissi, Z. and A. Zaks (2006), 'Is broadband the future? An analysis of broadband technology potential and diffusion', *Telecommunications Policy*, **30** (1), 64–75.
Richards, E., R. Foster and T. Kiedrowski (eds) (2006), *Communications: The Next Decade, a Collection of Essays Prepared for the UK Office of Communication*, Ofcom.
Salies, E. and J.-M. Glachant (2005), 'Consumers' switching costs in the GB electricity retail market', *GRJM Working paper* 2005-09.
Sharpe, S. A. (1997), 'The effect of consumers' switching costs on prices: a theory and its application to the bank deposit market', *Review of Industrial Organization*, **12**, 79–94.
Shelanski, H. (2005), 'Inter-modal competition and telecommunications policy in the United States', *Communications and Strategies*, **60** (4), 15–37.
Shy, O. (2002), 'A quick-and-easy method for estimating switching costs', *International Journal of Industrial Organization*, **20** (1), 71–87.
Spulber, D. F. (1999), *Market Microstructure – Intermediaries and the Theory of the Firm*, Cambridge: Cambridge University Press.
Stelzer, I. (2006), 'Creating an environment for R&D innovation', in E. Richards, R. Foster and T. Kiedrowski (eds), *Communications: The Next Decade, a Collection of Essays Prepared for the UK Office of Communication*, Ofcom.
Von Weizsäcker, C. C. (1984), 'The cost of substitution', *Econometrica*, **52** (5), 1085–116.
Wallis, J. and D. North (1986), 'Measuring the transaction sector in the American economy, 1870–1970', in S. L. Engerman and R. E. Gallman (eds), *Long Term Factors in American Economic Growth*, Chicago, IL: University of Chicago Press.
Wang, N. (2003), 'Measuring transaction costs: an incomplete survey', Ronald Coase Institute, Working Paper No 2.
Waterson, M. (2003), 'The role of consumers in competition and competition policy', *International Journal of Industrial Organization*, **21** (2), 129–50.
Waverman, L. (2006), 'The challenges of a digital world and the need for a new regulatory paradigm', in E. Richards, R. Foster and T. Kiedrowski (eds), *Communications: The Next Decade, a Collection of Essays Prepared for the UK Office of Communication*, Ofcom.
Williamson, O. (1975), *Markets and Hierarchies: Analysis and Antitrust Implications*, New York: Free Press.
Williamson, O. (1985), *The Economic Institutions of Capitalism*, New York: Free Press.
Williamson, O. (2005), 'The economics of governance', *American Economic Review*, **95** (2), 1–18.

15. The puzzle of regulation, deregulation and reregulation

Michel Ghertman

INTRODUCTION

Regulation of industries in its modern form has existed for over a century. It has roots in the commissioning of particular economic activities like stage-coach transport, maritime commerce or collecting tax levies by European monarchs since the Renaissance and before. The history of regulatory privileges and actions of Emperors, Kings and Princes is much longer than the history of regulation and deregulation in more or less democratic republics.

This benign observation has important theoritical implications. It puts regulation/deregulation/re-regulation under the lenses of multidisciplinary inquiries. Attempting to explain royal fiat solely by economic efficiency considerations is likely to miss crucial sociocultural and political determinants. When putting this issue in a historical and international perspective, there is advantage in mobilizing the complementary contributions of political science and sociology, on top of economics, law and organization. Unfortunately, theoritical and empirical efforts have largely been undertaken separately by each social science discipline while the topic would benefit from an integrated treatment. Regulation and deregulation have been analyzed almost exclusively by economists.

This chapter attempts to answer the following puzzle: 'How can each change from less to more regulation or vice versa be explained?' It starts with a review of selected economic theories pertaining to regulation/deregulation and continues with empirical findings. A research agenda largely based upon political science contributions and a discussion follow.

ECONOMIC THEORIES PERTAINING TO REGULATION: EQUILIBRIA # 1, 2 AND 3

This review does not intend to be exhaustive (see Peltzman, 1989; Joskow and Rose, 1989; Noll, 1989, for more extensive treatments). It is partially influenced by a focus on the comparative contributions of the Stigler/Peltzman and Williamson views as each is associated with a different type of equilibrium.

Regulation was justified by particular conditions of scale and scope for what were called 'infrastructure' or 'public utilities' and later 'network' industries. They were considered as natural monopolies, a case of market failure (Noll, 1989). Thus, they were exempted from anti-trust rules favoring competition on prices and quantities in other industries. For several industries in the USA and other English speaking countries, the legislator created regulating agencies as instruments of his policy to avoid monopolistic pricing from companies and protect social welfare. The main mechanism used by regulators to make consumers as well as producers happy was to set prices and allow increases if needed to enable private firms to reach a 'fair' rate of return on their capital. The welfare objective was to secure a sufficient and reliable quantity of consumption and service via a control of the price level. We call this Pigovian perspective equilibrium #1. Equilibrium is reached when the price level enables the regulator to fulfill the welfare objective subject to the constraint of the level of the rate of return for the operator. Market rules were replaced by regulation of many private monopolies in the USA. In most continental European countries, especially after World War II, few private operators were willing to put capital at risk in these industries. Some had done it before and had gone into bankruptcy. Governments used State-owned firms under the authority of Ministries of Industry, or similar institutions, to fill the gap. Ministries behaved as owners and to a large extent as regulators also with a mix of economic and political objectives, of which national interest and pride were not absent. In continental Europe and in the UK also, market rules were replaced by direct government intervention. On both sides of the Atlantic most of the conditions of contestable markets (Baumol *et al.*, 1982) were absent, especially free entry of new competitors. The State used its power through more or less direct intervention, in Europe and the USA respectively. The national interest was interpreted as a need for the State to act to reach equilibrium #1 in the USA, and create the infrastructure required for economic development in European countries.

Stigler's (1971) seminal article deeply revised the 'Economic Theory of Regulation'. Even though it had intellectual antecedents in other authors, his paper marked a complete turnaround in perspective. Stigler viewed regulation as an instrument by incumbent firms to prevent entry by newcomers. In his paper, regulation is analyzed as the result of demand for regulation by firms lobbying Government to protect their existing rents, and of supply of regulation by Politicians interested in maximizing their utility function through votes and campaign contributions. We call this type of regulation equilibrium #2. Using examples from airlines, truck transport, banks, mutual funds, professional licensing and oil, Stigler made a fairly convincing argument that firm lobbies were successful in using regulation to redistribute wealth in their favor as opposed to the previous view that they were 'controlled' by regulators for welfare purposes. He also argued that the benefits to industry were lower than costs to society if it opted for a market instead of a political process: the former has lower information costs and higher incentives. Thus Stigler viewed equilibrium # 2 as inefficient and argued for its replacement by market-oriented deregulation. A major appeal of Stigler's paper to many economists is that it uses the same assumptions, that of self-interested maximization, for both politicians and firms together, as well as the same tools, maximizing utility at the margin, to reach an equilibrium solution between demand and supply of regulation. In doing so, Stigler enabled economists to discuss the interface between the Polity, firms and society with familiar concepts and tools.

In retrospect Stigler, who was awarded a Nobel Prize in economics in 1982, can be considered the main theoretical antecedent to the movement of deregulation in the USA and the UK. He was an articulated and adamant proponent of deregulation in his writings (Stigler, 1982) and teaching as reported by Peltzman (1993). Among others, he proposed that customers use the State to auction off rights to sell electricity instead of regulation (Stigler, 1968). His ridiculing of the welfare impact of regulation fueled the arguments of opponents of any economic influence of the Polity, including groups on the Left traditionally opposed to the influence of 'big business' on the State. His theory struck a favorable cord among small businessmen and a large part of the population sensitive to the impact of lobbies on the redistribution of wealth as well as on the weight of Government bureaucracy in general.[1] As he viewed equilibrium #2 as inefficient because it has lower benefits to Society than market instruments, he called for the State to empower deregulation. The national interest was interpreted as a need for as little State intervention as possible. Stigler used his theory as a scarecrow to convince policy makers that equilibrium #2 must be avoided. By contrast, the authors of the two alternative theoretical approaches to regulation consider equilibria (respectively equilibrium #1 and #3) as norms to attain.

Peltzman (1976) contributed three refinements to Stigler's theory. First, he introduced the cost of coordination among industry members on the demand side. Stronger group cohesion and influence is associated with lower costs of internal coordination. This perspective contrasts Stigler's view that the larger the industry, the larger its influence, and this is clearly an improvement for scholars of organizations. Second, on the supply side, Peltzman introduced the need for the Polity to maintain a balance between influences from various interest groups. Third, he attempted to make the theory dynamic by explaining entry as well as exit from regulation as a sequential process. Entry occurs when coalition politics can favorably influence the distribution of wealth to its members. Regulation creates incentives for inefficiencies, such as cost increases. Uneven distribution of losses follows and changes the coalition promoting deregulation as a source of new benefits.

Another refinement to Stigler is provided by Becker (1976, 1983). He analyzed the importance of deadweight loss from regulation. Marginal gains by winners require the use of increasing political resources to offset those raised by losers to limit their losses. An Equilibrium still obtains, which is similar to Stigler's. However, regulation resulting in welfare losses will be avoided, since they are politically unpopular.

A third type of equilibrium regarding regulation is introduced by Williamson (1975). He constructed a theory amenable to explanations and observations of real economic exchange instead of the idealized neoclassical world of perfect competition with firms and their clients reduced to production and utility functions. To approach issues of regulation, he relies on the two main tenets of transaction costs economics (Williamson, 1976). First, alternative forms of economic organization like private monopoly, regulated monopoly, state-owned firm or franchise bidding must be evaluated on their comparative merits and failures, rather than being compared to an ideal solution. Second, this comparative assessment must take into account the redeployability of the assets used for transactions in different industries. In conditions of low asset specificity, deregulation resulting in more competition can be commendable. When higher levels of asset specificity exist, like in rail, gas and electricity, traditional telecommunications, or water networks, regulation can be more appropriate. We call this perspective equilibrium #3. It is reached when the Governance structure chosen among alternative solutions economizes on the costs of transaction in the context of existing attributes of transactions. Williamson (1998) considers that this kind of equilibrium lasts for limited periods. When governance choices are modified, because attributes of transactions differ, the previous equilibrium is replaced by a new one according to the same normative principle.

The conclusions initially based on inter-industry comparisons have dynamic properties when applied longitudinally to the same industry. If conditions of asset specificity – in one public utility industry or another – change towards comparatively lower levels, a change from regulation to deregulation can be warranted, provided that the costs of change do not overcome the benefits. Later, Williamson (1991) concluded that changes in the institutional environment act as shift parameters of the intensity of relative levels of costs associated to the main attributes of transactions, asset specificity, uncertainty and frequency. By changing the formal rules of the game toward more competition, the Polity can provide incentives for players to innovate and create new assets with comparatively lower levels of specificity than previous ones. Such innovations toward more easily redeployable assets can also occur as a result of the strategies of firms to alleviate existing barriers to entry in an industry.

It is worth noting that this line of reasoning applies to re-regulation as well as deregulation. If the Polity sees a need to create firm incentives to develop assets with a relatively higher level of specificity than existing ones, it might well be better to re-regulate. Therefore TCE can offer explanations of changes from one type of temporary equilibrium to the next, a considerable improvement over equilibria # 1 and # 2. The State provides the engine by changing the rules of the game for efficiency consideration, so as to offer the right incentives. The national interest is interpreted as a need for cost efficiency with pragmatic governance recommendations. Policy instruments can change according to industry and policy conditions unlike what is developed in the two other types of equilibria, in which instruments remain the same, independently of the situation.

As TCE did not exist in the early twentieth century, it cannot claim to be the explicit rationale used by the policy makers responsible for the initial wave of regulation of public utilities in the USA. However, although only developed later, TCE provides a quite convincing explanation to that movement. Before investing in non-redeployable public utility networks and infrastructures, firms can anticipate the risk of becoming unilateral hostages to potential Government opportunism. They need some kind of credible commitment to charge rates enabling profitable operations in spite of populist temptations by politicians to promise lower utility rates. Utilities are not primarily threatened by consumer opportunism, because of their position as sole suppliers. But rather, other parties to the transaction, public authorities and operators, are mutual hostages under the condition that rates are not set by operators alone. Otherwise, monopolistic pricing could obtain. Rate of return regulation protected utilities from Government, and consumers from Utilities.

In sum, for the three theories reviewed above, the role of the State is to make it possible to reach equilibrium # 1 (Welfare) or # 3 (Cost efficiency) and to avoid equilibrium #2 with Market instruments. The State is considered as a black box with one of the three efficiency objectives. All three theories are better equipped to explain equilibria rather than change. This is a quite disappointing answer to our initial question regarding determinants of change toward less or more regulation. TCE is the only theory offering an *ex post* explanation of the change from one situation of equilibrium to another. However it is not equipped to address the question of why the Polity and the State administration change their mind to act toward more or less regulation. Political reasons are obviously more important for politicians than efficiency considerations. Efficiency is on the agenda when it has a political influence and there is no apparent reason for its prominence over other issues.

EMPIRICAL ECONOMIC STUDIES

Before looking briefly at the empirical literature that came out of these approaches, a few definitions are necessary. We implicitly refer to a hierarchy of concepts, with policies on top, instruments of policy coming second and instrument mechanisms, or simply 'mechanisms' coming third. When Governments empower a specific policy, with the help of the legislature in some countries or by 'Fiat' in others, they can initiate or modify the goals of regulation or deregulation policies. In doing so, they can use two important instruments: regulatory agencies in case of regulation, market instruments in case of deregulation. Auctioning property rights or privatization of previously State-owned monopolies to several competitors are examples of deregulation mechanisms. Fixing rates of return or determining how costs for water consumption will be shared between end users and Government subsidies are examples of regulatory mechanisms. They are referred to as 'third-best' solutions for efficiency purposes by economists such as Spiller and Tommasi (2005), and as 'first-order' conditions by political scientists such as Hall (1993) because of the low political efforts necessary to change them. Conversely, first-best solutions for economists aiming at efficiency are third-order conditions for political scientists.

Let us now turn to some of the empirical literature associated with the theories described above. Stigler and Friedland (1962) were among the first to seriously challenge, through an empirical study, the Pigovian view that regulation contributes to welfare. They compared the influence on price and quantities of electricity consumption of a series of independent variables including regulation. They found a very small difference in price between regulated and unregulated States, with weak statistical significance. The welfare view was shown as wrong empirically. With the publication of 1971 paper by Stigler, the 'welfare' approach lost most of its former credit. The conclusions of both papers reinforced each other. It took 31 years to find that the results of the article published in the *Journal of Law and Economics* of 1962 included major errors, due to the coding and the use of common rather than natural logarithms (Peltzman, 1993). Correct results showed a price reduction of about 25 percent and a quantity increase of 50 percent in regulated versus unregulated States (Peltzman, 1993: 821). Academic endorsement of Stigler's theory might have been much weaker if proper results would have been available. The empirical recognition of some success of regulation in reaching welfare objectives came too late, once regulation was either abandoned or discredited. Moreover, the Stigler and Friedland data were from 1922 only. There is no reason to believe that additional empirical research replicating the same methodology over several years and different periods would give analogous results. With cross-section data for a single year, the efficiency record of the period of regulation, even though positive, does not stand on a sturdy empirical basis for electricity. Caution requires reserving judgment for other industries as well.

Peltzman (1989) made a non-statistical evaluation of the validity of the welfare/Pigovian approach versus the one developed by Stigler *et al.*, on railroads, trucking, airlines, long-distance telecommunications, stock brokerage, bank deposits and oil. He found five out of seven industries amenable to Stiglerian explanations and two (trucking and long-distance telecom) contradicting its predictions. Levine (1989) finds Peltzman's arguments overly generous to Stigler *et al.* He concludes for a prediction rate not higher than 50–50, analogous to chance, and thus a disclaimer of the empirical validity of the equilibrium '2 type'.

The record concerning equilibrium #2 can therefore be summarized as having raised considerable interest among economists in spite of serious empirical invalidation, including with respect to its conclusion against regulation. The empirical record for the welfare approach (equilibrium #1) is brighter than its reputation for at least a part of the post-World War I period for the electric industry. It does not perform better than the equilibrium # 2 approach the post-World War II period (Noll, 1989).

Transaction costs economics has been an empirical success (Williamson, 1999), mostly outside of the regulation literature, because of its numerous tests of the importance of determinants such as asset specificity and uncertainty on the choice of vertical integration versus market or the choice of a mode of governance for overseas operations. However, serious evaluation of the comparative efficiency of various forms of regulation taking into account the differences in the attributes of the assets used for transactions in a variety of industries is rare at best. Important methodological difficulties exist for ex post statistical studies. Based on our review of existing tests reviewed below, we realized that they are almost all ex post.We were not able to trace one ex ante study analyzing in a transaction costs perspective the feasibility of changes from regulation toward deregulation.

One of the most important empirical contribution to confirm the role of formal institutions on investment and welfare comes from Levy and

Spiller (1994). They analyzed the role of the credibility of Government commitments for foreign telecommunication firms purchasing previous State-owned operators after deregulation introduced privatization and competition. The credibility of Government commitments is inversely correlated with uncertainty, one of the attributes of transactions. Deregulation per se does not provide sufficient incentives for investors under conditions of high Government uncertainty. When local courts are under the notorious influence of politicians or subject to private corruption, as in Argentina, investment levels remain small, service availability does not increase, and prices do not fall as expected after deregulation. When courts have a tradition of independence toward the Polity and ethics impervious to bribing attempts as in Chile, efficiency obtains: investments increase, service improves and prices fall. Holburn and Spiller (2002) confirmed the results above with an international comparison in the electricity sector. Countries such as Australia and the UK with credible institutions attracted foreign investments after deregulation while Mexico, Turkey and Ukraine did not. This line of research has later developed in a direction that views institutions as a protection of the economy against direct Government intervention, which is one important source of uncertainty (Spiller and Tommasi, 2005).

Prior to his contributions to institutional studies, Spiller (1990; also Spiller and Urbitztondo, 1994) worked out of Agency Theory. He built a model using politicians and industry interest groups as multiple principals competing to influence regulator, refered to as a single agent. Using data for the career of bureaucrats from the Civil Aeronautics Board, the Interstate Commerce Commission and the Federal Communications Commission, he found that regulators were substantially rewarded by industry in the form of management positions with the operator once they left their regulating agency prior to 1978. This result decreased by approximately 50 percent after the US Congress passed the 1978 Ethics Bill prohibiting such practices.

Important empirical illustrations of the 'Contractual design' view and of the key role of supporting institutions can be found in the telecommunication (Levy and Spiller, 1996) and Water industries. Shirley and Ménard (2002) examined contracts for water and their implementation in the capital cities of Argentina, Chile, Guinea, the Ivory Coast, Mexico and Peru. They concluded that credible institutions together with well designed contracts were best performers and that cities embedded in less credible institutional environments were the highest beneficiaries of contractual arrangements, particularly when contrasted to organizations run by bureaucrats. Contracts can be designed to reduce information asymmetry, to provide incentives for increasing efficiency (lower costs and reduced waste as well as reduced pollution from sewage), and to set prices and bill collections at a level and with mechanisms preventing free-riding by powerful customers such as Government Ministries. One interesting example of an efficient regulatory mechanism comes from Santiago (Chile), where the Government subsidizes the utility for 60 percent of a maximum 20 cubic meters of consumption for customers certified as 'poor' by the City. They pay for the remaining 40 percent and can be severed from service for non-payment. Such cross-subsidies exist for connections also. Utilities thus have an incentive to service the poor who are motivated to avoid waste. Free riding is probably not completely avoided but large users such as businesses, churches, Ministries and wealthy individuals can hardly be certified 'poor' in Chile. The reverse could exist in countries where civil servants are either easy to corrupt or obedient to Government, military or religious injunctions. Such taxation by regulation (Posner, 1972) has more built-in incentives to avoid waste and increase price/output efficiency than an alternate regulation mechanism increasing the overall income tax rate and distributing free water to the poor. If cross subsidies favor large instead of small consumers, the opposite result may occur.

Empirical studies in the contractual design perspective acknowledge the importance of changes in formal institutions that favor a decrease in the uncertainty of transactions. They consider such first best changes as long-term and beyond the reach of their recommendations. However, without major shifts in the political power bases in these countries, welfare increases remain small, although not always negligible. When a military or religious coup or foreign military intervention replaces a dictatorship by another one, the institutions of the country remain the same.

Joskow and Kahn (2002) found that the California power shortages of the summer 2000 resulted from market power tactics used by electricity generators who took advantages of flaws in institutional design. They explain the lack of reliability of supply by the choice of 'unbundling', an unsatisfactory deregulation instrument. Had transaction cost considerations been included by the Californian legislator, uncertainty could have been examined and better anticipated ex ante, allowing to select deregulation instruments and mechanisms that could have avoided such power shortages. Indeed, transaction cost theory provides tools to identify and promote the right governance, that is, a governance that can lower costs and prices while avoiding overcapacity as well.

Joskow (2006) makes an interim assessment of the first ten years of deregulation policies in the electricity sector in the USA. He finds improvements in generating plant performance and consumer prices, but also uncertainties with respect to supply capacities and transmission congestion, which could well lead to additional power shortages in the future.

Improvements in market mechanisms and their institutional design are clearly required.

Two other recent studies have improved our knowledge of efficiency results of deregulation in electric utilities (Delmas and Tokat, 2005; Delmas *et al.*, 2007). They are summarized in Chapter 8 of this volume. Delmas *et al.* use Data Envelopment Analysis (Coelli *et al*, 1998; Majumdar, 1998) in both papers to aggregate several input–output efficiency parameters into a single measure of the dependent variable. The performance of each firm is benchmarked relatively to the efficiency frontier of the best performers. The first study (2005) shows a short-term decrease in efficiency due to deregulation. As it has no long-term data, results are interpreted as the cost of adaptation to deregulation. If future empirical work confirms that long-run inefficiency occurs, an alternative explanation will be necessary. As equilibrium #1 has a bad reputation, deregulation has the favor of the day to avoid the inefficient equilibrium #2, and equilibrium #3 has not been examined *ex ante* in this case, a consequence being that any result could be anticipated. Inefficiencies produced by deregulation should therefore not come as a surprise (Joskow, 1991). In their paper, Delmas and Tokat (2005) find that hierachy and market solutions show equivalent performance and are both superior to hybrid arrangements. With transaction cost reasoning validated for equilibrium solutions, but with results limited by the fact that their data come from a short period after deregulation, more empirical work is needed to see if one discrete form prevails in the long term.

When starting this review of the theoretical and empirical literature on regulation, deregulation and reregulation, we expected strong theories and sturdy empirical results supporting the advantages of deregulation in general and explaining recent reregulation in some instances. Hence our strong disappointment with the contribution of different and somewhat opposed economic theories. Noll (1989) characterizes equilibrium of type # 2 as the Chicago theory of Government because this theory goes well beyond economics. However, its insights on the power of coalitions and their changes are small when compared with the potential contribution of political science, as proposed in the next section to explain 'big bang' changes in the dominating paradigm. We came out with the conclusion that the approach initiated by Stigler was a very successful political success with a very thin academic base, and that the demise of the welfare approach that emerged in the period prior to World War II was based on extremely fragile demonstrations. On the other hand, the very limited influence of transaction cost theory over public policies and the relatively small number of empirical research papers on deregulation inspired by transaction cost theory 17 years after it was pointed out as a priority by Joskow

(1991) came as a further disappointment We surveyed a few additional and important empirical contributions to the study of regulation without pretending to be exhaustive. Joskow (1974) pointed to the importance of the behavioral theory of the firm (Simon, 1959) to understand the reactions of the regulatory agency. This line of research provides similarities and offers a transition with the literature coming from Political Science. The State, and the agencies it creates, does not only fuel the dynamics to reach one of the three equilibria reviewed above; it can also generate 'puzzle' (Helco, 1974) and it can learn (March and Olsen, 1984).

In sum the empirical literature reviewed provided little confirmation of the theories behind equilibria #1, #2 or #3. One paper (Joskow, 1974) introduced an interesting challenge to the traditional view that the State increased its powers for efficiency motives.The rare quantitative empirical work (Delmas and Tokat, 2005; Joskow, 2006) measuring *ex post* changes in the efficiency of deregulation reached interestingly mixed or negative results, even though their conclusions are temporary. It should also be noted that their methodology is not or only very partially derived from transaction cost economics.

Some of the most useful recent empirical work comes from the Contract Design view, which helps explain (and recommend) third-best changes, especially in countries with weak democracies. However, it does not address big bang changes from regulation to deregulation. Hence, our review of the empirical literature leaves us with a void; there is nothing really satisfying in that literature to make significant progress toward answering our research question. However, transaction cost theory performs relatively better on empirical studies relating to regulation when compared to the weak empirical contributions of the theories supporting the other two equilibria.

POLITICAL SCIENCE, INSTITUTIONAL ENVIRONMENT AND 'BIG BANG' PARADIGM CHANGES: A RESEARCH AGENDA

As the theories behind equilibria # 1, # 2 and # 3 seem not well equipped to explain changes from regulation to regulation or a potential move to re-regulation, we turned to the potential contribution of political science, an academic discipline accustomed to explain 'big bang' changes once they occurred.

Using some contributions from political science, we first distinguish three levels of policy changes. We then outline briefly a theory explaining paradigm changes (Hall, 1993). As theories of the State coming from political science share similarities with that domain of New Institutional Economics that focuses on institutions as an environment in which rules of the game operate (North, 1990; Williamson, 1998), concepts will be compared along the way. The research agenda follows.

Political science views the State as encompassing the Executive, the Legislature and the Court system (Hall, 1993), largely what North (1990) labels as formal institutions. The legislature creates or suppresses agencies as its policy instruments (Coase, 1984), regulation as well as State-owned firms being part of these instruments. In the USA, Courts can also act as regulators or deregulators. In the first section of this chapter we analyzed how the State (which then remains a black box) develops 'powers' needed to reach one of the three equilibria. Another view from political science is that the State (or formal institutions) does not necessarily reach efficient or satisficing solutions (Simon, 1959). It can hesitate and experiment, in other words it develops as a 'puzzle' (Helco, 1974). Helco relies on the behavioral theory of the firm. State actions are the result of a process in which administrative experts and officials 'puzzle' autonomously to produce outcomes most often if not always accepted by their Government.

Hall (1993) finds that States develop both 'power' and 'puzzle' strategies, depending on the level of policy analyzed. He proposed a taxonomy with three policy levels. We illustrate his classification with our own examples, coming from regulation, along with his own examples, coming from changes in macroeconomic policy in Britain between 1970 and 1989. In Hall's view, first order changes concern the fine-tuning of instrument mechanisms, like changes in sales prices by the regulatory agency, the composition of its board, or improvements in the renewal or monitoring provisions of a franchise contract. Politically, they are the least costly and risky changes. Economists call this level a 'third best solution' for efficiency considerations. Second order changes include regulatory instruments themselves, for example replacing a regulated monopoly with its regulating agency by oligopolistic competition with modified attributions for the regulator or via the sale of property rights with potential Court monitoring. In Williamson's language, second order changes involve alternate governance modes (or regulatory institutions), such as hierarchies, hybrids, or markets. For economists, these solutions are second best solutions in that there are always flaws. Hence the statement: 'get the Governance right' (Williamson, 1998). Changing the priority of objectives – from fighting unemployment to thwarting inflation in Hall (1993), or from social welfare to lower prices in this chapter – illustrates the importance of what political scientists call 'ideas' in the policy process: 'goals' and 'objectives' tend to be very close to informal institutions which include norms, values and beliefs (North, 1990). The replacement of accepted goals by others is a necessary but insufficient condition for third-order changes. 'Ideas' are supported by a consistent discourse integrating policy goals and instruments and mechanisms accepted by experts, policy makers; and a large part of the population. Hall (1993) labels 'policy paradigm' these discourses integrating the three levels of policy. For him, changing goals only is not sufficient to produce third order changes. Third order changes require changes in first and second order conditions, together with changes in objectives combined with a change in the dominating policy paradigm.

A policy paradigm is akin to a theory accepted as a basis to generate policy, instruments, and mechanisms. It becomes dominating when unquestioned, that is when there is no serious competing paradigm. However, it is subject to change according to the following theoritical pattern (Hall, 1993). Changes are due to heavy and repetitive dissatisfaction with previous policies. Incremental improvements of first and second order are proposed by Government bureaucracy experts rather than outside pressure groups at the outset. Their results are unsatisfactory and lead to further challenges to the existing paradigm. Third-order changes are the outcome of a political struggle between competing political forces. In Hall's example, Britain moved from a Keynesian to a monetarist paradigm for macroeconomic policy. It resulted from a struggle between Conservatives and Labour resolved by elections favoring the former. Margaret Thatcher espoused the monetarist paradigm as a consistent and instrumental line of discourse to replace the old Conservative party leadership in her favor and, later, Labour and its union base. The forces involved in the conflict over the paridigm were not political parties only. The media played a major role. Others included financial markets and numerous burgeoning think tanks in what Hall calls a 'market' for ideas. The role of industry pressure groups (the British Confederation of Industries) was found to be relatively minor. Thus the process of setting policy paradigms is conflictual (Weir, 1992). Conflict occurs with asymmetric power relationships *ex ante*. It can result in a reinforcement or a redistribution of the *ex post* power balance (Weir, 1992). Major third order changes are explained as a result of open political conflicts including several stakeholders, more than obscure pressures from interest groups as in the Stiglerian type of approach, while less important changes are more bureaucracy centered, at least in democratic political regimes. Hall finds first- and second-order changes consistent with Helco's State centric view, not third-order change.

We suggest that this model is relevant for analyzing the change that we have pointed out, that is, how and why deregulation replaced regulation to a large extent as the accepted paradigm for public utilities in the USA and Britain first, and in continental Europe more than ten years later. This proposition lays the ground for a challenging research agenda. The major difficulty in applying Hall's model comes from the variety of regulation and deregulation policies implemented in different industries, as opposed to a single policy in the case of Hall. The time frame also differs according to each deregulated industry. Therefore, we illustrate our research agenda with one industry at a time, with a special attention for the case of electricity, referring to first order conditions as analyzed by Joskow (1974, 2006) or Delmas and Tokat (2005).

Joskow (1974) used the behavioral theory of the firm (Simon, 1959; Cyert and March, 1963; Nelson and Winter, 1973) to explain the behavior of the electric utility regulator. The period starting in 1969 witnessed increasing costs, including those of inputs for electricity production, because of widespread inflation as well as the end of economies of scale in that industry. The result was lower profits and rates of return of firms below the level allowed by the regulator. Operators initiated numerous requests for reviews to obtain increased electricity and gas rates. Beside pressures from utilities, environment protection groups started to influence the regulator at the time. Its members proposed replacing the previous rate structure based on declining block rates parallel to increases in consumption by flat rates to take marginal social costs into consideration. As costs of producing electricity increased together with consumption, unlike before 1969, the flat rate structure stabilized the profits of firms and their rate of return and as a consequence their number of requests for reviews (Joskow, 1974: 316–23). The proposed change in the rate structure was clearly favorable to electicity firms, not environmentalist groups only. Rational self-interest seekers should have been happy. Yet, bureaucrats inside firms and the regulator resisted the change strongly at the outset. As Joskow reports with a sense of humor (1974: 318) they did not understand the concept of marginal cost and were surprised that the level of consumption and price could be related. They preferred to follow 20-year-old routines. The conclusions of Joskow (1974) are consistent with Helco's (1973) and Hall (1993) views of a puzzling State for first order changes. The example analyzed by Joskow brings two additional insights. First, puzzling is not only an intellectual process, it has an organizational, routine base rationale also. Second, first-order changes do not come only from regulators and experts. They can result partially from some kind of political conflict, with environmentalist groups playing an increasing role in the case summarized here, even though there was no paradigmatic change. Changes towards deregulation came in the industry much later and could not be analyzed in 1974.

Understanding the change in the dominating paradigm from regulation to deregulation goes well beyond the scope of the analysis of one single industry. Some synthesis of changes in a significant number of network industries is required as well as a look to broader changes. The change in the dominating paradigm, from Keynesian to monetarist policies, analyzed by Hall (1993) had major implications for accepted ideas and discourses on the necessity to downsize the role of the State in the economy. This shift in ideas was favorable to deregulation and squeezed advocates of the role of the State in the economy on a defensive position. Thus, while changes of first and eventually second-order conditions can possibly be analyzed for each industry separately in mixing behavioral theory and political influences, paradigm changes of the third order need borrowing from analyses of changes in informal as well as formal institutions in a wider context, including conflictual forces at work.

It might be possible that the change of the dominating paradigm, from regulation to deregulation, is not accepted to the same degree in different industries and different countries. Such differences in the degree of acceptance of the new paradigm may be a partial explanation of the slowing down of deregulation and even the resurgence of regulation in some instances, especially in cases of highly visible inefficiencies like the California power shortage of 2000 and the Enron bankruptcy. The dominating paradigm may not be completely dominating.

In sum, political science has the potential to contribute significantly to the explanation of paradigm changes from regulation to deregulation and eventually to reregulation. Strategic calculus probably obtains when social and political forces confront for the control and change of the legitimate policy paradigm to be implemented by formal institutions. Economists would benefit from integrating conflictual processes in their explanation of policy changes, including from regulation to deregulation and vice versa. Conflictual forces can be partly agents directly involved and partly 'outside' stakeholders such as political parties, media, professionals and scholars, as well as forces external to the industry, such as farmers and other interest groups. Collaboration between economists and political scientists is a promising avenue in spite of all the difficulties of cross-disciplinary research.

DISCUSSION

The puzzle we formulated in the introduction: 'how can changes from more to less regulation and vice versa be explained?' can find elements of answer, based on the theoritical and empirical insights reviewed above as well as on the research agenda stated in the previous section.

The framing of our question focuses on change instead of equilibrium. Movements toward or away from regulation are explained by the complementary insights from the institutional contributions of political science, law, economics and organization. These disciplines are not rivals but complements to answer the puzzle formulated at the outset of this chapter. Explanations of movements away from and back toward a dominating policy paradigm (regulation or deregulation) benefit from the dynamic properties of political science for third order changes (the paradigm), the dynamic properties of transaction cost theory for second order changes (regulatory instruments), and the behavioral theory of the firm and the contractual design view for first-order changes (regulatory mechanisms). The importance of each discipline varies, according to whether we focus on first, second or third order changes. Without these multidisciplinary contributions, no answer could encompass all the levels involved. The potentially conflictual influence of a variety of stakeholders and the self-interested implementation by politicians of new mental models, whether they already exist in the academia or not, is necessary to explain changes in policy paradigms. For that purpose, political science is more relevant than all forms of equilibria proposed by economists.

Enquiring upon the determinants of changes from one dominating policy paradigm to another leads to analyzing potential conflicts between stakeholders as well as to confront conflicting theories. By contrast, inquiries on the determinants of different kinds of equilibria tend to avoid political conflicts and how the sociological and ideological constructions of mindset frame issues. All the multi-level explanations above are formulated *ex post*. This remark is not a criticism of political science as it is not a predictive discipline, unlike the economic theories that are reviewed above. However, in the area of regulation and deregulation, the predictive capacity of the Stigler approach (equilibrium # 2) is far from validated (Levine, 1989; Peltzman, 1993) while transaction cost economics do a little better (Joskow, 2006), notwithstanding the paucity of empirical papers and lack of policy influence (Joskow, 1991).

Studies of possible changes toward reregulation could open an opportunity to move from *ex post* explanations found in the historical institutionalist literature (Hall and Taylor, 1996) to *ex ante* predictions. Such studies could focus on the three levels of changes (paradigm, instruments; mechanisms) and build propositions on the basis of the relevant social sciences. Reregulation could be motivated by a set of complementary forces. The relevance of the dominating policy paradigm is likely to differ amongst countries, or between states in the US, and may not resist overtime when its legitimacy is weak. Deregulation may not be totally accepted as a dominating paradigm in several political instances. A measurement or comparative assessment of the resistance of a policy paradigm to criticism and/or change would constitute an improvement. The efficiency of deregulation could become questionable in selected industries when temporary or long lasting failures affect a large body of customers/voters, especially if it creates a political opportunity for electoral competition. It may result in modifications of regulatory instruments, with or without changing the politicians in charge. For example, the need for investments with a higher level of asset specificity than existing ones to control pollution could possibly create a source of reregulation. Learning by Polity, regulating agency, producers, operators or consumers, could well lead to modifications of regulatory instruments in order to improve efficiency or to change the balance of costs and benefits in favor of one category of stakeholders to the detriment of others.

Reregulation is now on the policy agenda. For electric utilities, the *International Herald Tribune* likely pointed to an important issue when it posted as headline: 'Power deregulation creates US backlash: many states restore regulated systems' (*IHT*, 27 September 2007). The accompanying paper mentioned 'recent' US Energy Department statistics pointing to higher electricity costs in deregulated versus non-deregulated States (although the *IHT* did not provide the exact reference to the Department of Energy report). Reregulation is now part of the research and policy agenda in social sciences and among policy makers. However, there is apparently little intellectual effort to bring the regulation paradigm associated to equilibrium #1 back in. Fine-tuning of instrument mechanics and eventually of regulatory instruments themselves is clearly debated. The consideration of a possible reregulation by several American states reported by the *IHT* likely rests on a large dissatisfaction with price increase in electricity instead of the lower prices announced by advocates of deregulation. During peaks in demand, new investors in generation plants can obtain almost monopoly prices, while traditional utilities are forced to maintain constant prices, increases in their costs notwithstanding. Fine-tuning this artificial market segmentation ought to be found without going back to the previous regulatory instrument. It is worth noting that large electricity customers who were the strongest proponents of deregulation are calling for some form of reregulation, which may result in better market rules to prevent predatory pricing that favor specific suppliers.

The view on the influence of economists and other social scientists developed in this chapter is not that of scholars publishing and lecturing in their ivory tower. Scientists work at the advancement of knowledge for their own pain and pleasure, as well as for their own career, but they are also embedded in their society. So are politicians: in their quest for political survival, they shop around for theories and ideas, oriented by their political self-interest. They pick what they want as opposed to being under the influence of academic 'gurus'. The choice of politicians is motivated primarily by what can be useful for the next election. However, longer-term preoccupations of efficiency may not be absent, since their time horizon is often longer than a single term.

The normative conclusions of the Stiglerian type of approach are simple and can easily catch popularity: 'the smaller the size of Government, the higher the level of welfare'. Transaction cost economics carry a more complex message. As a result, even if TCE is better able to provide adequate answers to the issues at hand, it can hardly be as successful: it is not easy to communicate its message to the large audiences targeted by politicians. Focusing on uncertainties in quality and reliability of services instead of asset specificity might help. Possible changes of policy paradigm favorable to environmental concerns might offer opportunities to better communicate the message to the Polity. Uncertainties that could impact future elections, for example regarding service reliability and its impact on the health of voters and their children as well as on costs, may be more germane to the concerns of politicians than asset specificity. Institutional economists should not be bashful on the normative consequences of their work. They should provide their students and their clients in government, international agencies, business and the media with adequate policy tools. They would benefit from a user-friendly form, simplifying the academic jargon.

As regulatory arrangements can vary amongst different states, with similar institutional environment and within the same industry, as in the US, the efficiency of alternate regulatory arrangements can be researched (Stigler and Friedland, 1962; Delmas and Tokat, 2005; Joskow, 2006). This would hardly be possible if all states would choose the same mode of governance. Nevertheless, difficulties in doing so are huge. What was possible for automobile parts (Monteverde and Teece, 1982) or the coordination of subcontractors in naval construction of a ship (Masten *et al.*, 1991) is much more difficult for public utilities. Finding appropriate proxies to measure transaction attributes, particularly specific assets, is particularly challenging. Answers to this issue might be slightly better for some network industries, for example, the role of R&D or advertising in the telecommunications industry, and worse in others, for example urban water systems. These difficulties in measuring the attributes of transactions in public utilities likely explain the paucity of empirical work using these constructs and feed pessimistic forecasts on possible developments.

These difficulties are amplified when it comes to studies comparing several utility industries. What could be a common measure of asset specificity or uncertainty for air, road and rail transport, the post office, electricity, telecommunications and water? Furthermore, regulatory arrangements and their mechanics differ according to the utilities at stake.

So do the timing of changes from regulation to deregulation. The route of quantitative analyses is full of pitfalls and challenges.

The pessimistic conclusions above, regarding existing and future empirical studies based on transaction cost economics are better than those originating in the Stiglerian view as well as the Pigovian/welfare view. In that respect, transaction cost economics have been from the very beginning better grounded in empirical data and its ability to examine real regulatory alternatives and the kinds of assets involved provides a major advantage over alternative views. Difficulties of empirical tests do not weaken the value of the theory and its normative conclusion on the need to focus on transaction costs economizing between different regulatory instruments.

Academics should devote more of their time getting away from *ex post* empirical tests and rather focusing on recommendations regarding *ex ante* choices of efficient regulatory arrangements. The author of this chapter is persuaded that editors and referees of existing academic journals would help the advancement of economics if they would solicit such research.

CONCLUSIONS

This chapter reviewed selected theoretical and empirical works on regulation, deregulation and reregulation. It concluded that there was a paucity of well accepted theory or clear empirical results favoring one of them as well as to a methodological advantage for transaction cost economics among existing economic theories of regulation. In our view, TCE is better equipped to select alternative regulatory arrangements and mechanisms *ex ante*, according to the different kinds of assets existing in the various utility industries. Thus, the regulatory or deregulatory solutions it would recommend are likely to differ according to the utility analyzed.

This chapter found the contributions of political science for the *ex post* explanation of changes in regulatory institutions and dominating policy paradigm complementary to those coming from economics. The recent interest for reregulation seems to be the sign of a need for fine-tuning of the mechanisms of current instruments rather than their change per se. It is also possible that deregulation is not totally accepted as the dominating or acceptable paradigm in a few industries and countries. An ambitious research agenda based on the complementary contributions of political science, economics, law and organization theory might be what is needed for progressing in our understanding of shifts from regulation to deregulation and from deregulation to other, new forms of regulation.

ACKNOWLEDGMENTS

First, I thank Jackie Krafft, Evens Salies and the other participants of a GREDEG workshop for their valuable comments on an earlier version of this chapter. Second, I acknowledge the most valuable suggestions made by the participants to the 18–19 June 2007 conference held in Nice (France) on 'Deregulation or re-regulation: institutional and other approaches', particularly those of Oliver Williamson and Pablo Spiller. Claude Ménard offered most useful guidance on the last version of this chapter. I also thank Joel Gombin of the University of Aix-Marseille for pointing to an interesting selection of political science and sociology literature. Martine Naulet, GREDEG's librairian was most helpful also.

NOTE

1. For a more thorough treatment of this argument, see Derthick and Quirk (1985).

REFERENCES

Akerlof, G. (1970), 'The market for "lemons": qualitative uncertainty and the Market mechanism', *Quarterly Journal of Economics*, **84** (3), 488–500.
Baumol, W., J. Panzar and R. Willig (1982), *Contestable Markets*, New York: Harcourt, Brace Jovanovich.
Becker, G. (1976), 'Comment', *Journal of Law and Economics*, **19** (August), 245–48.
Becker, G. (1983), 'A theory of competition among pressure groups for political influence', *Quarterly Journal of Economics*, **98** (3), 371–400.
Breton, A., (1974), *The Economic Theory of Representative Government*, Chicago, IL: Aldine-Atherton.
Coase, R. (1984), 'The new institutional economics', *Journal of Institutional and Theoritical Economics*, **140** (March), 229–32.
Cyert, R. and J. March (1963), *A Behavioral Theory of the Firm*, Englewood Cliffs, NJ: Prentice Hall.
Delmas, M. and Y. Tokat (2005), 'Deregulation, governance structure and efficiency: the US electric utility sector', *Strategic Management Journal*, **26** (5), 441–60.
Delmas, M., M. Russo and M. Montes (2007), 'Deregulation and environment differentiation in the electric utility industry', *Strategic Management Journal*, **28** (2), 189–209.
Derthick, M. and P. Quirck (1985), *The Politics of Deregulation*, Washington, DC: Bookings Institution.
Fama, E. (1980), 'Agency problems and the theory of the firm', *Journal of Political Economy*, **88** (2), 288–307.
Ghertman, M. (1988), 'Foreign subsidiary and parent's roles during strategic

investment and divestment decisions', *Journal of International Business Studies*, **19** (1), 47–67.
Ghertman, M. (2004), *Stratégie de l'Entreprise: Théories et Actions*, Paris: Economica.
Giddens, A., (1986), *The Constitution of Society: Outline of a Theory of Structuration*, Berkeley, CA: University of California Press.
Hall, P. (1993), 'Policy paradigms, social learning and the state: the case of economic policymaking in Britain', *Comparative Politics*, **25** (3), 275–96.
Hall, P. and R. Taylor (1996), 'Political science and the three new institutionalisms', Max Planck-Institut für Gesellschaftsforschung working paper 96/6: 1–32.
Helco, H. (1974), *Modern Social Politics in Britain and Sweden*, New Haven, CT: Yale University Press.
International Herald Tribune (2007), 'Power deregulation creates US backlash: many states restore regulated systems', 127, September, 12.
Holburn, G. and P. Spiller (2002), 'Institutional or structural: lessons from international electricity sector reforms', in E. Brousseau and J. M. Glachant, *The Economics of Contracts*, Cambridge: Cambridge University Press.
Jensen, M. (1994), 'Self-interest, altruism, incentives and agency theory', *Journal of Applied Corporate Finance*, **7**, 40–5.
Jensen, M. and W. Meckling (1976), 'The theory of the firm: managerial behavior, agency costs and ownership structure', *Journal of Financial Economics*, **3** (October), 305–60.
Joskow, P. (1974), 'Inflation and environmental concern: structural change in the process of utility regulation price regulation', *Journal of Law and Economics*, **17** (2), 291–327.
Joskow, P. (1991), 'The role of transaction cost economics in antitrust and public utility regulatory policies', *Journal of Law, Economics and Organization*, **V** (7), 53–83.
Joskow, P. (ed.) (2000), *Economic Regulation*, Cheltenham and Northampton, MA: Edward Elgar.
Joskow, P. (2002), 'Transaction costs economics, anti-trust rules and remedies', *Journal of Law, Economics and Organization*, **18** (1), 95–116.
Joskow, P. (2006), 'Markets for power in the US: an interim assessment', *Energy Journa*, **27** (1), 1–36.
Joskow, P. and Kahn, E. (2002), 'A quantitative analysis of pricing behavior in California's wholesale electricity market during the summer 2000', *Energy Journal*, **23** (4), 1–35.
Joskow, P. and N.L. Rose (1989), 'The effects of economic regulation', in R. Schmalensee and R. Willig *Handbook of Industrial Organization*, Vol. II, 1450–98; Amsterdam: North-Holland.
Joskow, P. and R. Schmalensee (1986), 'Incentive regulation for electric utilities', *Yale Journal on Regulation*, **4**, 1–49.
Le Monde (2007), 'En Afrique, l'évasion des capitaux représente deux fois la dette', 28 September, 15.
Levy, B. and P. Spiller (1994), 'The institutional foundations of regulatory commitment: a comparative analysis of telecommunications regulation', *Journal of Law, Economics and Organization*, **10**, 201–47.
Levy, B. and P. Spiller (1996), *Regulation, Institutions and Commitment: Comparative Studies of Telecommunications*, Cambridge: Cambridge University Press.

March, J. and J. Olsen (1984), 'The new institutionalism: organizational factors in political life', *American Political Science Review*, **98**, 734–49.
Masten, S. (1992), 'Modern evidence on the firm', *American Economic Review*, **92** (2): 428–32.
Masten, S., J. Meehan and E. Snyder (1991), 'The cost of organization', *Journal of Law, Economics and Organization*, **7**, 1–25.
Meyer, J. and B. Rowan (1977), 'Institutionalized organizations: formal structure as myth and ceremony', *American Journal of Sociology*, **83**, 340–63.
Monteverde, K. and D. Teece (1982), 'Supplier witching costs and vertical integration in the automobile industry', *Bell Journal of Economics*, **13** (1), 206–14.
Muller, P. (1985), 'Un Schéma d'Analyse des Politiques Sectorielles', *Revue Française de Science Politique*, **35**, 165–89.
Nelson, R. and S. Winter (1973), 'Neoclassical versus evolutionary theories of economic growth: critique and prospects', University of Michigan Institute of Policy Studies, No. 46, (April).
Nelson, R. and S. Winter (1982), *An Evolutionary Theory of Economic Change*, Cambridge, MA: Harvard University Press.
Noll, R. (1989), 'Economic perspectives on the politics of Regulation', in R. Schmalensee and R. Willig, *Handbook of Industrial Organization*, vol. II, 1254–82; Amsterdam: North-Holland.
North, D. (1990), *Institutions, Institutional Change and Economic Performance*, New York: Cambridge University Press.
Peltzman, S. (1976), 'Toward a more general theory of regulation', *Journal of Law and Economics*, **19** (2), 211–40.
Peltzman, S. (1989), 'The economic theory of regulation after a decade of deregulation', *Brookings Papers* (supplement), 1–41.
Peltzman, S. (1993), 'George Stigler's contribution to the economic analysis of regulation', *Journal of Political Economy*, **101** (5), 818–32.
Pigou, A. (1920), *Welfare Economics*, London: Macmillan.
Posner, R. (1971), 'Taxation by regulations', *Bell Journal of Economics*, Spring, 22–50.
Riker, W. and P. Ordeshook (1968), 'A theory of the calculus of voting', *American Political Science Review*, **62** (March), 25–42.
Riker, W. and P. Ordeshook (1973), *An Introduction to Positive Political Theory*, Englewood Cliffs, NJ: Prentice Hall.
Shirley, M. and C. Ménard (2002), 'Cities awash: a synthesis of the country cases', in M. Shirley (ed.), *Thirsting for Efficiency: The Economics and Politics of Urban Water Reform*, New York: Pergamon Press.
Simmel, G. (1923), *Soziologie: Untersunchungen über die formen der Vergesellschaftung*, Berlin: Duncker und Humbolt.
Simmel, G. (1950), *The Sociology of Georg Simmel* (translation), New-York: Free Press.
Simon, H. (1959), 'Theories of decision-making in economics and behavioral science', *American Economic Review*, **49** (June), 253–8.
Spiller, P. (1990), 'Politicians, interest groups and regulators: a multiple principals agency theory of regulation (or let them be bribed)', *Journal of Law and Economics*, **33**, 65–101.
Spiller, P. and S. Urbitztondo (1994), 'Political appointees vs career civil servants: a multiple principals theory of political institutions', *European Journal of Political Economy*, **10**, 465–97.

Spiller, P. and M. Tommasi (2005), 'The institutions of regulation', in C. Ménard and M. Shirley (eds), *Handbook of New Institutional Economics*, The Netherlands: Springer Press.

Stigler, G. (1968), *The Organization of Industry*, Homewood, IL: Richard Irwin.

Stigler, G. (1971), 'The theory of economic regulation', *Bell Journal of Economics and Management Science*, **2** (1), 3–21.

Stigler, G. (1982), *The Economist as Preacher, and Other Essays*, Chicago, IL: University of Chicago Press.

Stigler, G. and C. Friedland (1962), 'What can regulators regulate? The case of electricity', *Journal of Law and Economics*, **5** (October), 1–16.

Touraine, A. (1977), *The Self-Production of Society*, Chicago, IL: University of Chicago Press.

Weaver, R. and B. Rockman (1993), *Do Institutions Matter?* Washington, DC: Brookings Institution.

Weir, M. (1992), 'Ideas and the politics of bounded innovation', in S. Steinmo, K. Thelen and F. Longstreth (eds), *Structuring Politics: Historical Institutionalism in Comparative Analysis*, New York: Cambridge University Press.

Williamson, O. (1975), *Markets and Hierarchies: Analysis and Antitrust Implications*, New York: Free Press.

Williamson, O. (1976), 'Franchise bidding for natural monopolies – in general and with respect to CATV', *Bell Journal of Economics*, **7** (1), 73–104.

Williamson, O. (1985), *The Economic Institutions of Capitalism*, New York: Free Press, Appendix to Chapter 2: Opportunism: A Digression, pp. 64–67.

Williamson, O. (1991), 'Comparative economic organization: the analysis of discrete structural alternatives', *Administrative Science Quarterly*, **36** (June), 269–96.

Williamson, O. (1998), 'Transaction cost economics: how it works, where it is going', *De Economist*, **146** (3), 306–42.

Williamson, O. (1999), 'Strategy research: governance and competence perspectives', *Strategic Management Journal*, **20** (12), 1087–108.

Index